How to Be French

How to Be French:

Nationality in the Making since 1789

PATRICK WEIL   *Translated by Catherine Porter*

DUKE UNIVERSITY PRESS

DURHAM AND LONDON

2008

Duke University Press gratefully acknowledges the support of
THE FLORENCE GOULD FOUNDATION, which provided funds toward the
translation, production, and marketing of this book.
We also gratefully acknowledge the support of the
FRENCH MINISTRY OF CULTURE / NATIONAL BOOK CENTER.
Ouvrage publié avec le concours du MINISTÈRE FRANÇAIS CHARGÉ
DE LA CULTURE — CENTRE NATIONAL DU LIVRE.

CONTENTS

ACRONYMS AND ABBREVIATIONS

ACE	Archives du Conseil d'État
AD	Archives diplomatiques
ADBR	Archives départementales du Bas-Rhin
ADI	Archives départementales de l'Isère
ADN	Archives départementales du Nord
ALR	Allgemeines Landrecht (Prussian legal code issued under Frederick the Great)
AMJ	Archives du Ministère de la Justice
AN	Centre historique des Archives Nationales
AP	Archives parlementaires (Senate and National Assembly archives)
APP	Archives de la Préfecture de police (de Paris)
ASDN	Archives de la sous-direction des naturalisations (archives of the Naturalization Bureau)
CAC	Centre d'archives contemporaines de Fontainebleau
CADI	Centre d'action et de défense des immigrés (Center for Action and Defense of Immigrants)
CAOM	Centre des archives d'outre-mer (Center for archives of France's overseas departments and territories)
CC	Cour de Cassation (Supreme Court)
CDJC	Centre de documentation juive contemporaine
CDS	Centre des démocrates sociaux (centrist social democratic party)
CE	Conseil d'État (Council of State)
CGQJ	Commissariat général aux questions juives (Office of the High Commissioner on Jewish Affairs)
CREDOC	Centre de recherche pour l'étude et l'observation des conditions de vie (Research Center for the Observation and Study of Living Conditions)

Dal.	Dalloz collection
DPM	Direction de la Population et des Migrations (Office for Population and Migrations)
FFI	Forces françaises de l'intérieur (French forces operating inside occupied France)
FFL	Forces françaises libres (Free French forces)
GPRF	Gouvernement provisoire de la République Française
INED	Institut national d'études démographiques
INSEE	Institut national de la statistique et des études économiques
JDIP (or Clunet)	Journal du droit international (periodical on international law founded in 1874 by Clunet)
JO	Journal officiel de la République Française (official organ of the French Republic, publishing legal texts daily)
MAE	Ministère des Affaires Étrangères (Ministry of Foreign Affairs)
MBF	Militärbefehlshaber in Frankreich (German Military Command in France)
MRP	Mouvement républicain populaire (a Christian Democratic political party)
ONI	Office national d'immigration
PC	Parti communiste
PS	Parti socialiste
RA	Revue algérienne et tunisienne de législation et de jurisprudence (legal journal co-edited in Algeria and Tunisia)
RCDIP	Revue critique de droit international privé (critical journal focusing on private international law; before 1934 called Revue de droit international privé, or RDIP)
RDP	Revue de droit public et de la science politique (journal focusing on public law and political science)
RFHOM	Revue française d'histoire d'outre-mer (journal focusing on the history of France's overseas departments, territories, and former colonies)
RHMC	Revue d'histoire moderne et contemporaine (journal of modern and contemporary history)
RPP	Revue politique et parlementaire (journal focusing on internal and external political and economic issues)
RPR	Rassemblement pour la République (right-wing political party)
RSHA	Reichssicherheitshauptamt (Third Reich central security office)
SD	Sicherheitsdienst (ss intelligence agency)

SFIO	Section française de l'Internationale ouvrière (left-wing political party, precursor of the French Socialist party)
SHAT	Service historique de l'armée de terre (historical service of the French land army)
Sir.	Sirey collection
STO	Service du travail obligatoire (bureau of mandatory labor)
UDF	Union pour la démocratie française (center-right political party)

Acknowledgments

❧ My thanks go first of all to those who made it possible to bring this history of French nationality into being. Savinien Grignon-Dumoulin and Fabienne Renault, heads of the Bureau of Nationality in the Ministry of Justice, allowed me to consult the archives maintained by their office, with the authorization of Alexandre Benmakhlouf, then director of civil affairs and the seal. Gérard Moreau and Jean Gaeremynk, successive directors of the Office of Population and Migrations, gave me access to the archives of the Naturalization Bureau in Rezé, where Jean-Claude Lattay was of invaluable help.

Patrick du Cheyron and the Mission for Research and Experimentation in the Ministry of Social Affairs (MIRE) agreed to finance a historical study of German nationality legislation. Franz Mayer, today an assistant professor of law at Humboldt University in Berlin, whom I put on the trail of the German archives, came back with kernels of gold. Floriane Azoulay, Stéphane Dufoix, Andreas Fahrmeir, Pierre-Olivier François, Andreas Paulus, Jay Rowell, and Howard Sargent also provided invaluable help on the chapter devoted to Germany.

Without the special authorizations I received from the Centre Historique des Archives Nationales (CARAN) and the Centre des Archives Contemporaines de Fontainebleau, this book would not have been written. I owe particular thanks to the Fontainebleau staff, the staff of the Archives Départementales du Nord, Martin Barringer, the Georgetown University archives, and Didier Fourny, library assistant at the Cour de Cassation.

Over a five-year period the conservators and staff of the Senate Library welcomed me week after week and allowed me access to their immensely valuable collection. Without the friendship and cooperation of the conservators and staff of the library of the Fondation Nationale des Sciences Politiques, my work would have been more complicated. The working conditions offered researchers by the Cujas library are without parallel, and deserve special mention.

The Woodrow Wilson Center for International Scholars and the Center for

European Studies at Harvard University welcomed me in 1995 and 1996; I am very grateful for these opportunities to carry out research in American libraries and archives.

On critical points this work benefited from information supplied by Vida Azimi, Alain Bancaud, Laure Blévis, François Galard, Claude Goasguen, Patrick Guéniffey, Bonnie Honig, Paul Lagarde, Laurent Lainé, Sébastien Laurent, Emmanuel Macron, Gerald Neuman, Denis Peschanski, Pierre Rosanvallon, Pierre-André Taguieff, and Gilles Vaillant.

Early versions of various parts of the book were the subject of presentations and always fruitful critical discussions. The chapter on the Revolution was presented in Géraud de la Pradelle's doctoral seminar at the University of Paris X-Nanterre; the chapter on Vichy was discussed by Robert Paxton and the participants in the New York Area French History Seminar led by Herman Lebovics. The material devoted to the status of women was discussed by Christine Bard at the Centre d'histoire sociale du XXᵉ siècle (University of Paris I), my CNRS laboratory where I find the serenity and stimulation I need to carry out my work.

All along the way, the intellectual support and friendship of Claire Andrieu, Olivier Beaud, Nicolas Bersihand, Marie-Claude Blanc-Chaléard, Laurent Joly, Jason Leddington, Jean-Claude Monod, Géraud de la Pradelle, Emmanuelle Saada, and Alexis Spire have been crucial. I owe special thanks to Peter Sahlins and Marc Joly, who read the manuscript with close attention.

Olivier Nora supported this project with his friendship and his professionalism, and Christophe Bataille at Éditions Grasset was an attentive reader.

Finally, Anne Simonin, who accompanied me from the beginning, knows how much I owe her.

Introduction

⤳ In the mid-1980s it became clear to many observers that the great majority of immigrants from France's former empire — mainly North Africa but also the southern Sahara — who had come to work would be settling permanently in France. Harsh political debates ensued, revealing a deep divide in French society over the critical question: "What makes one French?"

"One is French by blood, by descent," proclaimed the former French President Valéry Giscard d'Estaing, referring to the Civil Code of 1804.[1] *No*, the left responded, "it was blood for Vichy; one is French if one is born on French soil: this is a republican principle." *False*, declared the Constitutional Council in 1993: nationality by virtue of birth on French soil (*jus soli*) is not a fundamental principle of the Republic; it was introduced into French law only in 1889, "chiefly in response to the demands of the draft."[2] "One becomes French by choice, because one wants to," Alain Finkielkraut argued, invoking Ernest Renan's elective conception of the nation, as opposed to the ethnic conception that characterized Germany, where citizenship was traditionally passed on through bloodlines (*jus sanguinis*).[3] And while the French political and legal classes argued and disagreed over what made one "French," many young people of immigrant origin claimed that legal citizenship did not matter much in practice, that they were in any case still seen by others as foreigners. Such claims were articulated, for example, during the *marche des Beurs*, a demonstration organized by people born in France to North African immigrant parents (in 1983), and in suburban "riots" (in the fall of 2005).

Thus even today, in 2008, French nationality is less a subject about which we have a substantial body of knowledge and analysis than an object fraught with contradictory representations, beliefs, and stereotypes.

While significant scholarship deals with particular periods of French identity throughout history (Peter Sahlins on the Old Regime, Gérard Noiriel and Rogers Brubaker on the late nineteenth century, Miriam Feldblum and Brubaker again for the late twentieth century),[4] the history of French nationality has never been the object of a complete and systematic study. Whole facets of this important story have been left in the dark, and no one has taken the subject as an integrated whole and put it in perspective, especially in comparison with the American, British, German, or other foreign legislation from which the French have often borrowed, and upon which French legal developments have also had some influence in turn.

To fill this gap in comparative literature and reconstruct this history, I had first to overcome a substantial obstacle. The Ministry of Justice in France has no archives that can readily enable researchers to retrace the evolution of nationality policy. As a result, it took me eight years to complete the research for this book, not only in the archives of the national and departmental administrative offices with which the Ministry of Justice dealt over the years but also in private records left by some of the politicians and jurists who participated in formulating nationality policy over the past two centuries. I also explored numerous American, German and British archives and private collections. Without such a quest for these disparate and widely dispersed but essential materials, I could not have written this book, and I could not have discovered the hidden face of an as yet untold history of France.

French "persons" were first defined under the Revolution. At the time, the word "nationality" itself did not exist. The term in use was "quality of [being a] French [person]" (*qualité de Français*); at the beginning of the nineteenth century the word "nationality" came to define the bond that linked a state to its constitutive population by law.[5]

Nationality is a matter of law. In order to exist, every nation-state needs a population and a territory. Since individual human beings have a limited lifespan, states — to ensure their own continuity over time — have had to find legal tools that not only attribute nationality but also transmit it from generation to generation.[6] There are four such tools in modern democratic states:

1. Birthplace, or jus soli: the fact of being born in a territory over which the state exercises, or has exercised, or seeks to exercise, its sovereignty;

2. Parentage, or jus sanguinis: nationality is transmitted by a parent or a more distant ancestor;

3. Residency (past, present, or future) within the country's borders (past, present, or future);

4. Matrimonial status: marrying someone who comes from a country other than one's own may allow one to acquire the spouse's nationality.

If population and territory always coincided perfectly, that is, if all American, German, Japanese, and French people, and these alone, lived respectively in the United States, Germany, Japan, and France, then it would make no differ-ence whether nationality were attributed on the basis of birthplace, parentage, or residency. Since everyone, under this scenario, would be born in a particular country to parents who were citizens of that country, and would continue to live in that country, the choice of one or another of these criteria for the attribution of nationality would have the same effect. But if a citizen were to leave his or her country, marry a foreigner, or have a child abroad, or if a foreigner were to live, marry, or have a child in a country not his or her own, the situation would become much more complex. The choice of any one of these criteria—birth-place, parentage, residency—continues to include most of the people of each country (the vast majority of people are born in a country of which their parents are citizens, remain in that country, and marry compatriots), but it introduces a process of "selection" among people who are located in what we may call the "border zone" of nationality. As an example, let us take a child born in London to a French parent. If nationality is defined by birthplace in both Britain and France, the child will be British; if nationality is defined by the bond of parentage, he or she will be French. Thus in this border zone we find all those who have bonds (through birthplace, parentage, residency, or marriage) with not just one but two, three, or even more countries.

Nationality is also a matter of policy. The legislation governing nationality in France selects the criterion or criteria that will define a French person at birth. This legislation also stipulates the conditions that will allow people who find themselves "in the border zone" of nationality to cross over in one direction or another. For nationality is, as I make clear in this book, a boundary line that is constantly being renegotiated and crossed, not an enclosure.

What distinguishes France from other countries is that for as long as it has been defining its nationals, it has experimented with many ways of defining who is "French by birth," and has tried out virtually all possible rules for attributing or withdrawing nationality. Since the Revolution, France has changed its laws more often and more significantly than any other democratic nation has, and policies governing French nationality have been the object of continual political and legal confrontations.

At every stage these struggles have brought to the forefront a long and di-verse set of both well-known and obscure personalities and politicians: Napo-leon Bonaparte, Marie-Joseph de Lafayette, Pierre Daunou, Jean-Jacques de Cambacérès, and Emmanuel Sieyès during the Revolution; Adolphe Crémieux, Jules Favre, and Napoleon III in the mid-nineteenth century; Louis Barthou, Georges Clemenceau, Antonin Dubost, André Honnorat, Charles Lambert, and Louis Martin under the Third Republic; Marshal Philippe Pétain and his three

ministers of justice during the Vichy regime, Raphaël Alibert, Joseph Barthé-
lemy, and Maurice Gabolde; General Charles de Gaulle and the two "keepers of
the Seals" (ministers of justice) during the Liberation, François de Menthon and
Pierre-Henri Teitgen; finally, in recent times, Albin Chalandon, Jacques Chirac,
Harlem Désir, Valéry Giscard d'Estaing, Jean Foyer, Lionel Jospin, Jean-Marie
Le Pen, Pierre Mazeaud, François Mitterrand, and even Bill Clinton.

The debates over nationality have also been animated—in a public way or
from the sidelines—by jurists whose role was often a determining factor for
policy change: François Tronchet, who imposed jus sanguinis on Bonaparte in
1803 in the Civil Code; René Cassin, who convinced de Gaulle that Free France
should annul the Vichy law on denaturalizations; Camille Sée, who was the state
councilor responsible for reviewing nationality legislation from 1884 to 1920;
Georges Gruffy, who inspired numerous reforms during the Third Republic;
Georges Dayras, who served as secretary general of Vichy's Ministry of Justice; Raymond Boulbès, who drafted the Nationality Code of 1945; and Marceau
Long, who headed the Nationality Commission in 1987 and inspired the text of
the nationality law of 1993.

By studying these multiple confrontations and the laws that finally resulted
from them, we can discern *three principal stages* in the construction of French
nationality.

In the early days of the Revolution, the boundary between nationals and
foreigners was difficult to establish. One could not be a citizen without being
French, but during a four-year period—from 1790 to 1794—everyone living in
France was automatically naturalized as French. Modern nationality law entered
its first stage in 1803 with the Civil Code. Despite Bonaparte's opposition, the
new legislation broke with the Old Regime's "feudal" approach to nationality,
which made birth on French territory the principal criterion for possessing the
"quality of being French." From this point on nationality became a right attached to the person: like the family name, it was transmitted by fatherhood; it
was attributed at birth; it was no longer lost if its holder established residency
abroad.

By the late nineteenth century France had become a country of immigration,
the first such in Europe. Children born in France to foreign parents rarely claimed
French nationality, even though they had the legal right to do so. Thus for generations, and independently of the new migratory trends, France's foreign population had grown automatically by virtue of jus sanguinis and the infrequency of
naturalizations. The nationality law of 1889 reorganized the boundary between
French persons and foreigners. This was the second stage: it marked the return
of jus soli, but in a form that differed from the old legislation in that it was no

longer based on allegiance but rather on socialization. In other words, a socio-logical approach to nationality, based on education within French society, was added to, and somehow substituted for, the familial approach.

Beginning in this period, and to a greater extent after the First World War, depopulation emerged as a major problem. Nationality became—and this was the third stage in its development—an instrument of demographic policy; with a law passed in 1927, French nationality became available on a vast scale to immigrants who sought it through naturalization or marriage.

The first part of this book studies these three stages and retraces the construction of modern nationality law in France.

As this construction proceeded in the late 1920s, an approach to immigration and nationality policy with clearly racist overtones emerged. This approach was based on the assumption that foreigners were assimilable to varying degrees depending on their origins—national, religious, or racial. Accordingly, the architects of this approach—René Martial and especially Georges Mauco—sought to impose just these categories as criteria for differentiation in the selection of candidates for naturalization.

The "racist approach," as we may as well call it, triumphed under the Vichy regime. As early as July 1940 the French state established a comprehensive nationality policy, which the reader will find explained, for the first time, in this book. This policy provided not only for thousands of denaturalizations targeting Jews but also for the construction of a comprehensive new nationality code—one that never, owing to a veto issued from Berlin, came to fruition.

The racist approach did not disappear with the Liberation, and figures such as Georges Mauco came close to imposing a quota system for naturalization based on national origins. At the end of the twentieth century, racism and racist policies chiefly targeted North African immigrants and their children. Between 1978 and 1980 Valéry Giscard d'Estaing tried to organize the forced return of these groups to their countries of origin; this move was followed by an attempt—albeit unsuccessful—to deny these immigrants access to French nationality by eliminating jus soli more generally

The second part of the book examines three crises in French nationality, three moments—one "Nazi," one "American," and the last "Algerian"—marked by the emergence of racist options that triumphed only under Vichy but continued to be debated until very recent times.

It would have been possible for me to stop here, given that even throughout these periods of crisis, the overall body of French law governing nationality has remained relatively stable since 1889, when jus soli was reintroduced and French nationality was ascribed to children of foreigners born in France. Had I done so, the reader might have concluded that France is the model of a civic nation open to the integration of immigrants and their children, in contrast to Germany, an ethnic nation dominated by the principle of jus sanguinis ever since Prussia adopted this principle in 1842.

But the seeming contrast between France, as an open nation practicing jus soli, and Germany, as an ethnic nation practicing jus sanguinis, is actually much more complex.

1. The history of German nationality legislation, which I study in chapter 7, contradicts the myth, and demonstrates that in reality, *the nationality law of a given nation-state does not necessarily reflect the stereotypical representations of that nation.*[7] Nationality law has its own trajectory and its own characteristic features, independent from the history of citizenship.[8] Prussian and later German nationality legislation followed the "French" path, based on jus sanguinis; most European and Asian countries eventually did the same. In contrast, the United Kingdom retained the traditional jus soli, and the United States, Canada, and all the former British colonies followed suit.

2. In addition, each of the three major stages that I have identified in describing the construction of modern French nationality law — from the Civil Code to the law of 1927 — was reached at the expense of certain critical groups of French people whose history is analyzed here: women, Algerian Muslims, and newly naturalized persons.

The Civil Code instituted the right of nationality as an individual right in 1803, but this right, limited to men, was constructed at the expense of women: until 1927 a woman took the nationality of her spouse, automatically and obligatorily. In the 1920s 150,000 women had thus been made "foreign" by marrying men who were not French citizens, although they themselves had been born French and were living in France; they had become subject to the status of foreigner, and subject — in the case of divorce, for example — to the laws of their husband's country. The law of 1889 brought about the triumph of the "sociological" approach to nationality by allowing the gradual integration of foreigners and their children, but an increasingly inferior status was imposed on Algerian Muslims at the same time: their French nationality was merely formal, denatured, stripped of rights. These people were obliged — even though they were nominally French — to go through the naturalization process to obtain full nationality; only a few thousand succeeded in doing so before Algeria became independent in 1962. Finally, the law of 1927 opened up French nationality on a massive scale, but newly naturalized citizens were prevented from exercising their political rights and excluded from access to certain professions for a period of five to ten years; this discrimination lasted until 1983.

3. Lastly, in France as elsewhere there has often been a considerable gap between law and practice. The body of law governing French nationality today is a configuration of complex arrangements that have evolved over time. By examining modern nationality legislation and its concrete application in individual cases, in the final section of this book, we can complete the process of exposing and deconstructing the myths surrounding French nationality that have given us, until now, only a partial history of France.

PART ONE

The Construction

of Modern Nationality

Law in France

From the Old Regime to the Civil Code:

The Two Revolutions in French Nationality

❧ When the Revolution began, no explicit definition of a French person existed. Under the Old Regime the boundary between the French and foreigners, or rather—to use the terminology of the period—French people and aliens (*aubains*), was defined almost accidentally, in legal contests that arose over problems of inheritance and succession.[1] On the one hand, the royal right of escheat (*droit d'aubaine*) allowed the king to appropriate the possessions of any foreigner who died without a French heir.[2] On the other hand, children of a Frenchman could not inherit from their parents if they were deemed aubains, that is, if they had been born abroad. The *parlements*—the courts, under the monarchy—heard plaintiffs who contested their alien status; as judgments were issued in such cases, the definition of a French person began to evolve.[3]

At the beginning of the sixteenth century three conditions were still necessary for someone to be recognized as French: one had to have been born in France, to have been born to French parents, and to have one's permanent residence in the kingdom.[4] But by a decision dated 23 February 1515, the Paris Parlement introduced jus soli into French law:[5] whatever the origin of a person's parents (who could both be foreigners), birth in France bestowed the capacity to inherit property and thus French nationality, as long as the person in question resided within the kingdom.[6]

At the end of the sixteenth century the bond of parentage came in turn to transmit the quality of being French (*qualité de français*): birthplace was no longer a factor. On 7 September 1576, the Paris Parlement issued the Mabile decision,[7] a formal judgment recognizing as French a woman who was born in England to French parents; the court thus granted her the right to inherit her parents' property. That the claimant had settled in France, even though both parents had died, showed that she had kept "the spirit of return"; moreover, she agreed to give up all the possessions she had inherited from her forebears should she ever leave the kingdom.[8] Over time this decision became a legal precedent, and the requirement of a bond of parentage was even relaxed.[9] But just as much as birth within the kingdom or filiation, residence in the kingdom—not only at the time of the decision but also thereafter—was an explicitly mandated condition for acquiring the quality of being French, for it was the tangible sign of allegiance to the king.

Finally, the king had the power (the exclusive power, starting with François I) to grant letters of naturalization (*lettres de naturalité*) to those who were not defined by jurisprudence as French—in other words, to foreigners.[10] Naturalization transformed foreigners into French nationals and relieved them of all their legal incapacities, granting them in particular the capacity to inherit and to bequeath; the formula used in these letters allowed naturalized persons to enjoy the same "dignities, exemptions, privileges, liberties, immunities, and rights as the true and original subjects." According to Peter Sahlins's study, the king granted forty-five of these letters a year, on average; about six thousand were awarded between 1660 and 1789.[11]

Thus on the eve of the Revolution birth within the kingdom and the bond of parentage made it possible to establish the quality of being French, provided that a person's current and (above all) future residence was in the kingdom. To put it differently, under the Old Regime anyone who resided in France was French, provided that he or she had been born in France, or had been born to French parents, or else had been naturalized. Birth on French soil, jus soli, remained the dominant criterion, however. Thus when a child born to French parents abroad came to reside within the kingdom, he or she often asked the king for a lettre de naturalité to guarantee the capacity to inherit and thus to confirm the quality of being French; a child born in the kingdom of France to a foreign parent did not have to take this step.[12]

Between 1789 and 1803 the very definition of a French person and the way a foreigner could acquire the quality of being French were modified by two contradictory upheavals. In 1790 the first revolutionaries broke with what had been two symbolic representations of royal power with respect to foreigners under the laws of the Old Regime: the right of escheat and the power to naturalize.[13] For the first time nationality was defined by a constitution. However, in 1803 the Civil Code took the opposite tack. It reestablished the state's power over foreigners with regard to the right of escheat and admission to legal residency, and nationality disappeared from the Constitution. Most significantly for defining who was French by origin, the jus soli that had remained dominant through the end of the

Old Regime and had been reinforced during the Revolution was replaced by jus sanguinis.

1790–1791: The Definition of a French Person Enters the Constitution

In 1789 the revolutionaries were more concerned about the divisions within French society than about the boundary separating foreigners from the French. Privileges were abolished, professional bodies and corporations were suppressed, and under the principle of equality, the individual was placed at the heart of the new system for attributing rights.[14] First, serfdom was eliminated;[15] next, Protestants were reintegrated, and Jews obtained equal rights;[16] finally, slavery was abolished.[17] A new dividing line emerged among the French, who were henceforth equal under the law, with active citizens on one side—men who had reached the age of majority, and possessed certain resources, had the right to vote and to participate in the exercise of national sovereignty—and passive citizens on the other—women, minors, and the poor.[18]

In a decree dated 30 April–2 May 1790, the National Assembly nevertheless determined that foreign men who had established residency in France would be "known as French and allowed, upon taking the civic oath, to exercise the rights of active citizens after five years of continuous residence in the kingdom, if they [had], in addition, either acquired real estate or married a French woman or set up a commercial establishment or received letters of municipal affiliation [*lettres de bourgeoisie*] in some city."[19] Initially, the focus was on "border departments and coastal cities . . . filled with men born in foreign countries who are married and are long-standing owners of real property or have established businesses; they have held civic positions; some were officers in the former municipalities; others are officers of the National Guard; all have sworn the civic oath; in many cities they make up an eighth, a seventh, a sixth of the population: these are more friends you are acquiring for a constitution that seeks to make all men happy." With this decree, however, the right to naturalize was no longer a royal prerogative:[20] without the need for any further intervention by the government or for their own consent, foreigners became French if they met the conditions—for example, that of residency—prescribed by the law.[21]

Next, with the decree of 6 August 1790 the National Assembly abolished the rights of escheat and detraction,[22] without any conditions of reciprocity. Here too the point was to break with royal power. However, this particular break was more symbolic than practical. For several years many foreigners had already been exempted from the right of escheat either by virtue of particular privileges[23] or, more often, because they belonged to an exempt nation;[24] between

1766 and 1788 France had signed seventy-five agreements with other states providing for total[25] or partial exemption from the royal right of escheat.[26]

Finally, the law of 9–15 December 1790 restored the right to be French to descendants of the exiled Protestants. This provision signaled yet another break with the discretionary power of the monarchy: "All persons who were born in foreign countries and descend in any degree from a French man or woman who was expatriated for religious reasons are declared natural French persons and will enjoy the rights attached to that quality, if they return to France, establish their homes there, and swear the civic oath."[27]

A few months later the definition of a French person, inspired by the old jurisprudence, was included in the first constitution, dated 3 September 1791:[28] the quality of being French was granted to "those who were born in France to a French father; those who, born in France to a foreign father, have established their domicile in the kingdom; those who, born in a foreign country to a French father, have returned to establish residency in France and have sworn the civic oath."[29] In fact, the entire set of provisions dealing with nationality was inscribed in the constitution, for that document incorporated the law of 9–15 December 1790 pertaining to Protestants and that of 30 April–2 May 1790 pertaining to the naturalization of foreigners. For the first time in French history, legislation governing nationality had become explicit and applicable in a consistent way to the national territory as a whole.[30] From the legal and practical standpoints, the chief innovation lay in the way a foreigner could become French: either by exceptional naturalization or—most often—automatically.

1790–1795: Two Ways to Acquire the "Quality of Being French": Honorary Citizenship . . .

Article 4 of title II of the constitution of 3 September 1790 gave the legislature power to grant exceptional naturalizations: under special circumstances it could "give a foreigner an Act of Naturalization, without any condition other than establishing legal residence in France and swearing the civic oath."

Less than a year later, on 24 August 1792, Marie-Joseph Chénier[31] stood before the National Assembly, speaking for several citizens of Paris, to propose "the adoption of those who in the various countries of the world have ripened human reason and prepared the paths of liberty." France was at war with Austria and Prussia.[32] The fatherland had been declared in danger as of 11 July. On 1 August Parisians found out about the Brunswick manifesto threatening the capital's inhabitants with reprisals if "the least violence, the least offense" were committed against the royal family.[33] On 10 August the Assembly decided to suspend the rule of Louis XVI and put a provisional executive committee in the king's place while waiting for a Convention to be elected. On 19 August the Prussians entered France; the next day they were at the gates of the city of Longwy, whose inhabitants, under bombardment, forced the garrison to capitulate on 23 August.[34]

On 26 August 1792 the following decree was adopted:[35] "considering . . . that at the moment when a national Convention is about to establish the destiny of France, and perhaps prepare that of the human race, it behooves a generous and free people to call upon all sources of enlightenment and to bestow the right to join in this great act of reason on men who, through their sentiments, their writings, and their courage, have shown themselves eminently worthy; . . . the title of French citizen [is hereby bestowed on] Dr. Joseph Priestly, Thomas Payne, *Jeremy Bentham*, William Wilberforce, *Thomas Clarkson*, Jacques Mackintosh, *David Williams*, N. Gorani, *Anacharsis Cloots, Corneille Pauw*, Joachim-Henry Campe, N. Pestalozzi, *George Washington, Alexander Hamilton*, James Madison, *H. Klopstock*, and *Thaddeus Kosciuszko*."[36]

At the request of a member of the Assembly, the German publicist Giller was added to the list.[37]

The intent was not to apply article 4 of the constitution literally. According to the provisions of that article, the act of naturalization could take effect only *on condition that the recipient establish legal residence in France and swear the civic oath*. Neither Bentham nor Washington nor Hamilton, for example, resided in France, or swore the civic oath (nor would they). They were granted honorary citizenship, comparable in legal terms to what was bestowed on Lafayette[38] by the United States. As the U.S. Supreme Court ruled in Lafayette's case, the act of naturalization would take effect only if the beneficiary established actual residence in the country that had made him or her a citizen.[39] In France this was the case for two of those named, Thomas Payne and Anacharsis Cloots; moreover, both men were elected to membership in the Convention.

Given the context (the fatherland was in danger and the king had been arrested), the invitation to foreign intellectuals or legislators to participate in the founding of the French Republic marked the Republic's universal dimension. It was also a way of following Rousseau's advice: in *The Social Contract*, Rousseau mentioned that it was the custom in most Greek cities, in many modern Italian republics, and even more recently in the Republic of Geneva to confer upon foreigners the extraordinary task of establishing laws; they were acquainted with human passions, but as outsiders in the society that they were charged with organizing, they had no stake in its political conflicts.[40]

Finally, the attribution of honorary citizenship was the symbolic counterpart of the withdrawal of nationality inflicted on the French who were fighting their own country from abroad, the émigrés against whom measures had already been taken by decree: confiscation (27 July 1792) and sale of property (14 August 1792); further measures were to follow. Moreover, when Claude-Bernard Navier,[41] reporting a few weeks earlier on behalf of the committee on legislation, spoke in favor of three requests for exceptional naturalization that conformed to title I, article 3, of the constitution of 1791, support from the worthiest foreigners was the *chief consideration* that he invoked: "In our political situation of the moment . . . everyone will recognize how advantageous it is for the French nation to be in the position of countering the detractors of the Constitution and the Laws with the eagerness to subject themselves to them on the part of three men whose Enlightenment is beyond question and who value this constitution and these laws at a price that can be calculated in terms of the advantages they are renouncing in their birthplaces."[42]

These few exceptional naturalizations still have powerful symbolic value today; they signify openness to foreigners and a universalist outlook. A few months later, when war was declared, the foreigner, an ambiguous political figure in the landscape of the Revolution, took on the mask of enemy, traitor, or spy.[43] Decrees issued on 26 February and 21 March 1793 required foreigners to declare their presence. On 16 October 1793 the Convention decreed that "foreigners born subject to governments with which the Republic is at war will be detained until peace [is achieved]."[44] On 25 December 1793 foreigners lost the right to represent the French people, and Cloots and Payne were excluded from the Convention. By a decree issued on 26 December 1793, this interdiction was extended to French people born abroad. Only Frenchmen born within the national territory were authorized to participate in public life. On 15 April 1794, under the influence of Saint-Just, decrees were adopted forbidding foreigners born in countries with which France was at war to live in certain cities, and denying to all foreigners and nobles the right to join popular societies and surveillance committees, in communal or sectional assemblies.[45]

. . . and Automatic Naturalization

However, during the entire first phase of the Revolution, from the law of 30 April–2 May 1790 to 22 September 1795, the date when the constitution of Year III went into effect, a relatively stable common law governing naturalization remained in force. Neglected, badly interpreted, and yet radically innovative, it conferred French nationality on hundreds or even thousands of foreigners living in France. It did so automatically, with important practical consequences for men who were requisitioned and obliged to serve in the army or who were subjected, if married to a Frenchwoman, to the new legislation governing divorce.

Under the law of 1790, first of all, all foreigners were automatically French if they had been resident in France for five years, had acquired property, had set up a business, or had received a letter of municipal affiliation (a statement from a city attesting to residency). A foreign man who married a French woman was also automatically French. Men in this category could also, like other Frenchmen, become active citizens and thus vote, by swearing the civic oath. But even if they did not exercise that privilege they were no less French, according to the authorities responsible for military recruitment and the Supreme Court (Cour de cassation).[46]

Could the law of 1790 naturalize foreigners "without their express formal consent"? This question was raised in 1806 by Philippe-Antoine Merlin,[47] the state solicitor general attached to the Supreme Court, when the court had to rule on the case of Terence Mac-Mahon, an Irishman who had arrived in France in 1781 and married a Frenchwoman on 16 November 1789. Was naturalization not a contract "between a government that adopts a foreigner and the foreigner himself"? Merlin's answer was clear: naturalization could undoubtedly "be established by a contract that results from a request by the foreigner for this favor . . . but it may also be established by the sole power of the law, and without the foreigner's consent. The sovereign, by virtue of the simple fact that he is sovereign, may say: *I want all those who live in my states to be citizens*; and once he has said this, no one has the right to respond: *I do not want to be a citizen even though I live in your states*." After citing the emperor Antoninus, who "declared all the inhabitants of his vast empire Roman citizens," and the law of 23 February 1797, which had made all the inhabitants of Belgium French, Merlin finally added: "If sire Mac-Mahon had not wanted to be French, what would he have said, what would he have done, in view of the law that declared him such? No doubt he would have said: Since they want me to be French because I have my home in France, I withdraw, I leave the service and I abandon the territory of a government by which I do not care to be adopted; and, not content to say so, he would have done so."[48]

The logic of automatic attribution is not found in precisely the same terms in the constitution of 1791. Although the committee reviewer who presented article 3 to the Constituent Assembly indicated that it had incorporated the decree of 30 April–2 May 1790 and that he had "textually reported it just as" the Assembly had "long since decreed," the content is in fact different. In the formula adopted, "those foreigners who, born outside the kingdom to foreign parents, reside in France, become French citizens after five years of continuous legal residence in the kingdom, if they have, in addition, acquired property or [if male] married a French woman, or set up a business, *and* if they have sworn the civic oath." Swearing the oath had become one of the conditions of access to the "quality of being French"; this was not true of the law of 1790.[49]

Less than two years later, however, automatic attribution of citizenship was reestablished: article 4 of the constitution of 1793 no longer mentions the civic oath. It declares that "any foreigner" who is at least twenty-one years of age and who, "domiciled in France for one year, lives there by his or her work — Or acquires a property — Or [if male] marries a French woman — Or adopts a child — Or supports an elderly person is allowed to exercise the rights of a French citizen."[50]

Questions occasionally arise today about the extent to which the constitution that was adopted on 24 June 1793, approved on 10 August, and suspended by decree on 10 October of the same year actually went into effect, and about the way to interpret its article 3. Contemporaries — the courts, for instance — had no such hesitation: the constitution of 1793 had gone into effect, and proof of this "is found in the very decree of 10 October that suspends its effect."[51] In fact only the sections pertaining to politics and government were suspended; the decree of 10 October indicates that "the provisional government of France is revolutionary until peace is achieved." All other sections of the constitution of 1793 were thus considered applicable until the next constitution went into effect in 1795. So ruled the courts of Lyon, Colmar, Orléans, Douai, and Aix.[52] Article 4 of the constitution of 1793 was thus interpreted in conformity with the law of April 1790 on automatic attribution of citizenship; the courts deemed that people who met the prescribed conditions had acquired French nationality "without even a need for their volition or consent."[53]

The Colmar court thus ruled on the situation of a foreigner born on 15 September 1774, who had been living in France since 22 September 1790 and "continuously exercised a trade." In other words, he was supporting himself through his work in France; because he had reached the age of twenty-one on 15 September 1795 — that is, one week before 22 September 1795, "the day the Constitution of Year III was accepted by the French people" — he was declared to be French.[54]

Pierre François Lanau, born in Maubeuge on 22 November 1819, was also declared French inasmuch as he was the grandson of Pierre Joseph Lanau, a Belgian living in Maubeuge in 1793. His grandfather had married on 21 August 1793, when he was over twenty-one. According to the Douai court, he had acquired the quality of being French one year after his marriage, on 21 August 1794, because at that time he was still legally resident in Maubeuge and earning his living there as an armsmaker. The Aix court also declared Jean Martin to be French, inasmuch as he was the grandson of Jacques Martin, who was born in Turin in 1766, lived in Antibes from 1791 on, and was earning his living as a weaver when he married a Frenchwoman at Villeneuve-Loubet on 22 December 1794. In a decision dated 18 August 1858, the court specified that the constitution of 1793 "fully conferred the quality of being French without the foreigner thus naturalized *ipso facto* needing to manifest his intent or to make any declaration whatsoever."[55]

Thus, through the combination of the law of 1790 and the constitution of 1793, the vast majority of foreigners legally resident in France during the first years of the Revolution became French *automatically*, even without their consent; the short period during which the constitution of 1791 was in effect—a period during which swearing the civic oath was necessary—had had very little concrete impact.[56] The administrative authorities charged with organizing the conscription of Frenchmen took full advantage of the situation, moreover: a majority of the foreigners residing in France were thus enrolled in the army.[57]

Things changed for foreigners who arrived in France after 21 September 1795, when the constitution of Year III took effect: naturalization ceased to be automatic.[58] To become French, a foreigner who had reached the age of twenty-one had to take deliberate steps of his own volition: first he had to *declare his intention* to settle in France, and then he had to reside there for seven consecutive years. His naturalization took effect without any intervention on the part of public authorities as soon as he paid a tax, acquired real estate or a farm or business establishment, or married a Frenchwoman (article 10).[59] The constitution of 1799 maintained the same procedure, but the length of residency required after the declaration of residency became ten years, while the conditions of social status were eliminated for the first time; residency alone allowed access to the quality of being French.[60]

1803: Nationality Rules Incorporated in the Civil Code

The constitution of 1799, like its predecessors, thus specified how one was French at birth. But while various articles of the constitution of 1791 distinguished the definition of a French person from that of a citizen,[61] the constitutions of 1793 (Year I), 1795 (Year III), and 1799 (Year VIII) all embedded the definition of a citizen within that of a French national.[62] Following Condorcet's approach,[63] they spelled out the two definitions within the same articles, the one following from the other. For example, article 2 of the constitution of 1799 specifies that "every man born and residing in France" who, having reached the age of twenty-one, "has had his name recorded in the civic register of his communal district, and who has lived for a year since that time within the territory of the Republic, is a French citizen."[64] One might suppose today that this article, taken literally, defines only the citizen.[65]

On this point, contemporaries of the constitution did not yet harbor any doubt. They read, interpreted, and applied this article, as they did the corresponding articles of the constitutions of 1793 and 1795, in the self-referential way that these documents were conceived. Let us go back to article 2 of the constitution of 1799. Its first part, "every man born and residing in France," defines the Frenchman in a generic fashion, as Vida Azimi shows[66] — which is to say that every man and by extension every woman and every child born and residing in France are French. The second part of the article specifies who, among the French, is a citizen: only the male who, "having reached the age of twenty-one, has had his name recorded in the civic register of his communal district, and . . . has lived for a year since that time within the territory of the Republic."

In 1803 a new reading of this article took the definition of the Frenchman out of the constitution. The first title of the first book[67] of the Civil Code, "On the Enjoyment and Deprivation of Civil Rights," had just been promulgated. It contained a key provision, article 7, which specified that "the exercise of civil rights is independent of the quality of citizen, a quality that is acquired and retained only in conformity with constitutional law."[68] It follows from this that the constitution henceforth defined only citizens, while the definition of French persons was inscribed in the Civil Code and was to be constructed independently from — even in opposition to — earlier legislation. Since 1793 the successive constitutions, including the version from 1799, had asserted the exclusivity of the territorial principle: one was French if one had been born in France and resided there. With the Civil Code, bloodlines — jus sanguinis — prevailed: a French person was a "child born to a French father."

By the same token, article 2 of the constitution of 1799 had different meanings or effects depending on whether it was applied before or after 1803. Before 1803 this article also defined who was French: "every person born and residing in France." Thus the court in Nancy recognized the quality of being French in Jean-Pierre Jacques, born in 1800 in the Meuse region to a father from Luxembourg, for "at that time, there still existed the territorial principle by virtue of which one was [French if one was] born on French soil even to foreign parents" and "the constitution of Year VIII recognized *la qualité de Français* in every person born and residing in France." In the same way, the court of Douai decided that François Verhaeghen, born on 29 December 1800 near Hazebrouck in the north, was French, since "children born in France even to a foreign mother and father, before the promulgation of the *Civil Code*, found themselves invested by right, apart from their parentage, with the quality of being French."[69]

After 1803 this article of the constitution of 1799 was read on its own terms and no longer said anything but what can be read in it literally today: a (male) French person born and residing in France at the age of twenty-one was a citizen (that is, a person endowed with political rights), provided that he was included on the civic register.[70] And it was now the Civil Code that spelled out who was French: "a child born to a French father." But this victory of jus sanguinis was only achieved after a long struggle that began in 1799 and finally ended when a seventy-six-year-old jurist, François Tronchet, won out over the first consul, Napoléon Bonaparte.

Jus Sanguinis or Jus Soli?

The first clash between jus soli and jus sanguinis took place right after the coup d'état of 9 November 1799 (18 Brumaire, Year VIII) that put Bonaparte in power, with the drafting of the new constitution of 13 December 1799. Emmanuel Sieyès,[71] the leading figure behind the constitution under development, proposed to define French nationals by jus sanguinis: "The quality of being French is acquired by birth and can be acquired by adoption. It suffices in the first case to be born on French territory to a French father or a French mother, or even to be born in a foreign country to a father who had not lost the quality of being French. In the second case, adoption can be proved by a certificate (*brevet*), by letters of naturalization. . . . The Senate has the authority to make decisions in this regard."[72] But Bonaparte, supported by Daunou, chief drafter of the constitution of 1795 and secretary for the group that was polishing the definitive text of the new one,[73] managed to get the terms of the previous constitution reinstated: a French person was someone who had been born and was residing in France.[74]

A few months later, on 12 August 1800, work on drafting a Civil Code started up again, and led to a new debate. The first three drafts of the Civil Code, prepared between 1793 and 1796 under the leadership of Cambacérès,[75] were prepared, discussed, and rejected within parliamentary committees.[76] For the version of 1799 a ruling by the Consuls directed a commission of jurists to draft a new proposal. The commission was headed by Tronchet, the president of the Supreme Court (*Tribunal de cassation*), and its members included Bigot de Préameneu, a representative of the government on the High Court, and Portalis, a representative of the *conseil des Prises*.[77] Maleville, a member of the Tribunal, served as reporter.[78]

Some months later, on 21 January 1801, a draft was presented to the government and then submitted for comment to the Supreme Court and to all appellate courts in France. Finally, it followed the procedure for the adoption of a law that had been outlined in the constitution of 1799: the text was first polished by the Council of State in general assembly after having been studied by one of the Council's five specialized sections; it was then transmitted to be discussed by the upper parliamentary chamber, the Tribunate, which had to approve or reject it with no amendments; next, the lower Legislative Corps had to adopt or reject it without discussion, after hearing testimony by three representatives from the Council of State and three from the Tribunate. The Sénat Conservateur (constitutional Court) could intervene, finally, if an issue of constitutionality arose.

In these assemblies set up by the constitution of 1799 we often find actors left over from the earliest moments of the Revolution. In the new configuration, however, they were playing unfamiliar roles. Tronchet, whom Napoleon later called the soul of the Civil Code,[79] is an example of this transfiguration of roles and positions that gave a privileged place to the moderate jurists. Tronchet, born in 1726, was the senior member of the group drafting the Civil Code. The son of a prosecutor in the Paris Parlement, a lawyer at the Paris bar from 1745, he had just been named president of the bar when the Revolution broke out. He was elected to represent Paris at the Estates General without having sought the position; he later held a seat in the Constituent Assembly as a constitutional royalist. As a lawyer for Louis XVI, he went into hiding during the Terror; after 27 July 1795 (9 Thermidor) he opened a consulting office. He was also designated by the department of Seine-et-Oise as a representative to the Council of Elders (Conseil des Anciens), where he served until 1799. After the coup d'état of 9 November (18 Brumaire), Bonaparte appointed him to the Supreme Court, and his colleagues elected him president.[80] As head of the commission preparing the Civil Code he was responsible for the adoption of article 7, which removed the matter of nationality from the constitution. He played a decisive role in the invention of a new nationality law.

The discussion of the section of the Civil Code devoted to nationality began in the Council of State on 25 July 1801. In the proposal that Tronchet had prepared, only children born to a French father in France or abroad were French. But while the constitution no longer defined the quality of being French, it continued to define citizenship, stating in article 2, as we have seen, that "every man born and residing in France who, having reached the age of 21, has had his name recorded in the civic register of his communal district, and who has lived for a year since that time within the territory of the Republic, is a French citizen." On its face this passage indicated that every man born in France to a foreign father was a potential citizen. But could one be a citizen without being French? None of the framers of the Code had this in mind: "Something has to be done," Boulay (de la Meurthe) noted, adding that "one can hardly deny civil rights to a foreigner's son born in France, given that the Constitution gives him political rights."[81]

Tronchet acknowledged the problem, and proposed to require that children born in France to foreign parents must declare their intention to be citizens: "The population has always been willing to regard these individuals as French, provided that they expressly declare that such is their will."[82]

Bonaparte then intervened in the discussion. He was of a different opinion, and proposed quite simply to declare that "every individual born in France is French." Tronchet responded that "the fact of being born on French territory gives only the aptitude to acquire the enjoyment of civil rights; but this enjoyment must belong only to a person who declares that he wishes to accept it." He maintained that one could not "give the son of a foreigner the quality of being French without his consent."

Bonaparte replied that "if individuals born in France to foreign fathers were not considered rightfully French, then the sons of the foreigners who had settled in large numbers in France initially as prisoners or for other war-related reasons could not be subject to the draft or to other civic responsibilities." He thought that "one must consider the question solely in terms of France's interests. If individuals born in France to a foreign father have no property, at least they have the French spirit, French habits; they have the natural attachment everyone has for the land in which he was born; and, finally, they bear civic responsibilities. If they have property, the legacies that come to them from abroad arrive in France; those that they receive in France are governed by French laws; thus in every respect it is advantageous to admit them to the rank of Frenchman . . . Instead of establishing that the individual born in France to a foreign father will only obtain civil rights when he has declared that he wishes to enjoy them, we could decide that he is deprived of them only when he renounces them formally."[83]

The foreigners whom Bonaparte and Tronchet had in mind were probably not the same ones: Bonaparte's were of modest social status, available for the draft, while Tronchet's were of a more well-to-do class. Tronchet feared that if foreigners of the latter sort were granted French nationality against their will, their own countries would take reprisals against French nationals who had settled in these territories, depriving French emigrants of their right to inherit or to preserve their property. Tronchet tried to resist, but Bonaparte was decisively supported in the debate by Portalis, for whom "there was no reason not to declare that every child born in France is French, this principle being necessarily modified by the legal dispositions that govern the way in which a French person retains or loses the favor of his origin." Bonaparte accepted this approach, and the following week, on 2 August 1801, the version he had presented was approved: "every individual born in France is French." The Council of State, at Bonaparte's urging, thus reestablished the jus soli that Tronchet and his commission had sought to abolish. In parallel with jus sanguinis, which lost the exclusivity that Tronchet wanted to grant it, jus soli made it possible to attribute French nationality at birth.

Underlying the divergence between Tronchet and Bonaparte, there were two approaches to "nationality." As a lawyer under the Old Regime, Tronchet had pled on several occasions—for clients—in favor of jus sanguinis. Before 1789 legal challenges to the royal right of escheat were in fact rarely brought by people born in France, but rather by those born abroad to French parents, people whose French status had been called into question. Tronchet's archives, preserved in the Supreme Court, attest that to defend his clients and to convince the judges, Tronchet had carefully identified all court decisions from the mid-sixteenth century on that had validated the transmission of the French nationality through the link of parentage to the child of a French person born abroad.[84] He gradually constructed his own theory of nationality, at a considerable remove from the prevailing reality.[85] He argued with all the more conviction that jus sanguinis was superior to jus soli because it was inspired by Roman law, whose influence had expanded among jurists during the eighteenth century.[86] In the debates in the Council of State, Tronchet borrowed extensively from the last legal consultation he had prepared on the subject, in late 1783: "It is his origin that forms man's relation with the political state to which he belongs, and this is the true source of the respective rights and duties of the sovereign and the subject."[87]

Tronchet's desire to institute jus sanguinis can thus be traced to his *habitus* as a jurist. He built his theory on his experience with cases encountered in his own practice. Convinced that jus sanguinis was the legitimate criterion for attributing the quality of being French, he naturally used the position he occupied (when he became president of the commission charged with preparing the Civil Code), and the authority it conferred, to try to make this the dominant criterion of a new French law governing nationality.

Bonaparte's approach, based on a vision of the interests of the French state, was not without contradictions. On the one hand, for security reasons he was in favor of reinforcing state control over foreigners' access to France, the conditions under which they could establish residency or be naturalized. On the other hand, because a large population is an asset for state power, he was in favor of recognizing as French everyone who was linked to France by birth, whether through parentage or territory; on this issue his motto was that "there can only be advantages in extending the empire of French civil laws."

The politician Bonaparte and the lawyer Tronchet were thus opposed on jus soli, but in the debates that followed their views converged. First, they were both in favor of reestablishing the right of escheat: it had been abolished in 1790 with regard to foreigners in France, but foreign countries had not reciprocated with regard to French nationals residing on their territory. In his report, Roederer describes the failure of the Constituent Assembly's generous approach: "When Louis XV let it be known that he consented to the general abolition of the right of escheat provided there was reciprocity, a hundred States offered it to him, and a hundred treatises were signed . . . ; and, on the contrary, since the decrees of 6 August 1790 and 8 April 1791, no country, no State, has abolished either the right of detraction or the subject's right to inherit or even the right of escheat, although France had renounced those same rights."[88] Hence the wording of article 11 in the Civil Code: "The foreigner will enjoy in France the same civil rights as those granted to the French by the Treaties of the Nation to which that foreigner belongs."

Tronchet also supported Bonaparte's intervention to allow the state to control the attribution of a new status created for foreigners by the Code, the status of *admis à domicile*, "admitted to residency," halfway between resident and naturalized citizen. Initially article 6 read as follows: "The foreigner who has declared his wish to settle in France and become a *citizen* and who has resided in France for one year pursuant to that declaration will have full enjoyment of civil rights." Later this became: "The foreigner who *has been permitted* to declare that he wishes to settle."[89] The final text of the Civil Code thus distinguished among three types of foreigners: the one who was *permitted* to establish his legal residency in France and who enjoyed all the civil rights of French nationals; the one who enjoyed civil rights only according to terms of reciprocity with his country of origin; and finally, the one whose country of origin had no agreement with France and who was subject to the right of escheat.

Finally, Tronchet and Bonaparte together supported the extension of jus sanguinis by attributing the quality of being French to children born abroad to "Frenchmen who have abdicated their fatherland," if those children declared that they "intended to establish residency in France."

Tronchet had already intervened on this topic on 9 August 1791, borrowing from one of his pre-Revolutionary consultations to defend the right of all French expatriates, not just Protestants, to resume French nationality: "It has always been true that it sufficed for people who were originally French to return to

France and declare that they wanted to establish residency there for them to regain all the rights of French citizens." On 2 August 1801, supported by Boulay, he stated: "Expatriation is not in itself a civil offense; it is the use of a natural faculty that cannot be challenged in a person. One often leaves one's country for innocent reasons; most often, one makes the decision to do so in the interest of one's fortune. . . . But abdication has never effaced the favor of one's origin."[90] Bonaparte professed to approve of jus sanguinis as much as jus soli whenever doing so allowed him to achieve his goal of bringing in additional French nationals and "extending the empire of French civil laws." He thus backed Tronchet during the lively discussion devoted to what would become article 10, §2, of the Civil Code.

Those who had reservations were worried about the status of children of émigrés: Regnaud argued that there would be disadvantages in allowing sons of "Frenchmen who have freely adopted a new fatherland, who may simply have left France out of hatred for its regime, to regain the character of Frenchman, and to come to France to claim inheritances."[91] Sensitive to these concerns, Bonaparte ratified the initial version of the provision because it seemed to him to *favor the population*." Yet he got the Council of State to decide that a child born to an émigré would be viewed not as the child of a "Frenchman who had abdicated his country" but as the child of an individual who was dead in civil terms.[92]

On 19 November 1801 the Council of State adopted and transmitted to the Tribunate a text that extended—as Bonaparte wished—the empire of French civil laws further than ever by jus soli and jus sanguinis, and that provided for stricter controls over foreigners' access to residency and naturalization.

A Defeat for Bonaparte

The opening of the session of Parliament took place three days later, on 22 November 1801. Portalis introduced the Civil Code in a speech that was to become famous.[93] The subsequent debate in the Tribunate began in a tense atmosphere. A gathering of former members of the Convention who were attached to the principles of the Revolution, this assembly was disgruntled at having been marginalized in relation to the First Consul and the Council of State, and it was also troubled by various signs of reconciliation with the Old Regime, such as the concordat that had just been signed with Pope Pius VII. On the eve of the discussion of the first sections of the Civil Code, when peace treaties with England, Russia, the German and Italian powers, Portugal, and the Ottoman Empire were put up for ratification, a heated incident brought certain members of the

Tribunate into opposition with Bonaparte: France and Russia promised in their treaty "not to tolerate a situation in which any of their subjects should permit themselves to maintain a correspondence . . . with the internal enemies of the governments of the two states"; the émigrés were targeted in France's case and the Poles in Russia's, but the use of the word "subject" triggered a very strong reaction. The treatise was finally adopted with seventy-seven votes in favor and fourteen against, but Marie-Joseph Chénier and Benjamin Constant opposed it vigorously.[94]

The opposition manifested itself again with respect to the opening sections of the Civil Code. First, title 1 was rejected because it made the new laws non-retroactive. Then title 3 was adopted before title 2 — the one that concerns us — came up for discussion.

The Tribunate member Siméon, the reviewer presenting the first part of the text "on the enjoyment of civil rights," expressed particular reservations over re-establishing the right of escheat. He also challenged the attribution of the quality of being French to people who had simply been born in France: "The son of an Englishman may become French; but will this happen solely because his mother, passing through France, has given birth to him on this land foreign to her, to her husband, to her parents? . . . One's fatherland will depend less on the affection one attaches to it, on choice and residency, than on the accident of birth. . . . Every child born in England is generally a subject of the king, Blackstone tells us. This shows the effects of feudalism; it is not something to be imitated."[95] The Tribunate's opposition to jus soli converged with that of the jurists, but it was of a different nature. Like that of Sieyès, it was based on a determination to break with the feudal approach in order to make the nation the sole source of the quality of being French. The nation is like a family, and nationality must be transmitted the way the family name is transmitted: by parentage. Siméon concluded that the text under discussion should be rejected also because the passage concerning the "deprivation of civil rights" maintained the now-defunct institution of civil death. "The person condemned to that punishment loses all civil existence: he loses ownership of all his property; he can no longer accept or transmit any inheritance; his marriage is dissolved."[96]

In the debate that followed in the Tribunate, Boissy d'Anglas, Malherbe, and Chénier also opposed reestablishing the right of escheat, civil death, and attribution of the quality of being French to a foreigner's child who had not expressed the wish to be French. On 1 January 1802 the Tribunate voted to reject the proposed law.[97]

The same day, the Tribunate designated Daunou, rather than the candidate whom Bonaparte preferred, for a position as senator; the First Consul took this as a declaration of war. Daunou was the mind behind the constitution of 1795, he had drafted the constitution of 1799, and he had been the Tribunate's first president.[98] He had objected to the creation — in response to the attack on the First Consul in the rue Nicaise on 14 December 1800 — of special courts charged with judging political crimes and offenses.[99] After these courts were created, Daunou stopped serving on the Tribunate and declared that he would not serve again "as long as tyranny lasted."[100] A furious Bonaparte withdrew the proposals under discussion and thought about dissolving the Tribunate or the constitution.[101] But Cambacérès came up with another idea. One-fifth of the membership of the Tribunate and of the Legislative Corps had to be renewed that year (Year X). Instead of drawing lots as planned, why not have the Sénat Conservateur designate those members who were to leave, and eliminate the opposition that way?[102]

Tronchet, named to the Sénat Conservateur at Cambacérès's suggestion as of 28 February 1801,[103] played a decisive role in organizing the institution's complicity with the operation:[104] contacted by Cambacérès, he intervened in the Sénat Conservateur in favor of the proposed procedure for renewing the Tribunate, and he was the designated reviewer for the "commission on renewal" charged with studying its implementation.[105] On 13 March 1802 a senatus-consulte ruled on the forms in which the first renewal of the Legislative Corps and the Tribunate would take place; the Sénat Conservateur established the list of Tribunate members who were to remain in office. Four days later, the twenty strongest personalities of the Tribunate, who were also Bonaparte's most determined opponents, including Chénier, Constant, and Daunou, found themselves eliminated.[106] Tamed, the Tribunate then approved the entire set of thirty-seven proposed laws that constituted the Civil Code, with only a few modifications of detail.[107] Among these, as if by special arrangement, was Tronchet's proposal concerning nationality, which Bonaparte had previously rejected but which was nevertheless adopted after a final exchange of texts between the Tribunate and the Council of State.[108]

On 26 June 1802 the government again forwarded to the Tribunate's section on legislation the text adopted originally by the Council of State,[109] a text that provided for maintaining jus soli. But the section's reviewer continued to oppose the article stipulating that every individual born in France was French,[110] and the Tribunate proposed to eliminate it. In the name of the Council of State, Bigot de Préameneu finally suggested taking up virtually word for word what Tronchet had envisaged some months earlier:[111] "Every individual born in France to a foreigner can, in the year that follows the date of his majority, request the quality of being French, provided that, in the case in which he is living in France, he declares that he intends to establish his legal residence there, or, in the case in which he is living abroad, he submits that he intends to establish his legal residence in France, and that he establishes said residence in the year following the act of submission."[112]

With this version definitively ratified, the part of the Civil Code pertaining to the enjoyment of civil rights took effect on 18 March 1803.[113] To have jus sanguinis instituted as the *exclusive criterion* for attributing the quality of being French at birth, Tronchet had thus been able — in a quite particular political conjuncture, as head of a coalition of moderate jurists and with the support of the first revolutionaries — to get around Bonaparte. This break with jus soli, the reinterpretation of Roman law in the form of jus sanguinis in the name of the nation as the political extension of the family, marked the beginning of a lasting revolution. It inaugurated the era of modern nationality law in France and throughout Europe.

The Triumph of Jus Soli (1803–1889)

Codify: the word has important implications.
It implies that history and historians have in some sense been put aside.
Codification is a trenchant act on the part of the legislator, who cuts law off from
its origins, as it were; he bases it entirely on reason, justice, public interest, and
harmony and interdependence among its various articles, and he dispenses it
from seeking precedents or justifications apart from one authentic instant, be-
yond the day of its promulgation.
To anyone who might seek to go further back, the law itself seems to reply:
Why bother! There has been a liquidation of all that is past, and something like
a fresh start. —ÉMILE BOUTMY[1]

⤳ With the promulgation of the Civil Code, the legislation governing "nationality"—a new concept emerging in legal parlance to signify the "quality" of being French[2]—broke with the Old Regime and with the Revolution. Under the Old Regime and especially during the Revolution, the answer to the question "What is a French person?" was "A man or woman who was born in France and continues to live there." Once the Civil Code was adopted, only someone born to a French father, whether in France or abroad, was French.[3] Nationality was henceforth an attribute of the person, transmitted, like the family name, through fatherhood. It was attributed once and for all at birth, and no longer depended on residency on French territory, which had been a sign of allegiance to the sovereign under the Old Regime, and later a sign of support for the Revolution.

In practical terms, the first consequence of the new legislation was that a Frenchman living abroad kept his nationality and transmitted it to his children. The second, parallel result was that children born in France to foreign parents were no longer French: they received and transmitted their father's nationality.

Still, the Civil Code allowed them to request French nationality in the year after they reached the age of majority.

The Code contained an additional principle, the freedom to change one's nationality, which Napoleon quickly challenged. A Frenchman, who had been free to be naturalized abroad (although he would then have lost his French nationality),[4] very quickly found himself prevented from doing so. In 1809 Napoleon instituted the principle of perpetual allegiance, which kept such a person from being naturalized abroad without authorization from the French government; this principle remained in effect until 1889.[5] The point was to force the French to resign from enemy armies or administrations, to prevent them from evading the draft, or to have more control over them when they went off to serve states allied with the Empire.[6]

As for foreigners who lived in France without having been born there, the relevant provisions of the constitution of 1799, still in force, were applied, for the Civil Code remained silent on naturalization as such. French nationality was fully available to a foreign man by law ten years after he had registered his declaration of intent at the city hall in his place of legal residence. For Napoleon, this rule limited state power unacceptably in two ways: it was impossible for the state to naturalize foreign men who had less than ten years' residency, and more importantly, it was impossible for the state not to naturalize foreigners who had made a declaration of intent, once ten years had passed. The rule was thus modified to facilitate access to French nationality for certain carefully selected foreigners and to prevent access on the part of "undesirables."

Even before the Civil Code was promulgated, on 4 September 1802, a senatus-consulte had restored a mechanism for exceptional naturalization inspired by the provisions of the constitution of 1791.[7] The executive power could henceforth naturalize foreigners who had "rendered important services to the Republic, who [would] bring to it talents, inventions, or a useful industry, or who [would] form great establishments," a year after they had taken up residence in France.[8] Intended to be valid for only five years, this provision was renewed on 19 February 1808 with no time limit.

On 17 March 1809 foreigners' access to French nationality ceased to be automatic. Ten years afer a candidate's declaration of intent had been registered, his request had to be submitted for a decision by the emperor. "When a foreigner . . . has fulfilled the conditions required to become a French citizen, his Naturalization will be pronounced by us. Supporting requests for naturalization will be transmitted by the mayors of the [candidate's] domicile to the prefect, who will transmit them with his advice to our high judge, the minister of Justice."[9]

After 1809 the power of the state in matters of naturalization was never chal-lenged again. A major debate on the topic did take place on 8 November 1849, when the National Legislative Assembly discussed a proposed law on natural-ization.[10] The text did not address the role of the state as such, but rather the question of which authority within the state could deal most legitimately with naturalization. Under the Second Republic, as under the Fifth Republic today, two powers — the president of the Republic and the National Assembly — were elected by universal suffrage.[11] Jules Favre, speaking on behalf of the left, pleaded in favor of granting the National Assembly exclusive competence: "To admit a foreigner to the benefits and responsibilities of the quality of being French, to efface his origin and replace it with a different nationality, this is an act that depends essentially on complete sovereignty, on the exercise of power that was formerly called kingly power"; as that "one and indivisible" sovereignty has "passed from the king's hands to those of the nation . . . the nation as a whole delegates its power . . . not to the executive power, but to the National Assem-bly . . . which alone makes the laws."[12] Rouher, minister of justice under Louis-Napoleon Bonaparte, responded that the people had delegated its sovereignty to two separate and equal powers — the president of the Republic and the Assem-bly — of which each was thus only one of its constituents. The issue was settled by a compromise: the government definitively retained the power to naturalize that Napoleon had restored to it; the advice of the Council of State, whose mem-bers were designated by the Assembly in those years, was nevertheless required; in particular, the naturalized person's right to serve in Parliament could only be conferred by the National Assembly.

From 1810 French nationality was irrevocably attributed at birth and trans-mitted by parentage; it could be requested by a young foreigner born in France in the year after he or she reached the age of majority; for a foreigner not born in France, it could be acquired by naturalization. However, throughout the nine-teenth century most foreigners in France did not request naturalization — for the process was long, difficult, and costly, and military conscription dissuaded those born in France. When they found it necessary to secure better protection for their rights, foreigners opted for a status more advantageous than nationality, one that no longer exists today: admission to residency.

An Attractive Status: Admission to Residency

Around 1810 a few foreigners opted for the procedure of exceptional naturaliza-tion.[13] In one such case, a Scottish mechanic who had invented a new procedure made his declaration of residency on 12 March 1810 in Dreux and was naturalized two years later, in April 1812, thanks to a favorable report by the Ministry of the Interior and the Ministry of Manufacturing and Trade. Other examples included Adelsward, the son of one of Sweden's wealthiest families, a twenty-nine-year-old Swedish officer living in Longwy, and Cockerill and his three sons, who lived in Liège, then the administrative center of the French department of Ourthe.[14]

Others sought exceptional naturalization unsuccessfully: this was so for women, who could no longer be naturalized after the Civil Code was adopted. In 1808 M. Fitzsimmon of Nantes requested the naturalization of his foreign niece. She was his sole heir, and he wanted to be able to leave her his property,[15] something he could no longer do after the reestablishment of the right of escheat, which precluded foreigners from inheriting. The niece's naturalization was denied, but she was granted admission to residency.

The same fate was in store for the request made by Mme Copinger, widow Lawless. After the death of her husband in Dublin, she arrived in France with her three children on 20 November 1801, bringing with her "a rather considerable fortune (3,520,000 francs), and part of her capital [had] already been used to acquire real property in the nation." She had already "restored to cultivation one thousand nine hundred eighty-one hectares of swampy land in the Aude department." The local authorities supported her and wrote to the First Consul: "Already naturalized, as it were, in France, she lacks only legal naturalization, which she is requesting from you." On 16 May 1804 the minister of the interior wrote to the minister of justice that "the senatus-consulte of 18 October 1802, from which the petitioner solicits the application in her favor, has to do only with political rights that a woman is not capable of acquiring. Madame Lawless can lay claim only to civil rights, and these will be conferred upon her under the terms of the Civil Code, title 1, chapter 1, when she has obtained permission from the government to establish her legal residence in France. She must limit her demand accordingly." Her request for naturalization was transformed into a request for "authorization to establish her legal residence in France";[16] she obtained this authorization for herself and for her two sons and her daughter.[17]

In addition to the (few) women who were directed toward this new status, a number of men sought "admission to residency."

Before 1803 a male foreigner could acquire a legal residence in France without the government's permission.[18] Under the Civil Code he could still live in France without authorization from the central authorities.[19] The only requirement might come from the commune in which the foreigner sought to reside: it might be necessary to present a passport or some other document to prove that the applicant "was not in a state of vagabondage."[20] But until 1819 a foreigner who was simply a resident without legal standing was subject to the right of escheat,[21] unless French nationals were exempt from that right in the foreigner's country of origin. "Admission to residency" thus became a particularly attractive status. Instituted by article 13 of the Civil Code, it was a policing measure enabling the authorities to select the foreigners authorized to settle in France[22] as much as it was designed to welcome "virtuous and useful men" and to protect the foreigner who had transferred his legal residence to France, "if the legislation of his own country declared him bereft of his residence rights by [that] fact alone."[23]

Once the head of state granted authorization to establish legal residence in France, foreigners enjoyed all the civil rights reserved for the French;[24] moreover, their status was an independent one, different from naturalization.

In support of the request for admission to residency, a foreigner had to produce a birth certificate as proof of origin — that is, birthplace — and age, the passport used to enter France, proof of a status or profession assuring that he or she would not be a burden to the commune where he intended to live, and finally, attestations of good conduct, past and future.[25] Under the Empire most of the decisions granting admission to residency were not published. But a review of a sampling of dossiers in the National Archives[26] reveals that in the departments of Mont-Tonnerre (whose administrative center was Mayence), Bas-Rhin, and Haut-Rhin, where most of the accepted candidates were found, the great majority of candidates had married, or were preparing to marry, French women.

In 1803 Jean David Gerock, a thirty-five-year-old silversmith born in Stuttgart (Wurtemberg electorate), requested authorization to establish legal residence in Strasbourg. He explained that after working for eight years, "he had become engaged to marry a French woman, with the intention of settling permanently in France, to become constitutionally a French citizen." Antoine Gerstner, a twenty-five-year-old baker born in Weissenbach (Baden) and living in Strasbourg, requested admission to residency because he was engaged to marry Élisabeth Zitzner, and the bride's father Jacques Zitzner, a citizen — a fisherman born in Strasbourg — would consent to the marriage only if Antoine remained in France.[27] Jean Charles Hodel, a gardener and botanist, was engaged to a French woman native to Strasbourg, which he wanted to make his home.[28] Jean Gothard Giesé, twenty-five, a carpenter born in Schaken in Prussia, was engaged to be married in 1803. Bernard Gruber, who had been married for three years to a local woman, requested admission to residency in Guemar, Haut-Rhin.[29] Moyse Kirch, twenty-four, a Jewish schoolteacher and cantor, requested authorization to establish residency and marry in the commune of Krautergersheim (Bas-Rhin).[30]

Before the Revolution, in regions such as Alsace it was customary to view a foreigner married to a French woman as French himself.[31] During the Revolution that local custom had become the law of the land, since residing in France and marrying a French woman entailed automatic naturalization. With the Civil Code the rule was reversed and the custom destabilized: instead of the foreigner who married a French woman becoming French, it was the French woman marrying a foreigner who became a foreign resident in her own country. Admission to residency did not compensate for loss of nationality, but it helped to reduce the drawbacks by guaranteeing the civil rights of the henceforth foreign couple.

One might suppose that the attractiveness of admission to residency was only a passing phenomenon, spurred by the restoration of the right of escheat in 1803. But the definitive abolition of that right on 14 July 1819 changed nothing: in competition with naturalization, which was increasingly difficult to obtain, admission to residency took lasting hold as a substitute status.

Naturalization: More and More Disincentives

Just after the Restoration, naturalization seems to have attracted as many candidates as admission to residency: on average, 150 acts were signed each year until 1848. These figures are misleading, since these lettres de naturalité were *not true naturalizations* but rather, most often, declarations of maintenance or resumption of French nationality.

A law that went into effect on 14 October 1814 dealt with persons born on territories that had been reattached to France in 1791 but detached on 30 May 1814 by the Treaty of Paris and definitively separated after the "Hundred Days" in 1815 (Napoleon's Waterloo campaign): the law allowed these persons to retain or recover French nationality. From 1790 to 1815 France had undergone extensive territorial upheavals: it went from 85 departments in 1790 to 130 in 1812, when the French Empire extended from Hamburg to Rome and even reached into the Illyrian provinces (in today's Croatia and Montenegro).[32]

The imperial armies had recruited heavily from the "reattached" territories. The law of 14 October 1814 thus allowed recruits to remain French if they had already lived in France for ten years, or to recover their French nationality—which they had lost under the treaties of 1814 or 1815—as soon as they had ten years' residency in France: "We judged that the very act of reuniting their lands with France should take the place of an individual declaration on their part; and that if they exercised the rights of French citizens for ten years, it sufficed for them to declare the intention to retain those rights, to continue to enjoy civil and political rights."[33] Moreover, the law of 17 February 1815[34] left these soldiers no choice but naturalization if they wanted to continue to receive the retirement pay they had been getting before the treaty. They simply had to confirm, during the three-month period following the completion of ten years' residency, that "they persisted in the desire to settle permanently in France." Until 1819 the majority, those who had completed their ten years, registered and received "*lettres de déclaration de naturalité*."

The 2,789 declarations approved between 1815 and 1819, preserving or restoring French nationality to former Frenchmen, represented 41 percent of all the *lettres de naturalité* registered until 1848.[35] By virtue of the law of 1814, the king continued to approve declarations even after 1819, in response to requests by foreigners born in former territories of the Empire. Until 1847 these requests represented more than three quarters of the 150 decisions made on average each year.

In all, 85 percent of the decisions made between 1815 and 1849 were "declarations" rather than "naturalizations": they did not transform a foreigner into a Frenchman but rather reintegrated him into his original nationality; like the *lettres de déclaration de naturalité* issued under the Old Regime, they were retroactive to the time the candidate had been French,[36] and they applied to his wife and children as well.[37] Thus every year only a few dozen foreigners—natives of Switzerland, England, Spain, and Austria-Hungary,[38] territories that had never been attached to the Empire—were "naturalized" through the common law procedure incorporated into the constitution of 1799. Among these too, we find a large proportion of former soldiers, along with civil servants and inhabitants of Moselle or the Ardennes;[39] in these two forest departments, access to communal property—which was limited to French nationals—took on special importance.[40]

The Interlude of 1848

The revolution of 1848 was an interlude, but only as if to relaunch the restrictive approach with renewed zeal. On 28 March 1848 the provisional government of the Republic issued a decree temporarily authorizing the minister of justice to grant naturalization to all foreigners who had been living in France for at least five years. Candidates had to supply a document from the mayor of Paris, the prefecture of police in the Seine department, or the government commissioner of another department, attesting that they were "worthy, in all respects, to be admitted to the enjoyment of the rights of a French citizen."

The justification for this measure was both that "many foreigners played an active role in the glorious events of February" and that many of "these foreigners, although resident in France for several years, had not met or were unable to meet the conditions required by law to be admitted to the enjoyment of the rights of French citizens."[41] The publicity given to the decree (in the Nord department, for example, the prefecture had it posted in all the communes),[42] the reduction of the mandatory residency period by half, and the elimination of the obligatory prior declaration of residency led to a large increase in requests: "The number of foreigners who are asking to be naturalized as French is so great at this time that it has been necessary to establish a temporary bureau in the Ministry of Justice charged solely with examining these sorts of requests."[43]

Some two thousand naturalizations were granted over the course of a few months.[44] Many prefectures resubmitted — this time successfully — dossiers that had been rejected for various reasons in earlier years.[45] However, the majority of successful candidates belonged to two categories of foreigners, according to the minister of justice Adolphe Crémieux: political refugees, among the twenty thousand welcomed between 1830 and 1850, "who, for many years, were in our country and requested naturalization without receiving it,"[46] and, in this period of economic crisis during which many foreigners were led to leave France,[47] "a mass of foreign workers . . . whose existence was threatened, [workers] who were no longer wanted in France on the grounds that there was not enough work for French workers. Among these there were masses of eminently honorable individuals who had been working in France for more than five years, individuals to whom a hand had to be extended to prevent them from undergoing a disaster that would be cruel to them and to their families."[48] Pierre-Jacques Derainne confirms that "for the first time in France, several hundred workers, especially Savoyards, Belgians, and Germans, requested naturalization."[49] Coming primarily from the Paris region and the Nord department, the requests were made by day laborers, shop boys and office assistants, coachmen, metal workers, and the like. They were the target of protests and demands for "national exclusivity" voiced by a large number of French workers against foreign workers unless — and this is interesting to note — the foreigners were naturalized.[50] On 29 June 1848, after the *journées de juin* (the workers' revolt of 21–26 June), the decree was suspended pending the vote on new laws governing naturalization.

A Double Constraint

In reaction to what was perceived as an uncontrolled influx of population, the rather conservative Chamber of Deputies that had been elected in 1849 adopted an approach proposed by Louis-Napoleon Bonaparte's administration and passed legislation even more restrictive than before.

Until then a simple, voluntary declaration notifying city hall that residency had been established sufficed to initiate the ten-year waiting period required by the constitution of 1799.[51] In conformity with the law of 1814, even this step was not required when the waiting period was applied to a candidate born in one of the Empire's former territories. From 1849, however, no one could become French by naturalization without having first obtained "admission to residency" from the government. The new system for naturalization thus required two authorizations, ten years apart, after an investigation by the state. It also required paying the costly "seal fees"[52] twice; the government did not seem inclined to reduce these fees, although it was authorized to do so, because "in general one must avoid affiliating with the country foreigners who may later become a burden on the state."[53] Finally, the decision to naturalize could be made only after a favorable opinion from the Council of State.

It goes without saying that this procedure did not encourage naturalizations. Their numbers sank—lower than they already had fallen before 1848—while admissions to residency increased strikingly. More easily accessible and much more attractive than naturalization, admission to residency was advantageous in that it could be obtained without delay and produced immediate effects. In addition, those admitted were not subject to the military obligations that naturalized Frenchmen had to accept. In 1867 the delay between admission to residency and naturalization was reduced to three years, which led to a noteworthy increase in naturalizations. But except in Algeria, where admission to residency was not a prerequisite for naturalization as of 1865, admission by and large supplanted naturalization. In all, between 1849 and 1889 three times more admissions to residency were requested and obtained than naturalizations. Moreover, as admission to residency could have a collective effect—it could extend to the beneficiary's wife[54] and minor children[55]—the number of people admitted to residency was in reality much higher than the number of those naturalized.

Thus confronted with the difficulty of naturalization and the advantages of admission to residency, foreigners who came to live in France most often chose to remain foreign. This choice was also generally made by young men born in France to foreign parents, when they reached their majority and could become French: the draft was a powerful disincentive.

Children of Foreigners and the Draft: A National Problem

According to the Civil Code and the principle of jus sanguinis, children born in France to foreign parents were foreigners. They could request French nationality during the year after they reached the age of majority—and the framers of the

TABLE I

Statistics on Letters of Naturalization and Admissions to Residency in
Metropolitan France

	Letters of naturalization	Admissions to residency
1851	74	123
1852	42	204
1853	49	121
1854	31	240
1855	66	119
1856	37	145
1857	54	286
1858*	27	148
1859*	20	122
1860*	83	146
1861	51	204
1862	30	161
1863	50	233
1864	36	185
1865	51	223
1866*	42	218
1867	129	277
1868	159	300
1869*	80	234
1870*	385	658
1871	539	845
1872*	168	1,000
1873	137	594
1874*	179	313
1875	256	357
1876	282	349
1877	211	630
1878	169	539
1879	189	623
1880	209	658
1881	283	1,159
1882	303	1,178

TABLE I

Continued

	Letters of naturalization	Admissions to residency
1883	327	1,336
1884	498	3,085
1885	759	2,167
1886	663	2,203
1887	1,522	3,974
1888	1,959	5,082
1889 (before the law of 26 June)	720	2,152
1889 (after the law of 26 June)	2,223	741
1890	5,984	763
1891	5,371	631
1892	4,537	714
1893	4,212	729
1894	5,759	833
1895	4,468	587
1896	3,582	525
Total, 1851–1889	10,869	32,591
Total, 1889–1896	36,136	5,523

*These figures include naturalizations of foreign sailors and naturalizations that took place outside metropolitan France.

Source: Table constituted by the author with the help of the *Compte général de l'administration de la justice civile et commerciale en France* (annual publication).

Civil Code counted on their doing so. But why would they do this, especially if they were males? With respect to obligatory conscription, being French was of little interest compared to being a resident foreigner with no special status, and especially compared to being a foreigner admitted to residency.

The draft provided for by the Jourdan law of 1798 was abolished by article 12 of the Charter of 1814. But given the failure of voluntary enrollments,[56] it was reestablished on 10 March 1818 by the Gouvion-Saint-Cyr law. A contingent was created and found itself subjected to long-term service. In 1818 the contingent had forty thousand conscripts; the duration of active service was six years (plus six more in the reserves). In 1824 the contingent had sixty thousand members, and the duration of active service was six to eight years.[57] In 1831 the term of service was reduced to seven years, of which two were spent in the reserves; in 1840 the term was brought back up to eight years.

The contingent was filled by lot; unless they were exempted, those who were not selected in the draw were not immediately free. Those who were chosen could send replacements, for a fee. The more modest a man's social situation, the more likely he was to serve: those selected might not have the means to pay for replacements, and those not selected might be inclined to replace someone with greater means.[58]

The contingent established for each year was broken down by departments, then by cantons, in relation to population size. To evaluate the population of each canton and set the size of its contingent, nationals and foreigners were counted together.

But only French nationals were called up for the lottery and sent to do military service. Before the adoption of the Civil Code, children born in France to foreign parents were French by birth; once the Civil Code was in place they were foreigners, thus exempt from military service. Annie Crépin shows that this exemption was viewed as an unacceptable privilege from 1818 on, especially in border departments where many foreigners lived.[59]

Thus on 24 November 1818 the prefect of the Nord department wrote to the minister of the interior that in the Dunkerque district the draft spared not only those young men who had been born in Belgium (that is, in the Belgian provinces of the Netherlands), but also those who had been born in France, had lived there until the age of majority, and saw themselves (and were viewed by everyone else) as French.[60] In 1821 the Nord department's general council expressed chagrin that "sons of foreigners who have been living in France for several years are not subject to the law on recruitment, whereas they are counted in the population of the canton and are thus taken into account when the size of the contingent is fixed, which increases the burden and makes it fall on nationals alone."[61]

These complaints applied to Belgians in the Ardennes, Nord, and Pas-de-Calais departments, to Italians in the departments of Var, Corsica, and Hautes-Alpes, to Spaniards in Pyrénées-Orientales,[62] and to Germans in Bas-Rhin and Haut-Rhin. The prefects or general councils involved reminded the minister of the tradition according to which a child born in France was French, but to no avail. The central power stood firm behind the Civil Code and its article 9, and it rejected the demands and interpretations of local authorities.

On 11 August 1821 the mayor of Bastia sent a memorandum to the departmental review council:

> Among the inhabitants of Bastia there are a good many foreigners—dock workers, traders, laborers, and porters, most of them from Genoa—who have married, acquired real property and set up businesses. Where it is a matter of enjoying the privileges attached to the quality of being French, no one doubts the French nationality of these individuals.
>
> They take subjects of the king to court without surety; they take possession of the inheritances that have come to them on the Island; they occupy posts in the judicial magistrature and serve as officers of the National Guard; they intervene as witnesses in public acts; they vote in the assemblies of important businessmen.
>
> But when it comes to being exempted from fees, or avoiding the call for the army contingent, or going onto the Italian continent without a passport from the administrative authority of the Island, they are no longer French; they become foreign again. The Sardinian Consul claims as subjects of his king all those who were born in the former Republic of Genoa.[63]

In 1830 a first step was taken: the foreigners who had been counted in the population of each canton for the calculation of the quota were henceforth to be excluded. This measure was supposed to be calming, but it had little effect: the sons of foreigners generally remained on the eligibility lists and continued to count toward the quota; thus they participated in the lottery, and it was only when they drew a "bad number" that they remembered they were foreigners and were consequently exempted from the draft. The declarations that allowed male children born in France to foreign parents to claim French nationality during the year after they reached their majority were most often made at city hall, not on special registers but on separate sheets of paper; the declaration process was not centralized, and only the applicant knew whether he had taken that step, "so that he invoked it or kept silent about it according to his own interest."[64]

In 1831, when a proposed law related to army recruitment was under discussion, M. Passy, the reviewer for the project, argued that it was necessary to stop allowing foreigners the "exorbitant right" to live and die under the protection of a state without sharing in its responsibilities. He proposed, unsuccessfully, to attribute French citizenship automatically at the age of majority to any male child born in France to a foreign father who had himself been born in France.

Finally, the law of 7 February 1851 crossed a first threshold. It introduced what was to become one of the foundations and distinguishing features of French law, namely, the *double right of birthplace*, the double jus soli: children born in France to a foreign parent (initially the father, then the mother—after 1891, it made no difference)[65] who was himself born in France were French: the grandchild of a foreigner who came to live in France was thus French. But the law of 1851 still left open the option of repudiating one's French nationality at the age of majority, and this option was widely exercised to avoid military service.

Three years after the war in which France was defeated by Prussia and lost Alsace-Moselle, the law of 16 December 1874 sought to reinforce the constraint: from then on one could not repudiate the quality of being French without a document from another government attesting that the person in question had retained his original nationality. But this measure fared no better. For the cohort of 1882, of the 2,942 young men concerned, 1,554 invoked their foreign nationality and were exempted from service; in 1883, 2,478 of 3,186 did the same.

The Obstacles to Revising the Civil Code

Why, one may well wonder, did the members of Parliament, who discussed the question three times in a little more than forty years (1831, 1851, and 1874), take no further steps to impose French nationality on children born in France to fathers who had also been born in France, without any possibility of choice or repudiation?

In 1851, for example, the arguments invoked in favor of this position by the project reviewer Benoît-Champy[66] were very forceful. First among them was a *concern for equality* with regard to civic responsibilities. Since these children were French, if they were males they should be subjected like other French males to the conscription that governed military service at the time. Yet they were exempt: "These privileges are all the more detestable in that, generally speaking, these foreigners share the right to gather firewood and to pasture animals on communal lands, and they enjoy civil rights, sometimes even the most important political rights."

Another argument involved *state security*: "during the half-century since the Civil Code was promulgated, families of foreigners have become so numerous in France that there are villages on our borders in which they make up a tenth of the population: what would happen, in a few years, if the legislature did not consider means to regularize this abnormal situation?"

The third argument invoked in favor of the proposed law was that the children in question were *societally French*. "These foreigners who, after a long stay on French soil, had forgotten the language and sometimes even the name of the country where their ancestors originated—were they not French in fact and intention, through affections, values, and habits? Were there not serious disadvantages in tolerating the establishment, on our territory, of individuals destined, whatever the number of generations that followed, to remain indefinitely foreign to the great French family?"[67]

However, two main factors operated in 1831, 1851, and again in 1874 against the return of *jus soli*. First of all, the integrity of the Civil Code — which had been accepted as the foundation of modern law — was a subject of concern. This legislation had been renamed the Napoleonic Code on 3 September 1807 because, according to Council of State member Bigot de Préameneu, the title "Civil Code of the French" was no longer suitable for a code that was already viewed as the common law of Europe. With article 68 of the Charter of 1814, it became simply the Civil Code once again,[68] and it has been maintained as such by all regimes ever since. The classical authors were consigned to the storehouse of antiquities, and all the new generations of students and legal advisors who filled the courts applied its principles: "One must, so to speak, always have them in hand. This is the first thing one must use before undertaking an Affair, treating a question, giving an Opinion, or rendering a Judgment."[69]

The influence of the Civil Code spread throughout continental Europe; in the process, the principle of jus sanguinis as the exclusive criterion for nationality of origin became the common law almost everywhere in Europe; only England, Portugal, and Denmark remained faithful to the "feudal" principle of jus soli. In 1851 it was argued that "it was not without grave reasons that one should abolish a basic provision of our Code."[70] Antonin Dubost, the reviewer for the proposed law of 1889, later said that the National Assembly feared "modifying, by a provision added casually in a special law, the essential conditions of nationality regulated by the Civil Code"; it "thought that it could not override the prejudices of doctrine."[71]

Until the early 1880s the international consequences of unilateral decisions that France might make regarding residents of foreign origin were also taken into consideration. To impose French nationality by law on the children of foreigners might well produce reprisals with harsh consequences for children born abroad to French parents. The argument was invoked by legal scholars, since international law, which was developing rapidly, was based on reciprocity. But politicians were also sensitive to the issue, at a time when colonization efforts under the French flag were well under way not only in Algeria but also in Latin America.

Was France at that point more a country of immigration or a country of emigration? If the question had been raised in these terms, there is no doubt that in 1860 the answer would have been "emigration," and after 1870, "colonization."[72] An emigration bureau was opened in the Ministry of the Interior; the departures of French citizens were counted and recorded in ports. In a debate that took place in the Senate on 31 March 1865, the reviewer for a proposed law evoked the number and size of the establishments set up in foreign countries by Frenchmen: "it is estimated that more than 300,000 of our compatriots are living, have their legal residence or business, in the principal cities of Europe and America." This perception of the interests of France and the French abroad continued to justify the status quo for a long time.

The debate had advanced no further and seemed unlikely to do so when on 1 April 1882, the Orléanist senator Batbie,[73] who was also a law professor at the University of Paris, submitted the text of a bill concerning the naturalization of foreigners in France. Initially Batbie's objective was limited to harmonizing the various provisions governing the status of children born in France to foreign parents.[74] But the Council of State, following the lead of its reviewer Camille Sée,[75] proposed to go further and update all regulations having to do with *nationality*.[76] It was on Sée's initiative that this term was used for the first time as the title of a piece of legislation. However, Sée was proposing to go against the grain of all the legislation adopted since 1851 by Parliament, by reaffirming the primacy of jus sanguinis: on this point his views were not followed. The Senate did not adopt Batbie's bill until 11 February 1887, five years after it was submitted: it represented a timid step toward facilitating naturalization and access to French nationality for children born in France to foreign parents.[77]

This was too little in the eyes of the Chamber of Deputies, which reacted under pressure from representatives of the Nord department and from Algerian colonials. Since the previous debate on the subject, official statistics showed that while the French population was stagnating, the foreign presence in France had increased significantly. France had clearly become a country of immigration: the deputies concerned felt it necessary to "cut to the quick,"[78] to draw the consequences without delay.

Imposing Equality of Duties on Children in France

In 1876 foreigners represented 1.7 percent of France's overall population, numbering 655,036.[79] By 1886 the foreign population had doubled, reaching 1,127,000, or 3 percent of the total.[80] Between 1873 and 1896 France went through a serious economic depression, triggered by the abandonment of bimetalism in favor of the gold standard.[81] To cope with the decline in prices and profits, businesses sought to reduce costs by letting workers go, or by recruiting less expensive foreign workers. France, still heavily dependent on agriculture, was less affected, however, than its already highly industrialized European neighbors. A large number of foreign workers were thus coming to France in search of jobs.[82] This phenomenon did not fail to provoke xenophobic reactions, including demands for immigration controls and for protection of the national workforce — demands rejected by business and industry leaders.

At the same time, the first stirrings of demographic anxiety arose. In 1831 France was still the most densely populated country in Europe, with 32.6 million inhabitants, compared with 29.7 million in what was to become the German Empire and 24 million in the British Isles. In 1861, despite the addition of the Nice and Savoy region (645,000 inhabitants), France had a population of 37 million, Germany 38 million, and the United Kingdom 29 million. In 1871 the loss of Alsace and Moselle took away 1.5 million citizens.[83] By 1901 Germany had 56 million inhabitants, the United Kingdom 41 million, and France fewer than 39 million. In fact, between 1820 and 1901 Germany's population had increased by 123 percent, the United Kingdom's by 72 percent (127 percent for Great Britain alone), and France's by only 19 percent. The birth rate fell below the replacement rate, and a comparison of French and British statistics brings to light a significant aging trend and an underrepresentation of young people.

But what stirred up elected officials in the first place was the increasingly pronounced concentration of foreigners along France's borders and in the larger cities.[84] In 1831 members of Parliament from the Nord department had become aware that the foreign population in certain of their communes had reached 11 percent. In 1886 three fourths of the population of the commune of Halluin, half that of Roubaix, and one fourth of that of Lille were foreign.[85] The Nord department alone was home to 30 percent of the foreign population in metropolitan France, or 305,524 people. Almost half the members of this foreign population had been born in France and did not want to become French: among the 1.1 million foreigners counted in 1891 in metropolitan France, more than 420,000 had been born in France, 350,000 of them in the department where they were counted.

As it happened, a new bill on military recruitment was on the Chamber's docket; it provided for a shorter term of military service to be spread among a wider base of recruits. This "universal service" had been instituted in 1872, in the wake of the war of 1870,[86] but many exemptions and privileges remained, and those drafted had to serve for five years. At issue was an end to exemptions privileging teachers, priests, students, and young men from wealthy families. And to the list of privileged persons whose exemptions were to be eliminated, on 2 June 1885 Maxime Lecomte, a deputy from the Nord department,[87] proposed to add those born and raised in France whose foreign nationality seemed spurious, "a legal fiction ungrounded in social fact."[88]

According to the law we are currently discussing, all Frenchmen will spend several years in the barracks, this is clearly understood, and during this time a certain number of foreigners will remain in France in their homes. . . .

There is a shocking inequality here between the situation of the faithful Frenchman who will be obliged to leave his village and his profession for a fairly considerable number of years, and the situation of someone who ought to be viewed as French, who in everyone's eyes has been French, and who, at a given moment, in order to evade a military duty, claims that he is foreign.

. . . Allow me to pass around a letter written by a worker: its language is unsophisticated, but it has great impact nonetheless because it is very energetic and very sincere.

Here is what was written to me: "See any shop where Frenchmen and sons of foreigners are working. Imagine that they are all working as shop boys; they are sixteen to eighteen years old. Comes the draft, this is the moment when the workers were going to be promoted, this is what happens only for the foreigners, because the French boys are going to do one year, three years, forty months . . . and then come back to find themselves taking orders from their former companions, who are earning 2.50 or at most 4 francs a day."

Several voices. That's very true!

M. Maxime Lecomte. Now the author of this letter adds:

"Among us, all the foremen are foreigners. Something else; parents have a daughter to marry off and can give her money as a dowry: she is courted by a Frenchman and by the son of a foreigner, who both have about the same position . . ." (*Laughter.*) . . .

"The parents say to each other: this one will not do military service, or not much; he won't have the twenty-eight days, or the thirteen days [of required training]; he'll never go on a campaign if there is a war; our daughter will be much happier with him. You see the interest of the bosses and the interest of the families. This is how foreigners are taking our places, our jobs, our fiancées."[89]

What motivated Lecomte was not so much France's demographic needs, or the army's, as the principle of equality before the law. He himself estimated that there were fewer than 4,000 grandchildren of foreigners eligible for the draft; compared to the 300,000 French males who reached the age of service every year, foreigners represented only a marginal number. French nationality should be imposed on these young men, for "they are real Frenchmen claiming the quality of foreigners to the sole end of escaping the law on recruitment."[90]

The amendment that Lecomte presented, supported by Clemenceau, was rejected, however (159 votes in favor, 280 against), for it was seen as more pertinent to laws on nationality than to laws on recruitment. A few days later, on 25 June 1885, without waiting for Batbie's bill to make its way from the Senate to the Chamber of Deputies, Maxime Lecomte gathered thirty-three other republican colleagues, including ten of the eighteen deputies from the Nord department, and submitted a proposed law on "the nationality of the sons of foreigners born in France" that would impose French nationality on them.[91] Equality of duties, but also concern over the concentration of foreigners, motivated the Nord deputies.

This latter preoccupation was developing along parallel lines in Algeria. At the very moment when Camille Sée's report was published in 1883, the law school in Algiers, at the request of Louis Tirman, governor general of Algeria, presented its own proposal for a law that would make French any male person born in Algeria, unless he claimed the quality of foreigner within a year after reaching the age of majority.[92] In a speech delivered on 20 November 1884 before the High Council of Algeria, Governor Tirman explained his proposal: "The last census, in 1881, noted that the French population of European origin exceeds the foreign population by only a mere 14,064 individuals. This gap, which consisted of 26,248 individuals in 1865, is getting smaller every year, and in the Oran department the national element is no longer in the majority. Since we have no more hope of increasing the French population by means of official colonization, the remedy must be sought in the naturalization of foreigners."[93] The census of 1886 supported his analysis: in Algeria, 219,627 French nationals and 202,212 foreigners were counted, not including 17,445 Moroccans. The danger was that France would see its work of colonization challenged by Spain and especially by Italy, which had recently allied itself with Austria and Germany in the Triple Alliance, and which carried out a policy of active propagandizing in France's southern departments, where the Italian population had grown.[94]

When the Chamber of Deputies finally addressed the Senate proposal in 1887, the reviewer for the project, Antonin Dubost, went along with the converging recommendations of the Nord deputies and those from Algeria to establish a distinction "between [foreigners] who truly belong to a foreign nationality and those who, established in France for many years, no longer have any ties binding them to another nation." He deemed it impossible that "on the pretext of doctrine, or under the influence of overly inveterate legal prejudices, one should do nothing to forestall such a pressing danger." And with the full and unchallenged support of the Chamber, then of the Senate a few days later,[95] he secured the adoption of two provisions whose significance he himself noted: "As I see it, it is the law in its entirety that is being submitted to you."[96]

Article 8, paragraph 3, of the modified Civil Code declared that "every individual born in France to a foreigner who had been born in France" was French from birth. The grandchild of a foreigner, if the child was born in France to a parent[97] also born in France — this is what was called the double jus soli — was irrevocably French. The possibility of repudiation or renunciation that such a person had had since 1851 was thus eliminated.

A child born in France to parents who had not been born in France was French upon reaching the age of majority, if he or she still resided in France: French nationality was conferred automatically, with no declaration required. During the year after the young person reached the age of majority, he or she nevertheless had the possibility of repudiating French nationality in order to remain a foreigner (article 8, paragraph 4).

These two provisions had a certain logic: the incorporation into French nationality of foreigners born and educated in France was all the more obligatory in that the long-standing presence of the family in France was attested. The more the actual link with France was ensured, the less the person could refuse to be French. This quality was thus attributed automatically after two generations born in France (the rule known as double jus soli). With regard to a child born in France to immigrant parents, a double act took place. The state adopted the person by making him or her French at the age of majority. The consent of the young person was then presupposed if he or she did not refuse French nationality.

For "individuals who find their interest in not attaching themselves to any determined collectivity, in order to avoid its responsibilities," Dubost saw the two provisions as "indispensable," "the only way to oblige [them] to fulfill their duty as men and citizens and thus both to prevent them from living in a materially privileged situation and to keep them from becoming, in certain instances, a threat to public order." These provisions were, moreover, "without danger,"

for they will not make either a foreigner or a colonist leave France or Algeria. [Such people] will no doubt escape with satisfaction from social responsibilities when they can. But if these responsibilities are imposed upon them, they will submit to them without saying a thing, because the responsibilities cannot be compared to the advantages they gain from their residence or their establishment on our territory. Moreover, why would they leave? Is it not obvious that an individual born in France to a foreigner who was himself born there is a Frenchman from the standpoint of his mind, his inclinations, his habits, his values, and that one has the right to presume that he has a real attachment to the country where he and his father were both born, where he was brought up, where he has his interests, his relations, his friendships? Would he have continued to live in France for so long if he did not feel all this to a high degree?[98]

In this argument one finds, blended in what appears to be a fully virtuous circle, the principle of equality, an interest in the security of the state, the sociological affiliation of these young people with France, and a demographic preoccupation. And the compromise thus adopted satisfied both the republican left and a segment of the conservative forces.

The Restrictions with Respect to Foreigners

The deputies were divided, in contrast, over the naturalization of the most recently arrived foreigners, and the restrictive approach won out in the end. The new law did not particularly favor naturalization;[99] on the contrary, it shifted foreigners residing in France from a sometimes privileged status to an inferior status with respect to French nationals on the level of rights.

The opinion of the Council of State, required since 1849 for any naturalization, was no longer sought. Foreign men who had married French women could henceforth request French nationality after one year of marriage and residency. But the two common law provisions remained very restrictive: either foreigners obtained admission to residency from the state and could request naturalization three years after the date when admission was granted, or else they could request naturalization without admission after ten years of residency. The Chamber of Deputies did not want to go further and follow, for example, M. Escanyé, deputy from Pyrénées-Orientales, who had been seeking since 1877 to remove the "useless obstacles" that discouraged requests; he proposed a five-year period of residency as the sole condition of eligibility.[100] Similarly, the Chamber rejected almost without discussion an amendment offered by Paul de Jouvencel, who sought on the occasion of the centenary of the Revolution to introduce an exceptional naturalization procedure. Above all, the Chamber reestablished, "in the interest of French employees and workers," the seal fees of 175.25 francs which the Senate had decided to eliminate. M. de la Batut, who spoke in favor of reestablishment, wanted to subject to seal fees, "when their financial situation allows," foreigners who, "without having paid the tax of blood, come one day, because they find it in their interest, to claim the quality of being French," the enjoyment of which would confer rights upon them.[101] The reviewer Antonin Dubost invoked the importance, the demographic urgency, of naturalization, but in vain; he was defeated and his colleague Maxime Lecomte with him, by a majority of 341 to 175. Naturalization was thus not made easier, and candidates for naturalization were even less well served than before: they had to observe a waiting period before they could benefit from the right to be elected to a legislative assembly. In 1814 a distinction between what was called "simple naturalization" and full or "grand naturalization" had been established; only the beneficiaries of the latter could be elected to Parliament. This distinction was abolished in 1848, reestablished in 1849 owing to the left's mistrust of executive power, and abolished once again in 1867, to be reimposed durably in 1889: it was not abolished again until 1984.[102]

The status of the foreigner who was not naturalized was also diminished. The law of 1889 eliminated admission to residency, an autonomous status that gave its holders equality of civil rights with the French. Formerly, admission to residency was valid indefinitely; it ended only if it was revoked by government decree. Henceforth, this status was accepted only as the first step in the naturalization procedure, to accelerate it, since a candidate who had been admitted to residency could request naturalization three years after obtaining that status.[103] If he was not naturalized within five years, he lost his status and became a simple foreign resident.

And the simple foreign resident now had fewer rights: not owing to protectionist measures, proposals for which abounded,[104] but owing to measures intended to heighten control and preserve public order. In January 1887 foreigners who had recently settled in France had to be counted. In 1888[105] all foreigners residing in France were asked to declare themselves at the city hall in their place of residence. Under the law of 8 August 1893, identified as a "law concerning the legal residence of foreigners in France and the protection of the national workforce," every foreigner who had not been admitted to residency so that he could exercise a profession, business, or trade was required to fill out a declaration within a week of arrival. A memorandum from police headquarters dated 1 December 1893 listed the following categories of foreigner subject to this provision: industrialists, tradesmen, salesmen, artists, professors, artisans, agricultural workers, day laborers, employees, domestic servants, all those who drew remuneration from their work;[106] they had to sign a licensing register at city hall.

In addition, certain public professions were now reserved to the French, and some newly conquered social rights were denied to foreigners. This was true of the representation of salaried workers and social protections. Foreigners were also excluded from the right to be elected as union leaders or representatives of salaried workers by the laws enacted on unions in 1884, on delegates to mine safety boards in 1890, on conciliation and arbitration procedures in 1892, and on *conseils de prud'hommes* in 1907.[107]

With admission to residency eliminated and the rights of foreigners living in France reduced, a new hierarchy between French nationals and foreigners was thus established. It was intended to give increased value to French nationality and incite foreigners to seek naturalization. Only those petitioners judged "worthy" would be selected. Patriotic self-esteem, xenophobic anxiety, and demographic interest were all satisfied in a single stroke.

1889: The Reinvention of a Republican *Jus Soli* —for Metropolitan France

Since the Revolution the boundary between foreigner and French national had fluctuated. The law of 1889 solidified it in a double movement of nationalization and demotion of foreigners—inside metropolitan France. In concrete terms, foreigners were reclassified according to their degree of socialization, or more precisely according to the length of time they or their families had been in France. Foreigners born in France were automatically French if one parent had also been born in France (the double jus soli); otherwise they became French upon reaching the age of majority. Foreigners not born in France could request naturalization, but during the waiting period they had fewer rights than before the law of 1889 was passed. This nationalization, which was inscribed in the movement toward homogeneization of national sentiment reinforced by the war of 1870,[108] came about thanks to the return to jus soli, whose obligatory character was applied in stages. After almost a century of effacement (or discretion?), the new law reestablished jus soli at the heart of legislation on nationality, since in parallel with birth to French parents, birth on French territory was once again a sufficient criterion for attributing French nationality.

But the previous legislation was not simply reintroduced verbatim. By completely reversing the use that it made of the criterion of residency in its link with birth on French soil, the law of 1889 created the *republican use* of jus soli. This criterion of residency had been very important under the Old Regime: it was the sign of allegiance to the king. When recognition of the quality of being French could result only from birth abroad to French parents or birth in France to foreign parents, the parlements (the courts of the period) required that the candidate's *present and future residence* be fixed in the kingdom. This was the sign of present and future personal allegiance to the king of France. With the Republic, the requirement of present and future residence was transformed into a requirement of *past residence*. The link with the nation no longer resulted from personal allegiance to the king but from upbringing within French society; and past residence, noted at the moment of majority, was the guarantee. The law sought to translate "this constant truth that the milieu in which the individual lives acts upon him. The child born in France to foreign parents who were both born outside of our borders, and who have generally lived for a long time abroad, receives first of all from these latter foreign values, habits, and feelings. Little by little, living in France among schoolmates and workmates, he is impregnated with our civilization. As he grows up, his absorption by French ideas is accentuated; as his individuality is affirmed, the divergences of aspirations and teachings of his family offer in him weaker and weaker resistance . . . at bottom, this is just a simple question of fact."[109]

Growing up and continuing to live in one and the same society creates the bond of nationality, and this observation was made even before school or obligatory military service came to contribute, in the twentieth century, to the homogenization of society. Republican law took socialization rather than a voluntary and contractual act as the foundation for nationality. Nationality depended on the acquisition of social codes more than on origin or birthplace, which were in the end only signs of that potential acquisition. This logic of the effective sociological bond was not a passing trend; it structured French nationality law and gave it its permanence.

The correlation between *socialization* and nationality was not exempt from ethnic considerations, however; witness the fact that the law, owing to the influence of representatives from the colonies, was applied in Algeria, a French territory, only to people who were foreigners in the strict sense, i.e., Europeans; entry into full nationality remained virtually closed to Muslim natives of Algeria, who were French subjects. The law thus confirmed, in Algeria, a distinction between those who were "assimilable" and those who were not.

Soon, in metropolitan France, an approach of the same type, originating in the United States, was to be at the heart of political confrontations over nationality. Created to regulate the status of foreign residents, founded on a strategy that distinguished between generations, the law of 1889 soon became inadequate when the demographic question came to the fore and naturalizations seemed vital. The century just beginning was one of crises, extremely heated debates, and vigorous challenges that the apparent stability of the legislation fails to reflect.

3.

Naturalization Comes

to the Aid of the Nation (1889–1940)

⤳ When, at Parliament's request, the Ministry of Justice tallied the naturalizations that had been granted in 1890 (the first full year during which the law of 1889 was in effect), it was careful to adopt a reassuring tone: "Is there any reason to be apprehensive about the quality of the new elements thus introduced into the life of the nation? As far as naturalization by decree is concerned, we can answer in the negative without hesitation. This favor is granted, in fact, only after a thorough investigation, and the number of requests denied attests to the care taken in the process to admit into the French family only individuals who are worthy."[1] And it is true that naturalization was not granted lightly: 97 percent of the 5,984 people naturalized in 1890 had been living in France for more than ten years; 28 percent had been born in France, not counting those born in the former territories of Alsace-Moselle; 56 percent of the 4,796 men in the group were married to women who were French at birth.[2] The reports published in subsequent years indicate similar proportions: in 1896, for example, among the 3,582 persons naturalized, more than one fourth of the 2,741 men had been born in France, and more than half were married to French women.

The increase in the number of naturalizations (there had been only 1,959 in 1888) was short-lived. The years immediately following the passage of the new law saw a shift away from admission to legal residency—which was no longer of much use—toward naturalization. Admission was no longer a self-sufficient and permanent status: if people with that status did not request naturalization, their admission to residency expired after five years. As a result, candidates who had sought to request admission were oriented toward naturalization by civil servants.[3] Moreover, even people who had been granted admission to residency under the old law now had five years to request naturalization. When that time was up, in 1894, their status was no longer valid. That year, naturalizations peaked at 5,759. The number then dropped to around two thousand[4] and remained at that level for twenty years; this meant considerably fewer naturalizations than the pre-1889 totals of admissions to residency and naturalizations combined. Thus until the 1920s naturalizations were granted sparingly, for during that period the sole priority of France's nationality policy was the integration of second-generation residents.

This early period during which the law of 1889 was applied was in fact a time of profound mutation: it saw the invention of an administrative bureaucracy and the establishment of a nationality policy. Within the Ministry of Justice, the Bureau of Seals took charge of this policy and defined its own autonomous strategy, independent of both Parliament and the judiciary. The policy was extended in scope to include all legal mechanisms that provided access to nationality. The Bureau of Seals accentuated the distinction between first-generation immigrants, for whom naturalization remained tightly controlled, and their children, who conversely were encouraged, and sometimes even forced, to take on French nationality.

After the First World War naturalizations, which had been the object of some suspicion, became—in the name of the demographic imperative—the object of solicitation from all quarters. A law passed in 1927 spelled out as its goal the addition of more than 100,000 new French citizens each year. In the climate of economic crisis, political confrontation, and international tension that characterized the 1930s, a debate arose, spurred by those who wanted to select foreigners no longer according to individual characteristics but according to their national, racial, and ethnic origins, with the goal of singling out those who could be assimilated and eliminating those who could not. The partisans of the latter solution triumphed only after France fell to the Germans in 1940.

The Advent of the Bureau of Seals

In the early nineteenth century requests for naturalization were still written as they had been under the Old Regime, on separate sheets of paper, with the wording left to the candidate's discretion.[5] In 1827 requests were still written on separate sheets, but the formulation had become standardized: "In the year One Thousand Eight Hundred . . . before ourself Mayor of the commune of . . . came Mr. . . . the aforesaid residing in our commune, profession of . . . , who said and declared to us that he came to live in France on [date] and that he has the intention of settling definitively in the kingdom and that he is making the present declaration in order to obtain through the grace of His Majesty lettres de naturalité and the enjoyment of the quality of the rights of being French, submitting himself to all communal charges and promising to observe the laws and regulations of the Kingdom."[6]

In the 1840s this standard formulation was printed for the first time. Decisions on naturalization and admission to legal residency had been systematically published in the *Bulletin des lois* since 1831.

The division of the Bureau of Seals that dealt with matters of nationality originated under the Old Regime.[7] The king's decision to offer naturalization became definitively valid only after a letter patent had been presented for verification and sealed by the chancellor of the kingdom.[8] In 1802 Napoleon reestablished the system of seals that had been interrupted by the Revolution. A council on seals was created in 1808 to deal with titles; it was replaced in 1814 by a commission on seals. Initially independent of the Ministry of Justice, it was incorporated into the ministry under Louis-Philippe through a regulation dated 31 October 1830. From 1832 the division of seals, integrated into the Civil Section of the Ministry of Justice, was charged with certifying — "sealing" — name changes, marriage dispensations, titles, laws, letters patent, diplomas, and, finally admissions to residency, naturalizations, reintegrations into French nationality, and authorizations to serve abroad; dealing with the last of these soon became its primary activity.

Then in 1848 the Bureau of Seals began to acquire its "omnipotence," in stages.[9] The law of 3 December 1849 gave it the power to rule on requests for naturalization after it had investigated each case. In 1803[10] local authorities had become the determining bodies in procedural matters.[11] The mayor put the dossier together and his opinion was formally followed by that of the prefect, before the executive power made its decision. In fact the municipality played the key role: once the mayor issued a favorable ruling, the prefect most often seconded it and the central power followed suit. By replacing the intervention of local authorities with an investigation "into the foreigner's morality" undertaken by the central *government*, the law of 1849 thus marked a decisive break. In 1852 one mayor who had not fully understood this, and who had gone ahead with a public inquiry after a request for naturalization, received a warning from the Ministry of Justice: the investigation mentioned in article 1 of the law of 3 December must not be public, for "this way of proceeding cannot supply . . . any useful document"; the investigation "must be entirely confidential and consist in reports issued by government employees whom you have consulted, and who procure, by the means available to them, the necessary information to prepare the government's decision."[12] As an agent of the state, the mayor remained a cog in the machinery. But the prefects gradually came to rely on police investigations to manage and assess naturalization requests.

The power of the Bureau of Seals was nevertheless still limited in one respect: the Council of State controlled naturalizations, which had been submitted to it for a confirming opinion since the law of 3 December 1849 took effect. A law in 1867 made the Council's opinion non-binding; another law in 1889 eliminated it altogether. From that point on the Ministry of Justice made naturalization decisions on its own. Thus emancipated in turn from local power and from judicial control, invested with the power to conduct inquiries, the Bureau of Seals became autonomous. Codifying government practice in a seemingly anodyne document that was in fact of capital importance, a thirty-five-page memorandum dated 28 August 1893 and addressed to solicitors general as a group,[13] it put in place a "jurisprudence" of its own that would allow it to judge the validity of a naturalization request.

When a request reached the Bureau of Seals, it had been given a number followed by the letter x and then the year in which it had been registered; for example, 234x1897 would be file number 234 of the year 1897. Every request was examined by at least three people: an attaché or drafter, the assistant head or head of the bureau, then the director of civil affairs and of seals: in exceptional cases it was also seen by the minister.[14] Imperceptibly, the Bureau of Seals was transformed "into a veritable *Central Office of Nationality*," according to a writer from the period, "sometimes having its own decision-making power, always having a great and legitimate authority that extends to its simple opinions even when they are issued on a purely informal basis."[15] The Bureau of Seals was consulted on the quality of being French of specific applicants, and in the absence of a contrary judicial decision its opinion was tantamount to certification. Its reach extended beyond naturalization to all procedures governing access to French nationality: reintegrations, but also and especially the status of "second-generation" candidates; this latter area was the one in which the most critical issues arose.

The third generation in immigrant families was in fact French from birth, irrevocably except—from 1893—for children born in France to a mother but not a father[16] born in France: in such a case the children could choose to give up French nationality upon reaching the age of majority. For the second generation the law established the principle of favoring access to French nationality when a child reached the age of majority, but it did not impose nationality without at least the tacit consent of the person concerned. However, the bureaucracy did not appreciate this freedom, and it sought to control the legal destiny of second-generation immigrants.

A Goal: "Integrating" the Second Generation

If they took no special steps, children born in France to foreign parents were French when they reached the age of majority, provided that they still resided in France: this was "automatic naturalization."[17] But Parliament did not want to impose anything: it insisted on guaranteeing freedom of choice to adolescents nearing the age of majority. Young people could thus decline French nationality during the year after they reached majority.[18] The same logic meant that minor children of naturalized fathers became French at the same time as their fathers, but retained the possibility of giving up French nationality during the year after they reached majority.[19] The administration did not accept this possibility of choice that the law left open to children of the second generation, and sought to reduce it to a minimum.

On the one hand, it established a rigid framework for the procedure for renouncing French nationality. Declarations to this effect, formerly made before the mayor and then before the justice of the peace in the town of residence,[20] had to be registered with the Ministry of Justice and published in the *Bulletin des lois* beginning in 1893.[21] Any declaration that was not registered was invalid, which meant that the people concerned remained French in spite of themselves, as it were. Next, and most importantly, the Bureau of Seals favored irrevocable acquisition of French nationality by second-generation minor children well before they reached the age of majority.

To wait until the age of twenty-one to attain French citizenship could have been a handicap for certain young men. The delay could have irremediably postponed voluntary enrollment in the army or candidacy for public school entrance examinations — that of the naval academy, for example, where the minimim age for entrance was sixteen. The law of 1889 thus allowed adolescents born in France to foreign parents to proceed without waiting until the age of twenty-one; since they were minors and had no legal right to express their wishes, a father or even a mother could claim French nationality in the child's name. André Citroën, for example, became French at the age of eighteen through this procedure while he was enrolled in a class at Lycée Louis-le-Grand in Paris, preparing to take the entrance examination for the *grandes écoles*.[22] On 27 March 1896 his mother made a request in his name before the justice of the peace of the 9th arrondissement. On 30 April 1896 her declaration was registered at the Ministry of Justice.[23] Many young people became French this way, although not always voluntarily. Parliament had not established a minimum age, for any specification of age would have had the effect of "requiring incessant legislative modifications, every time new school or administrative regulations intervened to lower the age limit for admission to the various examinations."[24] Thus a parent could sign a declaration in the name of his or her minor child born in France up to the time of the child's twenty-first birthday. Beyond this, a provision that still remained an option, a convenience offered to adolescents or their parents, became a constraint under certain circumstances: the government decided to impose this declaration upon any father of minor children born in France who was himself a candidate for naturalization,[25] before responding favorably to his request. As long as he had not acquired French nationality for his children in advance, his own request was deferred. And the prefect of the department that dealt with the request received the following official letter from the Ministry of Justice: "Before ruling on this request, please point out to the candidate that the naturalization of the father and the mother does not suffice to establish the naturalization of the children irrevocably, but that the father can at this time definitively guarantee the quality of being French to his minor son born in France by subscribing for him before the justice of the peace of his district the declaration provided by articles 9, § 2, and 8, § 4, *in fine*, of the Civil Code. . . . If such is the candidate's intention, please give him the attached documents which he will have to produce before the magistrate who receives his declaration and who will supply all the necessary information. In any case I wish you to inform me without delay of the result of your efforts."[26]

The candidate often complied, but a problem remained: the law did not prevent young people declared French by their parents while they were minors from repudiating their nationality when they reached legal adulthood. Since the government wanted their French nationality to be definitive, the Bureau of Seals invented a procedure known as "renunciation of renunciation" to ensure that upon the father's declaration the child would irrevocably acquire the quality of being French. The same declaration on the father's part that won French nationality for the child included a renunciation clause to be used by the child upon reaching majority — the right to decline the quality of being French; the father forbade his son or daughter to renounce that quality. The acquisition of French nationality was thus rendered irrevocable. In 1905 the section of the decree of 13 August 1889 (article 11) that instituted the clause providing for "renunciation of renunciation" was ruled illegal and annulled by the Supreme Court.[27] But "renunciation of renunciation" was reestablished by a law passed under government pressure on 5 April 1909.

Year after year, the administration was thus able to observe that its goal — to integrate virtually the entire "second generation" into the ranks of French nationals — was being accomplished, except for a small minority: in 1893 the administration got legal approval for a provision that authorized it to refuse to register declarations of the desire to become French made by children born in France to foreign parents, "on the grounds of unworthiness." Such refusals could take effect only with the consent of the Council of State,[28] and in twenty-two years, between 1893 and 1915, they concerned a grand total of 124 persons.[29]

Most minor children of naturalized French persons were thus definitively French before their parents' naturalization process was complete. We may wonder why the government insisted on going to such lengths to incorporate children born in France to immigrant parents into French nationality in advance, as it were: Ministry of Justice statistics show that when these children reached the age of majority without already being French, only a tiny minority chose not to accept French nationality. Even in 1913, when the length of military service was extended to three years and renunciations were at their height, the number was small: 821 for the year. If we add the 495 repudiations made by those born in France to a mother born in France and a foreign father not born in France, the total comes to 1,316, or 5 percent of the population concerned (about 26,000 people).[30]

The fact remains that integrating the second generation, which was French by upbringing, was a fundamental principle of action for the Bureau of Seals and would remain so. Moreover, it was so that this objective could be achieved more fully that on 11 November 1913 the Ministry of Justice forwarded a bill providing for the irrevocable attribution of French nationality to all minor children of naturalized parents. But the First World War interrupted the examination of the bill and brought into France, as into all the warring countries, the winds of mistrust and restriction.

The Great War: Mistrust and Suspicion

As soon as war was declared, measures were taken to exert control over foreigners: a decree issued on 2 August 1914 obliged foreigners to request residency permits (1,160,000 foreigners had been counted in the census of 1911). The number of naturalizations was reduced: there were 2,117 in 1914, but no more than 538 in 1915, 803 in 1916, 418 in 1917, and even fewer—282—in 1918.[31]

But more than foreigners in general, citizens of enemy countries were the targets of the most stringent controls. Tens of thousands of Germans, Austrians, and Ottomans, but also, at the beginning of the war, numerous residents of Alsace-Moselle, were interned in "concentration camps" or "internee depots."[32]

Efforts were made to protect the "true French"—who might be "false Germans," moreover—and to protect the country from French nationals who might be enemy spies. Many French people suffered simply because their names sounded German. With them in mind, a proposal was put forward that would have made it easier to adopt a more "French" version of one's family name, but the attempt went nowhere. When they joined the French army, soldiers from Alsace-Moselle whose family names sounded too Germanic were authorized to take a borrowed name, that of a spouse for example,[33] to avoid being subject to "reprisals" if they were taken prisoner by the Germans. There was concern too about the situation of French women who had married Germans; having become German by marriage, these women were sometimes interned.

But the biggest concern throughout the war involved naturalized persons of enemy origin. The first priority was to react to the Delbrück law, a new German law on nationality that went into effect on 1 January 1914, and especially to article 25, whose objective (according to the Ministry of Justice) was "cynically acknowledged at the Reichstag court itself": to allow Germans living abroad "to acquire a nationality of pure show for the preservation of essential interests, in order to be able to be admitted to the London Stock Exchange, for example, or to acquire property in Russia" — prerogatives denied to foreigners — while continuing to serve Germany, which "remained their only true homeland, by propaganda, espionage, voting, and if necessary the use of arms."[34]

In the journal he kept in 1914–15, the historian Jacques Bainville, an influential chronicler who wrote for *L'Action Française*, denounced German espionage camouflaged behind naturalization:[35] "*L'Information* points out that many Germans have been naturalized as Americans and thus live in France protected from the draft and from sequestration. We are discovering at last the Delbrück law (the text of which was printed by Léon Daudet a hundred times before the war), which allows German subjects who have been naturalized abroad to keep their German nationality. But naturalizations of that stripe can be found all the way up to the Joint Chiefs of Staff."[36]

On 14 January 1915 the Catholic deputy Jean Lerolle[37] proposed to amend the law of 1889 to include an article that would rule out the possibility of dual nationality.[38] But the government and Parliament chose another path, one that had been adopted by the United Kingdom in August 1914.[39] Laws passed on 7 April 1915 and 18 June 1917[40] instituted — under the control of the Council of State and then of the Supreme Court — a procedure for stripping French nationality from naturalized persons of enemy origin. Of this group, 25,000 had their situation reexamined; in all, 549 naturalized men and women of German, Austro-Hungarian, or Ottoman origin lost their French citizenship through the application of these two laws.[41] The majority of the 473 men involved — often former members of the Foreign Legion — lost their nationality on the grounds of insubordination.[42]

But suspicion toward all naturalized persons of enemy origin — fear that

Germans had infiltrated the heart of the French economy and finance systems through the application of the "Delbrück strategy"—persisted and increased as the war went on. In April 1918 a service for the "control of naturalized persons" was created within the National Police under the jurisdiction of the Ministry of the Interior: "the ever-increasing number of questions that arise concerning former foreign subjects" led to the establishment of an office whose purpose was to "bring together and deal with all matters concerning those individuals who, not being French by birth, have become French through the benefit of the law."[43]

To begin with, this office undertook a complete inventory of naturalized citizens and classified them by profession. Then it launched an inquiry into "the insidious invasion or rather the infiltration" into financial markets in Paris and the world at large on which Germany had purportedly embarked.[44] Since on the London market "the great German banks [had] just recently been caught *in flagrante delicto* in a general and concerted exercise of influence," the service for the control of naturalized persons decided to launch an investigation into "the 153 members of the bankers' syndicate who [had] standing in the Paris stock market." Its report, issued in September 1918, concluded that twenty-six of them, leaders or associates, "seemed" to be naturalized Frenchmen of enemy origin. In addition, 90 percent of the assets of the twenty-six firms represented were thought to have been contributed by underwriters who were not French nationals by birth. Finally, the police investigation into this group noted eighteen ties of kinship, ten of business, and nine prewar ties of friendship or social relations in enemy countries. The conclusion? That following the model of limited or special partnerships in economic affairs, the naturalized French citizens had "supplied German policy with its favorite instrument, the 'interposed person.'" "The acquisition of French nationality was for Germans a conquest like the others."[45]

The service for the control of naturalized persons consequently recommended that union members be obliged to note on their business documents whether they were "French" or "naturalized"; that more stringent guarantees for naturalizations and for access to nationality on the part of persons born in France be put in place; and finally that the adoption of the new bill currently under discussion in Parliament be treated as an urgent matter. On 31 October 1918 the Chamber of Deputies in fact adopted a text that accelerated the procedure by which someone could be stripped of French nationality. If this text had become definitive, the administration could have avoided "the guarantees of a laborious procedure with the double faculty of appeal and of appeal to the Supreme Court" for which the law of 1917 provided,[46] and it could have deprived naturalized citizens of their French nationality more rapidly, on the grounds of "unworthiness" or "their attitude toward the national point of view," by means of a simple decree issued by the Council of Ministers. But the armistice signed on 11 November 1918 interrupted the review process, and the service for the control of naturalized persons disappeared. France counted its dead—1.3 million plus seventy thousand more from the colonies—and its wounded. The demographic question arose again at the end of the war with unprecedented urgency. And naturalized citizens, still objects of suspicion, soon became precious commodities.

The Demographic Imperative

On 11 October 1919 Georges Clemenceau, head of government, concluded his presentation of the Treaty of Versailles to the Senate as follows: "And then I have another recommendation to add. The treaty does not state that France is committed to having a large number of children, but that is the first thing that ought to have been included. (*Applause.*) For, if France gives up having large families, you can put the finest clauses you like in treaties, you can take away all the German cannons, you can do whatever you like, but France will be lost, because there will be no more Frenchmen. (*Applause.*) . . . I beg you to stand together in an act of unity and seek the means of legitimate aid that are necessary to lead the French people to accept the responsibility of having large families. (*Widespread applause.*)"[47]

The demographic imperative—the perception that an increase in the French population was a vital necessity—once again meant first of all taking measures to increase the birth rate or lower the infant mortality rate; however, these measures could be effective only in the middle or long term. Thus there was also an opening to immigration, which was an immediate possibility. Workforce agreements were signed with Italy, Czechoslovakia, and Poland. A private company, Société Générale d'Immigration, founded by the committee on coal mining and the central office for agricultural labor, organized the recruitment of foreign laborers and their importation into France.[48]

Parliament did not immediately see what impact this call for immigration might have on nationality questions. Still under the influence of wartime fears and suspicions, it went back to the proposal of 1913, which had never been adopted, and added a feminist provision offered by Senator Louis Martin in February 1916. On 24 January 1922 and 12 April 1924, the Senate and the Chamber respectively approved a text whose only significant opening had to do with the status of married women: out of concern for French women and their children, a French woman would be allowed to retain her nationality even if she married a foreigner.

Since 1803 the Civil Code had included a provision according to which a woman automatically took her husband's nationality when she married.[49] For some, this provision had led to complicated, even absurd situations. G. Verberkj-moës attested to this in a letter to Adolphe Landry, deputy mayor of Ajaccio, on 18 August 1919:[50]

> As a result of her marriage, my mother, French by birth, having married my father who was Belgian, became Belgian.
>
> Now during the course of his marriage my father was naturalized as a French citizen, but despite this my mother remained Belgian, since naturalization of the husband did not entail naturalization of the wife and children.
>
> As for me, I was born Belgian, 86 years ago, and I became French only because at the age of 21 I opted for the quality of Frenchman.
>
> From this imbroglio resulted a real reshuffling: my mother, born French, died a Belgian, and my father, born Belgian, died a Frenchman.[51]

The story of that mother is not just a "Belgian joke"; during the war it applied to French women who had become German by marriage, and after the war to many "Italian" women, since the Italian nationality moved to first place among mixed marriages in 1924. For half a century the overrepresentation of men among immigrants had meant that many more French women were transformed into foreigners by marriage than foreign women into Frenchwomen. The imbalance grew much more pronounced after the war, for, beyond the fact that 1.4 million men had died and 700,000 women were widowed, businesses tended to recruit mainly single male immigrants, for reasons of productivity.

Between 1914 and 1924 France had "lost" almost twice as many Frenchwomen (103,000) as it had gained (53,000). The proposal adopted thus provided that a Frenchwoman who married a foreigner would keep her own nationality unless she explicitly declared that she wanted to take her husband's; the latter step became obligatory only if she lived abroad (article 8). In addition, a Frenchwoman married to a foreigner transmitted her nationality to her children born in France (article 1, item 3). Similarly, a foreign woman kept her own nationality unless she requested her husband's, or her own national legislation specified that she must take it. However, in 1924, in the climate of suspicion that had ruled during the war, legislators tended to impose more constraints on naturalization in the strict

TABLE 2

Marriages between French Citizens and Foreigners, 1914–1924

	Foreign women and French men	French women and foreign men	Change in number of French women
1914	3,700	4,400	−700
1915	2,200	2,900	−700
1916	2,700	4,700	−2,000
1917	3,200	6,700	−3,500
1918	3,200	8,600	−5,400
1919	6,000	17,300	−11,300
1920	8,736	14,178	−5,442
1921	6,686	11,672	−4,986
1922	5,773	10,792	−5,019
1923	5,395	10,877	−5,482
1924	5,782	11,363	−5,581
TOTAL	53,372	103,482	−50,110

Source: Depoid, *Les naturalisations en France*, 61.

sense. The bill about to be put to a vote proposed legislation that would require publicizing naturalization requests in a local newspaper, in city hall, and in the prefecture where the applicants resided, so that neighbors and acquaintances could express their opinions and thus their reservations, if any.[52] And although control was not restored to the Council of State, the power of the Bureau of Seals was limited through the institution of a commission reporting to it that was charged with issuing an opinion on each request.[53]

The victory in the legislative elections of 11 May 1924 of the Cartel des Gauches — an alliance between the Radical party and SFIO, the Socialist party — led the administration to change its mind.[54] The new administration decided to be less severe in evaluating current candidates for naturalization. Formerly, candidates who were "mobilizable at their age and healthy" but had not "agreed to participate actively in the national defense" were rejected; henceforth candidates who had children or who were young enough to produce children would be considered more favorably.[55] In two years the number of naturalizations more than doubled, from 5,224 in 1924 to 11,095 in 1926.

Given the danger of depopulation, these results were judged insufficient for many "populationist" members of Parliament. Unlike natalists, who believed that only birth in France to French parents should be privileged, populationists held that "any surplus in population [was] worth having."[56] Between 1921 and 1926 the census revealed a 60 percent increase in the number of foreigners in France, a shift from 1,532,000 to 2,409,000, or roughly 6 percent of the population. In addition to workers from Italy, Poland, and Czechoslovakia, France took in a significant number of political refugees of various origins, in direct relation to the political events disrupting Europe: Russians driven out by the Bolshevik revolution, then Armenians, Georgians, and Jews from Eastern Europe, then Italian anti-Fascists.

With respect to the demographic imperative, it now seemed necessary to correlate the rhythm of immigration with the pace of admissions to French nationality. The administration acknowledged as much: "The fact is that, of two million foreigners currently living in France, each year there are relatively few requests for naturalization: 15,000 to 20,000."[57] More candidates thus needed to be naturalized, and for that two obstacles had to be overcome. The first was the cumbersome procedure that discouraged potential applicants. Candidates usually had to prove ten years' residency; this waiting period was further lengthened by the requirements imposed on minor children, and by the shuffling of dossiers back and forth between the prefecture and the ministry when—as often happened—the latter deemed them incomplete. To be sure, the waiting period could be reduced to three years if the candidate obtained admission to residency. But in such cases seal fees were assessed for both procedures, and these fees were high, so they served as disincentives.[58] They could be reduced in proportion to the candidates' income, but the applicants were rarely informed of this possibility.[59] Moreover, a portion of the seal fees remunerated the three surviving members of the Compagnie des Référendaires au Sceau de France. Created by an order dated 15 July 1814 and abolished through attrition in 1892, until the last of its members died this company retained a monopoly on delivering naturalization certificates and receiving seal fees. This outdated privilege contributed still further to the feeling that the procedure was somewhat obscure, even mysterious.[60] In addition, référendaires could be intermediaries for the presentation of naturalization requests.[61] Thus requests could be submitted either to a prefecture, to a référendaire du sceau, or directly to the Ministry of Justice. The ministry, to lighten its own burdens, required as of February 1926 that requests be submitted initially to prefectures. But because requests kept increasing in number from 1924 on, this measure too had little effect.[62]

The cumbersome nature of the services operated by the Bureau of Seals became a second obstacle. The bureau had no more means at its disposal than it had had in 1914. Consequently, it took longer for dossiers to be processed, and delays accumulated. It was decided that as of 1 January 1924 naturalizations would be announced in the *Journal officiel* rather than in the *Bulletin des lois*.[63] This reduced the delay by four or five months, but the gain was immediately offset by a delay in registering requests when they arrived in the bureau — that took another four or five months. Le Foyer Français,[64] a private association set up to support naturalizations, was charged with receiving candidates and preparing the dossiers.[65] At the same time, an old practice continued to be respected: each candidate from the Seine department was called in for a personal interview with a member of the Bureau of Seals. Like the number of dossiers registered, which went from 13,200 in 1920 to 21,500 in 1924,[66] the number of interviews greatly increased, and the time saved on one end was lost on the other. Clearly, it had served no purpose to make naturalization requests easier without restructuring the services involved.

1927: Consensus around a Bold Project

Louis Barthou[67] took on the task of reform as soon as he returned to the Chancellery on 23 July 1926 in Raymond Poincaré's national unity government, without waiting for a law to be passed. On 3 August 1926 Barthou set up a commission reporting to him under the leadership of André Honnorat, a former minister and at the time a senator from Basses-Alpes; Honnorat had founded the Alliance against Depopulation in 1896 and had been the spokesman for Le Foyer Français in its dealings with public authorities since 1924.[68] The commission's reviewer was Charles Lambert, a Radical deputy from the Rhône department and one of the most ardent partisans of an open naturalization policy.[69] The commission worked quickly: it submitted its report on 18 August, two weeks after it was formed.[70] It noted that the organization of the Bureau of Seals no longer corresponded to the needs that had "grown considerably," owing to "the size of the immigration movement that had developed since the war." It added that "the bill currently pending before the Chambers would in fact remain inapplicable if changes in the current state of affairs were not made right away."[71] Louis Barthou ratified all the commission's suggestions. In a few weeks he had recruited eighty new civil servants, including twenty-one magistrates, and arranged for the service to be transferred to new offices at 24 rue de l'Université in Paris. The service was reorganized so that its director would not have to examine each and every dossier when it arrived and again before it was released, and would not have to review all correspondence.[72] In less than three months, in October 1926, the new organization was ready to go.

In a parallel development in the Senate, under direct pressure from the Ministry of Justice, the commission charged with pursuing the discussion on the current bill took up the text adopted in 1924 and "cut to the quick."[73] It reduced "the waiting period required for a foreigner to request naturalization" from ten to three years.[74] This reduction, proposed by Charles Lambert in 1925,[75] went much further than the five-year period the government had envisioned.

This amounted to a departure from the traditional approach to naturalization. When there was a long waiting period of ten years, "assimilation under the law confirmed a state of assimilation in fact." With the shift to three years, "prognoses" were substituted for "diagnoses."[76] Foreigners residing in France were to be naturalized even if their socialization was not yet complete, on a wager that naturalization would encourage socialization. It was pointless to worry, since naturalization remained a favor that the state could either grant or deny. Worry was all the less useful in that the broad new opening had as its counterpart a clause allowing French nationality to be withdrawn by legal means, in exceptional cases. Since it was of vital importance to France to absorb its foreign population as quickly and as broadly as possible, naturalization was to be granted on a broader scale;[77] however, it was appropriate "that henceforth the French state be defended against fraudulent naturalizations, which are more to be feared in the future precisely owing to the reduction in the waiting period."[78] This clause shocked a segment of the left, but as Barthou acknowledged, it was the condition for Parliament's adoption of the populationist scheme and thus for achieving the 100,000 naturalizations a year sought by Lambert and Honnorat's commission:[79] "If you adopt M. Lafont's amendment [which proposed the suppression of the clause allowing nationality to be withdrawn] the law is lost," Honnorat exclaimed. The amendment was finally rejected by a vote of 385 to 31,[80] and the law of 10 August 1927 was finally adopted—almost without opposition—by a large majority of the Senate and the Chamber of Deputies, fourteen years after the initial proposal was officially presented.

Like many legal texts adopted under the Third Republic, this one was a compromise. It was balanced throughout, but the balance was unmistakably tilted toward openness; according to its reviewer in the Senate, Emile Lisbonne, the text was inspired by "the following guiding principles: make French the largest possible number of foreigners who are attached to our country either by birth or by blood ties; avoid imposing our nationality, however, on those for whom constraint could not create attachment; make naturalization as easy as possible; protect the state, nevertheless, against imprudence or abuse resulting from hasty decisions."[81] The law did not go as far as Lambert and Honnorat would have liked. Honnorat sought to facilitate the assimilation of naturalized citizens by allowing them to make their family names more French. Lambert wanted the second generation to become French automatically upon reaching the age of majority, without the right to make a contrary decision. But on the whole, it was a clear victory for the populationists, who were in favor of increasing the French citizenry through naturalization. Charles Lambert saluted a law that "includes, perhaps for the first time, a truly effective remedy against a terrible evil [depopulation] that is afflicting the country, an evil that, like a cancer, is gnawing away at [the country] and at the sight of which, too often, we close our eyes."[82]

This success came about thanks to the determination of a few men and to their skill at mastering the rules for building a majority in Parliament under the Third Republic.[83] Situated at center-left or center-right on the political chessboard, they all saw increasing the French population by naturalization as an urgent and necessary matter of national interest. Charles Lambert, "the most active, the most eloquent propagandist"[84] for naturalization in the Chamber, who fought tirelessly for the adoption of the new law from the time he was elected in 1924, was convinced that it was a "vital necessity" for France to rebuild its strength;[85] Louis Barthou, once he was back in the administration with Poincaré, thoroughly reformed the Ministry of Justice, and according to Lambert's testimony, he was "committed with clairvoyance and energy to resolving the grave problem of naturalizations, whose full importance he grasped;"[86] in the Senate, finally, from 1913 on André Honnorat—a populationist from the outset—defended a naturalization policy that would be a weapon against the danger of German militarism and nationalism.[87] Until 1932 he headed the naturalization commission that Barthou had created in 1926.

"Paper Frenchmen?"

The policy's few opponents, on the right or the far right, clearly understood what was at stake. Before the adoption of the law, Marie de Roux had warned in *L'Action française* against "the illusion that we can create one more Frenchman thanks to a decree inserted into the *Bulletin des lois* . . . , akin to the illusion that we can create wealth by running the printing press to produce bills. Let us beware of inflating nationality and let us not make paper Frenchmen."[88] After the vote on the law, François Coty, director of the daily newspaper *Le Figaro*, expressed his views with unusual vehemence in a front-page editorial:[89]

> Three million vigorous, healthy, honest Frenchmen have been shipped to the slaughterhouse so they could be replaced by the world's vermin . . . We go so far as to recognize that it is useful to fill the holes dug by the war and to compensate for our weak birth rate by adding elements *of good quality, duly verified, really assimilable* to the French people. What is being prepared is the exact opposite. The hidden administration of the Three Hundred, which Walter Rathenau has defined and which constitutes the true *Internationale*, has decided to replace the French race in France with a different race; it began by arranging for the destruction of true Frenchmen; then it arranged for the introduction of neo-Frenchmen; and the internationalist demagogues are carrying out its orders.[90] The naturalized enemies can no longer be expelled; they are at home just as we are; they have the same rights as we do within our walls — what am I saying, the same rights! They are setting themselves up as political leaders, intellectual leaders, social leaders; they are giving us civics lessons; they are imposing their no-homeland doctrines on our young people and our workers — while waiting to drive us out or to exterminate us. The French people, distracted by other difficulties, other dangers, have not followed the preparations for these supreme machinations; now that M. Barthou is keeper of the Seals and M. Poincaré president of the Council of State, the blow has been struck. We take note of it for the final accounting.[91]

The effect of the law was immediate: naturalizations doubled, from an average of 10,000 in 1925–26 to 22,500 in 1928 and 1929.[92] Then the pace slowed: except for a peak in 1933 (24,763), the average fell to around 17,000 in the following years, with a low point of 15,024 in 1936. But the number of anticipatory declarations made on behalf of minor children born in France went up. Between 1929 and 1934 there were about 10,000 such declarations each year; it is hard to compare this number with the pre-1927 figures, which included minor children of naturalized parents.[93] In addition, the balance of acquisitions through marriage, which had been negative by more than 5,000 before 1927, when more French women were marrying foreigners than the reverse, shifted to the positive side and increased steadily once a French woman could keep her nationality when she married a foreign man, and a foreign woman marrying a French man could easily become French: there were 2,541 such moves in 1928, 2,710 in 1929, 2,881 in 1930, and 3,402 in 1931. All in all, the net number of acquisitions of French nationality — after the losses are taken into account — remained stable throughout this entire period, at around 65,000 a year.[94]

But in the early 1930s the effects of the stock market crash of 1929 were felt in France: the economic crisis was settling in and unemployment was on the rise. Xenophobia was progressing in 1931 when the census counted 2,715,000 foreigners,[95] a record 6.58 percent of the French population. The law of 10 August 1932 allowed the government to issue decrees, at the request of labor unions and business organizations that established the maximum proportion of foreign workers — quotas — in private industrial or commercial enterprises. Some foreigners left the country voluntarily. The restrictive immigration policy left others fearing that they might be required to leave. To protect themselves against forced return, some of these workers — Italians in the Paris region, for example — requested naturalization.[96] Janine Ponty shows that Poles registered their children born in France so that the children would become French.

The Bureau of Seals chose this moment, in November 1932, to assess the impact of the law of 1927. Since that law was passed, more than 350,000 foreigners had acquired the quality of being French (about 170,000 of them through naturalization or reintegration). The Ministry of Justice wanted to know "whether these new French people" had "through their loyalty, their behavior, their morality, and their probity shown themselves worthy of the favor that had been conferred upon them," "whether their assimilation to our populations [had] in fact been accomplished and whether their admission to the French collectivity [had] been favorably welcomed in the social and economic milieus in which they tended to live." The Bureau of Seals recommended that prefects investigate "the effects of the new legislation as much from the national viewpoint as from the social and economic viewpoint"; it asked them to verify the conditions under which nationality was granted, "the advantages, and the disadvantages, if any, that appeared to result" from the law.[97]

The response of the Nord prefect seems straightforward and favorable to the legislation in force: "As for my department, no foreigner who has become French has been the object of unfavorable observations." But the statement was in fact ambiguous, and it encompassed all the issues of the day: "Naturalized foreigners, who are generally of Belgian origin and who work in modest professions for the most part, had already been assimilated to the French population before they were naturalized. The favor that was granted them only sanctioned what already existed. Their admission into the 'French collectivity' has not been the object of justified criticisms."[98] If these two elements — professional situation (modest) and national origin (Belgian) — constituted determining criteria for the assimilation of new French people, should they not become selection criteria for the acquisition of French nationality? If this question could be raised implicitly in an administrative report, it was because it had already begun to be raised in public and vigorously debated.

Populationism versus Selection according to Origin:
The Struggle of the 1930s

Until the First World War Germanophobia had "chloroformed" the racialist approach to immigration and nationality policy—that is, the idea of selecting foreigners on the basis of their national, racial, ethnic, or religious origins. Since the German Empire had annexed the Alsace-Moselle region in the name of race and ethnicity, the battle to recover the lost provinces made it difficult to defend national identity in the name of the French race. When opponents of France's nationality policy deemed it too liberal, they used a discourse that came to be called "individually restrictionist," advocating a more stringent selection to weed out swindlers or delinquents.

The war allowed these sentiments to be expressed somewhat more freely in the context of an anti-German struggle: haunted by an obsession with treason, some saw traitors in all naturalized citizens of enemy origin. As Pierre Baudin, a former minister, wrote in *Le Figaro* on 17 January 1915: "The experience that we have just had commands us to regard every German living on our territory as a spy." He thus proposed—with support from Léon Daudet, writing the very next day in *L'Action française*[99]—that French nationality be withdrawn from "all Germans naturalized after a certain date" and that a more important place be given to jus sanguinis, while making all grants of naturalization permanently conditional.[100] After France's victory the residents of Alsace and Moselle were not reintegrated into French nationality as inhabitants of other annexed lands had been, on the basis of legal residence: that would have meant integrating, alongside the people of Alsace-Moselle annexed in 1871 and the children born to them afterward, "the immigrants, the Germans who had come as conquerors to swoop down on the country and subject it to the worst vexations and the greatest moral tortures."[101] But once peace returned, these xenophobic ideas had difficulty making headway in a France in which reconstruction and the demographic imperative had priority.

During the debates over the law of 1927, the selection of candidates for naturalization by national origin had already been suggested by Léon Baréty.[102] Without asking "for preferences for anyone, of course," this deputy from Alpes-Maritimes wanted "the most assimilable elements, that is, not only Italians but Belgians, Spaniards, French Swiss, and so on, to be naturalized as quickly as possible," and he wanted a special procedure for withdrawal of citizenship to be set up for "crimes or misdemeanors committed by people who had recently become French, most of whom are of Levantine or Oriental origin"; moreover, he accused these latter groups of obtaining naturalization too easily by virtue of their residence in Paris (let us recall that all applicants from the Seine department were received individually at the Bureau of Seals) and because of the help they received from associations in preparing their dossiers.[103]

In this context, in the 1930s the idea of reforming immigration and nationality policies by selecting foreigners based on their origin took on a new dimension. The economic crisis and unemployment persisted, agriculture and the artisanate continued to draw immigrants, and refugees kept coming. New "specialists," in the name of a purported "science" of assimilation, tried to lend legitimacy to this approach.

Old immigration "specialists," often lawyers or economists, were also interested in assimilation. For Georges Gruffy, a lawyer and André Honnorat's principal source of inspiration, "there is no such thing as the French race. France is essentially a land of immigration, an old country of immigration, as Argentina is a new country of immigration. Any lawmaker who does not rely on this idea will not produce a viable nationality law. . . . It is not a matter of diminushing the number of naturalizations or the dominance of *jus soli* . . . Rather, we must achieve the true fusion of naturalized citizens. How? By education."[104] But Gruffy wrote these words in 1920. In the 1930s the new "science," which established hierarchies of immigrants by origin so as to distinguish the "assimilables" from the "unassimilables" among them, appeared more promising. It was patched together from eugenics, the study of races, biology, anthropology, sociology, criminology, psychology, and even psychoanalysis. It was ultimately influenced and legitimized by new American legislation that had instituted quotas by national origin and drastically reduced the number of immigrants, after sociological studies had been conducted on their "assimilability" according to ethnic origin.[105] Moreover, the same confrontation that was developing in France over the way to select foreigners or candidates for naturalization had taken place in the United States a few years earlier, opposing two approaches, individual and racialist: under the first, foreigners were selected according to their individual physical, mental, or moral characteristics, while under the second, selection was based on membership in a national, racial, or ethnic group.[106]

Theoretically, one could support both individual and restrictionist selection — that is, be in favor of restricting the number of immigrants or of naturalizations by selecting on the basis of individual characteristics. Similarly, one could be racialist — that is, in favor of using national or ethnic origin as the criterion — without being restrictionist (wanting to reduce the flow of entrances) or racist (wanting to exclude people on the basis of their supposedly "unassimilable" origin). One could want to take origin into account to ensure the ethnic diversity of a country, for example, a policy embodied in current American legislation.

Moreover, as soon as it came to acting on these matters, to translate theories or ideas into legal terms, proposals often combined the different approaches. For example, the populationist Lambert advocated a racialist selection of new immigrants, but he was a partisan of liberal integration—according to individual characteristics—of naturalized citizens, for he thought that all immigrants admitted into the country should aspire to become French.[107]

In practical terms, however, during the 1930s the partisans of selection on the basis of individual characteristics were almost always liberal populationists, and the scientific racialists showed themselves to be racists as well. Like their American counterparts, they often proceeded under camouflage in order to get their projects approved. In the United States from 1894 there were proposals to select immigrants by means of a literacy test; such a test was finally adopted in 1917. Robert A. Divine noted that "outwardly, it conformed to the tradition of individual selection, adding an educational qualification to the physical, mental, and moral requirements previously established," but he added that "a new principle, group selection, was evident in such discrimination directed against the new immigration, and this concept of judging men by their national and racial affiliations rather than by their individual qualifications was to become the basic principle in [American] immigration legislation of the postwar period."[108] In France the distinction between "immigrant" and "refugee," the applicant's professional status, and the difference between rural and urban occupations all played a similar role.

Among racist experts, the figure of Dr. René Martial stands out.[109] Born in 1873, he earned his medical degree in 1900, specializing in public health, and took an interest in immigration very early in his career.[110] He was in charge of the "immigration course" for the Institute of Health at the medical school in Paris; he published a treatise on immigration and interracial "grafting" in 1931, and a book on "the French race" in 1934.[111] By then he was an authority in the field of immigration.[112] Beginning with his earliest writings (in which he showed himself to be tolerant of foreigners, moreover: the employers "who threw them out onto city streets without any precautions" were the ones to be condemned),[113] he advocated the selection of immigrants.

The American method struck Martial as a model to be followed in both of its dimensions: individual inspection of immigrants in ports of entry (chiefly Ellis Island in New York), and especially selection by ethnic or national origin, even within the "white race," in particular through quotas. Martial thus proposed to create five "land ports" for inspecting immigrants along France's borders, but he did not take up the American system for calculating quotas. In the United States the worldwide immigration quota of 150,000 a year had to be distributed according to the contribution of race or nationality to the American population, calculated retroactively on the basis of the census of 1890.[114] This theoretical calculation, conceivable for a country made up of immigrants or descendants of immigrants, could not be applied to a country like France.

Martial thus sought another method for choosing among immigrants in terms of origin, and in 1928 he thought he had found one. The "scientific" approach to human groups allowed him to assert that the French race was, like every "race," "the entirety of a population whose latent or manifest psychological character- istics (language in particular) and anthropobiological features constitute in time (history) a distinct unit."[115] From this standpoint, affinity through bloodlines was essential. An unlimited opening to immigration, and consequently to natural- ization, would bring in a disordered racial mixing that would risk eradicating the distinct unit, for "blood type subtends psychology"; "this phenomenon is unconscious, instinctive."[116] In this view immigration is like a horticultural graft; it has the same effect on a people as blood transfusions have on individuals. Just as there are incompatible donors and recipients (one does not transfuse type O blood to a type A recipient), one can only achieve a successful immigrant trans- plant if there is adequate "biochemical" compatibility between the entering and receiving groups. Martial was thus a partisan of racial selection of immigrants on the basis of a biochemical index of proximity[117] that he began to develop in February and March 1933. Each population was assigned a "biochemical index" in relation to the proportion of each blood group within it, calculated according to the following formula:

$$\frac{A + AB}{B + AB}$$

The number of Bs increases as one moves from northwestern toward south- eastern Europe, and the coefficients of the groups of people decrease corre- spondingly: Englishmen, 4.5; Belgians, 4.4; Alsatians, 4.01; Swedes, 3.7, French- men, 3.2, Germans, 3.1; Dutch, 3.08; Scots, 2.7; Italians, 2.6; Danes, 2.5; Czechs, 2.4; Greeks, 2.25; Armenians, 2.01; Jews, 1.6; Arabs, 1.6; Russians, 1.4; Poles, 1.2; Negroes (American), 0.9.[118] The English have too high an index; this ex- plains why they have never emigrated into France.[119] Transplants can have good outcomes only if they involve races with biochemical indexes that are not too far apart. The choice of "racial ferment" must involve "a very limited number of peoples, immigrant families selected methodically and primarily through an effort to group blood types: keep the Os and the As, eliminate the Bs, keep the ABs only if the psychological and physical examinations are favorable."[120]

Martial wrote a great deal and lectured widely; he was known and cited. He was not taken seriously, however, when it came to transforming his ideas into concrete policies. This is attested by the critique of an "old specialist," William Oualid, a law school professor in Paris and a respected authority on immigration.[121] He challenged the claim that what was "true for blood transfusions [would be] true for the racial mixing obtained by marriage or sexual intercourse." The proof is that

> nothing is farther apart than the biological indexes of the Belgians and the French. Consequently, if it were true that the biological index were the index of total incompatibility, nothing should bring them together. Yet everything is in place to show that of all the ethnic groups represented on French soil, none is closer to the French than the Belgians. . . . Secondly, alongside this methodological and scientific objection, we must also invoke the reluctance of the French people to assimilate individuals to animals from the standpoint of physical selection. It suffices to allude to the protests that arise among us when certain methods of physical selection are introduced and applied on the pretext of eugenics in neighboring countries, for example the sterilization or castration of elements reputed to be physiologically or morally undesirable. . . . In the name of human dignity, in the name of the equality of all men before divine law, Catholics rise up against the prenuptial certificate . . . In the same way, in the name of human equality and of the equality of all men before the law, in the name of the universal rights of man, we shall rise up against this selection process whose expected and achieved results, moreover, are not certain to be those sought.[122]

This reservation was not shared by Georges Mauco, who soon came to be viewed as the leading expert on immigration.[123] He defended his doctoral thesis, on the economic role of foreigners in France, on 13 February 1932.[124] A geographer, he applied himself to meticulously describing the recent evolution of immigration patterns in France, which he examined in terms of territory, profession, and national origin. Seeing himself also as a demographer, he situated the migratory phenomenon within the development of the French population, evaluating "problems of integration" and finally the degree of "assimilability" of immigrants according to their origin. To measure assimilability and justify his approach, he turned (and would often turn again, into the 1950s) to a "mini-survey" carried out in 1926 involving department heads in a large automobile manufacturing firm that employed 17,229 workers, 5,074 of whom were foreigners or North Africans. The aptitudes of each nationality were categorized on a scale from 1 to 10, with "the maximum score applying to the very good French workers." The survey noted physical appearance, absenteeism, productivity, discipline, and comprehension of the French language. On average, Arabs came in at the bottom of the scale (2.9), then Greeks (5.2), Armenians (6.3), Poles (6.4), and Spaniards (6.5); Italians (7.3), Swiss (8.5), and Belgians (9.0) came out on top.[125]

In 1932, however, Mauco was prudent. His approach by way of assimilability was common at the time, under the influence of American policies and studies, and its general nature camouflaged deep divergences among those who professed it.[126] He concluded the book that he drew from his thesis the same year by evoking the "peril of a peaceful invasion," thus betraying his proximity with François Coty or Charles Maurras and *L'Action française*. "One day," he said, "the newcomers notice that they are masters of the entire productive life of the country, and act accordingly." Elsewhere, Mauco noted optimistically that factors favorable to the assimilation of foreigners outweighed the unfavorable factors, and that the liberal naturalization instituted by the law of 1927 was not entirely a bad thing. His work was greeted with positive reactions from opposing political horizons.

This recognition led in turn to official appointments. In 1935 Henry de Jouvenel offered Mauco the position of secretary general of a committee that Jouvenel had just created to study the problem of foreigners.[127] In 1937 the Center for Foreign Policy Studies commissioned Mauco to prepare a report that was presented as the French contribution to the permanent conference of High International Studies in the League of Nations.[128] Then he was appointed to the cabinet of Philippe Serre, the first, if ephemeral, undersecretary of state responsible for immigration and foreigners' services under Camille Chautemps, head of government, from 18 January to 10 March 1938.[129]

Enough Refugees!

In fact, throughout the 1930s and right up until the Second World War broke out, France's immigration policy was disorganized, subject to upheavals on the economic and political stage. Immigration was pursued, for example, in agriculture, to which the law of 1932 did not apply. In industry the government was lackadaisical about applying the rules governing the distribution of foreign labor. It was not until November 1934 that the Flandin government began to increase the pace of decrees limiting the number of foreign laborers in certain industrial sectors. The same year, a decision was made to stop granting work permits to new migrants, which meant halting the legal immigration of salaried workers. A decree issued on 6 February 1935 allowed the non-renewal of foreigners' work permits for persons who had not been in France more than *ten years* when they worked in a sector where unemployment was rampant. In practice, foreign workers who were fired were often required to leave the country. The same year, 20,500 repatriations took place in a climate of "total indifference."[130] As Janine Ponty indicates, children with French nationality had no protections: "the convoys that took families of unemployed workers back to Poland included children who were already French."[131]

With the Popular Front the legislation did not change, but it was applied more flexibly. In May 1938, at the request of businesses, the quota system set up in 1932 was eased; a simple ruling applicable to a given sector or the consent of the inspector was now sufficient for making an exception. Also in 1938, to stabilize the most solidly established immigration streams the authorities announced the delivery of identity cards, valid for longer or shorter periods according to the length of the foreigner's stay in France. While this reform was not applied as such, political control over the presence of foreigners in France became increasingly stringent, along with police enforcement: every change of residence had to be reported to the authorities. The Ministry of the Interior could require a foreigner to live in a specific place, or could expel him or her with no motive other than the authorities' wishes (decree of 2 May 1938). This repressive approach did not distinguish between "irregular" foreigners and those who had been established in France for years, for example when the documents needed for proof of identity had been confiscated by the immigrant's country of origin. Above and beyond this disorder and confusion, public policy respected a certain hierarchy of norms, independent of origins, which distinguished between "regular" and "irregular" foreigners, and between refugees and immigrants, with refugees given the greatest protection.

For in the late 1930s refugees continued to arrive in France. The decision to shut down immigration, made in 1934, was thus not supposed to apply to refugees, for whom the decree-law of 2 May 1938 ensured special protection for the first time. As early as 1933, 25,000 to 30,000 refugees from Germany and then Austria found asylum in France; in all, on the eve of the Second World War the number of refugees from Germany was approximately 100,000 (of whom about 60,000 remained in France) and from Austria 10,000 (most of whom remained in France).[132] Maintaining the principle of asylum and protection was often unpopular: the refugees were perceived as responsible for importing foreign political conflicts onto French soil, as when a president of the Republic was assassinated in 1932, or when the foreign minister Barthou was killed along with the king of Yugoslavia in 1934 in Marseille. But asylum for refugees, beyond being increasingly guaranteed by specific agreements, constituted for Edouard Herriot "one of the essential elements of republican doctrine."[133]

Martial noted: "As of 1933, new entry of German Jews expelled from Germany. Entry not controlled. No French government agency, civil or police, ministerial or prefectoral, can say anything about the number of these entries, estimated in turn to be 3,000, then 6,000, then 25,000. The latter figure is in all probability closest to the mark, but still inexact. Happily, the Germans take pains to inform us via the National Socialist party's press service."[134]

That from 1933 on most refugees were Jews, first from Germany and then from Austria or Poland,[135] posed both political and theoretical problems for Martial and Mauco. Martial did not want Jews, either as immigrants or as naturalized citizens. Yet a study in 1932 showed that the biochemical index Martial was using to justify "scientific selection" was, for Jews, close to the one for the nations to which they belonged: the index for German Jews resembled the one for Germans, the index for Polish Jews approached the one for Poles.[136] Martial thus proposed — since blood typing did not condemn Jews systematically — to justify their undesirability by their psychology: they were "unstable and also anxious" half-breeds, "perpetually demanding something."[137] When Mauco defended his thesis in 1932, he classified foreigners according to differing degrees of "assimilability," without feeling a need to distinguish refugees from other immigrants within a given nationality, whereas political refugees were already numerous in France — Italians, Russians, and Armenians.

The arrival of Jews driven out by Hitler led Mauco to introduce a "scientific turning point," a distinction between desirable immigration (that of workers), which should be encouraged, and imposed immigration (that of refugees), which should be rejected. This new categorization allowed him to distinguish Jews from non-Jews within a given national origin — Polish, for example. In 1939, speaking before the High Committee on Population,[138] which was studying the question of Spanish and Jewish refugees, Mauco added an additional distinction. Taking a stand against the positions of Claude Bourdet, who wanted to integrate both Spaniards and Jews into agriculture (for the Jews, he used the example of their integration into Palestine) and against the National Police within the Ministry of the Interior, which sought to use the artisanal and industrial qualifications of Jews in the service of the national economic interest,[139] he differentiated according to the refugees' professional classifications: "France is becoming a country of high-level white-collar workers. Foreign immigration is thus a necessity for France, but an immigration of workers and farmers, a complementary immigration. In contrast, all immigration directed toward cities, toward 'white-collar' activities — liberal, commercial, and artisanal professions — does not correspond to any need. . . . That immigration began with the arrival of Russians and Armenians. It expanded right after the war, around 1920, with Israelite, Polish, Romanian, and Hungarian minorities, and this has continued without pause. More recently, there have been refugees from Germany, Austria, Czechoslovakia, almost all non-laborers and clustered in cities. . . . comparison is possible between such an emigration and the emigration of ardent young colonists, leaving with faith in a new land."[140] On that basis Spanish refugees were desirable, in Mauco's view, while Jews were not.

The continuous arrival of such refugees was not without consequences for nationality legislation, moreover. A law passed in April 1933 limited the practice of medicine to the French alone, or to people who had come from countries placed under France's protection, provided that they had earned their medical degrees in France. Foreign doctors were in fact very few in number, 750 out of a total medical population of some 25,000, although they were concentrated in the Paris region.[141] Some of them requested French nationality, but few obtained it. When a request for naturalization came from a doctor or a dental surgeon or a student in medicine or dentistry, it had to be reviewed by the Ministry of Health and by the local doctors' or dentists' union; the drawbacks of this requirement were stressed by Rémy Estournet: "The local union can issue only a partial opinion, dictated by the immediate material interest that consists in preventing the establishment of a future rival. . . . Certain doctors' unions [have] appropriated for themselves the right to summon candidates and subject them to a detailed interrogation focusing especially on their legal antecedents and their families."[142] With tradesmen and industrialists the opinion of the Chamber of Commerce was also requested, but as Estournet noted, the refusal to naturalize did not have the same consequences for the candidate's professional activity — the immigrant could continue to practice his trade.

Lawyers protected themselves in a different way: fearing the arrival of refugee lawyers from Germany, they succeeded as of June 1934 in getting a law passed that forbade recently naturalized French citizens to practice public professions instituted by the state or to register with the bar before the end of a ten-year waiting period.

At the end of 1938, to satisfy a segment of public opinion, an "antifraud" measure was passed. The decree-law of 12 November 1938 made the conditions for marriage more stringent: a foreigner could no longer marry without having obtained a residency permit for a period greater than one year. A foreign woman marrying a French man had to declare her wish to become French before the wedding; this declaration took effect only after a six-month waiting period, during which a decree of opposition could be signed. In addition, the procedure for withdrawing nationality could henceforth be initiated "when a foreigner knowingly [had] made a false declaration, presented a document containing an untruthful or erroneous declaration, or used fraudulent maneuvers to obtain naturalization."[143]

Naturalization Nevertheless!

Until 1939 the Bureau of Seals continued to approve two to three times as many naturalizations as it had before 1927. But this increase in absolute numbers must not obscure the fact that the majority of requests were not granted. In the first place, the prefectures were very selective, and transmitted to the Ministry of Justice only a portion of the dossiers submitted for examination—in Paris, fewer than 40 percent.[144] In addition, the Bureau of Seals applied its own criteria to individual cases, making the process even more selective. Thus for 1938, 44 percent of the dossiers transmitted to the Ministry of Justice by the prefectures were rejected or postponed.[145] And while in that same year 23,500 adults were naturalized and more than 100,000 foreigners acquired French nationality through various procedures,[146] this was first of all because the number of applications to be dealt with had increased: the Bureau of Seals, again seriously deficient in means, was reinforced at the end of 1937 and could thus catch up in 1938 on some of the backlog.[147] Another reason was that in the prewar "frenzy"[148]—the war was looming and immigration policy was hardening—many foreigners who again feared forced repatriation made declarations allowing their minor children born in France to become French: their number went up nearly threefold in a single year, from 13,663 in 1937 to 36,485 in 1938.

Throughout this entire period, however, the overall nationality policy varied little in its principles. In a general directive issued in early 1939, the head of the Bureau of Seals reminded its services of the following: (1) The presence of foreigners in France posed above all a problem of immigration policy that might need to be revisited, but one that fell under the purview of other ministries. Nevertheless, as soon as a foreigner came to reside in France "it [was] necessary to assimilate him to the French citizenry," because one had to "avoid allowing the creation of ethnic minorities in France" and because it seemed logical that "people who participated in the economic life of the country should be a part of it legally." (2) The most important measures for assimilating foreigners were birth in France and marriage: "These modes of automatic integration of foreigners, which have the advantage of seizing individuals in their early years, constitute in a way the normal mode of progressive integration of foreigners into our collectivity . . . naturalization is only an 'accidental mode of integration.'"

As far as naturalization was concerned, each dossier was *a particular case examined as such*. Naturalization had to be merited: the candidate had to be in good physical condition, display good morals, and be well assimilated. Naturalization also had to be of some interest for the country: the candidate's contribution might be professional or familial in nature. Finally, since military service was a heavy responsibility for the French citizen, naturalization must not allow foreign males a way out and thus privilege them with respect to the French. Priority was thus given to young men in a position to do their service, and to parents of minor children.[149] The criterion of profession or trade was rarely taken into account: having a rural occupation might allow someone to escape the veto that applied to people seeking exemption from military service; conversely, candidates in business or invested in a financial enterprise could find their applications deferred if the tax information they supplied was unsatisfactory. In contrast, the criteria of national, ethnic, racial, and religious origin were not taken into consideration.

From 1939, when war was imminent, naturalizations were granted in large numbers. Foreigners were encouraged to rejoin the French army; as for refugees, a decree-law of 12 April 1939, passed after the arrival of the Spanish republicans and aimed partly at them, provided "that foreigners benefiting from the right of asylum would henceforth be subject to the obligations imposed on the French by the laws of recruitment and by the organization of the nation in wartime." To avoid complications with Mussolini,[150] the enrollment of Italians in the Foreign Legion was put off, but their enrollment as Frenchmen was facilitated, as soon as they had been discreetly naturalized. By a secret memorandum of 13 April 1939, the Minister of Justice ordered the prefects to move quickly to forward the dossiers of Italians they deemed naturalizable, marking them with the notation "memorandum of 13 April 1939."[151] When the war broke out Parliament pressed for naturalization,[152] easing the naturalization of Belgians, Swiss, Italians, and Spaniards who had been living in France for at least five years and were candidates for military service: the investigation went more quickly, no longer requiring the opinion of the prefectures, and the chancellery fees that had replaced seal fees were eliminated.[153] For this reason 1939 was a record-breaking year: 44,498 men and women were naturalized and, counting their children, this meant that a total of 99,081 foreigners became French that year through naturalization, and more than 130,000 through all procedures combined. The equivalent numbers were 29,140 during the first half of 1940 alone, and 55,589 until the military defeat. Among these, Italians constituted the majority (60 percent), although they represented only 31 percent of the foreigners in France.

When Georges Mauco testified in February 1939 before the High Committee on Population,[154] he was probably aware of the presence, among those naturalized in 1938, of 1,899 Germans, most often Jewish refugees, or 8 percent of the total number (23,544), the highest proportion since 1927. In any case, he put twenty years of nationality policy on trial: "Since the war, a veritable industry has developed: too often money, relations, politics, or cleverness have been the determining factors in certain naturalizations." According to him, the Bureau of Seals refused "to naturalize worker and peasant families who had been in France a long time . . . [and] who were much better assimilated, for these were in a way new elements, raw, so to speak, and thus more educable. They became more profoundly French in contact with the [French] people and acted less directly on the community. In contrast, [foreign] city-dwellers and [their] urban activities act directly on the nerve centers of the country. Some may have a notable influence, for example doctors, professors, film-makers, and even foreign businessmen or salesmen, and this without even having been imbued with the qualities proper to the collectivity. Moreover, becoming French is much more difficult — despite appearances — for individuals who are already evolved: their previous education counters an in-depth assimilation of the quality of being French." And he concluded: "A serious review of the naturalizations granted during the last twenty years would produce some surprises."[155]

For a long time, the proposals of these immigration "specialists" were aimed only at establishing new rules for selecting in terms of origin in the future. The review of the naturalizations that had taken place "during the last twenty years" — that is, since the end of the First World War — was something that Hitler had decided on in Germany in 1933. Before Mauco, the anti-Semitic Louis Darquier de Pellepoix had again put the idea before the Paris city council.[156] This was in 1936. Once the defeat of 1940 was consummated, the "suggestions" made by Mauco and Darquier de Pellepoix were soon followed.

PART TWO

Ethnic Crises

in French Nationality

Vichy: A Racist and Anti-Semitic

Nationality Policy

⇝ What we have known up to now about the Vichy regime's nationality policy can be summed up in three figures: 15,154 denaturalizations, 446 withdrawals of French nationality, 110,000 Algerian Jews demoted from citizen to subject.[1]

A "law" passed on 23 July 1940 made it possible to withdraw French nationality from all French citizens who had left France without government authorization between 20 May and 30 June 1940.

Inspired by the second section of the Nazi law dated 14 July 1933,[2] deprivation of nationality was intended primarily to punish and degrade members of the Free French Resistance, whom the Vichy regime termed "dissidents"; among these were General Charles de Gaulle, General Georges Catroux, René Cassin, Alexis Léger, General Philippe Leclerc de Hauteclocque, Pierre Mendès-France, and later on Maurice Couve de Murville and Admiral Darlan. The property of those affected was confiscated, sequestered, and then liquidated, and the profits were deposited in the National Aid bank (Secours National).[3] The "law" of 23 July 1940 was completed on 23 February 1941, when it was made to apply to every French person who, "outside the metropolitan territory, betray[ed] by his actions, speeches, or writings the duties incumbent upon him as a member of the national community."[4] Most of the decisions were made by a commission consisting of three military officers and headed by General Julien-Claude-Marie Dufieux, at the Ministry of the Armies.

The Nazi law of 1933 also directed, in its first section, that all naturalizations granted between 9 November 1918, the symbolic date of the fall of the German Empire, and Hitler's seizure of power—thus during the entire period of the Weimar Republic—could be revoked if "naturalization [did] not appear desirable."[5] Following this model, the "law" of 23 July 1940 concerning review of naturalizations established the symbolic limit of the law of 1927—one of the most open and liberal components of legislation. The Vichy law made it possible to withdraw French nationality without cause from anyone who had acquired it after 10 August 1927. The law was only the visible portion of a much broader program, however: a complete recasting of French nationality was an immediate priority for the new regime.

The plan of action projected by the Vichy government had three facets: first, denaturalizations, to "rectify" past errors; next, restrictions on new naturalizations; finally and most importantly, new legislation, under development since July 1940, that would create a new French nationality code. The implementation of this plan brought out a conflict between two distinct approaches. While both "restrictionists" and "racists" sought to limit access to French nationality, their reasoning differed, and they remained in opposing camps until 1944.

The "restrictionists" wanted to be more rigorous in granting access to nationality or entry into national territory; they wanted closer control over who was to become French. They were in favor of barring criminals and delinquents from holding French nationality, they often viewed Jews with suspicion, and they saw national or ethnic origin as one criterion among others for evaluating an applicant's capacity for assimilation; each application was to be assessed individually. The "racists," partisans of selection on the basis of racial, ethnic, or religious origin, wanted the criterion of origin, especially Jewishness, to be the exclusive principle of selection for access to French nationality.[6] Adherents of both approaches were already present in the late 1930s, but they were counterbalanced by "liberals" who supported a policy of openness in matters of nationality and immigration. Now, with liberals sidelined by the military defeat and the Vichy regime, with immigration blocked and the status of Jews determined, the new nationality policy became the main battleground for the two groups. The Vichy government did not have anti-Semitic laws (for example, laws governing the status of Jews) on the one hand and xenophobic laws (for example, the law allowing denaturalizations) on the other. The anti-Semitic and xenophobic projects were not complementary: they were in competition. As we look at the process by which texts were developed and applied, we find that the rival projects were often overlapping or intertwined.

For the anti-Semites whose overall goal was national "regeneration," the status of Jews—who were clearly targeted—and the new nationality policy—which was more neutral in appearance—belonged to one and the same framework. The way to recast nationality was still being debated in 1942 when Charles Rochat, general secretary of the Ministry of Foreign Affairs, signed the following judgment, in a letter addressed to the minister of justice, also often known as the keeper of the seals: "Since the armistice, our Government has had a racial policy. On the one hand, a commission from your Chancellery is undertaking to review naturalizations that were granted too readily; on the other hand, recent legislation more or less eliminates the Israelites from the French economy. It seems abnormal to keep open an unregulated access route to our nationality for descendants of elements that we exclude otherwise from our nationality or our economy because they are considered unassimilable."[7]

This anti-Semitic framework thus had its own logic, its strict interpretations, its justifications, and its principles. We find these defined and reiterated, for instance, in each of the reports that the Council of State member Louis Canet submitted to his colleagues when his opinion as "clerk for Jewish affairs"[8] was sought.[9] Put in order and juxtaposed, Canet's reports to the Council of State have implacable legal coherence.

On the one hand, there were the French Jews. As the reviewer of the bill designed to institute a quota for Jewish lawyers,[10] Canet drafted a note justifying the new status of the Jews in sweeping terms.[11] The French tradition was originally a good one, according to Canet: "The concordat regime that came out of Napoleonic policy led to the constitution of a Jewish Gallicanism that incorporated the Israelite community into the French community." Action had became necessary because the Republic had perverted everything: "If France had stuck with that doctrine . . . it would have received fewer Jewish immigrants; those it did receive would have been easily assimilated. . . . The law of 1905, in giving churches almost unrestricted freedom, took away from the Jewish community the possibility of assimilating newcomers and allowed certain segments of French Judaism to submit to the latter's influence, and thus to tend to become less French."

The hierarchy in the exclusion of French Jews was thus justified. Potentially exempted from this status were the Jews who "remained French," who had to be separated from the "*défrancisés*," those who had become "un-French." The principal index of "Frenchness" was the length of time the family had been in France and evidence of having served the nation, for example by fighting under its flag: "The text of article 8 in the law of 2 June 1941 marks a return to the traditional doctrine in that it allows derogations for those whose family, established in France for at least five generations, has rendered exceptional services to the French state."

Louis Canet proposed very few such derogations, even fewer than had been proposed to him by the Commissariat-Général for Jewish Affairs, hardly a liberal agency on this point, and he responded in the negative to requests from Pierre Laroque, Claude Lévi-Strauss, Jacques Valensi, Jean Wahl, and others.[12]

Then there were the foreign Jews, whom Canet wanted to see driven out of France. On 26 November 1941 Canet reviewed a proposed decree intended to regulate Jews' access to commercial, industrial, and artisanal professions.[13] He approved it except on one main point: the exception to the principle of exclusion that the Vichy government planned to allow for ritual Israelite businesses: "There is scarcely any business that, for the Jews, has not been ritual and could not become so again (for example the wine business and the clothing business) . . . and because (where the meat business is concerned) the adoption of a single mode of slaughter with a pistol or an automated cleaver, already imposed for horses by order of the police prefect in Paris, would have the effect of removing from France the unassimilated and unassimilable Jews of Eastern origin."[14]

Lowering the status of French Jews—with a few exceptions denying "unassimilated and unassimilable" foreign Jews the right to stay in France—what were the "racists" proposing in the three facets of nationality policy? And would they win out over the conservative approach of the "restrictionists"? The answers to these questions have to be sought deep within the inner workings of the Vichy government. The analysis of texts produced by government services under an authoritarian regime presents a special challenge, however. Even in normal times, the hierarchical French administrative system and the management of careers that depends on it inhibit the expression of disagreement or conflict; in an authoritarian period when the risks are greater—internment, reassignment, revocation—it is even more difficult to find expressions of dissent. One often has to scrutinize the texts and their contexts, looking for elements that may mark resistance or zeal; in short, one has to try, as Leo Strauss suggested, to read "between the lines."[15]

The Bureau of Seals in the Office of Civil Affairs at the Ministry of Justice continued to play the central role in the conduct of Vichy's nationality policy. The bureau now housed the secretariat of the Commission on Denaturalizations, and the regime took care to put a man it trusted in charge. Paul Didier,[16] who had headed the bureau since 1937, was the only magistrate who dared refuse to swear allegiance to Marshal Pétain; he was thus replaced, on 22 September 1940, by Henry Corvisy, who was loyal to the new regime and close to Action Française.[17] But to prepare and implement the new policy, the Ministry of Justice worked much more closely than usual with the Ministries of the Interior, Labor, and War, as well as with the Council of State, the Commissariat-Général for Jewish Affairs, the prefectures, and the public prosecutors' offices. Finally, within the Ministry of Justice itself, the Bureau of Seals—which had remained in Paris—had a representative in Vichy, and it acted under the authority not only of the three consecutive ministers who served during this period (Raphaël

Alibert, Joseph Barthélemy, and Maurice Gabolde), but also under the supervision of their cabinets and of the ministry's general secretary, Georges Dayras; he had direct authority over the Commission on Denaturalizations, which had been created *ex nihilo*. The Vichy government's nationality policy was the product of all these interactions.

The Failed Attempt to Produce a New Nationality Code (1940–1943)

Establishing new legislation on nationality was unquestionably an absolute priority for the new regime. As early as July 1940, the minister of justice Raphaël Alibert[18] asked his staff to give him proposals for reforming the nationality code. In the response submitted to Alibert on 31 July 1940, the chief proposal focused on naturalizations. The law of 1927 had opened up access to nationality by reducing the required length of stay in France before a candidate's application could be considered, from ten years to three. The ministry's staff proposed to tighten the conditions by means of a simple memorandum, as "naturalization is a favor that the government can refuse without cause." They proposed lengthening the required stay in France to eight years, not without a certain involuntary humor: "the weakening of France's influence might lead to a decrease in its capacity to assimilate, which is naturally a supplementary reason for caution where naturalizations are concerned."[19]

They also proposed transforming into criteria of acceptability certain factors that had previously been used to evaluate the quality of a dossier: that the candidate was leading a "good life" with "good morals"; had not been the object of any reproach regarding behavior, morality, or professional activity; had never been condemned for infractions of common law either in France or elsewhere; had clear proof of means of subsistence; had assimilated French mores and customs; could speak and understand the French language; was in demonstrably good physical and mental health; and presented sure guarantees of attachment to France and its institutions. But they did not want to go much further: "Thus while it is indispensable to have very strict guarantees in the naturalization process, it does not seem to be necessary to interrupt the operation of this institution given that it is useful to the country."

The proposal that Georges Dayras transmitted to the Council of State on 9 August 1940 was much more restrictive. The waiting period for naturalization was extended not to eight years but ten, in a return to the pre-1927 system.[20] The procedure chosen had been in place between 1849 and 1889, a period when naturalization could be granted only with the approval of the Council of State, which was done no more than a few hundred times a year.[21] The right of foreign parents to have their minor children become French by a simple declaration was suppressed; between the ages of sixteen and twenty-one these children could only become French by registering a declaration of intent, but the Ministry of Justice could reject a candidate through a decree issued by the Council of State. At the age of twenty-one such children could become French only if they possessed a certificate of residency delivered by the Ministry of the Interior for a minimum of three years (instead of one year, as before).

On 16 August 1940 the Council of State responded to a request for its opinion[22] by approving the government's proposal, during its first meeting since the new regime had established its new seat at the Hôtel Thermal in Royat, a suburban city near Clermont-Ferrand. However, the Council added several restrictions suggested by the Ministry of Foreign Affairs[23] or by the reviewer.[24]

At the end of September the Ministry of Justice rejected an amendment proposed by the Ministry of the Interior that was intended to restrict the right of foreign women who married Frenchmen to become French. On 14 November 1940 the Council of State ratified the most stringent position, that of the Ministry of the Interior: henceforth a foreign woman marrying a French man would have to go through the constraining procedure of naturalization.[25] The Council's reviewer, Armand Guillon,[26] also won approval in principle for a wholesale recasting of the bill.[27] On 30 January 1941 the Council approved a text presented as a complete new nationality law (earlier it had taken the form of amendments to the law of 1927). Now the proposal was close to being signed. On 22 February 1941 the new minister of justice, Joseph Barthélemy,[28] wrote to the minister of war that "the forthcoming promulgation of the new nationality law will allow the Chancellery to regain responsibility for investigating naturalization requests, on which it has not been able to rule since the events of June 1940."[29] The inter-ministry discussions resumed several weeks later, however, on an unprecedented scale.

In a letter to Barthélemy on 15 March 1941, Admiral François Darlan, who had become vice-president of the Council on 9 February and was also minister of the interior, took the critique onto new territory. According to Darlan and his staff, what was missing in the proposal — "it is silent on this point" — were conditions "having to do with the candidate's ethnic origins": "If France means to move consciously toward a policy of directed naturalization, she must base it principally on the ethnic origins of the individuals that she desires to integrate. Following the example of what is done in countries where immigration is controlled, such as the United States, contingents, actual 'quotas' by race or nationality of origin, could be set annually for candidates for the definitive immigration that is naturalization. The problem presents some difficulties, but a technical committee could resolve them easily. . . . It would not be opportune . . . to indicate these 'contingents' in the law itself; it would suffice to specify in the text that interministerial rulings would establish them annually."[30]

On 22 April 1941 the Bureau of Seals in the Ministry of Justice expressed opposition to the system of "quotas by race or nationality of origin" established annually. It had consulted the American embassy in Vichy, which reported that the system of quotas in the United States did not exist for naturalization; it was "applied only to immigration": "It would be illogical and arbitrary to want to envisage it directly for access to nationality in a country which, like France, has never had an immigration policy, and in which the number of foreigners is so high that their legal assimilation by naturalization becomes almost a necessity if one wants to avoid creating veritable foreign colonies on one's own soil. . . . If we were to go down the path of establishing quotas for naturalization on the basis of race or nationality of origin, we would have to complete the measure by establishing quotas for acquisition of French nationality *jure soli*, which would entail a complete recasting of our nationality law and an absolute modification of the rules that have been gradually imposed on legislators (owing to the demographic situation of our country)."[31]

The Ministry of Justice recalled, in addition, that naturalization could be freely denied "to foreigners who demonstrably satisfy the legal conditions," and that if the proposed new text were adopted, naturalization could no longer be granted without the approval of the Council of State. Finally, the ministry questioned the determining character of ethnic origin: "As the truly constitutive element of the nation is the family, one may wonder whether naturalization, a measure of integration taken in the national interest, should not be conceived essentially in relation to the candidate's family situation. In reality, family situation, race, nationality of origin, and profession all count as elements for evaluation that must be completed, moreover, by information about the applicant's morality, health, and degree of assimilation. Consequently, nationality remains in spite of everything a question of specific cases, and in this area objective rules have to give way to subjective utility."[32]

After the offensive of the Ministry of the Interior, the second assault came from the Commissariat-Général for Jewish Affairs. This agency, created on 29 March 1941, was charged in particular with "proposing to the administration all legislative arrangements and rulings as well as all appropriate measures for implementing the decisions of principle taken by the administration with respect to the status of Jews, their civil and political capacities, their legal right to hold jobs and exercise professions." The new commissioner general for Jewish Affairs, Xavier Vallat, wrote twice to the minister of justice, on 5 June 1941 and again on 4 August, to propose radical changes in the proposed nationality law. He suggested that no more Jews be naturalized, and that nationality should never be granted to a foreign Jewish woman who married a Frenchman. He also proposed completely withdrawing from foreign Jews the right to make anticipatory declarations of nationality for their children born in France, although he did not want to prevent those children from gaining access to French nationality when they came of age: "that solution would have the disadvantage of . . . favoring the concerned parties over French nationals required to serve in youth work groups."

On 14 August 1941 the keeper of the seals responded to Vallat with a wholly legalistic objection: "as for naturalization by decree, . . . you have quite rightly pointed out that in this matter . . . the public authorities were invested with a sovereign liberty of decision. It is thus perfectly useless to envisage a text through which the Government would forbid itself in advance to grant a determined category of persons a favor that it always remains free to deny them. It is desirable, moreover, to keep open the possibility of accepting requests by Jews who have particular qualifications for naturalization."

As for acquisition of nationality by children born in France, either while they are minors (article 3 of the Civil Code) or after they have reached the age of majority (article 4 of the Civil Code):

> These two models of acquiring French nationality are intimately linked, and it would be contrary to logic as well as to the traditional spirit of our legislation to seek to prevent Jews from making the declaration provided for by article 3 between the ages of 16 and 21 if later on they become French automatically upon reaching the age of majority by virtue of article 4. Now you seem to consider that making Jews ineligible for the application of article 4 could have undesirable consequences by favoring the concerned parties with respect to Frenchmen required to serve in youth work groups. If such is indeed your sentiment, I suggest also abandoning the interdiction directed toward article 3, since the specific option provided by this text is in reality only an anticipatory manifestation of the desire of the parties to invoke the benefit of article 4 upon reaching the age of majority.

The Commissariat-Général for Jewish Affairs went no further.

But a final offensive in favor of an anti-Semitic approach to nationality came from the Ministry of Foreign Affairs. On 17 December 1941 it asked the keeper of the seals to suspend the "planned promulgation of the new law."[33] On 8 March

1942 Charles Rochat, general secretary of the Ministry of Foreign Affairs, addressed a note to the minister of justice:[34]

> Article 3 of the proposal allows children of foreigners born in France to request our nationality between the ages of 16 and 21 by means of very simple formalities. Article 4 gives French nationality to any foreigner born on our soil who is living there at the age of majority if he possesses a three-year residency permit and if he has not declined our nationality; it does specify that the keeper of the Seals can refuse to grant nationality after the Council of State has issued its opinion. But nothing is provided, in the text, to set up the controls that the current circumstances impose. . . . France, under the pretext of a liberal tradition that the Anglo-Saxon democracies have not imitated, has admitted to its territory practically without restrictions a considerable quantity of Eastern refugees of whom many are Ashkenazy Jews driven out by pogroms or Armenians expelled from Turkey. . . . These elements have family and social traditions that are absolutely different from those of our country. They live grouped together and according to their own habits. . . .
>
> Births of children of foreigners who came to our country under the conditions spelled out above went up to 25,000 in the early years, later reaching a maximum of around 60,000 before subsiding. . . . A considerable number of boys and girls remain eligible for French nationality at the age of majority without any formality. Now, since the armistice, our Government has had a racial policy. . . . It seems abnormal to keep open an unregulated access route to our nationality for descendants of elements that we exclude otherwise from our nationality or our economy because they are considered unassimilable.
>
> Rochat thus proposes setting up strict controls on the acquisition of nationality by a commission composed of representatives from the ministries concerned (Justice, Foreign Affairs, Interior, Health, and Family) and headed, for example, by a Councilor of State. . . . It would set simple criteria on the basis of which applications would be presented for examination. For example, the unassimilable Eastern Israelite elements would not be accepted. Candidates born in neighboring French-speaking countries would benefit, in contrast, from a favorable predisposition.

Ethnic selection would be applied to children born in France to foreign parents (articles 3 and 4 of the law) as well as to naturalizations, and would have to be carried out on a "scientific" basis: "Rules of an anthropological order intended to determine the populations whose absorption would be judged particularly advantageous for the French race could be determined by the 'French Foundation for the Study of Human Problems' created by the law . . . of 14 January 1942 . . . which is charged among other things with studying, from all angles, the most appropriate measures 'for safeguarding, improving, and developing the French population in all its activities' and the search for 'any practical solution . . . in view of improving the physiological, mental, and social state of the population.'"[35]

The Ministry of the Interior proposed selecting candidates for naturalization on the basis of ethnicity, with first-generation Jewish immigrants as the main target for exclusion: the Commissariat-Général for Jewish Affairs proposed to prevent this group from becoming French. The Ministry of Foreign Affairs proposed to go even further and extend the ban to the second generation, children born in France to foreign Jewish parents. The arrangement proposed by the Ministry of Foreign Affairs, clad in the scientific trappings of the day, appeared "solid" enough to seduce Armand Guillon, the Council of State's reviewer for the bill: "The concern that dictated this proposition is obtaining in all such cases, a jurisprudence based on carefully studied racial policy. I share this concern, for my part, but could [such a policy] not just as well guide the competent section of the Council of State?"[36]

Guillon approved of the racist approach, and of its extension to children born in France to foreign parents; his only worry was that the Council of State would lose control. Thus he suggested combining the new commission sought by the Ministry of Foreign Affairs with the maintenance of the Council's prerogatives: "The work of the Council of State would be reduced and simplified."[37]

But the Ministry of Justice did not accept Guillon's proposal. In interministry discussions it agreed without difficulty to restrict naturalizations, that is, to restrict access to nationality for first-generation immigrants. But since 1889 access to French nationality on the part of children born to that first generation had become such a fundamental principle of action in the Bureau of Seals that the ministry had no intention of departing from it. A few weeks later, on 20 May 1942, two days after Laval succeeded Darlan, a meeting took place between Dayras, general secretary of the Ministry of Justice, and the director of the Chancelleries in the Ministry of Foreign Affairs. On 17 August 1942 the keeper of the seals sent the minister of foreign affairs — who was also the head of government — a letter enacting the compromise that had been reached in the meantime: the bill remained as it had been. The control envisaged over access to nationality on the part of children born in France to foreign parents

can only exist if all persons belonging to this category are required to constitute a dossier with the Ministry of Justice or at least to make the date of their majority known, and if the failure to complete this formality is sanctioned by the withdrawal of the benefits of the provisions of article 4. At that point, the automatic character of French nationality would disappear from the legislation.

Now it seems impossible to give up a traditional (and nevertheless republican) principle of this importance, and the right of refusal that belongs to me under the terms of the new draft of article 4 seems a sufficient weapon to forbid access to the national community on the part of undesirable and unassimilated elements.[38]

The minister of justice gave his consent to the creation of "an agency centralizing all information concerning naturalizations and acquisitions of French nationality, in order to extract from the entire set of facts a general doctrine that could be used, in the light of the demographic problems, by the agencies — Council of State or Bureau of Seals — that [were] responsible for applying the new law." He added that he felt "personally very firmly that no modification should be made to the final version of the bill, and that its promulgation should not be further delayed."

Barthélemy accompanied that note of 17 August 1942 with a handwritten message to Laval:[39] "I respectfully call the attention of the Head of the Government to the necessity for finally completing a law on nationality. The collaboration among the various ministerial departments must not degenerate into the systematic organization of a general paralysis."[40]

The Ministry of Foreign Affairs confirmed the terms of the agreement on 31 August 1942: in exchange for maintaining the law in the form presented by the Ministry of Justice, the decree implementing the new law would contain precise means for keeping second-generation "undesirables" from gaining access to French nationality. In addition, a new immigration policy set by the new High Council on Foreigners would make it possible to limit their influx.[41]

In January 1943 the definitive draft of the bill seemed ready for the German authorities' approval. But the debate started up again over a new question raised by the seals staff: for the pending naturalization applications that had been accumulating since 1940, should the old law or the new one be applied, and if the new, at its date of publication or its date of promulgation? On 23 March 1943, profiting from Joseph Barthélemy's replacement by Maurice Gabolde,[42] the Justice Ministry's staff tried in vain to reopen the question of the new control function exercised by the Council of State for each naturalization.[43] A definitive text was finally ready in August 1943, accompanied by an introductory summary and the draft of a decree of implementation.

Even though it appeared to preserve the traditional policy of the Ministry of Justice in favor of integrating the second and third generations, the bill was very restrictive. Where state control already existed, it was reinforced: the minimum length of stay in France required before naturalization went from three to ten years, contingent on a residency permit valid for three years;[44] every naturalization dossier would be submitted for a ruling by the Council of State.[45] In addition, restrictions were created where they had not existed before—for foreign women marrying Frenchmen. Children of foreigners born in France could still become French upon request between the ages of sixteen and twenty-one, or automatically upon reaching majority (twenty-one), contingent in either case on their having a residency permit valid for at least three years. Finally, their access to nationality could be denied by the keeper of the seals, after a ruling by the Council of State. In contrast, the double jus soli was maintained: "Nothing has changed in the former legislation concerning the attribution of French nationality at birth."[46]

On 15 October 1943 General Secretary Dayras confirmed that the new nationality law had been signed, adding this note: "The Parc[47] is waiting for the Chancellery to indicate that the German authorities are in agreement or that there is no need to communicate with them." The Chancellery had in fact communicated the text of the bill to the German authorities, and their verdict arrived several weeks later. The answer was no.[48]

This is how Barthélemy characterized the entire process:

> The French government found itself forbidden to publish a law in the *Journal officiel* before being authorized to do so by the occupying authority. It sometimes happened that that authority deferred its authorization for a long period of time, or indefinitely. It happened more often that it responded with a formal and naturally (dare I say) unexplained rejection. I had had my staff undertake a very careful study of a major law on nationality; the Minister of Foreign Affairs had subjected it to stringent examination; I had to defend myself at length against the obstructiveness of the Ministry of the Interior; the Ministry of the Family, pursuing with tenacity the impossible enterprise of justifying its own existence, demanded to add its own grain of salt in turn. When everything was finally ready, after two years of preparation, I sent the text to the head of the government, who submitted it to the German authority. But "Majestic answered 'no,'" as they said then. The German authority refused to approve it, without explanation or pretext.[49]

This account contains two misstatements: first, it was not Barthélemy but Alibert who originated the project; second, the negative ruling of the German authorities was clearly motivated: the "no" was based both on Germany's interests and on its racial policy.[50]

The veto came straight from Berlin, from a university institute that had been consulted owing to the divergence of opinions between the two structures representing the Nazi administration in Paris.[51]

A note dated January 1943 from the military command in France (Militärbefehlshaber in Frankreich), in principle the highest German executive authority, accepted Vichy's proposal. It observed that "the chief provisions bring no change to the current legal situation," but that "from the viewpoint of the occupying power, the bill in question does not give rise to any objections." But on 21 January 1943, in contrast, the commander of the security police and the Security Service in France (Sicherheitsdienst, or SD) — reporting to the Central Office of Security (Reichssicherheitshauptamt, or RSHA), which was directed from Berlin by Himmler and Heydrich and commonly known as the Gestapo — issued a negative opinion: "The new bill . . . contains important elements of *jus soli*. Its provisions lead to naturalization of as many persons born in France as possible. This regulation cannot be accepted by us inasmuch as it infringes on the interest of the German *Volkstum* [character of the people]. . . . The bill contains no provision regarding the Jews. Consequently, according to this law, foreign Jews can acquire French nationality under the same conditions as other foreigners. The elements of *jus soli* mentioned above apply equally to them. . . . Previous revisions to this bill have all been incorporated into it; with one remarkable exception: only the law of 2 February 1941 has not been inserted, a law whose provisions made it possible to denaturalize dissidents (Darlan, Giraud)."[52]

On 11 February 1943 the military commandant in France maintained his stance and proposed to consult a third authority. On 19 April 1943 the German embassy in Paris, headed by Abetz — the third official Nazi authority in Paris — transmitted the bill and the divergent opinions of the military command and the Gestapo to the Ministry of Foreign Affairs in Berlin, and suspended approval of the bill in the interim.

In Berlin it was thus the Institut für Staatsforschung of the University of Berlin, responsible for the "scientific" preparation of important works for the state and the party,[53] which was officially consulted. Integrated into the wartime infrastructure[54] by a decree from Himmler dated 29 August 1938, the institute was consulted until 1944 by the Nazi party Chancellery (Parteikanzlei), the Reichsführer SS, the Ministry of the Interior, the Wehrmacht High Command, and the Ministry of Education[55] for research or expert legal opinions on questions of constitutional and administrative structure, first purely German ones and then, increasingly, questions on the constitutional and administrative law of the other European states.[56]

The institute was headed by Reinhard Höhn, born in 1904, a member of the

Nazi party since 1 May 1933,[57] and a member of the ss as of 1934. He went to Berlin from the University of Heidelberg in 1934–35, with an appointment as professor. At the same time, in 1935 he became section chief (Hauptabteilungsleiter) of Heydrich's sd staff in Berlin. With Ohlendorf, Best, Six, and Schellenberg, Höhn was part of the group of "young lions," Nazi intellectual technocrats grouped around Heydrich.[58] For his work with the sd Höhn had the secret services of the ss, including the Gestapo, at his disposal. In 1936 he used this position to arrange the surveillance of Carl Schmitt,[59] who had become one of his chief rivals among Nazi legal scholars. Höhn was one of the principal forces behind Schmitt's fall in 1936.

Höhn had to leave the sd in 1937, because he had supported for a position as director of a historical research institute a candidate who had been rejected by Hitler.[60] But after his departure he maintained close contact with the regime: in January 1939 Himmler awarded him the rank of colonel (ss-Standartenführer); in November 1944 he became ss-Oberführer; in 1945 he was promoted to general (Generalleutnant der Waffen-ss). Until the end of the war Höhn made numerous trips abroad, traveling principally to occupied countries to participate in conferences on legal topics. Moreover, he was invited by the Deutsches Institut in June 1944 to give a lecture in Paris on the theme "Staat und Volk in der deutschen Rechtswerdung" (the state and the people in the development of German law).[61]

In terms of productivity at the institute, Höhn characterized his chief assistant, Berthold Hofmann,[62] as one of the best among the young generation of academics.[63] Hofmann's expertise included international public law, constitutional law in the Reich and the occupied territories, problems of contemporary administration, and the analysis of contemporary legal publications.[64] The institute's only full-time employee, he was in charge of finances, and he took over as director when Höhn was away. He received the rank of ss-Obersturmführer when the institute was integrated into the wartime infrastructure, on 20 April 1940; he became ss-Hauptsturmführer in September 1940. In this capacity he reviewed all the expert opinions issued by the institute, and he drafted the most important ones himself. On 16 October 1943 it was he who signed the institute's position paper on the French nationality bill;[65] in an interview with me on 12 April 1996 Höhn indicated that this was an isolated occurrence.[66] The document was addressed to ss-Brigadeführer Otto Ohlendorf, one of Höhn's close associates in the group around Heydrich.[67]

The reservations expressed about the bill were general at first: "The text does not break with the French tradition which seeks through the angle of *jus soli* to integrate an immigrant population in order to reinforce the faltering French population." In addition, the bill did "not satisfy the requirements of a modern nationality law that would conform to the ideology of the people [*völkisch*]": "In fact, it brings French nationality law back to the situation in effect before the law of 10 August 1927 was promulgated. The goal of this bill is essentially to abolish the liberalizations introduced into the naturalization procedure by the law of 8 August 1927, which were designed to increase the number of French citizens. . . . Consequently, the bill does not constitute a recasting of French nationality law. By the return to the legal situation in effect in 1927, the bill is situated along the general lines pursued by Marshal Pétain: even while abolishing the legislative creations characteristic of the Popular Front, it extends the constitutional law of the Republic, petit-bourgeois and formal, and conservative in spirit — the typical sign of the property-owning bourgeoisie."

Subsequent reservations concerned specific points in the text that harmed "the interests of the Reich." These interests were then divided into two groups "according to the measures to be taken." On the one hand, there were the clauses that "even while affecting the biological interests of the German people, should not lead the Reich as an occupying power to oppose the promulgation of the new codification" — for example the application of the principle of jus soli to children born to German soldiers and women of French nationality, which made the children French.[68]

But two other provisions, which according to Hofmann bore upon "the interests of the Reich as a belligerent power," required "the maintenance of German objections to the adoption of the proposal so long as these provisions are not modified. a) Nowhere does the bill prevent members of the Jewish race from acquiring French nationality. Consequently, according to the bill, in the future as at present, any Jew who satisfied the other legal conditions could acquire French nationality. b) The bill fails to establish a legal basis for depriving dissidents of their nationality and preventing them from recovering it too easily." In short, it might have been acceptable for children born in France to French women and German soldiers to be French. But it was not acceptable that Jews could still become French and that Gaullists could retain their nationality.

On 15 October 1943 Vichy was informed of the German veto; on 21 April 1944 the commandant of the security police and the SD wrote to the military commandant in France and asked him to agree to "maintain the objection against the French nationality bill of 20 August 1943, and to let the French government know that a new codification of French nationality law [was] undesirable during the period of armistice." Thus owing to Berlin's veto, Vichy's proposed new legal code on nationality was definitively buried.

Preventing "Undesirables" from Becoming French

During the entire time when reform of the law of 1927 was under discussion and going nowhere, this law remained in force.

It provided for mechanisms of access to nationality that were contested by the new regime, as we have seen: children born in France to foreign parents could obtain French nationality easily, either through a declaration by parents on their behalf before they reached the age of majority, or automatically when they turned twenty-one. First-generation immigrants, for their part, could request naturalization after three years' residency.

The government allowed the mechanism for integrating children to keep working,[69] except when the children were Jewish: on 1 July 1941, in response to a proposal by the director of civil affairs,[70] Joseph Barthélemy ordered prosecutors' offices[71] to suspend registration of declarations of acquisition of nationality made on behalf of Jewish children born in France to foreign parents.[72] In most cases this order was carried out. The records of registration in the various courts of appeal that I consulted show that until mid-1941, the parents of Jewish children born in France who declared their child French had the declaration registered quickly: in Clermont-Ferrand a declaration made in the name of Daniel L. on 30 December 1940 was registered on 8 January 1941; in Besançon a declaration made on 4 May 1940 was registered on 3 July 1941; but the declaration made on 1 July 1941 in the name of Abram R., transmitted to the public prosecutor's office in August 1941, was registered as no. 241 only in December 1944.[73] In Clermont-Ferrand from July 1941 the designation "Jew" was added to the records, and the registration of some ten declarations thus designated was suspended until early 1945. With a few exceptions (for example, Villefranche-sur-Saône and Lille) the same designations and the same waiting periods appeared elsewhere: in Pont-l'Évêque,[74] Orange,[75] and Bordeaux, where the prosecutor's office showed its zeal by requiring, more often than elsewhere, that before declaration was granted certificates must be provided indicating that the candidate did not belong to the "Jewish race."

As for decisions on naturalization and reintegration, they were interrupted in June 1940. They did not resume until 15 February 1941, the date of a decree that naturalized one couple and reintegrated four women who were French by birth and had become foreign by marriage. From this date until the end of the war, the vast majority of decisions by the public authorities in this area involved not naturalizations but the reintegration into French nationality of women who were French by birth, had become foreign by marriage, then after a divorce or

TABLE 3

Naturalizations and Reintegrations from 1939 to 1946

	1939	1940	1941	1942	1943	1944	1945	1946
Adult natu- ralizations	47,099	31,122	136	633	980	923	3,377	14,154
Adult reintegra- tions	4,501	1,523	512	708	853	707	903	744
Minors upon the death of parents	29,552	12,661	36	149	207	178	703	3,216
TOTALS	81,152	45,306	684	1,490	2,040	1,808	4,983	18,114

Source: INSEE, *Acquisitions and Losses of French Nationality Regulated by the Ministry of Justice, Office of the Deputy Director for Naturalizations (1940–1947).*

their husband's death sought to have their nationality restored. Between 1941 and 1944 there were more reintegrations than naturalizations (2,780 as opposed to 2,672), whereas during the years 1939, 1940, 1945, and 1946, adult reintegrations represented fewer than 10 percent of the adult naturalizations (5,597 as opposed to 73,737). As we shall see later, there were more denaturalizations than naturalizations.

Between 1940 and 1944 Marshal Pétain's government granted only a few hundred naturalizations, in the strict sense, each year. Several factors contributed to the declining pace of activity. The Nationality Service lost much of its staff: there had been forty-four staff members in 1939, but only nineteen in 1941 (some members were prisoners of war, and the Jews had been eliminated). Moreover, while the drafting of new legislation designed to restrict access to naturalization was under way, the process of investigating dossiers was interrupted. The anticipated law was applied to the cases that were addressed: a minimum of ten years' residency was required as well as special ties to the French state (factors that counted in addition to the long period of residence included military service or a bond of marriage or filiation linking the candidate to a French national).

But these were not the decisive reasons. French naturalization policy bore the traces of the Vichy government's racial policy, but also of the diplomatic caution imposed on it by its position vis-à-vis the conquering countries, Germany and Italy. Racial selection and political prudence together contributed to a reduction in the number of decisions and to a change in composition of the population of successful candidates. While the decrease in naturalizations was very striking (from 15,914 adults, men and women together, in 1936 and and 23,542 in 1937, to 127 in 1941 and 562 in 1942), its distribution—that is, the decisions made case by case and nationality by nationality—was especially telling. In 1937 and 1938 Italian and Polish nationals figured in the majority of favorable decisions (46 percent and 15 percent). In 1941 and 1942 Spaniards and Armenians came first (18.5 percent and 17.3 percent), then Italians (11 percent) and Belgians (10 percent). The English represented 5 percent of the decisions, whereas they had accounted for only 0.4 percent before the war.

The distribution of nationalities was in fact the object of numerous exchanges among ministries. At the top of the "scale of caution" were the Germans and the Italians. However, on 10 January 1941 the minister of labor René Belin announced in a letter to the prefects in the unoccupied zone that because certain Italian workers who had specialized skills and were hard to replace with French workers had returned to their country of origin, he had arranged with the Ministry of Justice to speed up the process and act favorably on naturalization requests from particularly well qualified Italian workers whose applications were pending and who would be identified by the prefects. On 22 February 1941 the Ministry of Justice requested the opinion of the Ministry of Foreign Affairs on this initiative. The answer came on 23 July 1941, and it was negative: "It is to be feared in fact that, under the present circumstances, the attribution of French nationality to too great a number of Italians or Germans might give rise to reactions and protests on the part of the German or Italian authorities."[76] While waiting for the new policy on immigration and naturalizations "that the planned new High Council on Foreigners [was] to propose,"[77] only exceptional cases, about which the keeper of the seals would inform the political section of the Ministry of Foreign Affairs,[78] could be the object of favorable decisions. The rule was extended to everyone who originated in a country "at war" with France. It had particular impact on Italians, who represented the principal nationality of origin before 1940. However, in September 1941 the minister of the interior, who had come back to the subject in April, succeeded in getting naturalizations resumed case by case for Italians, giving priority to "those who had fought."[79] In early April 1942 it was even decided to respond favorably, although cautiously, to requests from Germans who were members of the Foreign Legion, by selecting "the most interesting candidates, in order of merit, and in a sufficiently dispersed manner so as not to attract attention."[80] In practical terms, exceptions came into play only for a few men who had volunteered for the French army, and some Legionnaires.[81]

So that in the decrees the handful of Italians and Germans could be "swallowed up among other foreigners,"[82] the rhythm of naturalizations was increased again, timidly, under the vigilant control of the Ministry of Foreign Affairs. Until then the few dozen naturalizations and reintegrations that had been granted were the result of interventions and decisions by the minister of justice or the secretariat general of the ministry.[83] In the months that had followed the defeat, the English were especially sought after as candidates for naturalization. Because the English stock was soon exhausted, non-refugee Spaniards, Portuguese, Luxembourgers, and Swiss candidates who posed no political or ethnic problems were favored.

For at the top of the scale of racial undesirability, there were the Jews: on 5 June 1941 Xavier Vallat asked to be consulted on all requests for naturalization by foreigners of the "Jewish race," and he also proposed to "withdraw from Jews the right to benefit from the provisions of article 3 of the law of 10 August 1927 on nationality."[84] On 27 June 1941 he received satisfaction on the first point from Joseph Barthélemy. Naturalizations of Jews were subject to a veto by the Commissariat-Général for Jewish Affairs and they were most often the object — in the rare cases when they were considered — of decisions to postpone.[85] The prohibition on naturalizing Jews probably contributed to the decline in the number of Poles naturalized: this decline resulted also from the low ranking of the "Slavic" Poles in the hierarchy of assimilability that was in fashion at the time.

The Armenians were a special case that merits examination: the political or racial criteria used by the regime should actually have excluded them. Such at least was the view of the two French immigration specialists, Georges Mauco and René Martial. Mauco ranked Armenians at the bottom of his scale of "desirability," just above Jews and far below Russians.[86] As for Martial, who was president of the Institute of Anthroposociology and the founder of a course on the anthropobiology of the races in the medical school in Paris,[87] on 17 June 1943 he had called the attention of the keeper of the seals to the naturalization of Armenians.[88] Martial insisted on the difficulty of assimilating them, and argued that naturalizing them did not appear desirable from the racial standpoint.[89]

But the regime had already decided to include Armenians, because of the services they had rendered in the French army as stateless persons, and especially because they were Christians. On 24 December 1941 the head of Marshal Pétain's civil cabinet, a devout Catholic who belonged to Action Française until the movement was excommunicated, wrote to the minister of justice:

> For a long time the Marshal and his Cabinet have taken a very kindly interest in the Armenian refugees in France . . . over the centuries, and from the Middle Ages on, people from that nation have linked their destiny to that of French and Christian civilization . . . there is hardly any need to recall that the last royal Armenian dynasty was a family of French crusaders, the Lusignans; that the Armenians have always been traditionally considered as French protégés . . . during the 1914–1918 war, as during the war of 1939–1940, the Armenians fought generously and courageously with the French Armed Forces. All the reasons just mentioned seem indeed to indicate that the Armenians deserve privileged treatment in comparison with the regime of common law reserved for foreigners . . . it seems that special good will ought to preside over the examination of individual cases among Armenians . . . especially for naturalizations.[90]

On 26 January 1942 the keeper of the seals made it known that "in response to the desire expressed by the Head of State, [he had] ordered . . . that requests for naturalization made by this category of foreigners be examined in a spirit of particular good will." As a result, in 1943 and throughout the three years of Vichy naturalizations the Armenian nationality was the number one nationality of origin, although the total number of naturalizations nevertheless remained low.

For between 1941 and 1944 every naturalization dossier was submitted for the marshal's signature. It included a presentation of the candidate and spelled out the reasons for the decision: a long period of residence (more than twenty years) was often mentioned; and men were often prisoners of war, veterans, or volunteer soldiers, or, as we have already seen, Legionnaires[91] who benefited as of 15 February 1941 from more favorable treatment than in the past.[92] Wives or mothers of Frenchmen also had priority if their good reputations had been verified, especially if they could show evidence of religious activity or ties to a Catholic institution.[93]

As of 12 April 1943, a few weeks before Barthélemy was replaced by Maurice Gabolde as minister of justice, every dossier submitted for Pétain's signature mentioned the candidate's race and nationality of origin: "Madame Marguerite X, widow of Y, residence 48 years, Italian, Aryan, who has five children of whom four are French by choice. . . . M. Ephrème X, Russian, Aryan, residence 23 years, married to a Frenchwoman and who has three French children"; and so on.

The last naturalization decree signed by Pétain is dated 14 August 1944, and it was published in the *Journal officiel* on 20 August 1944. In all, in a little more than three years, fewer than two thousand adult naturalizations were granted. This is because in addition to the political and racial criteria for selection, and the new regime's suspicion of foreigners, the task assigned to the staff was not so much to naturalize as to denaturalize, and the work required to prepare and implement denaturalization decisions was considerable.

The Target of Denaturalizations: The Jews

From 1940 to 1944, in applying the law of 22 July 1940, the Vichy regime thus proceeded to review the naturalizations that had been granted since the law of 1927 was promulgated.[94] In projecting withdrawals of French nationality, Vichy — in appearance — was doing nothing new, either in comparison with other countries or in the French context.

In the United States, for example, since 1906 a law had allowed the federal government to proceed for the first time to annul a naturalization that had been obtained fraudulently or illegally; no time limit was set for this procedure. In addition, for any person who went off to reside in his or her country of origin or in another foreign country within the first five years after naturalization, American nationality was automatically withdrawn.[95] Between 1906 and 1940 more than fifteen thousand naturalizations were annulled through the enforcement of this law.[96] During the First World War both the United Kingdom, in 1914, and France, in 1915 and 1917, adopted withdrawal procedures: in France these were aimed at naturalized citizens from a country with which France was at war and who were suspected or convicted of disloyalty.[97] The United Kingdom, by an act promulgated on 8 August 1918 that remained in force after the war, authorized the withdrawal of naturalization in a whole series of new circumstances: failure to reside in the British Empire (for more than seven years); condemnation to at least twelve months in prison or a fine of at least one hundred pounds; acts of a political nature; lack of loyalty to the sovereign or connivence with the enemy during a war; or remaining a subject of a state that was at war with Great Britain.[98] In France, in compensation for the broadening of access to French nationality that this law introduced, articles 9 and 10 of the law of 1927 included permanent clauses providing for withdrawal of nationality in cases of lack of loyalty and, from 1938 on, in cases of fraud or unworthiness.[99]

But in its objectives, in the procedure chosen, and in its effects, the Vichy law of 22 July 1940 was different in nature, and it marked a break with the previous system.

American, British, and French "democratic" laws penalized individual acts of a specified nature. The law of 1927 included three reasons for withdrawal of nationality: (1) carrying out acts against the internal or external security of the French state; (2) committing acts benefiting a foreign state that were incompatible with being a French citizen and were contrary to France's interests; (3) failing to carry out obligations resulting from laws on military recruitment.

The Vichy law did not indicate any particular causes: withdrawals could be made without justification. What was repudiated was not any individual act but rather a policy, the liberal policy that had been followed since the promulgation of the law of 1927. Thus any foreigner who had become French since that date could lose his or her nationality owing to a decision made simply by administrative fiat.

Furthermore, under the law of 1927 withdrawal of nationality had been an oppositional procedure that obliged the administration to refer the matter to a judge or — from 1938 — to obtain the approval of the Council of State, and naturalized citizens retained the right to defend their cause; they could go to court or to the Council of State to contest a decision to revoke their nationality.[100] Under Vichy denaturalizations were decided by the administration, free of all external controls; the concerned parties had no opportunity to exercise their legal rights. Against these decisions there was no recourse.[101]

The mandate of the Vichy law was very broad, much broader than is suggested by its title, "Related to the Review of Naturalizations." Indeed, persons naturalized by decree — foreigners not born in France who sought to become French and who obtained a favorable decision from the public authorities between 1927 and 1940 — were not the only ones who could lose the quality of being French. All persons born to foreign parents in France who had acquired French nationality by declaration when they were minors (according to article 3 of the law of 1927), or automatically upon reaching majority (article 4 of the same law), or by marriage to a French citizen, were also susceptible to withdrawal: a total of 900,000 people![102] Since the measure could be extended to the wife and children of any concerned party (for example, a French woman married to a foreigner who had acquired French nationality before or after their marriage, and their children), far more than a million people were potentially affected by the law. Between 1927 and 1940, 261,000 adults had been naturalized, and 16 had lost their citizenship. Between 1940 and 1944 there were just under 2,000 adult naturalizations, as compared to 15,154 denaturalizations.

A commission set up by the decree of 31 July 1940 and headed by the Council of State member Jean-Marie Roussel[103] was charged with studying the files of these hundreds of thousands of people. The administrative work of the commission (that is, the search for dossiers and the implementation of decisions) was handled by the Bureau of Seals. But the examination of the files was carried out by reviewers and associate reviewers appointed by decree; these came from outside the government services, as did the members of the commission who made the decisions.

The commission met for the first time on 21 September 1940, and it immediately made several key decisions[104] about its working methods. On 30 October 1940, on the eve of the signing of the first denaturalization decree, it published an official communiqué:[105] "The Commission for the Review of Naturalizations which . . . has been actively at work currently meets several times a week. While reserving priority for the cases that have especially attracted its attention, it has undertaken the systematic examination of all the dossiers (about 450,000) that fall within the field of law enforcement, in particular those that have been processed from 1936 on. The work accomplished is already considerable, as attested by the decree, [which] targets nearly five hundred individuals, including a fairly large number from Central Europe whose assimilation has been particularly difficult, various political agitators whose incorporation into the national community presented more danger than interest, with, in each of these categories, a significant percentage of Israelites."[106]

The commission worked with rapidity and zeal. For this first decree including nearly five hundred names, it gave priority to people whose naturalization resulted from a political decision that ran against the views of the civil servants involved; these cases could be located easily and dealt with rapidly. The commission also studied files that had been transmitted through the intervention or the intermediary of one of its members. For the rest, it decided to begin by "treating" the 510,690 people who had been naturalized between 1 January 1927 and 4 June 1940, before examining the dossiers of children born in France to foreign parents. Still, when a file concerned persons who had acquired French nationality through some means other than naturalization, the commission did not hesitate to use the power the law had granted it.[107] In some cases it agreed to denaturalize women and children, even if they had acquired French nationality before 1927 or had been born after their parents were naturalized — and even if they were French by birth.[108]

To carry out this task the commission split into three subcommittees, led by Jean-Marie Roussel, André Mornet, and Raymond Bacquart. Each subcommittee met three times a week, the full commission twice a week. But the number of files to be examined was impressive, and in all, in 1944 the commission ended up handling 666,594 cases:[109] in other words, given at most twelve meetings a month, the commission handled an average of 830 files a meeting,[110] or in the most active months, 30,000 a month and 10,000 for each subcommittee.

The commission thus did not undertake systematic examinations, and from the very first weeks of its activity, it adopted a two-pronged approach. It reexamined the entire set of files beginning with 1936—the year of the victory of the left-wing Popular Front. The files were taken by agents of the Bureau of Seals to the commission's reviewers and associate reviewers. This process of reexamining all the naturalization files, year by year, focused above all on identifying and denaturalizing Jews, unless they presented some "exceptional interest" for France or were prisoners of war.

From the beginning of its work in September 1940, the commission thus tallied Jews separately, month by month. It kept count of the number of files examined and the number of "withdrawees" (retrayés, in the official terminology); in a special column one finds the number and thus the proportion of Jews. To distinguish Jews the commission did not use special records, neither those of the Prefecture of Police in Paris[111] nor more generally those established in the Northern Zone at the request of the German occupying authorities (the Militär-befehlshaber's order dates from 20 September 1940, and the deadline for declarations was 20 October 1940).[112] Yet in September and October 1940 the commission produced categories of denaturalizations that distinguished between Jews and non-Jews and were applicable in both the "free" and the occupied zones.[113] To categorize the dossiers the commission referred to "indices" such as family names or first names, documents stemming directly from the naturalization files, or birth certificates that appeared to have been produced by religious authorities in certain of the naturalized Jews' countries of origin.[114]

The commission very quickly ran into difficulty. It had begun to denaturalize Jews by examining their dossiers directly. But its policy was also to suspend the denaturalization of prisoners of war. Now in the absence of a complementary investigation, having focused on the situation of each person at the time of his or her naturalization, the commission had, in some of its early decisions, denaturalized prisoners of war.[115] Thus it decided to organize a systematic inquiry at the prefectoral level. On the one hand, the reviewers and associate reviewers examined all the files to identify Jews. As soon as a dossier was selected, it was sent to one of the subcommittees; then, through the intermediary of the director of civil affairs and the seal at the Ministry of Justice, the commission wrote a letter to the prefect of the department where the person resided, asking him or her "to be so kind as to direct, in the shortest possible time, that a very complete investigation be carried out concerning this ex-foreigner, and the members of his or her family if any. This investigation is to bear in particular on conduct, morality, and attitude from the national viewpoint. Military service in time of peace and during the war (wounds, citations, captivity) must be carefully spelled out, if indicated. In addition, you will please formulate explicitly your opinion as to the appropriateness of a decision either to maintain or to withdraw French nationality from the concerned parties."[116]

Then the prefecture replied. For example, the Paris police prefect wrote on 24 February 1941 to the keeper of the seals: "You have asked me for information about . . . I have the honor to inform you that the party in question, incorporated into the 21st regional regiment on 27 August 1939, part of the 19th Company (Anti-parachutist Intervention Group), was discharged on 16 August 1940. He has a complimentary letter from his former company commander. . . . He practices the profession of traveling salesman and earns on average 500 francs per week. He has not been the object of any remarks concerning either behavior and morality or political and national viewpoints; his loyalty does not seem to be in doubt. [The record kept internally by the commission then notes:] *Of no national interest* (Jew); obviously did nothing extraordinary during the war."

The decision of the first subcommittee was handed down on 7 June 1941; the entire family was denaturalized by a decree dated 19 July 1941.[117]

The "typical" itinerary of a Jew's dossier was thus the following: preselection by the denaturalization commission; a request for a complementary investigation and for the prefect's opinion; favorable or neutral opinion regarding maintenance of French nationality in the majority of cases. The letter often concluded in the following way when the dossier came back to the Prefecture of Police in Paris: "X has not been the object of any particular notice. He has not attracted attention from the political and national points of view." But the opinion of the commission was almost always unfavorable, and the decision to denaturalize was made because the person was Jewish and "of no national interest." The commission knew the Jewish origin of the person involved, because while the prefect's report was neutral, all the accompanying information sheets filled out by the Central Direction of General Intelligence noted each person's religion.

After exhausting the naturalization files from 1936, the commission took on those of 1939, then 1940. At the end of 1941 it had examined the vast majority of the decisions made in 1939 and a portion of those made in 1940. At the beginning of 1942 the commission went back to examining files year by year, beginning with those closest to 1936 (1937, 1938), then going backward in time (1935, 1934, 1933) to 1927.[118]

The commission also worked in close collaboration with the Ministry of Public Health (questions having to do with doctors, dentists, and so on), with the

Order of Barristers, and with the Commissariat-Général for Jewish Affairs. This coordinated effort permitted the commission to apply an implacable logic and to strike two successive blows: first, exclusion from the profession; next, exclusion from nationality. On 30 March 1941 the secretary of state for families forwarded a list of the naturalized Jewish doctors, dental surgeons, and pharmacists who had been forbidden to practice their profession ten days earlier, through the implementation of article 1 of the law of 16 August 1940. The dossiers of all these doctors, surgeons, and pharmacists who had become French through naturalization were submitted to the commission, which decided to withdraw French nationality "in most cases."[119]

In a parallel procedure also targeting Jews, certain naturalization dossiers followed a different itinerary, a "bottom-up" instead of a "top-down" approach. On 10 August 1940 the minister of the interior asked all prefects to inform him of persons eligible for denaturalization because they had committed offenses or crimes, or because they had manifested opinions or acted in ways contrary to the national interest. He reiterated this in a memorandum dated 12 October 1940. In reply to a note from the Prefecture of Police in Paris, which complained of not being informed quickly enough "about the condemnations pronounced against persons susceptible to motivating a proposal to withdraw our nationality,"[120] Georges Dayras, general secretary at the Ministry of Justice, asked the general prosecutors on 9 August 1941 to inform the Chancellery without delay of what infractions had committed by naturalized foreigners, what proceedings had been undertaken, and what condemnations had been imposed.[121]

Italians constituted the largest foreign community in France and the largest national group among the "withdrawees" subject to the bottom-up procedure of "notification." The 4,476 Italians who were denaturalized can be grouped in two broad categories, according to the files I have studied: those who had committed criminal offenses, often minor ones, and those who had "political" affiliations, often Communist. "Condemned 7 March 1941 to two months in prison and a fine of 100F for theft of harvests not detached from the ground," "identified by the Prefect, Communist," "ex-militant of the Popular Front hostile to the work of national renovation," or "is said to have declared: 'To hell with Marshal Pétain and the Legionnaires, British bombs ought to fall on Vichy; they were right to bomb Dakar.' Denounced by X, a fellow worker, to the police." Among those condemned by the *sections spéciales* (the special courts set up to expedite judgment of "terrorists" — Gaullist Resistance members, Communists, and so on), any who had been naturalized were denaturalized. A few pro-Italian cases also deserve mention, "defeatist pro-Italian talk having led to 6 months in prison."

Finally, there are those who were denaturalized at their own request: having become French on the eve of the war for the most part, they wanted to be Italian again; denaturalization was the condition for their return to Italy.[122] Until 1943, to satisfy the Italian government, the Ministry of Justice denaturalized Italians upon request. In early August 1943, after Mussolini's fall, the ministry changed policy to keep these "Franco-Italians" from being exempted from the obligatory work service: "Such an obvious proof of their lack of loyalty has justified, up to now, in their regard, the withdrawal of French nationality, pronounced summarily by virtue of the law of 22 July 1940 relative to the review of naturalizations. But such a measure, despite its dishonorable nature, amounted to giving these individuals, who were not of much interest, full and complete satisfaction."[123] As of 2 August 1943 these Italians were subject to a procedure of "liberation from bonds of allegiance"; this procedure allowed a French person to request that his or her ties with France be severed, but it was a long and tedious process, and — most importantly — it was available only to people living abroad.

In the end, the two procedures reflected the two contradictory forms of logic at work:[124] Jews were denaturalized in the vast majority of cases — 78 percent of the dossiers examined — unless they represented some "national interest" for France or were prisoners of war. Non-Jews were denaturalized only exceptionally, if they had committed acts or expressed opinions that led them to be perceived as undesirable elements in the nation.

Despite the commission's zeal, in early 1942, when statistics for 1940–41 were published (the commission had issued 9,608 withdrawals of which 3,479, or 36.2 percent, involved Jews), the rhythm did not correspond entirely with the government's objectives. In particular, the number and proportion of Jews failed to satisfy the occupying authorities.

The commission's work slowed abruptly, first of all owing to its own working methods. To select the files of people presumed to be Jews, it had initially sought to look at naturalization decrees in the order in which they were issued. But since the dossiers were filed according to the order of their arrival and registration in the agency, this procedure had led to considerable confusion. A number of files had been mixed up, and others were nowhere to be found.[125] In short, as an agent from the naturalization service testified later, "quite soon we stopped going by the order of decrees and took up the dossiers by year, that is, we followed the chronological order in which the applications had been registered."[126] The commission's work was further slowed by the need to manage an appeals procedure that had not been programmed at the outset.

Among the five hundred people denaturalized by the initial decree of 1 November 1940, some had powerful supporters in the Vichy government. This was true of Angelo Tasca and George Montandon.

TABLE 4

Balance Sheet: Denaturalizations by Nationality, 1940–1944

	Naturalized, August 1927– December 1940		Denaturalized, 1940–1944 (estimate)		Denaturalized as percentage of naturalized
Italians	259,640	53.5%	4,476	29.5%	1.7
Poles	48,205	9.9%	2,963	19.6%	6.1
Spaniards	55,131	11.4%	1,062	7.0%	1.9
Russians	14,918	3.1%	1,013	6.7%	6.8
Romanians	3,971	0.8%	756	5.0%	19.0
Turks	9,113	1.9%	629	4.1%	6.9
Germans	19,719	4.1%	468	3.1%	2.4
Belgians	31,042	6.4%	277	1.8%	0.9
Greeks	2,383	0.5%	242	1.6%	10.2
Swiss	13,645	2.8%	233	1.5%	1.7
Hungarians	2,516	0.5%	228	1.5%	9.1
Czechs	4,985	1.0%	171	1.1%	3.4
Austrians	1,388	0.3%	105	0.7%	7.6
Portuguese	4,209	0.9%	93	0.6%	2.2
Yugoslavs	2,042	0.4%	52	0.3%	2.5
Unknown nationality			1,733	11.4%	
TOTAL	485,200	100.0%	15,154	100.0%	3.1

Source: Laguerre, "Les dénaturalisés de Vichy," 10.

Angelo Tasca was a co-founder of the Italian Communist party, an anti-Fascist who arrived in France in 1930 and became an active member of the Socialist party SFIO. He was naturalized on 7 August 1936, while the Popular Front was in power, by a decision of the keeper of the seals that went against the recommendation of the naturalization services.[127] This action caused a stir at the time. *Action française* published a copy of a letter of intervention addressed to Marc Rucart, keeper of the seals, by Pierre Viénot, undersecretary of state at the Ministry of Foreign Affairs and a friend of Tasca.[128] On 25 September 1940 the

TABLE 5

Balance Sheet, 8 September 1943: Denaturalized Jews

	Naturalized 1927–1940	Withdrawals proposed			Withdrawals as percentage of naturalizations, 27 August 1943
		26 August 1943	27 August 1943	8 September 1943	
Jews	23,648	6,307	7,053	7,055	29.8
TOTAL	485,200	16,508	17,964	unknown	3.7
Jews as percentage of total	4.9	38.2	39.3	unknown	

Source: Laguerre, "Les dénaturalisés de Vichy," 12.

Bureau of Seals was visited by a Parisian, Monsieur de M., who had denounced that intervention, demanding that Tasca's dossier be submitted to the commission. This was done. Angelo Tasca was among those listed in the naturalization decrees of 1 November 1940. On the one hand, having taken "part in political struggles in the country, [he had] been seriously lacking in the reserve that foreigners ought to maintain in France"; on the other hand, his naturalization had been "obtained only thanks to powerful political interventions, despite the opposition of the services." Finally, "his entire family had remained in Italy; naturalization without interest from the national standpoint."[129] Tasca appealed this measure on 12 November 1940, and he attached several supporting letters from "left-wing" members of the new regime. René Belin, minister of industrial production and labor, Gaston Bergery, Henry Moysset, Jacques Fouques-Duparc, L. O. Frossard, the founder of the French Communist party and a former minister, and Paul Rives, deputy from the Allier department, testified in his favor. François Chasseigne, deputy from the Indre department (SFIO), went so far as to write: "At Vichy, during the National Assembly and afterward, Tasca played a decisive role in rallying to the Marshal a number of Socialist deputies who held his counsel in particular esteem. He first pushed them one by one to the vote in the Assembly. Since then, when some were giving way to doubt, he has tirelessly sought them out and won them back." On 28 November 1940 Font-Réaulx, chief of staff of the minister of justice, asked the Commission on the Review of Naturalizations to "send him a new recommendation as soon as possible." On 4 January 1941 the seals cabinet was growing impatient: it informed Jean-Marie Roussel, president of the denaturalization commission, that "the cabinet desires a rapid decision, favorable to the concerned party." On 11 January 1941, in plenary session, the commission decided by majority vote "not to oppose the rescinding of the decree of withdrawal."

The commission was also led to reexamine the case of George Montandon when the extreme right-wing fringe of the Vichy regime intervened in his favor.

Born in Switzerland in 1879, Montandon was a medical doctor who arrived in France in 1925 and worked until 1927 in the anthropology laboratory of the Museum of Natural History. In 1931 he held a teaching position at the School of Anthropology in Paris. In 1933, the year when he requested naturalization, he was appointed by Louis Marin to be director of the school and a chaired professor of ethnology.[130] His naturalization was blocked because Montandon had expressed Bolshevik sympathies in Switzerland and had even participated in Communist activities from 1922 to 1925. At all events, he was identified by the French Consul as head of the Soviet party and as having been condemned for subversive activities in Switzerland. He was naturalized thanks to Louis Marin, who had become minister of state; Marin intervened decisively on 15 January 1936, in a communication to the keeper of the seals: "I was not unaware of the attitude taken at the time by this scholar, but I also know, since I know him and have observed him for ten years, that he has completely evolved." It was because of his past political activities and because of this intervention that Montandon was denaturalized on 1 November 1940. As of 1937, after his naturalization, he had begun to specialize and to publish overtly anti-Semitic articles in increasing numbers.[131] The characteristics of the Jewish ethnic group — "whorish" — justified its proscription in his eyes. Thus in April 1940 he declared: "To claim that I am obeying Hitlerian suggestions is nonsense. It is rather Hitler who has picked up mine — carrying them out in the middle of a war and without reciprocal agreements."[132] In July 1940 he created the journal *L'Ethnie française*, which supported Pétain's policy and Franco-German rapprochement, and he collaborated with *La Gerbe*. When Montandon wrote to Marshal Pétain on 10 December 1940 to request that his denaturalization be rescinded, he was supported by representatives of the regime's extreme right wing: the publishers Jacques Bernard (*Mercure de France*) and Georges Payot, the lawyer Félix Colmet-Daage, and Louis Darquier de Pellepoix, a member of the Paris municipal council and a future commissioner general for Jewish affairs.

Louis-Ferdinand Céline also intervened, writing to the commission president on 16 January 1941 proposing, as a connoisseur, to confer a certificate of anti-Semitism:[133]

> Monsieur le Président,
>
> I can attest that Professor Montandon, whom I have known for some years, has never shown evidence, in my presence or in public, of any Marxist, Soviet, Bolshevik, or anarchist sentiment.
>
> I know Professor Montandon only through his scientific work and his anti-Semitic publications.
>
> I may be permitted to observe that it seems to me very difficult to be as resolutely anti-Semitic as Prof. Montandon is and to be a Communist at the same time. These two professions of faith are still currently irreconcilable and M. Montandon is certainly the most resolute anti-Semite that I know, the most determined, the best armed, the most steadfast.
>
> I beg you, Monsieur le Président, to accept the assurance of my most respectful sentiments.
>
> L.-F. Céline

A few days later the commission met and by majority vote issued the cautious opinion that "it did not believe it should oppose the measures of good will that the government believed it should take."

To allow the annulment of its decisions, however, a "judicial framework" was needed: since the law of 22 July 1940 had not provided for this, a law promulgated on 21 March 1941 authorized the review of denaturalizations upon request; the time period for application was three months, or six months in special circumstances (with prisoners, for example): the concerned parties could invoke new factors that had come up after their naturalization.[134] The decree reintegrating Tasca was issued the very next day, 22 March 1941, the one reintegrating Montandon on 27 July 1941. From then on, applications for review drove the commission's activity. They came pouring in, their numbers increasing because, under the leadership of its vice-president, the Council of State for its part had decided that it would not consider appeals for review of denaturalizations.[135]

And these applications for review slowed the activity of denaturalization even more as the committee appeared less resolute. In the beginning the procedure seemed legitimate; the commission was unanimous and eager. Mornet, the future prosecutor general at Pétain's trial, was on the commission; he later declared that the review of naturalizations granted to foreigners "who had shown themselves unworthy of benefiting from it . . . seemed [then] in correlation with the search for elements that had contributed to the defeat."[136] But certain members of the commission, or certain agents of the central administration, gradually began to change their views.

In August and September 1941 the commission held only two plenary sessions a week instead of nine subcommittee meetings plus the two regular plenary sessions. Moreover, these two weekly sessions were often devoted to examining applications for review of previously issued naturalization decrees: "The Commission in fact has deemed it necessary to bring the greatest diligence to this important task; it is indeed important that the concerned parties and the public be assured that the review of naturalizations is not a biased operation."[137] In contrast with the 30,000 dossiers handled in the previous quarter, 14,477 dossiers were examined. Furthermore, in the third quarter of 1941, that is, just when the first arrests of foreign Jews were taking place (14 May 1941), the work slowed down: 975 withdrawals as compared to 1,173 in the second quarter of 1941.

In the fourth quarter of that year productivity went back up (1,885 withdrawals), and it remained high in the first quarter of 1942 (1,729). Then, during the second quarter of 1942, withdrawals were interrupted: more precisely, no decrees were issued between 28 March and 3 August 1942 — that is, as Bernard Laguerre has emphasized,[138] between the departure of the first convoy of deportees for Drancy and the implementation of the Franco-German agreements in July that sealed the collaboration of the French police in arresting and deporting Jews, leading most notably to the roundup of 16 and 17 July 1942 (known as the *rafle du Vel d'Hiv* because the victims were interned in a stadium in Paris used for winter bicycle racing). Before then, denaturalized Jews were liable either to be interned in a special camp or to be assigned to a foreigners' work group.[139]

Testifying in 1948, Mornet stated:

However, the anti-Semitic campaign that was taking shape in certain documents at the discretion of the occupying authorities continued to trouble me. It did not take me long to realize that the members of the commission were acting in perfectly good faith, trying to judge in full objectivity and in complete independence, and in most cases rejecting with distaste the idea of a policy of collaboration with Germany; but the majority of them, blinded by their trust in Pétain, made themselves auxiliaries of his racial policy and, even while denying that they were anti-Semitic, alongside decisions that were justified a hundred times over they nevertheless pronounced withdrawals of nationality that only a preconceived idea regarding Jews could explain. Under these conditions, I announced my intention to resign, and I would have done so if the pressing intervention of friends that I count among the Jews urging me insistently to stay in order to exercise the influence that will doubtless be judged not without utility if one refers to the letter written by Brinon to Laval in the month of August 1942.[140]

It was actually on 2 August 1943 that Brinon wrote to Laval to explain "the derisory results obtained up to now" by "the influence of council member Mornet [who is] more and more hostile to denaturalizations . . . [and is] powerful in the commission. The paralysis being seen now must be attributed to the influence he exercises over his colleagues."[141]

In addition to Mornet's influence, efforts at resistance within the Bureau of Seals appear to have been real, if we believe the testimony of Dautet, a member of the Inspection des Services who intervened in January and February 1944, on the occasion of a conflict between two agents in the bureau, one of whom was accused of withholding a certain number of files involving Jews from his district to keep them from being examined by the commission. Dautet mentions that in the course of his investigation, he was told in confidence that "when the staff of the Bureau of Seals took an interest in some situation that was presented unfavorably from the standpoint of the commission's jurisprudence, it strove to direct the dossier toward the subcommittee headed by President Mornet . . . Not all those subject to review could benefit from that appearance of favor."[142] The examination of two hundred naturalization decisions shows that on several occasions, the more favorable decisions taken by the second subcommittee were later reversed in the plenary assembly. In reality, fewer and fewer dossiers of Jews were sent to that subcommittee, which dealt with people of all foreign nationalities condemned for crimes or offenses, plus a few pro-Fascist Frenchmen of Italian origin.

The lack of zeal was reflected at the prefectoral level as well: in August 1942 twenty thousand dossiers were awaiting a complementary review process.

The slowdown did not escape the occupying authorities for long. On 3 June 1942, when the *Journal officiel* published a decree annulling withdrawals of French nationality from a group that included Jews, the authorities seized the occasion to intervene. On 18 August 1942 Lieutenant Colonel Heinz Röthke, head of the Gestapo in France, interrogated the commissioner general for Jewish affairs, who immediately asked the Ministry of Justice for "the reasons that motivated the annulment of certain decrees pronouncing the withdrawal of French nationality from Oriental Jews or foreigners who had emigrated from Italy."

The deputy director of seals replied that "the information requested by the commissioner general for Jewish Affairs is clearly confidential in nature. What is more, it appears all the more difficult to satisfy the request attached in that the details that would be provided would make it possible to restrict decisions taken by the Government by virtue of its discretionary power." His opinion, seconded by the minister of justice, was that "it is appropriate to inform the commissioner general for Jewish Affairs that it is not possible to fulfill his request."[143]

On 26 May 1943 the Commissariat-Général for Jewish Affairs transmitted a note from Röthke dated 18 May 1943 to the keeper of the seals: "I confirm to you for the third time my previously-cited letters (letters of 18/8/42, 2/5/43, and 26/2/43) and ask you to respond with all possible speed. I beg you also to let me know for what reason there has been no response to these letters up to now and to take measures as appropriate against the civil servant or employee at fault. I point out to you that I am not inclined to respond to such a dilatory manner of proceeding with regard to a request on my part by a third reminder, but that I reserve the right to take other measures as needed."

Darquier de Pellepoix wrote to Röthke[144] that he hoped to obtain the reasons for the decisions from the new minister of justice, Maurice Gabolde, as he had not been able to get them from Barthélemy.[145]

The number of cases handled was minimal with respect to the number of denaturalizations. The beneficiaries can be categorized as follows:

Some had exceptional qualifications. One man who was denaturalized on 21 June 1941 had his nationality restored on 29 May 1942 because he "had rendered great services to our country by putting his exceptional qualities as an engineer and contractor at the service of French aviation, and that he was currently ensuring the execution of important construction projects"; another, D., naturalized on 5 May 1938 and "withdrawn" on 1 June 1941, had his rights restored as a result of "new elements of evaluation submitted to the Commission" showing that he had been "a doctor whose honorability and professional conscience [were] attested by various notable figures and in particular by several of his fellow doctors."[146] Some had brilliant records of military service or had been taken prisoner during wartime operations. In one case the person's Jewishness had been presumed by mistake, on the basis of a family name.[147] In another, the keeper of the seals had intervened personally on behalf of a woman who taught at the law school in Paris: she had been born in France to German Jewish parents, had been naturalized in 1913, and had her naturalization withdrawn in 1918, restored in 1936, and revoked again in 1940.[148]

In any case, on 4 June 1943 the keeper of the seals replied to the Commissariat-Général for Jewish Affairs

that there had been a response in a letter of 28 September 1942 to the request for information that you had already sent in this connection on 26 August 1942. Owing to the insistence of the Occupying Authorities, I believe I must specify that the law allows individuals who are the objects of a decree of withdrawal of French nationality to formulate an appeal against the measure that has been taken against them. This appeal is submitted for examination by the Commission for Review of Naturalizations, which issues an opinion. . . . Respect for the opinion of the High Magistrates who compose [the Commission] and who deliberate in complete independence on each individual case, suffices to justify these measures. This procedure, instituted to correct errors that may have slipped into the large volume of refining work undertaken on the impetus of the Commission for Review of Naturalizations, has made it possible to remedy injustices.

This incident undoubtedly contributed to the exasperation of the occupying authorities, who decided to act as soon as the first letter was sent. In any case, as of September 1942 the Ministry of Justice seems to have turned over the matter of massive Jewish denaturalizations to Pierre Laval and then René Bousquet, secretary general for the police at the Ministry of the Interior since May 1942. As the French police and the French government did not want to be associated with the arrest and deportation of French Jews, negotiation began over the possibility of denaturalizing as a group all Jews who had been naturalized since the law of 1927 went into effect. Laval gave his consent to hand over Jews who had acquired French nationality since 1933.[149] The Commissariat-Général for Jewish Affairs proposed to go back to 1927. Finally, in early April, René Bousquet asked Gabolde to prepare a law and a decree denaturalizing Jews who had been naturalized since 1 January 1932. The original, signed by Gabolde, was transmitted to Bousquet on 10 April 1943 at 7:00 p.m. The enforcement decree was ready; it repeated the terms of the bill: "are annulled by right the decrees of naturalization issued since 1 January 1932 in favor of foreigners regarded as Jews under the terms of the law of 2 June 1941." Exceptions were made for military veterans and prisoners of war. Bousquet transmitted his proposal to Hagen on 12 April 1943. On 21 May the SD representative in France, Colonel Knochen, insisted on going back to 1927, which would make it possible to include—and thus to deport—many more Jews. Darquier held the same view, and finally, on 11 June 1943, Jean Leguay, Bousquet's representative in the occupied zone, sent Röthke the definitive government proposal, which set the date of 10 August 1927. In anticipation of the imminent publication of the law, the German authorities solicited the Prefecture of Police and announced a roundup for 15 July 1943, which they later postponed until 23 and 24 July.[150] But on 22 July the police prefect, Bussière, alerted Gabolde to the German plans and questioned him about the interpretation of the law he had signed, at Bousquet's suggestion: Was it necessary to apply article 1 of the law, according to which a Jewish woman who had married a denaturalized Jew lost her nationality, even if she was French by birth? And what was to be done with minor children who might not be Jewish, or might be French by birth or by choice, and not through naturalization?[151]

On 25 July Laval decided to stop the promulgation of the law. Two factors seem to have been involved in this about-face. First, the assessment of a new context: the Soviets were advancing in the Ukraine after the fall of Stalingrad on 2 February, the Allies had landed in Sicily on 10 July, and Mussolini fell precisely on 25 July.[152] And then there was the position of Pétain himself: it seems he was impressed by a visit from Msgr. Chappoulie, who in the name of the episcopate had brought a message from Pope Pius XII, now "very upset" to learn that Pétain was about to permit new anti-Jewish measures in France. The pope was "concerned about the Marshal's soul."[153] Pétain later confirmed to Brinon, who came to see him on 24 August, that he could not take responsibility for denaturalizing French citizens so that the Germans could immediately deport them. He wanted to continue to have each case examined individually, and promised to work as quickly as possible. In any event, the commission was denaturalizing the majority of Jews whose dossiers it received—78 percent[154]—but it was doing so according to its own methods, and it did not intend to let the Nazis tell it how to be anti-Semitic.[155]

On 7 August Laval confirmed definitively to Knochen, who was trying to get him to ratify a slightly modified version of the bill, that he would not sign a new law on denaturalization. The denaturalized Jews would be deported to Germany, and he did not want to "serve as rabatteur and beat the woods for the hunted game."[156] On 27 August 1943 Brinon informed Knochen and his adjunct, Major Hagen, of the "desires expressed by the Marshal and spelled out in the instructions" he had been given to relaunch the activity of the denaturalization commission.[157] He indicated in a telegram to Laval that the German authorities would maintain their consent to the procedure envisaged only insofar as significant results could be communicated weekly. Pétain received Roussel, the commission president, on 28 August 1943.[158] Thanks to a considerable increase in the seals staff, a special examination of all the dossiers in the general files was undertaken, making it possible to find dossiers of "presumed Jews" that had never been screened and submit them to investigation.[159] The commission resumed its work: in the third quarter of 1942, 1,473 decisions to withdraw nationality were made; in the fourth quarter, 1,441; in the first quarter of 1943, 425; in the second quarter, 1,197; and during the month of September 1943 alone, 1,555 withdrawals were carried out.[160]

At the time of the Liberation the commission on denaturalizations kept on working inexorably: it was waiting for the results of its requests for investigations into the fourteen thousand Jews whose cases it had not yet examined.[161] Then it was planning to undertake the review of acquisitions of French nationality by children born in France to foreign Jewish parents, acquisitions that came about simply because of a declaration made by their parents—this was to be a "particularly delicate review, affecting a large number of people and one that [would] impose on the Bureau of Seals the responsibility for a very large number of inquiries."[162]

But on 19 August 1943 the Gestapo had already denounced the agreement made with Bousquet, namely the provisional exception allowing French Jews not to be arrested for deportation in exchange for the arrest of foreign or stateless Jews in both zones.[163]

In June 1944, of the Vichy regime's projects there remained only the 15,154 men, women, and children deprived of their French nationality:[164] most of these were Jews whose denaturalization had contributed to the deportation to Germany.[165] For four years more than one million French citizens had lived under the threat of losing their nationality and, if they were Jews, in the well-founded fear of being handed over to the Nazi occupier.

These four years can be interpreted from the standpoint of the conflict between a racist logic founded on ethnic, racial, or religious unassimilability on the one hand and a restrictionist individual logic on the other. The racist logic that would have kept Jews from any access to French nationality under new laws governing naturalization during the Occupation and that would have denaturalized all the Jews naturalized since 1927 triumphed only in the policies that were subject to direct control by the regime: in the area of naturalizations, where biological racism (mention of Aryan origin) was at work even at the end of the Vichy period; and in denaturalizations, even if the special procedure aimed at Jews was increasingly difficult to implement.

In contrast, the racist logic was defeated, if only within the French administration and provisionally, when it was a matter of preparing a new law. If the restrictionist Ministry of Justice carried the day against the racism of the Ministry of the Interior, the Commissariat-Général for Jewish Affairs, the Council of State, and the Ministry of Foreign Affairs (in increasing order of expression and action),[166] it was probably because this was the sector of nationality policy in which political power could be the least present, and professional jurists the hardest to contravene. Here making law was a matter of legislating for the future, in an impersonal and general fashion: the "judicial knowledge" of the staff, the invocation of tradition, jurisprudence for the past and prudence for the present, the assessment of the practical consequences of the options chosen, had more weight than in the two other sectors of nationality policy. In the realm of naturalizations and denaturalizations, the decisions were individual, had immediate impact, and were under the influence of the political authority, either directly (with naturalizations, filtered by the cabinet of the minister and submitted for the personal signature of Marshal Pétain), or indirectly (through the establishment of exceptional procedures for denaturalizations): most members of the commission and the external reviewers at the Bureau of Seals were partisans of the racist approach.

As early as July 1940 the Vichy regime had thus sought to make nationality a symbol of its so-called national revolution. Free France was not mistaken about this when it sought to make nationality the symbol of reconquest, beginning in July 1940. But at the Liberation, the trial of the Third Republic's "liberal" nationality policy was not over. Nor was the debate concerning a hierarchy of "assimilable races."

The Difficult Reestablishment

of Republican Legislation

The Free France Register

Free France too had turned its full attention to nationality policy. From the first weeks after the headquarters of the Free French Forces were set up at 4 Carlton Gardens in London,[1] René Cassin opened "a register comparable to the one in the Ministry of Justice in France,"[2] intended to record declarations pertaining to nationality.[3] "A very short time after my arrival in London, as early as August," he wrote later, "I set up a double-entry nationality register, which was kept with the greatest care by M. Marion, head of the Chancellery Service of the London National Committee."[4]

While the policy of denaturalization and recasting of French nationality was being put in place in Vichy, from 23 September 1940 to 15 September 1943, in a simple notebook with lined pages bearing the insignia of the administrative services of the British Kingdom (George Rex), Free France maintained the French law that had been in force before June 1940 by recording 462 handwritten declarations "of acquisition, maintenance, or consolidation of French nationality."[5] The majority of those concerned were women, most often British,[6] preparing to marry soldiers from the Free French Forces. They made voluntary prenuptial declarations of their intent to acquire French nationality, in conformity with the laws in effect until 1940.[7] Most of them had addressed written requests to General de Gaulle.[8] Once the requests had been recorded, the women received receipts signed by René Cassin. Record no. 1, dated 23 September 1940, was in the name of a British woman, Jacqueline Watson: she made her declaration before marrying André Millet, who served with the Free French Forces. Next came Laure Tombet, Swiss, who declared that she wanted to become French before marrying Sergeant Lucien Trochon; and then Yvonne Pinder, British, engaged to Sergeant Ludovic Delanoë.

This register kept by Free France had multiple uses from the outset. Births were recorded there, for example: on 3 December 1940 Count and Countess Alfred d'Hollosy registered the birth of their daughter Suzanne, "for whatever purpose it might serve." At the same time they asserted their fidelity to France, "come what may." Many of the earliest declarations recorded were also acts of "conservation" of French nationality, as René Cassin called them; these were carried out by French people threatened with denaturalization by Vichy. On 18 October 1940 Sigismond Jarecki and his wife Helen—both born in Lvov (Poland), naturalized in 1930, and married in Paris on 6 January 1944—asked to remain French "no matter what happens," and they addressed "an act of fidelity to Free France." On 8 September 1941 Eberhard Gunther, born in 1892 in Germany, "in his own name and that of his wife," who had been naturalized along with him in 1938, had "drawn up an act of fidelity to France and expressed their desire to remain French come what may."

Finally, requests for naturalization were recorded, but no official rulings were made as to their status. According to Cassin, "General de Gaulle and the National Committee did not want to grant naturalizations or reintegrations during that period, but they kept careful account of the official declarations made to them by private individuals, and they gave them very detailed receipts." Abraham Dzialozynski, born in Poland on 15 May 1917, a member of the Foreign Legion since May 1937, wounded at Narvik on 28 May 1940, had been enrolled in the Free French Forces since July 1940; on 7 November 1940 he addressed an act of fidelity to Free France in which he asserted that whatever happened, he wanted to remain tied to France and to acquire French nationality. He became French only after the war, in 1952. In all this, René Cassin was strictly applying the law as it stood until 1940.

That law did not authorize the naturalization of a foreigner living outside France. But it did authorize granting French nationality to the wife of a Frenchman, even if the two lived abroad. Cassin's caution, his punctilious respect for the law, can be explained also by the precarious status of these records in the eyes of the Free France leaders: they noted that "it is appropriate to warn the applicant that this transcript does not have the official value of one made at the French Consulate General; it has only provisional value and will have to be subjected to regularization at the end of the war." They added that "the transcript made in the Register of the Free French Forces is rather a declaration of fidelity to Free France . . . and, if the applicant is not a Volunteer, it would be appropriate for him or her to address a letter of support to General de Gaulle."[9]

What had begun as a way of bringing French people together around Free France and of grounding its legitimacy, and also as a way of protesting and combating the measures taken in Vichy against naturalized citizens and resisters outside the country, took on official value as the international recognition of General de Gaulle and Free France grew. From December 1941 the declarations no longer included oaths of fidelity to Free France; legal terminology was used. As of 15 September 1943 the register was closed; the French consulate general took over for declarations of persons residing in Great Britain. And on 30 March 1944 in Algiers the French Committee for National Liberation, led by de Gaulle,[10] issued its first naturalization decrees, based on the report of François de Menthon,[11] commissioner of justice. These decrees involved foreigners residing in Algeria, thus in France. Others followed in April, May, and June, until the last decree was signed in Algiers by the provisional government of the French Republic on 14 August 1944.[12]

On 9 September 1944 the provisional government began to operate in Paris, and the registers that had been inaugurated in London in August 1940 were delivered to the Ministry of Justice by René Cassin as soon as he arrived in Paris, along with all the corresponding dossiers and archives. With the Liberation, all these declarations took on even more official value in that—as Cassin recalls—"the recognition of the provisional government of the French Republic, first by the French people, and then by foreign powers, confers a veritable legal authority on all the dossiers prepared by the Chancellery of the National Committee in London."[13]

On 30 September 1944 Jean Nectoux, director of civil affairs, who had served in Vichy since 23 November 1942, was suspended[14] and replaced by Louis Bodard,[15] who had exercised the same functions in Algiers from 23 July 1943 on.[16] The members of General de Gaulle's provisional government, henceforth established in Paris, faced two urgent tasks: they had to finish the work of revising the Vichy "laws," which had been difficult to undertake in Algiers, and they had to deal with pending naturalization requests. One might imagine that the break with Vichy's racist policy was a matter of course. But to make this assumption would be to neglect the influence and persistence of the ethnic approach—since the mid-1930s—in the debates over immigration and nationality policy. The ethnic approach could take two forms. In the racialist version, origin was viewed as one criterion in the selection of candidates for naturalization, set alongside other, sometimes more important considerations (population size, respect for equality, age, the candidate's professional or familial situation). In the racist version, origin topped all other criteria; it was the sole principle for selecting, or rather for eliminating, applicants for French nationality. Under the Third Republic the racists had failed to influence nationality policy. Under Vichy they had won out over the restrictionist approach.

In the provisional government of the French Republic, in Algiers and then in Paris, the racist criterion came to the fore. But once again it came up against a republican, egalitarian conception of nationality and immigration policies.

The Difficult Abrogation of Vichy's "Laws"

Three Vichy "laws" provided for the withdrawal of French nationality.

The law of 23 July 1940 authorized withdrawing nationality from 446 French persons who had left France between 20 May and 30 June 1940 without permission from the Vichy government[17] — de Gaulle, Catroux, Cassin, and the early members of the French Resistance. This law was also applied to Admiral Darlan and General Giraud, who headed the North African administration in turn after the Allied landing in November 1942. On 14 March 1943, moreover, General Giraud declared Vichy's constitutional acts, laws, and decrees null and void after 22 July 1940. The law of 23 July 1940 providing for withdrawal of nationality was thus formally annulled. To give this act greater solemnity, General Giraud issued an ordinance dated 18 April 1943 explicitly abrogating the law of 23 July 1940: de Gaulle, Giraud, and the 444 other French citizens who had been targeted by that Vichy law were "fully reintegrated into French nationality, with all legal consequences."[18]

Another Vichy law, dated 7 October 1940, abrogated the Crémieux decree of 24 October 1870 that had naturalized all Jews in Algeria; the new law revoked the citizenship of 110,000 Algerian Jews. Alongside his declaration of 14 March 1943 abrogating the decisions made by Vichy after 22 July 1940, General Giraud took care to promulgate one exception: the Crémieux decree remained abrogated.[19] Since Admiral Darlan and later General Giraud had taken the administration of North Africa in hand, the anti-Semitic legislation instituted by Vichy, more severe in Algeria than in metropolitan France, had been maintained and justified as a way of reestablishing "equality of status" between Jews and Muslims. Giraud in particular was convinced, as Marrus and Paxton remind us, that "the Jews were 'responsible for the defeat' and that the racial laws were 'one of the essential conditions of the armistice.'"[20] Giraud's ordinance of 14 March thus produced strong reactions: the Gaullist French National Committee made its disapproval known officially on 24 March,[21] and the American press protested. The Algerian Jews mobilized, and finally the CFLN (Comité français de Libération nationale) stated on 21 October 1943 "that the Crémieux decree was now in force." The Algerian Jews were thus reinstated as full-fledged citizens.[22]

For the 15,152 denaturalizations that had been carried out under the law of 22 July 1940, abrogation was an even longer and more difficult process. While in his ordinance of 14 March 1943 General Giraud annulled the acts that Vichy had carried out *after 22 June 1940*, the very same day he issued another ordinance stating that "laws, decrees and instructions promulgated after 22 June 1940" were temporarily valid, until such time as rulings on each of them were issued.[23] A few months later, on 9 September 1943, François de Menthon, one of the earliest members of the Resistance, who had just been appointed by de Gaulle as *commissaire à la Justice* (that is, Free France's minister of justice), directed René Cassin, president of the Legal Committee of Free France, to address questions of nationality.

On the subject of the law of 22 July 1940, which allowed a review of all naturalizations granted since 10 August 1927, Menthon wrote: "I envisage the maintenance of this new institution."[24] In his eyes the annulment of Vichy's denaturalizations "could in certain cases present the gravest disadvantages." Besides, "the too numerous naturalizations, in the years immediately preceding the war, of dubious Israelite elements have provided a pretext for an anti-Semitism that could pose a certain problem on the day of return. It would not be a way of staving this off in advance to annul *a priori* all the withdrawal measures that have been taken."[25] This was not the opinion of André Mornet, vice-president of Vichy's commission on denaturalization: in a text that reached the Legal Committee, Mornet proposed to abrogate retroactively the law of 22 July 1940, reversing all the denaturalizations brought about through its application.[26] On 11 January 1944 the Legal Committee of Free France, which was in a sense its council of state, adopted a text that reads like a stinging rebuke to Menthon:[27] "Vichy's legislation in this area constitutes one of the regime's most shameful chapters. It will always remain linked, for the French and for all peoples accustomed to respecting France, with the memory of the persecutions carried out against the patriots who refused to bow to defeat, and also with the infamous measures taken to hand over to the enemy the foreign and stateless refugees who had become French, covering [these measures] with a legal pretext. The French Committee for National Liberation would assume a heavy responsibility, vis-à-vis the nation and the world's conscience alike, if it did not break categorically with the unjust measures taken by the men of Vichy. . . . Vichy's laws form a whole within which one cannot establish any real distinctions."

The Legal Committee thus proposed to annul all the Vichy laws that had not yet been annulled and to reexamine each denaturalization decision made by Vichy in the light of the pre-war French legislation, which was "sufficiently reinforced in 1938–1939 to avoid the massive review of naturalizations that had had to be improvised during the war of 1914–1918." However, Menthon did not comply: on 10 February 1944 he sent the Legal Committee the text of an ordinance that annulled the law of 22 July 1940, but only for the future, "in order to avoid . . . [letting] this annulment lead to a massive and automatic reintegration . . . that would come about without regard for the actual circumstances that might have provoked the measures taken." He proposed to validate the denaturalizations carried out by Vichy in the past, but to allow denaturalized persons to appeal those decisions within a six-month period following the end of the war.

The Legal Committee reacted once again, even more strongly, in a report by François Marion: "The agency that currently calls itself 'Government of the French State' . . . has arrogated to itself, in matters of nationality, powers that are exorbitant and contrary to human rights and to international law . . . It has made numerous withdrawals of naturalization that have, among others, afflicted foreigners who had obtained their naturalization after a long wait, who had given proofs of their attachment to France, but who, in the eyes of the Vichy leaders, were guilty of having continued the struggle against the enemy in France as well as abroad, or of having manifested their hostility to the politics of collaboration or treason."

It added that "even if those naturalizations had been too numerous and granted without due consideration to non-assimilated individuals who did not present sufficient guarantees . . . , such objections were sufficient to justify a refusal to grant French nationality, but they would in no case be able to justify the withdrawal of naturalization once it had been granted."[28] The committee recalled, finally, that "article 10 of the law of 1927 and the subsequent texts give the Government the necessary powers" to revoke the naturalization of those who had become unworthy. It thus proposed to nullify the law of 22 July 1940 along with all of Vichy's denaturalizations and, if the need arose, to submit "naturalized persons who merited withdrawal [of nationality]" to the previous legislation.[29]

The views of René Cassin and the Legal Committee were finally endorsed. On 24 May 1944, in conformity with the deliberations (on 18 February and 26 March 1944) of the Legal Committee of the French Committee for National Liberation in Algiers, the act called "law of 22 July 1940" relating to the review of naturalizations was annulled.[30]

After the provisional government returned to Paris, all the denaturalization dossiers were reexamined by a team of four magistrates from the Bureau of Seals. They verified whether those dossiers fell under the pre-war legislation on withdrawals. Most dossiers were examined very rapidly and filed away without further action, so that denaturalization was in effect rescinded. Sometimes, in cases of "disloyalty" toward the Resistance, further information was requested from the prefect of the department where the denaturalized person lived. But even where denaturalization had come about at the request of the person concerned—for instance, someone seeking to return to his or her country of origin—and even when denaturalization had been imposed as a penalty for support of Fascist Italy, the administration took a liberal approach and closed the files.[31] In contrast, it took steps to withdraw nationality from active collaborators or draft dodgers; by 10 December 1953 these procedures had led to a total of 479 withdrawals.[32]

The Return of the Ethnic Approach

But the most important question remained that of naturalization requests: 200,000 dossiers had accumulated in the prefectures since 1940. As early as October 1944 Menthon, who had become keeper of the seals, asked the prefects to return the requests that had been forwarded to them beginning in July 1940, giving priority to the people who had participated in "France's war efforts, either in our armies or in the Resistance, themselves or through their ascendants or descendants, and on condition that they are completely assimilated to our mores and our customs and that they speak our language fluently."[33] A new memorandum from the minister of justice to the prefects on 5 February 1945 specified that *all* naturalization requests had to be sent to the ministry. This was a revolution in the handling of requests: let us recall that before the war, the prefectures—in particular the Paris Prefecture of Police—made their own selection and transmitted only a limited number of the applications that they had received.[34]

From that point on the Bureau of Seals within the Ministry of Justice was charged with examining dossiers on its own and choosing candidates suitable for naturalization. To this end, on 19 March 1945[35] the minister of justice set up an interministry commission on naturalizations that was to identify and coordinate "the principles that should presumably preside over the examination of naturalization requests by the administrative authorities." The commission included representatives from all the ministries concerned: justice, foreign affairs, colonies, labor, public health, defense, national education, prisoners, deportees, and refugees.

At about the same time (3 April 1945),[36] a High Advisory Committee on Population and the Family was created. In the speech in which he set forth his program before the Consultative Assembly on 3 March 1945, General de Gaulle proclaimed that "the lack of men and the weakness of the French birth rate are the underlying cause of our misfortunes" and "the principal obstacle in the way of our recovery." He went on to be more specific: "In order to call to life the twelve million beautiful babies that France will need in ten years, to reduce our absurd rates of infantile and juvenile mortality and illness, to introduce over the course of the next few years, methodically and intelligently, good elements of immigration into the French collectivity, a grand plan has been drawn up . . . so that the vital and sacred result will be obtained whatever the cost." The High Committee was charged with preparing new immigration laws, and Georges Mauco, viewed as the best expert on immigration of the period, was appointed its secretary general.[37]

A prudent analyst before the war, Mauco waited for the defeat in 1940 before expressing himself openly. In an article titled "Revolution 1940,"[38] he advocated "a totalitarian government that must impose an economic community and the value of work," as well as a "Fascist revolution," a third way between liberal democracy and the Communist revolution. Mauco was a contributor to *L'Ethnie française*, a newspaper published by Montandon, and in 1942 he used this forum to publish an article reproducing almost word for word the written testimony he had given on 3 September 1941 before the Supreme Court that had been set up in Riom by the Vichy regime to judge the leaders of the Third Republic.[39] In these two texts Mauco challenged the immigration policy of the Third Republic — "the egalitarian political tendencies of governments prevent them from acting consequentially and ensuring the ethnic protection of the country"[40] — before going back to his theory about the distinctions between refugee and foreigner that he had already developed before the war. In the category of "refugees," from which Mauco had taken care to exclude Italians and to some extent Spaniards ("they belong to a country close to France in civilization and language"), he described the ethnic characteristics of Russians, Armenians, and Jews that made them, in increasing order, more and more unassimilable: "While the Russians are far from the French people in many respects, they generally have a cultural level that allows contact. With the Armenians, even this contact is difficult . . . They have been living for generations in a situation of enforced inferiority, and they have been chronically terrorized. With the exception of some isolated individuals, this has shaped a soul adapted to constraint in which character gives way to shifty obsequiousness."[41]

All the undesirable features of imposed immigration appear finally, according to Mauco, with Jewish refugees. "Physical and psychic health, morality, and character are equally diminished. . . . Here again, one has souls shaped by the long humiliations of a servile state, in which repressed hatred is masked by obsequiousness."[42] Justifying Vichy's anti-Semitic policy toward Jews both foreign and French, he added: "More seriously still, [that hatred] was awakened by contact, among the Frenchified Jews, and it made them lose, in part, the [desirable] qualities they had managed to acquire." Thus Mauco, who evinced an early interest in psychoanalysis, put this discipline at the service of his core belief in the irremediable and total determination of personality by ethnic origin: "The alteration of character—[which] is found in the Jew . . . is serious, for it is the product not only of education and the environment on the individual, but in part of heredity. Modern psychology—and especially psychoanalysis—has shown that these features, transmitted through parental influence from the child's earliest years, modified the subject's very unconscious and could only be reabsorbed after several generations [had been] subjected to satisfactory conditions and had completely escaped from the influence of the hereditary milieu."[43] Mauco collaborated on *L'Ethnie française* until 1943.

In early 1944, however, Mauco joined the Foch-Lyautey resistance group of the FFI and participated in liberating the Auteuil district in Paris. In September 1944 he sent Charles de Gaulle's cabinet a note advocating that the provisional government set up a High Advisory Committee on the Family and Population.[44] This was done, and Mauco was named the committee's secretary general, probably at the suggestion of Louis Joxe, who was secretary general of the provisional government.[45] Before the war Joxe had involved Mauco in the activities of his center for the study of foreign policy,[46] and in 1937 he had asked him to do a study on the "assimilability" of foreigners. In this new position, which put him in direct contact with the secretary general of the government, Mauco was charged with setting up the new immigration policy that had been entrusted to the High Committee.

To translate his ideas into public decisions, Mauco relied on the work of the General Delegation for Equipping the Nation, a precursor to France's General Planning Commission (Commissariat Général au Plan).[47] This work had been developed under Vichy, in 1943 and 1944, with the collaboration of the French Foundation for the Study of Human Problems (led by Alexis Carrel). Robert Gessain, secretary general of the "population" team of the foundation, had been asked to draft an "anthropological" study;[48] Robert Sanson had been asked to do a special report on North Africa. In March 1944 Louis Chevalier, *chargé de mission* with the delegation, had taken responsibility for synthesizing the "scientific" and administrative views on "assimilability" and thus on the selection of immigrants according to origin. Observing that "knowledge of phenomena relating to population, ethnic types, the constitution of human groups, and racial mixing was insufficient at the present time to found a totally objective immigration policy," he had deduced that "the safest position, and the one that should make it possible to set aside any risk of modifying the French population profoundly and any risk of disaster from the cultural standpoint, is certainly the one that consists in seeking immigrants whose 'ethnic type' is already represented in the 'French mosaic.'"

Chevalier thus suggested identifying the countries "from which it is appropriate to stimulate immigration": Belgium, Luxembourg, Germany (the Palatinate and the Bade region but also the Rhenish provinces and Bavaria), Switzerland, Italy (Piedmont, Lombardy, Frioul, Sardinia), the Spanish provinces of Leon, Aragon, Navarre, Catalonia, and the Basque country, and also Holland, Ireland, Scotland, Denmark, Sweden, and Norway. He also proposed to accept Slovakian Austrians, Portuguese from the northwest, French Canadians, and Americans of European ethnic descent. Among those "whose nationals can be admitted to France only with certain reservations, in particular regarding their number," he ranked Germans from regions not mentioned above: Serbs, Croats, Czechs, Bulgarians, and agricultural workers from Greece and the southern regions of Italy, Spain, and Portugal. Finally, he judged that people "from the other European or overseas countries with white populations" could only be admitted "on an exceptional basis."[49]

Mauco took his inspiration directly from Chevalier's report,[50] but for "zest" he also added a touch of the American approach. To categorize their immigrants according to origin, the Americans had grouped all foreigners who entered the United States into five major races (Teutonic, Celtic, Iberian, Slavic, and Mongoloid), without regard to their nationality: Mauco took this "grand" classification and proposed to distinguish between northern Europeans, Latins, and Slavs. In 1921, to select immigrants on the basis of quotas, the U.S. Congress relied on the origin of immigrants as indicated in the census of 1890, in which the presence of the new "undesirable" immigration was still weak. Mauco suggested an approach that while less rigid than the American quota system referred to "the composition of the foreign population in the censuses of 1881–1891, in which the sources of emigration were in balance." Thus when the High Committee headed by General de Gaulle met on 18 May 1945, it adopted a proposal for a "general directive"[51] that would organize the admission of immigrants according to a determined order of "desirability."

First in this ranking were the "Nordics" (Belgians, Luxembourgers, Dutch, Swiss, Danes, Scandinavians, Finns, Irish, English, Germans, and Canadians); their overall proportion in immigration was fixed at 50 percent. The "Mediterraneans" came next, for 30 percent (Spaniards from Asturias, Leon, Aragon, Galicia, Navarre, Catalonia, and the Basque country; Italians from Lombardy, Piedmont, Venetia, Liguria, Emilia, Tuscany; Portuguese from the Beira region). The Slavs (Poles, Czechs, Yugoslavs) were limited to 20 percent. Immigration by "all foreigners of other origins" was strictly limited to "individual cases presenting exceptional interest." Unlike Chevalier, who took pains to set apart "the case of stateless persons and political refugees, so as to keep France's traditional customs of generosity in this respect," Mauco proposed to be extremely restrictive toward political refugees and "fugitives."[52]

As for naturalizations, following the approach of Vichy's Delegation for Equipment,[53] Mauco sought to apply the same outlook as the one advocated for immigration policy: thus he tried to take naturalization policy in hand and to circumvent the action of the Ministry of Justice, the only agency empowered to deal with naturalizations.

The Defeat of Georges Mauco

The Bureau of Seals in the Ministry of Justice was instructed to give priority to naturalizing members of the Resistance and others who had fought for Free France. But this did not suit Mauco. As soon as he was appointed to the government and given an office in the Secretariat General in the Hôtel Matignon, he oversaw every naturalization decree. His notes to Louis Joxe[54] struck repeated notes of warning: "Naturalizations are being carried out right now with no overall vision. In particular, there is no directive regarding ethnicity, profession, geography, or even health. The only criterion is belonging to the Resistance. Hence: in the decree attached, a considerable proportion of Mediterraneans, Armenians, and Russian or Polish Israelites."[55] And again: "This cohort of Frenchmen is, like the previous ones, especially devoted to Mediterranean and Armenian elements. Of 50 naturalizations, 38, or three fourths, are attributed to Italians, Spaniards, Armenians, and Portuguese. The professions practiced by the Armenians do not seem a priori to be of any particular interest ('employees,' soccer players, painters, decorators, 'hairdressers,' etc.). In contrast, very few naturalizations for the Nordics: only 5 Belgians and no Swiss, Luxembourgers, Dutch, etc., whereas 200,000 naturalization requests have been on hold for four years and many are from agricultural workers and miners, whom the country urgently needs." As the decrees were numerous, Mauco selected those that included the greatest number of "Mediterraneans" for his commentaries, thus truncating the facts.[56]

A few days later he tried again, giving Joxe the draft of a letter to be sent to the minister of justice. On 12 June 1945 Mauco's note to Louis Joxe was transformed, with a few modifications, into a letter addressed[57] by de Gaulle to Pierre-Henri Teitgen,[58] who had become minister of justice on 30 May 1945:

> The High Advisory Committee on Population and the Family is currently studying proposals that will constitute its opinion concerning Government policy on immigration.
>
> From now on it is important that naturalizations be carried out according to an

overall directive. It would be appropriate in particular to make them no longer exclusively dependent on the study of particular cases, but to subordinate the choice of individuals to the national interests in the ethnic, demographic, professional, and geographic realms.

a) On the *ethnic* level, limit the influx of Mediterraneans and Orientals who over half a century have profoundly modified the human structure of France. Without going so far as to use, as in the United States [*which has had the same preoccupations*][59] a rigid system of quotas—it is desirable that priority be granted to Nordic naturalizations (Belgians, Luxembourgers, Dutch, Swiss, Danes, Scandinavians, Icelanders, English, Germans, etc.). [*With reference to the composition of the foreign population in the 1881–1891 censuses, where the sources of emigration were balanced*:] Given the large number of dossiers currently pending in the prefectures, one could envisage a proportion of 50% of these elements.

b) On the *professional* level, France especially needs directly productive workers: agricultural workers, miners, construction workers, and so on. In contrast, to retain our country's power of assimilation, it is desirable that the liberal professions, commerce, banking, etc., not be too broadly open to foreigners. It is to the extent that foreigners can acquire their own intellectual and economic frameworks in France — even naturalized—that they retain their particularism more fully. There is an interest in limiting naturalizations in these professions, and in urban professions more generally.

c) On the demographic level, it is important to naturalize individuals who are young or who have children. [*It is not desirable to grant French nationality to individuals more than 70 years old.*]

d) On the geographic level, limit naturalizations in cities [*very*] strictly, especially in Paris, Marseille, and Lyon, where the influx of foreigners is not desirable for many reasons. In contrast, naturalizations can be encouraged and multiplied in the provinces and especially in rural milieux.

I beg you to be so kind as to give instructions to the prefectures such that the study and forwarding of dossiers will be informed by these directives and desirable naturalizations will be produced according to need.

Ch. de Gaulle

When Pierre-Henri Teitgen received this letter, he took its instructions only as working hypotheses: "You have been so kind as to communicate to me overall directives that *could* be followed in matters of naturalization," he wrote to de Gaulle on 25 June 1945.[60] To signal his disagreement, he added that the decisions made by the Chancellery "have never depended exclusively on the study of particular cases. . . . The petitioners' family situation, their nationality of origin, their assimilation and their profession were the principal elements that were to be retained at the moment of decision." In each conjuncture, certain criteria carried more weight than others: "From 1936 to 1940 more particularly, the candidates' age and aptitude for armed military service was of capital importance. At the present time . . . the Seal of France takes into account especially, for admission into the heart of our community, the attitude taken and the services rendered since the beginning of the hostilities by foreigners who desire to become French." Finally, he attached to his letter to de Gaulle the report produced by the Interministry Commission on Naturalizations, instituted by the decree of 19 March 1945 and charged with establishing criteria for dealing with the 200,000 dossiers still outstanding.

The interministry commission on naturalizations, set up on 17 March 1945 with the charge of identifying principles that would preside over naturalization, met eight times between 11 April and 1 June 1945.[61] It began by settling the issue of quantity: M. Pagès, director of foreigners and passports in the Ministry of the Interior,[62] stressed the need "to naturalize foreigners living in France as broadly as possible, without too much consideration of their professional background,"[63] while the Ministry of Labor proved to be in favor of a restrictive policy that would "discourage candidates." Alfred Sauvy,[64] after a report on the demographic situation in France, finally brought the commission to unanimity by proposing to establish a number of acquisitions of French nationality equal to the anticipated number of new immigrants, or 130,000 a year — so that the proportion of French people would remain constant.[65] Since entry into nationality could also take place through automatic or declarative procedures, this amounted to setting a goal of 45,000 a year for naturalizations in the strict sense.

On 11 May the commission attempted to answer the following question: "Is it appropriate, for granting naturalization, to give primary consideration to the candidate's family situation, or his profession, or his nationality of origin?" Each minister produced his own ranking.[66] The minister of foreign affairs advocated giving primacy to origin, with a ranking similar to Mauco's. Pagès, speaking for the Ministry of the Interior, proposed to give priority to foreigners who had resided in France before the war, to heads of families, and to adults under the age of twenty-five, ranked according to the following three categories: (1) originating from Nordic countries, Italy, Spain, or Poland, or stateless persons, subject to the same military obligations as the French; (2) originating from the countries of central Europe and Germany; (3) Slavs. Furthermore, he did not want to take the candidates' professions into account. Sauvy, for his part, proposed that among the 200,000 dossiers those who had immigrated before 1914 should have priority. He suggested the following ranking: (1) family situation; (2) stability of employment; (3) national origin. The last criterion struck him as the least important since the children of all these immigrants would be French in any case.[67] In the view of the minister of labor, finally, priority should be granted according to profession, in the following order: (1) industrial workers; (2) agricultural laborers; (3) businessmen; (4) liberal professions.

The preferences of each were then consolidated: as for the public directives to be given to the prefectures, there was agreement on the following priorities: first, veterans of the Second World War and candidates who had played an active role in the Resistance;[68] next, parents of three (or more) children and foreigners under the age of twenty-five eligible for armed military service; finally, parents of two children, and foreigners aged twenty-five to thirty eligible for armed military service.[69]

A ranking of the candidates by a complementary criterion, nationality of origin, was also to be carried out. "It will remain in the Chancellery and will be known only to the magistrates called upon to make decisions."[70]

A few days after receiving the commission's report, Louis Joxe, the provisional government's secretary general, wrote a letter to Teitgen that was accompanied by instructions from the High Committee on Population and that completed the letter of 12 June 1945 signed by de Gaulle.[71] The tone was less menacing, but the High Committee reiterated to the minister of justice its desire to see taken into account in naturalization decisions directives that were first ethnic, then demographic, and finally professional and geographic. He requested that naturalizations deemed particularly desirable and useful for the country be encouraged and accelerated — Nordic elements, directly productive workers — and that only limited study be given to "less desirable candidacies: commercial, liberal, artisanal, and urban professions, and in a general way candidacies from the large cities." Then, to accelerate the processing of dossiers, the High Committee proposed that the power to award naturalizations by decree be transferred from the prefectures to civil tribunals: every naturalization receiving unanimous support from the judges of a tribunal would be granted; only the dossiers remaining would be transmitted to the ministry.

Responding on 3 August 1945, Teitgen rejected the High Committee's proposals. He rejected the decentralized procedure relying on tribunals, for fear that it would allow the naturalization of "certain individuals whose role [had been] harmful during the Occupation." He reiterated his request for supplementary funding and resources for handling naturalizations at the level of his ministry and the prefectures alike. He guaranteed that under these conditions, the processing of dossiers would see no further delays. He did not mention the general directives on the selection of candidates, but the practice of his services stood as a response. Mauco was under no illusions, moreover, when he remarked to Louis Joxe on the composition of a new decree: "The directives recently addressed to the Ministry of Justice as to the ethnic, profession, geographic choice, have not yet been applied. The military services (Resistance) alone determine the choice."

Mauco's battle seemed definitively lost when, with the support of Adrien Tixier, minister of the interior,[72] Teitgen succeeded in getting the rulings on naturalizations incorporated not into the ordinance on foreigners prepared under the aegis of the High Committee but into the Nationality Code that the Ministry of Justice had been discreetly preparing over the past year.[73]

A New Nationality Code

On 8 September 1944 the cabinet of the Ministry of Justice had given the green light to the Bureau of Seals for reexamining the law of 10 August 1927 along with all the provisions that had subsequently been added to it, "with the goal of simplification."[74] Raymond Boulbès, head of litigation in the Bureau of Seals, set to work at once to review the law. A magistrate who had worked with the bureau since 1931, Boulbès was responsible for the legal consultation service under Vichy. In this role he had made some crucial decisions. In a memorandum of 12 October 1941, in view of "harmonizing . . . the strict conditions for delivering these certificates [of naturalization] with the importance of the quality of being French," Vichy's minister of justice Joseph Barthélemy had decided to attribute the exclusive right to deliver certificates of nationality to justices of the peace, under the supervision of the prosecutor's office (see chapter 9). But for candidates whose parents had not always been French, he had instructed justices of the peace to suspend judgment and consult the Chancellery. The effect had been immediate and impressive: the number of consultations, negligible until then, had gone up to 12,973 in 1942 and 18,966 in 1943.[75] In this activity, in which the Bureau of Seals enjoyed relative autonomy (compared to the control exercised over naturalizations and denaturalizations), it seems that Boulbès managed to "deliver naturalization certificates as quickly as possible to many naturalized persons, reintegrated persons, or Jews who sought them,"[76] perhaps saving them from a grim fate.

To draft his nationality code, Boulbès sought advice from his former professor at the University of Toulouse, Jacques Maury, one of the leading specialists on nationality[77] and—a less well known fact—a Resistance member from the start. In October 1940 Maury commented on the Vichy legislation in a respected journal, La Semaine juridique.[78] Far from practicing the complacency evinced by many jurists,[79] he criticized the legislation by mocking it, using the technique of inversion.[80] Concluding his discussion of the status of Jews, naturalized Frenchmen, and sons of foreigners, he showed that the Vichy laws had created "a privileged category of Frenchmen by origin." "To this group, which includes the vast majority of [France's] nationals, moreover, the legislature reserves rights, jobs, professions or trades from which all the other French people are, with a few exceptions, definitively and even retroactively excluded. It is no longer a question, as in the earlier texts, of imposing a certain waiting period for the enjoyment of determined rights on individuals who have become French through naturalization; it is no longer a matter of ensuring a progressive adaptation that will lead to total assimilation. The differences established, the inequalities pronounced, are lasting, permanent, they are based on the idea of a quality inherent to the person, an essential quality."[81]

Once the nationality code had been drafted, its author (Boulbès) and its source of inspiration (Maury) sat together with other legal experts under the direction of M. Loriot, president of a section within the Council of State,[82] on a commission that examined the proposal officially between 23 June and 30 July 1945.[83] Submitted to the keeper of the seals, then to the government, and finally to the Council of State, the new Nationality Code was promulgated on 19 October 1945; the High Advisory Committee on Population and the Family had not been consulted.

In the words of Professor Maury himself, "the code [was] essentially the work of the Direction of Civil Affairs and the Seal . . . it [was] the doctrine of the Bureau of Seals that [was] consecrated in a very coherent way by the Code."[84] The goal was not to modify the legislation in force in any significant way but primarily to profit from the brief opportunity in 1945 when the government could act by issuing ordinances, without intervention by a legislative power that had not yet been elected, to bring about a legal and formal recasting that had already been prepared in the late 1930s.

The law of 1927 included fifteen articles, the Code of 1945 more than ten times as many — 156. "The legislator, taking inspiration from the tradition that goes back moreover several thousand years (the Hammurabi Code, 2,000 years B.C.E.) made an effort to introduce into each article a single, concise provision, corresponding to a single idea. The disparate elements, sometimes mingled in a confused way in each of the articles of the 1927 law, were the object of rigorous analysis and were categorized according to a logical order that makes them easier to read and to apply."[85] A few years later Jean Foyer was less appreciative of the work that Boulbès had described to his own advantage: "This code is chatty.

Multiplying distinctions and subdistinctions, multiplying references from one article to the next, it looks more like a practical repertory — a *vademecum* — malicious tongues would say a recipe book — than a legislative monument marked by *imperatoria brevitas.*"[86] At bottom the modifications are minor, reflecting at the same time the demographic preoccupation and the desire to reinforce the state's prior control over acquisitions of nationality.

The national interest and demographic considerations prevailed when it was decided that henceforth a child born to a French mother would be French, even if he or she were born abroad. Demographic concerns also justified restricting the freedom of a foreign woman who married a French man: she found herself automatically granted French nationality, whereas the law of 1927 had allowed her to express her own choice.[87]

As for naturalization, the length of prior residence required of the candidate before a decree could be granted was extended from three years to five. In compensation, the Code provided for cases in which this minimum delay would be reduced: foreign men who were married to French women, or held advanced degrees from a French institution, or had rendered important services to France (by making scientific, industrial, or literary contributions) had to wait only two years. Finally, no waiting period was required of a father of three (or more) legitimate minor children or of someone who enrolled voluntarily in the French or Allied armed forces. For candidates eighteen years of age or more, the Code added four conditions of acceptability that had earlier served simply as criteria for evaluating the dossiers: actual residence, morality, assimilation, and good health.

Finally, and this is the Code's chief innovation, a unified and centralized mechanism for proving nationality was provided for the first time: the certificate of nationality was to be attributed by a small claims court judge, under the control of the Ministry of Justice.

Naturalizations versus Child Protection

All in all, the new Nationality Code sounded like a victory for the Ministry of Justice. Why, then, a few weeks after the Code was promulgated on 10 October 1945, was the handling of naturalizations taken away from that ministry and transferred to the Ministry of Population? During the weeks that preceded the adoption of the Code, at the height of the conflict between Mauco and the Ministry of Justice, no one had proposed or hinted at such a transfer. On 2 November 1945 Justice Minister Teitgen sent his instructions for handling naturalization requests to the prefectures. On 29 November 1945 he presided personally over an interministry meeting in his office to examine the assignment of supplementary staff in the prefectures to deal with naturalizations.[88]

The creation of a separate Ministry of Population under the direction of Robert Prigent[89] (MRP) in December 1945 altered the situation and led to the unexpected transfer. The establishment of an autonomous ministry implied transferring a certain number of administrative responsibilities and staff from other ministries.

A decision handed down by General de Gaulle[90] at the beginning of December provided that the Office of Child Protection would be transferred from the Ministry of Justice to the Ministry of Population, where a large Office of Childhood was to be created. But this decision was not accepted at the Ministry of Justice.[91] Mauco, who had become aware of the resistance, and who was as interested in childhood as in immigration, sent a note to Louis Joxe on 12 December 1945 to ask him to inform de Gaulle immediately: "It would be regrettable in all respects if the Ministry of Population could not obtain the service of Child Protection from Justice. [This attribution] had received the approval of all the specialists and all the agencies interested in the protection of childhood. They saw it as a step toward a necessary unity of action. A single department was to be charged for the first time with the health, protection, and reeducation of endangered, handicapped, or ill-adapted children."[92]

However, a new ruling had been handed down a few days earlier: the Office of Child Protection was to remain with Justice. In exchange, the Ministry of Justice agreed to allow naturalizations and declarations of nationality to be transferred to the Ministry of Population. The Ministry of Justice would doubtless have preferred to retain all its prerogatives, but as it was refusing above all to give up Child Protection, it agreed to yield naturalizations as a tradeoff. Probably considering that the management of that service posed especially thorny problems, and that the new responsibilities it had been assigned by the Nationality Code could compensate for the loss, the Ministry of Justice had agreed to an internal bargain.

To handle the dossiers that had accumulated in the prefectures, the administrative machine had taken some time to get back in gear. The transfer of dossiers had been slowed by a lack of means, both in the prefectures and in Paris in the Bureau of Seals under the Ministry of Justice, as well as by the obligation to consult the Ministry of War. On 30 May 1945 the head of seals, André Levadoux, had sent to the Justice Ministry's cabinet a note appealing for help for his overburdened staff:[93] "It is absolutely certain that if this situation is not corrected in a very short time there will be a scandal, despite the complete devotion of all the staff in the Service." An assessment mission had already been launched, and because experience had "proved irrefutably that a single magistrate already experienced in the service [could] not handle more than 25 dossiers a day," Levadoux proposed that the service as a whole be assigned seventy magistrates, of whom some forty—a director, ten reviewers, and thirty drafters—would work exclusively on naturalizations and reintegrations, whereas the Nationality Service as a whole included only twenty-five magistrates.

For Levadoux, moreover, the remedy did not lie simply in increasing the number of magistrates; it also required an improvement in their training. "The questions involved in naturalization are very different from the ones that are addressed in the Courts and Tribunals. They require a long apprenticeship. It is appropriate, for this reason, to have specialized Magistrates [in the service] on the rue Scribe. Yet apart from the magistrates of the central administration who remain there for several years, the people charged with making decisions are recruited in the provinces, under undesirable conditions (either through recommendations or because of an inaptitude, for example, to preside from the bench, or to take the floor in a hearing). In any case, these collaborators remain only a very short time in the Chancellery and the examination of the dossiers unquestionably suffers from this obvious lack of stability."

Levadoux thus asked that "as quickly as possible, the Seals of France be endowed with Substitutes called to spend a major part of their career" in its service. But he did not get what he wanted. What is more, the new Nationality Code had institutionalized the certificates of nationality and confirmed the direct competence of the ministry regarding declarations. To the 200,000 naturalization dossiers were thus added 500,000 pending dossiers of declarations of nationality, plus the 90,000 dossiers in that category that had to be investigated each year, without counting 36,000 legal consultations, 30,000 name changes, and "40,000 interventions of the Cabinet, members of Parliament, highly placed civil servants, veterans' associations, or the applicants themselves." To be relieved of naturalizations was thus to reduce that excessive burden of work. The new competencies of the Bureau of Seals, especially in legal cases where nationality was contested, allowed the minister of justice to remain the minister of nationality, carrying out and expressing the law in this area.[94]

On 8 December 1945 Teitgen thus proposed the decree that would finally be retained by the Council of State: "The minister of Population is charged with preparing and presenting, after confirmation by the keeper of the Seals, [who is] the minister of Justice, decrees of acquisition, denial, loss, or withdrawal of French nationality, and decrees of admission to the rights of French citizen; to examine and record the declarations signed in view of reclaiming, declining, or repudiating French nationality, or renouncing that faculty of repudiation."[95] As of January 1946 the minister of population became responsible for naturalizations.

New Ministry, New Criteria

The 200,000 pending dossiers were then processed at a steady pace. At a meeting of the parliamentary group MRP on 6 August 1946,[96] Robert Prigent highlighted the change in rhythm: in June 1945 83 naturalizations had been granted; in June 1946, 2,157. In 1946 there were 17,351 naturalizations altogether (minor children included); in 1947 there were 83,317, beating the record set in 1937 of 76,169; the total number of recorded acquisitions of French nationality had reached 111,736.

How can these results be explained? Speaking before the MRP, Prigent indicated the criteria applied by his services. The applicant's attitude during the war remained primordial. Thus in 1946 the length of residency required of a candidate was in practice seven years, even though the law specified only five; this was to be able to take into account "the attitude at the time war was declared and the territory was occupied." Priority was given to those who had distinguished themselves during the war, then to foreigners who had three or more children, then to miners.

Poland had incorporated the Silesian mines within its new borders, and it sought to "recuperate" those of its miners who had settled in France: France and Poland signed three successive agreements, on 20 February and 28 November 1946, and then on 24 February 1948, providing for the orderly repatriation of volunteers.[97] But in an effort to avoid such a repatriation as much as possible, the word went out to make naturalizing Polish miners an absolute priority;[98] the dossiers of mine workers that had been deferred before the war were treated as urgent matters. In the end certain Polish miners went back to Poland nonetheless, and, according to Janine Ponty, those who remained in France were in no hurry to be naturalized. In contrast, the priority given to members of the Resistance was respected. Janine Ponty cites the case of Marian D., who was born in Poland in 1925 and arrived in France two years later, in Aubin-Cransac. Having joined the maquis, he was naturalized in 1945, at the age of twenty. In another case, Euphrosine C., born in 1908 in Galicia (Poland), arrived in France in 1931 as a servant on a farm and lost her Polish husband in the massacre of Oradour-sur-Glane. She was offered French nationality in 1949, which allowed her to receive a war widow's income and a pension to raise her children as wards of the nation.

TABLE 6

Naturalizations and Other Acquisitions of Nationality, 1937–1948

	Metropolitan France				France	
	Men	Women	Minors	Total	Total naturalizations	Total acquisitions of nationality
1937	11,299	4,624	8,516	24,439	25,309	40,412
1938	16,307	7,237	13,137	36,681	38,899	77,870
1939	28,774	15,724	28,561	73,059	76,169	118,300
1946	9,237	3,932	2,788	15,957	17,351	38,869
1947	43,408	20,014	13,573	76,995	83,317	111,736
1948	30,126	15,892	8,646	54,664	58,823	70,925

Source: INSEE.

According to her testimony, without that intervention by the authorities this possibility would not have occurred to her.[99]

The dossiers that had priority were dealt with quickly, as they were few in number. Did the next step entail favoring the naturalization of "Nordics" and agricultural workers, as proposed by the High Committee of which Prigent was a member? Not really, even though article 15 of decree 45–2698 spelled out on 2 November 1945 how the ordinance of 19 October 1945 was to be applied, indicating that nationality of origin would be one of the criteria (although not the primordial one) in any naturalization request to be considered by the administration.[100] In the first place, the so-called Nordics had not requested — and thus had not obtained — naturalization in large numbers. Then too, restrictionism was off the agenda, inasmuch as openness to mass naturalizations was once again perceived as a demographic imperative, in a climate that was somewhat reminiscent of the 1920s — a climate of alarm over Germany's demographic power.[101] In addition, in the political climate of 1946 and 1947 the principle of ethnic selection was even less legitimate than it had been in 1945, since the majority of the National Assembly membership belonged to the Communist party and to the

Socialist SFIO, governing in a tripartite coalition with the MRP. Ethnic selection was openly criticized by the associations for the defense of foreigners and by Abbot Glasberg, who challenged "certain theoreticians influenced by Nazi doctrines" and rejected any distinction based on origin: "It was believed earlier that the natural ease with which Mediterraneans could be assimilated into French civilization made their immigration desirable. . . . But now we have voices rising up against these 'gypsified' and 'negrified' peoples on the pretext that France is already sufficiently 'gypsified' and 'negrified' itself, and they recommend the introduction of 'Nordics' with complementary racial qualities. . . . However, the hazards of migration hardly make it possible to anticipate a considerable number of 'Nordic' contributions. . . . Thus, given the uncertainty of a woolly-minded ethnic pseudo-science, attention must be focused not on racial selection but simply on human selection, on a physically and mentally healthy immigration."[102]

At the Ministry of the Interior the head of the division of foreigners was Pagès, who was favorable to mass naturalization. His goal was to get the accumulated pending dossiers from the prefectures as quickly as possible and to rule on new requests promptly. All the prefectures had to handle an increased number of applications, but the ones with a large foreign presence, in urban zones, had the largest stock. From the Seine department, for example, which included Paris and the surrounding communes, the Prefecture of Police transmitted dossiers of candidates of all origins who were more often laborers or employees, businessmen, industrialists, or doctors than miners or agricultural workers.

The files were finally transmitted to the Ministry of Population, which processed them all according to the order of priority established by the Interministry Commission on Naturalizations.[103] The dossiers of mine workers, parents of three children, and veterans were examined first, and with a certain leniency, for example where matters of morality arose: "if a worker is reproached for incidents without real gravity, these [must] not be an obstacle to a favorable decision."[104] For other categories of applicants, age and family situation were taken into account. As Jacques Mérot[105] indicates, candidates lacking priority were also naturalized, but the waiting period was longer. Naturalization was even granted "to those who [were] elderly, without children, without profession, and who [had] not rendered any service to our country, provided that they [had resided] in France for a long time and were the object of favorable information." Twenty years of residency was all that was asked of such persons.[106]

The determination to get through the backlog accounted for the record number of naturalizations in 1947, the year in which the rate of favorable decisions was the highest (93.3 percent).[107] Italians still constituted the largest group of successful candidates, even if their proportion had decreased (37 percent in 1947 as opposed to 50 percent in 1937). Poles progressed from 14 percent to 18 percent. Then came Spaniards, who remained stable at a little more than 11.5 percent. Armenians were on the increase, from 2.7 percent to 7.5 percent, ahead of Belgians, who remained, between 1937 and 1947, at around 6 percent. The groups that Mauco wanted to introduce — Americans, English, Luxembourgers, Monegasques, Dutch, Norwegians, and Swiss — represented in all only 2 percent of the citizens naturalized in 1947, a far smaller proportion than Bulgarians, Romanians, Russians, Czechs, and Yugoslavs, who accounted for more than 10 percent of the successful candidates in 1947.[108] As for the new citizens' places of residence, the Seine, an urban department par excellence, progressed significantly: it represented 20.5 percent of the naturalizations in 1946 and 19 percent in 1947, as opposed to 12.87 percent in 1938. The evolution in terms of profession was described by Mauco:

We can deduce from this that except for mine workers (who were not counted before the war), the groups that experienced the strongest progression were industrialists and businessmen, and in somewhat smaller numbers white-collar workers and doctors.

After 1947 most of the dossiers left pending during the war had been taken care of, and the rhythm of naturalizations slowed, falling to around 35,000 in 1950.[109] The dossiers were studied case by case, and a decision was made after the criteria of age, family situation, nationality of origin, profession, and length of stay in France had been taken into account. But naturalization was granted broadly; the rate of unfavorable decisions (rejection or deferral) stabilized at around 20 percent. Each new National Assembly after 1945 was confronted with the same draft legislation proposed by Jacques Bardoux, a deputy from Puy-de-Dôme,[110] who sought to institute jus sanguinis as the sole means for attributing French nationality at birth.[111] France's naturalization policy did not change. However, restrictive inflections arose at certain moments. The cold war thus had its impact. On 15 June 1950, for example, a note within the service from the director general of population and mutual aid recommended seeking the opinion of the minister of the interior regarding the dossiers in which membership in a political party, sympathy for an extremist ideology, or professional activities directed toward political ends were mentioned.[112] The staff was thus in effect ordered to take the candidate's loyalty (in reality, this meant political commitment) into account in evaluating a dossier. On 23 April 1952 there was a short-lived change in direction — instructions sent by Paul Ribeyre instituted the ethnic criterion as a discriminating factor: "One must avoid naturalizing elements that, by virtue of their origin, would be hard to assimilate and could alter the ethnic and spiritual

TABLE 7

Professions of Naturalized Men (Metropolitan France)

	1937	1938	1939	1945	1946	1947	Average increase, 1938–1947: ×2.5
Owners of income property	11	22	24	4	8	113	×5
Liberal professions	580	327	366	65	225	517	×1.6
Industrialists, businessmen	407	565	1,242	228	1,298	6,435	×13
White-collar workers	720	1,094	1,650	233	969	4,215	×4
Petroleum industry workers	6,003	8,901	6,219	435	2,204	11,083	×1.3
Farmers	—	—	2,099	125	649	3,352	
Agricultural or forestry workers	1,413	2,210	2,443	135	768	3,802	×1.7
Factory workers	1,763	2,440	3,848	269	1,414	7,208	×2.9
Mine workers				74	1,066	3,747	
Sailors, fishermen	31	48	83	4	13	115	×2.5
Military personnel				286	161	247	
Doctors		71	24	46	131	289	×4
Dentists		14	6	8	21	44	×3
Pharmacists		2	1	3	4	9	×1.5
Medical and dental students		35	12	4	17	56	×1.5
Other students		172	185	26	100	283	

Source: G. Mauco (AN, AP 577/5).

characteristics of the French nation. . . . In order to avoid a break in the equilibrium between the Mediterranean and the Nordic contributions whose blend characterizes the French ethnic 'composite,' there is reason to favor to the fullest extent possible the naturalization of foreigners originating in countries of Western Europe (England, Scandinavia, Holland, Belgium, Luxembourg, Switzerland)."

The "right origin" did not suffice, moreover, to allow naturalization. It was with "prudence [that one must integrate] the elements that are in fact already blended with the French populations and that [are] worthy of being naturalized. In no case must the requests present any counter-indications."[113] The immediate effect was that the rate of acceptance dropped considerably: from 80 percent in 1950–51 to 63.5 percent in 1952–54.[114]

1953–1973: Twenty Years of Liberalism

Very quickly the acceptance rate returned to the levels of 1950–51 (77.6 percent in 1955, 82.9 percent in 1957). A new instruction dated 23 November 1953 rejected national origin as a criterion for selection: "To proceed thus would be to demonstrate an unacceptable racism."[115] From 1953 and for more than twenty years thereafter, the criterion of origin was absent from the debates over nationality and from naturalization practices. A liberal breeze was blowing over naturalization policy in particular and nationality in general.

Demographic concerns played a major role. For example, they pushed the government to look more favorably on naturalization requests that had been rejected earlier: parents with just one child, elderly people, and even, from 1953 on, foreigners without proper papers if they exercised "a useful profession."[116]

From 1967—a new liberal turning point[117]—the logic behind the way naturalization dossiers were handled was reversed: whereas the only dossiers judged acceptable had been those of candidates who could show some contribution to the national community, now the only ones eliminated were "foreigners corresponding to certain negative criteria."[118] The criteria of assimilation (including five years' residence) and of family unity became dominant. The rate of acceptance went back up above 85 percent after 1967, whereas it had tended to drop down to around 77 percent in the early 1960s.[119]

After that, decolonization was the occasion for new legislative advances. After the signing of an agreement between France and Vietnam on 16 August 1955, a whole series of treaties organized France's legal separation from its colonies, and transformed most of the former French subjects into independent citizens of the new states. The law of 28 July 1960 determined the conditions under which the populations of sub-Saharan Africa and Madagascar could maintain French nationality: all persons residing in these countries who were originally from the territory of the French Republic (metropolitan France or the overseas departments and territories) could retain their nationality, as could their spouses, widows or widowers, and descendants, along with all those originating in those countries who could prove that they had been domiciled in France or abroad. The ordinance of 21 July 1962 based the distinction for those originating from Algeria on the criterion of personal status. French persons who benefited from common law status retained the right to French nationality. Those having local law status—the vast majority of the Muslims—could only acquire full French nationality by establishing their residence in France and subscribing to a "declaration of recognition"[120] before 22 March 1967. Another law in 1961 eliminated any requirement of legal residency before one could request naturalization. Above all, it did away with any requirement of length of stay for people seeking naturalization who were originally from countries over which France had exercised sovereignty.[121]

The great legislative reform of the period—a symbol of the prevailing liberalism—was the law of 9 January 1973, which ensured the equality of women and men with regard to nationality, and thus facilitated the access of spouses of French citizens to French nationality.

At the outset, for the government it was simply a question of cleaning up the Code of 1945. A commission of legal experts, headed between May 1969 and May 1970 by Professor Batiffol, had been charged with preparing a text. The government turned this text into a very modest bill, which it submitted in 1971. The proposal was simply to unify nationality law in metropolitan France and the overseas territories, and to include provisions allowing a child born out of wedlock to a French mother to be granted French nationality. But under the leadership of Jean Foyer,[122] designated by the National Assembly to review the bill, the text took on a broader scope. Foyer had been keeper of the seals from 1962 to 1967. It was on his initiative that Professor Jean Carbonnier had been charged with thoroughly reforming French civil law.[123] The regime of guardianship, the regimes of matrimony and succession, parental authority, and filiation had been modified, primarily to ensure definitive equality between men and women and between "natural" and legitimate children. However, this equality between men and women was not yet guaranteed in nationality law.[124] Despite reservations and pressure on the part of the Ministry of Justice,[125] Foyer got the National Assembly's commission on laws to approve a new text that extended the progressive reforms in civil affairs into the domain of nationality law.[126]

The law of 9 January 1973 placed women on an equal footing with men for the first time since 1803 where nationality law was concerned, in matters relating both to marriage and to transmission of nationality. Marriage between two persons of different nationalities no longer had an automatic effect on the nationality of either one; each spouse kept his or her own nationality, whereas earlier a foreign woman marrying a Frenchman became French automatically.[127] In contrast, access to French nationality for the non-French spouse of a French person was facilitated: until then, a foreign man marrying a French woman could only become French through naturalization; henceforth he could—just like a foreign woman married to a French man—become French through a voluntary declaration made immediately after the marriage.[128] Both spouses could transmit their own nationality to their children. Finally, natural children had the same status as legitimate children.[129]

It has often been said that the liberal law adopted in 1973 was unrelated to the immigration that had taken place very broadly during the Thirty Glorious Years from southern Europe (Italy, Spain, Yugoslavia, and especially Portugal) but also from North Africa (Algeria after 1945, then Morocco and Tunisia). In reality, Jean Foyer was perfectly aware that his law opened French nationality to immigrants of all origins. Prolonging a state of mind that had pervaded thinking about naturalization issues since 1967, he took responsibility for this choice, concluding his report to the National Assembly as follows:

Despite an improvement in its demography between 1946 and 1964, France is and will remain, like all its neighbors, a country of immigration. Like the Romans of the sixth century refusing to serve in the imperial legions, the Europeans of the twentieth century refuse to carry out painful, dirty tasks. Today, as in that time, immigration is a necessity. Does it perhaps entail the same dangers? However that may be, an immigration policy is a necessity. The features of such a policy are not always easy to discern. But whatever that policy may be, those immigrants who have no desire to return will have to be integrated into the National Community. Our renovated Nationality Law will allow this to happen without the ineffective restrictions that caused useless vexations. In the course of her long history, France has been a marvelous melting pot. Of Gallo-Romans and Germans it has made Frenchmen. The amended bill that we are proposing to you will facilitate this melting with other ethnic groups. Racism is an odious stupidity that has led to the greatest crimes in History.[130]

A few months later, on 3 July 1974, the immigration of new foreign workers was interrupted, and the words of Jean Foyer were quickly forgotten.

6.

The Algerian Crisis in French Nationality

꙳ On 3 July 1974, a few months after the oil crisis, the government stopped bringing in new foreign workers. Immigration in France at that point was kaleidoscopic: the census of 1975 counted 758,000 Portuguese residents, 710,000 Algerians, 497,000 Spaniards, 462,000 Italians, 260,000 Moroccans, and 139,000 Tunisians. There were also Yugoslavs, Turks, and sub-Saharan Africans, for a total of 3,442,000 foreigners, or 6.2 percent of the total population. This diversity obscured the harshness of the confrontations that took place throughout the Thirty Glorious Years over the "desirability" of immigrants according to their origins. In 1945, let us recall, the High Advisory Committee on Population and the Family had approved a "general directive" that would have made it possible to select immigrants through quotas calculated according to their "degree of assimilability": 50 percent of the foreigners admitted to French territory would have been northern Europeans, 30 percent Latins from the northern regions of Spain, Italy, and Portugal, and 20 percent Slavs. The entrance of foreigners of other origins would have been "strictly limited to individual cases presenting exceptional interest." To apply these provisions, Georges Mauco, secretary general of the High Advisory Committee, proposed a plan for controlling immigrants of all origins, first through rigorous selection on the basis of physical and mental health, then by keeping tabs on length of stay, housing, and permanent residence. But the interior minister, Adrien Tixier,[1] and the labor minister, Alexandre Parodi,[2] had strongly opposed this plan because of its policing aspect, its intrusive control over the foreigners admitted, and the concomitant rejection of refugees. The government had accepted the possibility of selecting foreigners according to origin and requiring them to settle in a specific department, but the last-minute arbitration of the Council of State[3] had prevented this from happening. The ordinance ultimately adopted on 2 November 1945 represented France as a country of continuing immigration, bringing in workers but also families. At the outset of this new immigration process the salaried workers—in agriculture or industry—who were given priority were brought in only with the promise of a job or a work contract; in the United States, in contrast, at the urging of the labor unions Congress had passed laws to ensure that immigrants would be "free" of any work commitment upon arrival. An immigrant worker in France could be accompanied by his wife and children, whereas Germany opened up in the late 1950s only to the temporary immigration of single workers.

The ordinance of 2 November 1945 was not without ambiguity, however. On the one hand, the state as a legal entity (*l'État de droit*) guaranteed immigrants an increasingly stable situation: as their initial authorization to stay in France was renewed and their integration into society was presumed to be under way, the state granted residency permits for longer and longer periods—one, three, and then ten years. Furthermore, the administration did not distinguish according to national or ethnic origin in selecting new immigrants; formally, it was supposed to treat Turks and Italians alike. On the other hand, the state as an active agent (*l'État acteur*) fostered an implicit selection by setting up the headquarters of a new National Immigration Office in Milan rather than in Istanbul. These offices were responsible for recruiting a foreign labor force; northern Italians were clearly more likely to turn up at its windows than Turks.

As of 1946, moreover, organized immigration came from southern rather than northern Italy, in numbers smaller than had been hoped. But this European immigration was very quickly rivaled by that of Muslims from Algeria, a population considered "undesirable" during that period by most of the immigration policy makers. On 20 September 1947 the attribution of citizenship to Algerian Muslims legalized their free movement toward metropolitan France, a process that had already been under way since 1946. Thus between 1949 and 1955, 180,000 Algerian Muslims settled in France, as compared to 160,000 workers from all foreign nationalities combined. In 1956 the French authorities reacted by formalizing the regularization procedure that allowed companies to hire on the spot foreign workers who had arrived by their own means; this was a way of favoring the arrival of Italians and Spaniards by giving them the same rights as Algerians. In 1962, however, at the request of the French authorities (who thought at the time that many French citizens would remain in Algeria), the Évian agreements provided for free circulation between France and Algeria for citizens of both countries. When it became clear that that clause benefited only Algerians seeking work in France, the authorities in charge of French immigration policy continually attempted—from 1962 to 1973—to renegotiate that provision, or to favor Portuguese but also Tunisian and Moroccan immigration and thus slow the arrival of Algerians.

Formally, the foreigners present in France in 1974 had equal rights. The

Algerians even had "superior" rights in relation to other foreigners, because theirs were guaranteed by the Évian agreements. Over a ten-year period the status of Algerian immigrants, and more generally the status of all immigrants of North African and African origin, became a critical political issue. When an initial consensus was reached in 1984, guaranteeing all legal immigrants regardless of origin the right to a permanent stay, the Nationality Code became the object of a confrontation taken to the extreme: the children of immigrants were at stake in the debate.

Ten Years to Guarantee the Status of North African Immigrants (1974–1984)

From July 1974 to 1976 the French government was not concerned about the economic recession, believing that it would be short-lived. While the influx of immigrant labor was interrupted, the status quo was more or less respected in other areas. Under the leadership of Paul Dijoud, state secretary in charge of immigrant workers, the procedure for family reunification was even modernized, and a social policy favorable to immigrants and their families was developed. But by 1977 the economic crisis appeared likely to last, and unemployment became France's primary concern: Valéry Giscard d'Estaing decided to make the return of non-European immigrants to their own countries one of his first priorities. After promoting voluntary returns without success in 1977, between 1978 and 1980 he sought to organize the forced return of most North Africans who were long-term residents in France; the prime targets were Algerians. Giscard tried to persuade Algeria to cooperate with his project, but he also threatened to get Parliament to approve legislation that would allow—without Algeria's consent—the forced return of tens of thousands of Algerian immigrants. The Évian agreements would be repudiated, quotas of non-renewal of residency permits would be created for each department, residency permits would be withdrawn in cases of unemployment lasting more than six months, or in cases of late return from a paid vacation. Overall, the goal was the forced departure of more than 100,000 foreigners a year, thus 500,000 in five years; the majority of these would be Algerian.[4]

This plan for forced returns failed owing on the one hand to the traditional mobilization of churches, associations, unions, and left-wing parties and on the other to the more discreet action of central administrations, foreign governments, two parties from the current presidential majority (RPR and CDS), and the Council of State.

After François Mitterrand's victory in the presidential elections of May 1981, the newly empowered left veered away from the previous policy, liberalizing the rules for entering and staying in France and regularizing the status of 130,000 undocumented foreigners. But after the left lost in the municipal elections in 1983, it steered its policy back toward the center. In June 1984 the National Assembly unanimously adopted a law providing for a "single ten-year permit." Foreign residents were guaranteed that their stay would become permanent regardless of their nationality or origin, and the right to residency was dissociated from employment status.[5] This law symbolized the first consensus on immigration policy between the parties on the right (UDF, RPR) and those on the left (PS, PC), and it signaled the end of forced return policies. But no sooner had the residency status of Algerian immigrants been settled than a new agenda surfaced, and the focus of debate shifted to the nationality of these residents' children.

The Real Stakes in the Nationality Debate: The Second Generation

In the early 1980s it began to be perceived in France that the children of Algerians were French, by virtue of article 23 of the Nationality Code, through the effect of the double jus soli: they were born in France to a parent born in Algeria before 1962, when Algeria was French territory.

This provision, which had imposed nationality since 1889 without the possibility of repudiation (a possibility left open for children born to foreign parents — children of Moroccans, for example),[6] created a certain number of problems for these Algerian children, and especially for their parents, some of whom had fought for Algerian independence. But as long as the problem of dual nationality was simply a problem of identity for these children and their parents, or a diplomatic problem for France and Algeria, the matter went no further.

From this standpoint, 1982 was a political turning point. In the absence of a bilateral agreement, the first contingent of young men with dual nationality, French and Algerian, had to perform their military service in both countries. A number of civic associations, under pressure from certain Algerian consulates, organized a campaign to eliminate bonds of allegiance to France for these young men who were "Frenchmen in spite of themselves."[7] Algeria had always wanted France to modify article 23 unilaterally so that its compatriots would be exempt, but Paris had consistently opposed such a change, for it would have meant admitting that Algeria had not been a French territory before 1962. At an interministry meeting in April 1982, however, the interior minister Gaston Deferre obtained agreement in principle on a revision of article 23 along the lines demanded by Algeria. In exchange, he presumably obtained real concessions — or at least promises — regarding border control policy, which was his chief concern at the time. The political danger was still the same, however: the acceptance of Algeria's long-standing claim risked being interpreted by a segment of public opinion as de facto recognition of the illegitimacy of the French presence in Algeria—which was the Algerian authorities' aim. That solution—which would also have raised numerous technical problems regarding proofs of nationality for people who had been repatriated from Algeria—was quickly abandoned. Article 23 was not going to be revised.

The problem of "dual national service" was finally resolved through a shift in the Algerian position. The Algerian state had always maintained a traditional discourse regarding the return of its citizens who had "temporarily" settled in France. Facing the fact of their definitive settlement, it envisaged using the Algerian community in France in a strategy of lobbying based on identity politics along American lines: from this perspective, dual nationality was no longer a disadvantage but a tool that Algerian leaders believed they could adopt. An agreement about military service was thus signed with France: it specified that young Franco-Algerians, despite their residency in France, could carry out their national service either in France or in Algeria, as they chose. France was satisfied, for it had not yielded on a traditional element of its own nationality law. However, in 1983 a segment of the French right began to propose abandoning that tradition, because it led to the integration of children of Algerians into French nationality.

The Right Radicalized

In the municipal elections of March 1983 the left suffered heavy losses. These elections marked the emergence of the National Front on the French political scene; the European elections held in 1984 confirmed this trend, with 11 percent of the vote going to the National Front. For the new voters in Jean-Marie Le Pen's party, public safety and immigration were the main concerns, and the National Front made ridding France of its non-European immigrants a primary focus of its struggle.[8] A debate over national identity was initiated by the Club de l'Horloge[9] and spread rapidly. Because the belief in the link between national identity and nationality law was deeply entrenched, the debate came to bear quite naturally upon nationality legislation and in particular upon the situation of children of Algerian immigrants, a paradoxical and legally complex situation.

On the right, a book published in 1984 by Alain Griotteray (UDP deputy and regular contributor to *Figaro Magazine*) launched the debate. In *Les immigrés: le choc*,[10] Griotteray questioned whether it was possible to assimilate immigrants from a culture that was "too different," that of Islam, and whether Muslim immigrants even wanted to assimilate. He rejected a multiracial France and wanted to see the Code revised in such a way that nationality would henceforth be "chosen" and not "imposed." He invoked Ernest Renan's concept of the nation as a choice on the part of its members, and his notion that a "desire clearly expressed for a common life" must be a foundation for acquiring French nationality. And Griotteray proposed to replace jus soli, which attributed nationality automatically to children born in France to foreign parents, with a voluntary act that would take on legal value only on condition of "good integration."

In the spring of 1985 a radical revision of the Nationality Code—not far removed from the National Front's approach[11]—was thus included in the common platform that RPR and UDF put forward in view of the legislative elections: "Nationality will have to be requested and accepted: its acquisition cannot result from purely automatic mechanisms."[12] At the same time, François Mitterrand put back on the table the issue of foreigners' voting rights in local elections.[13] In 1981 the demand for voting rights had been among the 110 proposals included in Mitterrand's program when he was the Socialist candidate in the presidential election. The announcement on 9 August 1981, by the current minister of external relations Claude Cheysson, that this provision would be implemented in the municipal elections of 1983 provoked hostile reactions on the right, while the left's reaction was lukewarm (with the exception of the Federation of Associations in Support of Immigrant Workers—FASTI). The strong hostility of public opinion and the unconstitutionality of the reform had forced the government to backtrack.[14] In April 1985 President Mitterrand let it be known that he remained in favor of voting rights for immigrants. However, fully aware that the measure could not be put through either politically or legally, he indicated that since public opinion was not ready to accept such a measure he would not propose it, even if the left won the legislative elections.

But it was the right that won the legislative elections of 10 March 1986, with 291 deputies out of a total of 577 in a proportional vote that allowed the National Front to make its entrance into the National Assembly, with 35 deputies. From the outset the government of the new center-right prime minister Jacques Chirac launched a modification of immigration law and a parallel reform of the Nationality Code that seemed unlikely to encounter any obstacles. Several bills were drafted and presented to Parliament. The RPR group's proposal[15] was radical: it entailed the suppression of jus soli, which had been part of French law since at least 1889, on the grounds that the military and demographic justifications for it had disappeared. The institution of a strict jus sanguinis would lead to attributing French nationality at birth only to the child of a French father or mother.

Children born in France to foreign parents would have to request naturalization; this would not only oblige them to take voluntary action but would also allow the state to proceed to a "selection" among them as it saw fit.

This radical project was profoundly transformed — and moderated — in three stages.[16] First, the administration decided to submit its own bill. The Bureau of Nationality, successor to the Bureau of Seals at the Ministry of Justice, had prepared itself for the takeover of power by the right. The majority of its staff wanted to recast the Code: this had not been modified since 1973, except for the laws of 17 July 1978 and 20 December 1983, which had eliminated the last remaining restrictions on the rights of naturalized citizens.[17] But this group of civil servants did not want to see the double jus soli challenged. First, this principle had been an unquestioned component of French nationality law since 1889, even under Vichy. Then "double" birth in France had become the easiest means of proving French nationality for the majority of French people when they had to supply a certificate of nationality. The birth of two generations on French soil was easily proved by two birth certificates. Abolishing the double jus soli would transform the administration of that proof into an often insurmountable ordeal.[18] Should the application of double jus soli be questioned only for births on Algerian territory, as Gaston Defferre had agreed four years earlier? But that proposal was rejected at once by the Ministry of Justice staff and by the interior minister Charles Pasqua, on the argument that it could "excessively complicate the process of proving French nationality for children whose parents [were] of non-Algerian origin as well as for the children of Harkis [Algerians who had fought on the French side in the Algerian war]."[19]

The Bureau of Nationality ultimately built its proposal around four goals: (1) abolish automatic acquisition of nationality by the children of foreigners born in France and require that children in that position who wanted to be French must manifest that desire; (2) reform the acquisition of nationality through marriage by replacing the system of declaration — viewed as facilitating fraud[20] — with the more tightly controlled regime of naturalization; (3) eliminate the attribution of French nationality to children born in France to a parent from one of France's former colonies, to purge legislation of anything that might contravene the policy of restricting "African" immigration, and (4) eliminate the possibility that parents could declare their minor children French, a move that had protected the parents of those children against expulsion.[21]

The administration proposed to add to these arrangements an oath that would be required of all foreigners becoming French, and a whole series of regulations forbidding access to French nationality for people who had been sentenced to prison for more than six months. These last two points were very controversial:

the oath of allegiance is not part of the French tradition, and prison sentences could prevent people born in France from ever acquiring citizenship simply because of some youthful infraction.

The bill went to the Council of State on 7 October 1986; a month later the Council issued a negative opinion on its most important points. In particular, it refused to require that a young person born in France to foreign parents manifest a desire to have French nationality: "The Council of State has not found any reason to modify a system that has been in force for nearly a century and that has not demonstrated disadvantages in practice."[22] This opinion, widely publicized in the press,[23] led the administration to correct its proposal: the requirement of an oath was eliminated; and while the procedure of naturalization for acquiring citizenship through marriage was maintained, a limit was set: if the authorities did not issue a decision within eighteen months, naturalization would be acquired automatically.

The bill submitted on 12 November 1986 by Chirac's government thus maintained the attribution of French nationality to children born in France to a parent born in France (double jus soli). But it eliminated acquisition of nationality by marriage upon simple declaration, requiring that the spouse of a French person go through the naturalization process. Most importantly, it required that young people born in France to foreign parents manifest their desire to become French between the ages of sixteen and twenty-three.[24] In this form, as Rogers Brubaker points out, "the bill satisfied no one." For those who rejected the integration of some 400,000 children of Algerians into French nationality, what should have been abolished was article 23 of the Code; but the bill did not touch that article, offering only symbolic modifications.[25] On the left, in contrast, the proposal was criticized for restricting access to nationality, for calling into question the droit du sol, and for tampering in this way with a republican tradition according to which, since 1889, a child born in France to foreign parents became French at the age of majority.

The debate was starting up when the administration suffered a major defeat over a university reform bill that had been presented in June 1986 by Alain Devaquet, minister in charge of research and higher education. On 17 November and 4 December 1986, 200,000 and then nearly 500,000 students demonstrated in the streets against the "Devaquet project," whose goal was to institute a selection process for university entrance. In the early morning of 5 December, Malik Oussekine, a young student of Algerian origin, died after being struck by police officers who were breaking up the demonstration. The strength of the student movement, the emotion stirred up by Oussekine's funeral, which drew 200,000 students on 10 December, and the divisions within his own administration, forced Chirac to announce Devaquet's resignation on 8 December and to withdraw the higher education reform bill. Immediately afterward, Chirac's ministers discussed the proposal for reforming the Nationality Code. In the Council of Ministers where the text had been adopted, François Mitterrand had already expressed his opposition. The League for the Rights of Man had started a campaign against the reform, and the association SOS Racisme had launched its own mobilization.[26] Finally, in the wake of Malik Oussekine's death, the student movement appropriated the criticisms of the proposal to reform the Nationality Code. Albin Chalandon, who as justice minister had directed the preparation of the bill, informed Chirac at this point that he would not present it to Parliament, considering that it would be inopportune and unwise to persist. He saw the bill as primarily symbolic, since the reforms it would bring to nationality law were no longer fundamental; it thus risked provoking an unnecessary explosion.[27] Chirac decided in favor of Chalandon, and announced the abandonment of the project on 15 January 1987.

A Commission of "Sages"

A few months later the administration asked a commission of "sages," headed by Marceau Long, vice-president of the Council of State, to study several possible approaches to reforming the Nationality Code. The commission was made up of four law professors (Berthold Goldman, Pierre Catala, Yvon Loussouarn, Jean Rivero), three top civil servants (Marceau Long, Pierre-Patrick Kaltenbach, and Jean-Jacques de Bresson), three historians (Pierre Chaunu, Hélène Carrère d'Encausse, and Emmanuel Le Roy Ladurie), two sociologists (Alain Touraine and Dominique Schnapper), two doctors (Salem Kacet and Léon Boutbien), one lawyer (Jean-Marc Varaut), and one filmmaker (Henri Verneuil). It was set up on 22 June 1987, and on 7 January 1988 it submitted a report titled "Être Français aujourd'hui et demain." Meanwhile it had transformed — to borrow Miriam Feldblum's expression — "an untenable revision into an admirable reform."[28] At Henri Verneuil's suggestion the commission had organized fifty public hearings between 16 September and 21 October 1987, most of them televised live. Through the wide range of opinions expressed,[29] a broad public was introduced to nationality law, became aware of the complexity of immigration issues, and came to realize the extent to which one's relation to France could have an affective component. A consensus gradually developed, symbolized on the one hand by Pierre Chaunu's "conversion" to the idea that nationality could be acquired voluntarily but easily, for young people born in France to foreign parents, whereas a few months earlier he had been in favor of a jury and a probationary period for "people who belong to a fundamentally different cultural system."[30] On the other hand, Alain Touraine came to support the idea of integration, whereas he had previously appeared as an advocate of the right to difference.[31]

The commission proposed that young people born in France to foreign parents should manifest their desire to be French instead of having French nationality attributed to them automatically upon their majority. In this it was conforming to the charge conveyed in a letter from the justice minister Albin Chalandon to Marceau Long on 19 June 1987. Chalandon expressed his wish that a declaration be instituted "whereby the foreigner [born in France] would clearly manifest his will to acquire French nationality."[32] But the commission decided to propose a very liberal approach to application. Under the previous legislation, young people born in France to foreign parents were French upon reaching the age of majority (eighteen), but had to prove that they had resided in France for the five years preceding their eighteenth birthday. Anyone who had left France for a year, at fifteen for example, was not French. The commission still required five years' residency, but under its proposal the request could be made between the ages of sixteen and twenty-one, which helped soften the condition. There was no more question of taking an oath, or of being excluded from French nationality for minor legal condemnations. In addition, the declaration could be made with a minimum of formality at a city hall, a police station, or a small claims court. The point was to allow people to exercise free choice, not to prevent them from becoming French.

Unlike Chalandon's bill, Long's report no longer proposed to require a spouse of a French national to go through the naturalization process if he or she wished to become French; the system of declaration was maintained, while the minimum length of marriage required before the declaration could be made was extended from six months to one year.[33] The report suggested many other modifications in the Nationality Code, for example eliminating the possibility that parents could declare their minor children French without the expression of the children's intention, and eliminating the attribution of French nationality at birth to children born in France to parents who had come from a former French colony.

The report was well received — on the right unsurprisingly, but also on the left, where people felt relief at having escaped something worse. The press saluted the performance: Robert Solé noted in *Le Monde* that "in the future, legislators will be unable to ignore this key document."[34] In *Libération* Jean Quatremer paid homage to "a radically liberal reform of the current code."[35] On the extreme right, Jean-Marie Le Pen manifested his hostility to a "very negative" report.[36] On the left, the chief opposition was from SOS Racisme. That association was not seduced by Marceau Long's declaration that it would be possible "to become

French more easily,"[37] since according to its president Harlem Désir, certain young people would not have to do anything to become French, while others would have to take steps to "validate their rights."[38] SOS Racisme thus advocated an "integral" droit du sol: every child born in France would automatically be French.

Should One Have to Manifest Intent?

A few months before the presidential election of 1988 Jacques Chirac's administration chose not to put the Long commission's proposals on Parliament's agenda. François Mitterrand froze all reform projects after his reelection. The debate continued nevertheless. From 1989, helped by Jean-Jacques de Bresson, a member of the Nationality Commission, Pierre Mazeaud "translated" the Long commission's proposals into a bill.[39] In September 1991 Valéry Giscard d'Estaing attempted to radicalize the debate on the right. In an article in *Figaro Magazine* he pointed out the risks of foreign invasion and proposed to eliminate all provisions of the Code that allowed nationality to be attributed by virtue of birth in France (jus soli); his new version would allow transmission of French nationality solely on the basis of parentage (jus sanguinis), following the German model. But this approach, resembling the one advocated by the Front National, was no longer convincing.[40] In 1993, when the right returned to power, Pierre Mazeaud got the new prime minister, Édouard Balladur, to put the Long commission's proposals before the National Assembly.[41] The president of the Assembly's Commission on Laws sought to make only a symbolic modification: nationality legislation was reintegrated into the Civil Code, from which it had been removed in 1927 in favor of an "autonomous" Nationality Code.[42] Parliament adopted Marceau Long's bill and its principal provision: a young person born in France to foreign parents would have to manifest his or her desire to become French between the ages of sixteen and twenty-one, rather than acquiring nationality automatically at the age of majority. Under pressure from the right wing of its majority, led by Philippe de Villiers, Parliament nevertheless toughened the original text. Concerning the acquisition of nationality by marriage, the law that was adopted imposed a waiting period of two years instead of six months for the spouse of a French person who sought to become French by declaration.[43]

Finally, to address a particularly vexing situation, a child born in France to a parent born in Algeria before 1962 would be French at birth — through the effect of the double jus soli — only if the parent could prove that he or she had resided in France for at least five years.[44] The new provision was adopted in the context of new immigration laws: the consensus had unraveled. The left espoused the criticisms leveled earlier by SOS Racisme. Speaking in the name of the Socialist party, Michel Rocard deemed the reform "a bad law, troubling in its motivations, unjust in its intentions, and dangerous in its provisions." SOS Racisme argued that "by maintaining the voluntary act only for children born in France to foreign parents, the current code ratifies an artificial and unacceptable discrimination."[45]

For the left, the meaning of the reform, from the standpoint of the history of nationality law, had been clearly identified by Professor Paul Lagarde when he testified in 1987 before the Nationality Commission: "The legislation [is taking] into consideration the intensity of the bonds that link an individual to the population. If these bonds are very strong, then nationality will be attributed to the individual without anyone asking his opinion. Individual desire will play no role. In contrast, if the bonds are real but not sufficiently strong, then there can be an appeal to the positive desire of the interested party to strengthen those bonds which, on their own, would not have been sufficient."[46]

Since 1889 being born in France and residing there upon reaching the age of majority had sufficed as evidence that one was French. With the law of 1993 these conditions were no longer deemed adequate, and a manifestation of desire was demanded as supplementary proof of belonging. More was being asked, in 1993, of the son of a Moroccan, a Portuguese, or a Turk than had been asked of the son of an Italian, a Pole, or a stateless person before or after the Second World War; France was thus breaking with a deeply rooted egalitarian practice of recognition.[47]

The arguments focusing on the non-European origin of children of immigrants, or the ineffectiveness of the traditional instruments for republican assimilation—school and the army—were highly debatable, to say the least. Acculturation continued to take place, even if its forms had evolved, as Marceau Long recalled in the conclusion to the report of the High Council on Integration in 1997:

School remains—it is more than ever—the soul of this melting-pot. Children start school earlier and earlier, and stay in school longer and longer. . . . The army—and especially military service—are no longer at the heart of the melting pot, as they were for such a long time, very effectively. Work no longer holds the same place, either: access to employment is difficult; the condition of a salaried worker may be precarious; the world of workers, unions and their activists, no longer has the same influence. . . . But, in the face of these declining factors, the last few decades have confirmed the prodigious effects of voluntary associations and of the media, which were only modest factors in integration fifty years ago . . . they play an essential role in conviviality, knowledge of oral expression in French, initiation to knowledge of our country and to the various forms of social, cultural, professional, and sporting activities . . . they are pillars of our melting pot.[48]

The opposition to the new law also rallied the young Algerians whom it concerned more symbolically than practically. A few years earlier these young people could proclaim their refusal to be French "in spite of themselves"; by 1997 the situation had changed, in an evolution perceptively analyzed by Abdelmalek Sayad:

> The beneficiaries of [French] nationality that has been acquired without being requested in advance make the most of it, and no circumstantial protests (which may be perfectly sincere, moreover) can convince of the contrary. Those around them, who would not have accepted the act of naturalization according to the ordinary procedure, turn out to be relieved, after the fact, that French nationality ("French papers," as one says) has come on its own, like a collectively-imposed constraint: it is the common lot of all and not the result of an individual and voluntary act through which some people would be singled out and separated from the others. . . . Despite the protests of all sorts that it is good form to produce, despite the feeling of guilt or simple unease that continues to haunt naturalized citizens, naturalization that is said to be "forced" ends up giving rise to a satisfaction that, for a whole series of reasons, seeks to remain secret, and sometimes resigned. No further proof of this changed attitude is needed beyond the desire more and more frequently expressed by all those families that are "divided" with respect to nationality: they want to reestablish their unity and thus acquire a relative homogeneity, even at the price, if necessary (and it is necessary), of naturalization.[49]

The Quest for a New Synthesis

During the electoral campaigns of 1995 and 1997 the left expressed its desire to reestablish the earlier situation. After his victory in the legislative elections of June 1997, Prime Minister Lionel Jospin asked the author of this book to prepare a report on the "conditions of application of the principle of *droit du sol* for the attribution of French nationality."[50] The goal of the project was limited to one specific point in the nationality legislation: the status of children born in France to foreign parents.

The ministers in the "plural left" administration who were affected by this proposal wanted to break with the previous legislation and return to jus soli; the right rejected any modification of the law; legal experts on all sides were reserved in their views on repeated modifications of the nationality law. The report thus sought a synthesis: in July 1997 a first evaluation of the law of 1993 was possible.

The new procedure for declaration between the ages of sixteen and twenty-one simplified the legal situation of children born in France to two foreign parents not born in France. In the 1980s, owing to the modifications made in the legislation since 1889, the situation of such children had become complex, to say the least. Before the age of sixteen, such a child:

— would have been French at birth if he or she had been born to a parent born in Algeria or on the territory of a former French colony — in this case French nationality could not be repudiated;

— could have been declared French from birth by his or her parents without knowing it, or without having been asked for an opinion and without the possibility of repudiation;

— could have become French by the naturalization decree of his or her parents.

A child who had not become French by the age of sixteen faced several choices, about which he or she was not always informed:

— between the ages of sixteen and eighteen, he or she could request French nationality with parental authorization;

— between the ages of seventeen and a half and eighteen — thus in the short six-month period preceding the age of majority — he or she could decline French nationality;

— at eighteen, if the child had taken no action, he or she became French.

In the first two of these last three cases, a minor child born in France to foreign parents could have acted under familial pressure or on the contrary could have let the opportunity to decline French nationality go by because he or she had not been informed about it. In the third case, the child had to bring proof of five years of continuous residence before the age of eighteen, something that was not always easy to do.

The procedure for manifesting the will to become French thus simplified things, and fears that it would be boycotted by young people — fears often expressed when the procedure was adopted in 1993 — turned out to be groundless, for the majority of young people concerned chose to request French nationality. The declarative system that was substituted for automatic access at the age of majority nevertheless had some gaps.

Certain young people had trouble accessing the procedure when they wanted to, because they confronted various obstacles. First, they might experience parental pressure: in some families sons were "authorized" to manifest their will while daughters were not. Then—and this was the most problematic situation— a young person who wanted to manifest his or her will might find it hard to prove *continuous* residence in the five years that preceded the date of manifestation.[51]

After leaving the school system at sixteen, young people could find themselves unemployed and unable to prove any connection with an institution. Lack of proof of continuous residence was the primary reason for refusing nationality (42 percent in 1996). In addition, the small claims courts, for example, which were responsible for registering declarations, implemented different "policies." The rejection rate at the national level had been stable for two years, at 2.6 percent. Yet very significant inequalities existed from region to region, with no coherent explanation. The rejection rate was 10 percent or higher in 1996 in seven departments: Morbihan (41.2 percent), Gers (24.3 percent), Alpes-de-Haute-Provence (20 percent), Dordogne (17.5 percent), Meurthe-et-Moselle (10.9 percent), Lot (10.4 percent), and Orne (10 percent); three regions had a rejection rate between 5 and 7 percent: Basse-Normandie (7 percent), Lorraine (5.3 percent), and Bretagne (6 percent). In reaction, a veritable rating system for the small claims courts emerged, with some courts reputed to be liberal and others restrictive.

The most serious issue was probably that some of the young people who did not participate in the procedure did not know they would not be French, because they believed they already were. A study carried out in Alsace[52] attests to this: certain young people born in France felt themselves to be French and, not having been well informed about their situation as foreigners, might unwittingly let slip the deadline coinciding with their twenty-first birthday.[53] In fact, information was disseminated unevenly, and this may explain the large variations in the rates at which the desire to be French was manifested within a single region (Alsace: 68 percent in Mulhouse as opposed to 42 percent in Strasbourg); unequal access to information probably penalized the most disadvantaged youth. There was thus a risk that in every cohort of young people, 10 to 15 percent would not be French at the end of the window of opportunity allowed them, not by choice but because they were ignorant of their real status or because of the difficulties inherent in the procedure. In the old legislation, which had become so muddled, a child could become French without knowing it or desiring it; with the law of 1993, a child could remain a foreigner without wanting to or without knowing that this was his or her status.

The legislation adopted in 1998 sought to bring about a synthesis between the principle of equality of access to French nationality (instituted by the law of 1889) and the requirement of autonomy of will (reinforced in 1993). The principle of equality was reaffirmed, because the law provided that at the age of eighteen, any child born in France to a foreign parent was automatically French if he or she still lived in France and had lived there during adolescence. The five-year residency period, which was still required, could be discontinuous between the ages of eleven and eighteen. The law thus allowed young people to prove residency simply by producing school certificates.

But the young person's autonomy of will was also better respected. The power of parents to declare their minor child French without the child's approval was not reestablished, despite the proposal made by the National Assembly's reviewer for the bill, Louis Mermaz, and supported by a large minority within the Socialist group.[54] In the six months that precede their eighteenth birthday and especially during the year that follows — thus after reaching the age of majority — adolescents can declare that they wish to remain foreign and decline the quality of being French. Finally, from thirteen to eighteen they can anticipate the state's recognition of their quality of being French and manifest their own will to be French (with parental authorization required between the ages of thirteen and sixteen).[55]

After fifteen years of vigorous debates and two changes in legislation, the logic adopted in 1889 presupposing the progressive integration of the children and grandchildren of immigrants seems no longer to be in question today.

Conclusion to Parts One and Two

➤ At the end of this chronological analysis of the multiple changes that have come about since 1789, we can distinguish three major stages in the development of French nationality. Under the Revolution the definition of a French national was made explicit for the first time, but it was embedded in the definition of a citizen. The first turning point was reached with the Civil Code in 1803. Nationality took on autonomy: it was defined independently of citizenship and became a personal right. It was transmitted through filiation — jus sanguinis — just like the family name. It was no longer lost through a transfer of domicile outside the country, but only by a voluntary act on the part of a French person who wanted to take on a foreign nationality.

At the end of the nineteenth century, when France had become a country of immigration, the sociological approach was added to — or even substituted for — the familial approach to nationality. This was the second stage in the development of French nationality, with the return of jus soli, but a jus soli henceforth based on socialization rather than allegiance. From this point on, just like a child born to a French national, a child born in France to a foreign parent who had been born in France was irrevocably French from birth: this was the double jus soli. As for the child whose foreign parents had not been not born in France, he or she became French upon reaching the age of majority, when socialization — education — had done its work. After the First World War, under the pressure of depopulation, French nationality was used as an instrument of demographic policy. In the third stage of its development, naturalization was thus opened on a massive scale to new immigrants.

Alongside this integration of children of immigrants into French nationality and the opening to the immigrants themselves, the racist option began to surface in the debates over nationality. Proponents of this option — which had been continuously present since the 1920s — sought to base selection for entry into French nationality on origin: national, ethnic, religious, or racial. The racist option was manifested, for example, in the anti-Algerian and even anti-Muslim crisis of the late 1980s, but its only real triumph came during the Vichy regime, in its anti-Semitic form.

Still, it is important not to confuse racialism and racism. As Hervé Le Bras emphasizes,[1] most of the experts who have written about French nationality policy or participated in its development, before or after the Second World War, attributed differences in value to foreigners depending on their origin. The opinion of specialists rubbed off on nonspecialists, and politicians who thought differently were rare. But while everyone reasoned in terms of preference according to origin, French thinking at the time cannot be reduced to this approach. As Jean Leca notes, "not every hierarchist is exclusionary, or even in favor of discriminatory measures."[2] Racialists considered that origin should be one of the criteria for selection among candidates for naturalization, along with population goals, respect for equality, age, and the candidate's familial or professional situation. Racists, for their part, placed origin above all the other criteria and made it the principle for selecting — or rather for eliminating — candidates for entry into French nationality.

Since the 1920s the racist option has always been present, promoted by experts, politicians, and even certain ministers or institutions responsible for nationality policy. But in each of its stages, nationality *policy* has been the object and the product of competition among several options. If the racist option triumphed under Vichy (and only then), it was because it dominated in the government, and because the only surviving alternative was restrictionist individualism. In other periods it came up against a republican, egalitarian conception embodied in the 1930s by Charles Lambert and André Honnorat, in 1943 by Teitgen — a conception that won out every time. In the analysis of a public policy, acts — that is, concrete propositions and their anticipated effects — are often more important than what is said or written.

Even if Valéry Giscard d'Estaing's public discourse was in appearance less "racist" than the "racialist" discourse of the 1930s, when he advocated the complete elimination of jus soli in 1991 he was going further to block the children of Algerian, or Muslim, immigrants from access to French nationality than any republican government had ever sought to do.

Thus despite these crises the law of 1889, which based access to French nationality for children of immigrants on the principle of sociological reality and not, as the Constitutional Council wrongly asserted, on a response to contemporary concerns about conscription,[3] has never been called into question. Not in 1927, or in 1945, or in 1973, or in 1993, not even under Vichy, when the minister of justice put forward "logic as the traditional spirit of our legislation" in resisting a challenge to the law of 1889.

Does the persistence of jus soli over more than a century reflect a particular identity that would characterize not only French nationality law but also the French nation itself, one that would differentiate France from a closed, ethnic Germany based on jus sanguinis? The study of German nationality law will allow us to verify or invalidate this hypothesis. This will be the first step in a reexamination from different perspectives — comparative and practical — of the history of nationality whose major stages we have just retraced.

PART THREE 🖋

Nationality in Comparison

and in Practice

Jus Soli versus Jus Sanguinis:

The False Opposition between

French and German Law

Comparative history, to be an independent field of scholarly endeavor, would have to compare historical processes, *i.e. change over time, developments over time, with . . . other processes . . .*

Yet, if we aim at discoveries, comparison of the obviously similar or dissimilar will be less fruitful than that of homologies . . . Webster explains "homologous" as having the same relative position. Therefore the word homology in the terminology of the comparative historian will connote phenomena that, regardless of their appearing heterogeneous and incomparable at first sight, nevertheless can be juxtaposed. They may fulfill identical functions in the historical process or in different countries or civilizations or different stages of development or merely in the frame of different institutional set ups. —FRITZ REDLICH[1]

May we deduce from the presence of jus soli in French law—for more than a century, through and beyond periods of crisis—that it reflects an open conception of the nation? The opposition between jus soli and jus sanguinis seems self-evident. France would be the model of the civic nation open to the integration of immigrants and their children, since it reintroduced jus soli into its legislation in 1889 and retained it thereafter; Germany would be the seat of an ethnic nation dominated, ever since 1842 when Prussia adopted it, by jus sanguinis.

Yet the equation jus sanguinis = ethnic conception = Germany, as opposed to jus soli = non-ethnic conception = France, does not hold up to an examination of the comparative history of German and French—and beyond these, European—nationality law.

If we plunge into the history of German law at the time it was being developed in Prussia, between 1830 and 1842, far from finding traces of a Prussian or Germanic conception of the nation, we discover a perhaps surprising French influence instead.

French Influence on Prussian Law (1830–1842)

When Prussia issued an edict in 1842 establishing legislation that defined what it meant to be a subject, it was hardly the first of the thirty-nine German states to do so:[2] Austria had already taken that step in 1811, for example, and Bavaria in 1818.[3] But it was Prussia that would inspire the legislation adopted for all of Germany in 1871. Thus it is important to understand how Prussia's legislation came about.[4]

Until the early nineteenth century the need for such legislation had not been felt in Prussia. Belonging to a commune sufficed. Peasants were bound to the lands of their lords: hereditary subjection to landowners (*Erbuntertänigkeit*) determined where they had to live. The Frederick Code, the *Allgemeines Landrecht* (ALR), in force in Prussia at the end of the eighteenth century, contained terms such as "citizen," "resident," "resident of the country," and "resident of the state," without any coherent correspondence among these notions.[5] The ALR allowed provincial laws to determine how people could acquire the quality of subject (*Angehörigkeit*); according to the Prussian minister of foreign affairs, the sources of Prussian legislation in this area were at once the Frederick Code, jurisprudence, and the collection of ordinary laws.[6]

For anyone not born Prussian, jus domicili constituted de facto "the principal criterion for acquisition of the quality of subject."[7] Applied in blunt fashion, this "domiciliary law" could create problems. In 1817, for example, the French embassy in Berlin informed the Prussian government about the situation of certain French nationals who had been enlisted in the army some months before settling in Prussia to do business there. In response, on 13 June 1818 the Prussian minister of foreign affairs spelled out the criteria of access to the quality of Prussian subject: "Foreigners . . . become *Prussian Subjects* effectively . . . when they manifest the intention to choose their *fixed domicile* in the States of H.M. the King of Prussia. This intention may be *manifested explicitly or tacitly*. The laws of the Country presuppose [this intention] in all Foreigners, who in the Prussian States, take on an employment that requires their continuous presence; or devote themselves to a branch of trade or industry that requires a habitual sojourn; or, finally, acquire what belongs to a regulated household or domestic economy."[8]

The reforms undertaken between 1807 and 1820 by Stein's and Hardenberg's administrations, in reaction to the wars and the Napoleonic victories, brought about a gradual change in the situation. The edict of 9 October 1807[9] abolished serfdom; on 7 September 1811[10] the obligation of corporations (*Zunftszwang*) was lifted.[11] These reforms compensated and encouraged the mobilization of soldiers; they reinforced love of the fatherland, national cohesion, and attachment to state power.[12] But by liberating peasants from obligatory labor on the lord's farms and fields, and by abolishing the artisan-worker's obligation to belong to a corporation, the reforms left these groups free to move about and to live anywhere in Prussia: nothing prevented anyone from settling in some other commune.[13] The mobility facilitated in this way attracted a population from the Prussian countryside that was often poor to the fledgling industrial zones, but it also drew in more and more people from the thirty-eight other German states (members of the Germanic Confederation). From 1823 to 1840 immigration into Prussia produced a demographic surge of 700,000 people.[14] Certain communes refused to let these newcomers settle on their territories[15] or even expelled them on the grounds that they could become a public charge. When these measures affected Prussian subjects, they were illegal. The state thus decided to rule on three intimately related questions: Prussians' freedom of settlement, the obligation to care for the poor, and the definition of a "Prussian subject," thus making it possible to control immigration from the other German states.

In a first phase, on 20 April 1830, the king of Prussia charged his minister of the interior, von Schuckmann, to take measures against "undesirable" immigrants until a new law on the Prussian fatherland ("*Preussische Heimatgesetz-gebung*") was passed. But Johann Peter Ancillon, the minister of foreign affairs, very quickly persuaded his colleagues that priority should be given not to the question of foreigners but rather to legislation on "the acquisition and removal of the relation of subjection," conceived in a way that would be compatible with the laws of the other German states. On 5 November 1832 the king finally gave Ancillon responsibility for preparing a bill on Prussian nationality.[16]

The German states, seeking to define the quality of subject with precision, had done this previously in two distinct ways:

—Unilaterally and directly, by establishing internal rules of law.
—Contractually, through international treaties that determined which people from each German state residing illegally on the territory of another German state should be repatriated,[17] or by rendering an economically independent person immune to expulsion[18] after a certain length of residence (often ten years) or after marriage to a citizen; these treaties naturalized such persons de facto.

During the 1820s the majority of the German states had not yet completed internal legislation but had signed treaties defining a form of de facto citizenship based on length of residence.[19] Often the combination of the two approaches made the legal situation particularly complex. For in certain cases (Austria, Brunswick, Hamburg, the Danish territories, Hanover, Lippe, and Hesse Darmstadt) the treaties did not contradict the internal law that provided for automatic acquisition of citizenship after a period of residence not exceeding ten years.[20] But in other cases, the adoption of different, stricter rules for explicit naturalization created a discrepancy between the internal law and the treaties. This is what happened with Prussia.

It was not until 31 December 1842 that the law on Prussian nationality was promulgated.[21] In the meanwhile a battle raged over a ten-year period among the concerned ministers and then among the various factions within the Council of State.[22] The question was not how to define a native Prussian. That definition was directly inspired by the French and Austrian codes — "the present work has taken into account the Austrian Civil Code and the French Civil Code in a comparative fashion," Ancillon wrote[23] — and there was unanimous agreement on the principle of paternal filiation: one was Prussian if one's father was Prussian. The controversy bore rather on how Prussian nationality could be acquired by someone who did not have it from birth. Those who favored an explicit decision by the public authorities (the procedure called naturalization in France) were in conflict with those who defended the criterion of domicile: "automatic" access to nationality after ten years' residency (a provision included in the Austrian Civil Code of 1811).

Rejecting the principle of mechanical acquisition of Prussian nationality through entry to and prolonged residency in the territory,[24] the minister of foreign affairs, Ancillon, wanted to establish clear and incontestable signs of recognition that would make it possible to determine easily who could be defined as a foreigner and be expelled,[25] and who could be defined as a subject and be called up for military service or recruited by a public agency.[26] That was why he proposed a naturalization system grounded in respect for four conditions: (1) freedom from bonds of allegiance toward another state; (2) a good reputation; (3) the ability to work; (4) a fixed domicile as a member of a commune.[27]

The minister of justice, Baron Karl von Kamptz, remained partial to the traditional system, which provided automatic access to Prussian nationality after a certain period of residency. As he saw it, by automatically eliminating an emigrant's status as subject and by automatically granting such a status to an immigrant, a number of useless formalities could be avoided without necessarily sacrificing state security, since it would always remain possible to prevent unwanted immigration by strict border controls.[28]

At the end of 1834 two of the four ministers involved remained radically opposed to their colleague at Foreign Affairs: von Kamptz and also von Rochow, minister of the interior and the police, who joined his colleague at justice[29] in proposing to maintain a prolonged stay in the country as the criterion for access to the quality of Prussian subject.[30] Ancillon, convinced of the impossibility of getting his proposed law passed within the collective apparatus of the Ministry of State,[31] then tried to bring opinions closer together by setting up a nine-member commission that included representatives from each of the ministries involved, along with a member of the commission charged with reviewing legislation.

The decisive vote ultimately bore on the question: "whether by merely staying in the country — even without explicit authorization from the government — the right of quality of Prussian subject can be acquired or not?"[32] Ancillon's position prevailed, but only by a five-to-four vote.[33] It was thus by a single voice that the "French model," requiring an explicit act of naturalization to become Prussian, was chosen over the alternative "Austrian model" of automatic acquisition of nationality by virtue of residency.[34]

But the matter did not rest there. It took three more years for the Council of State[35] to examine the project, between 4 February and 8 July 1841. The Council's reviewer, von und zu Mühlen, spoke against the bill because it granted the quality of subject only by an explicit decision, and not through domicile, duration of sojourn, or property ownership; it was thus not compatible either with pending bills on entry to the country and on the poor, or with the existing legislation on the obligation of military service or place of jurisdiction, which made domicile the determining criterion.

Trying to convince his colleagues on the Council of State, Mühlen chose to rely, as Ancillon had done in 1833, on Austrian and French law, but with an entirely different interpretation. He first cited the provision of the Austrian code that made it possible to acquire Austrian nationality by residing in the country for ten years.[36] That Austria had not abandoned the principle of domicile was important from the standpoint of unifying German legislation. Then Mühlen looked to French law and showed how, in their effort to draw on it, the authors of the proposed law had misunderstood it.[37] He cited *in extenso*, and in French, articles 8 and 17 of France's Civil Code: "The most important of the articles in question here is article 13 [on admission to residency]. In France, it has been settled for a long time that foreigners have to ask to establish residency in order to obtain full use of civil rights. There is thus indeed legislation that allows access to French nationality only by explicit agreement (naturalization), but one cannot be naturalized without having been admitted to residency by the government."[38]

However, admission to residency had not been included in the Prussian proposal. Any foreigner could settle freely in Prussia; by virtue of mutual agreements adopted by the German states among themselves, foreigners became exempt from expulsion after ten years' residency, but they did not become Prussian at that point (unless they requested naturalization). "Far from clearly distinguishing the inhabitants of the country from foreigners, the bill would instead help create a class of persons living in Prussia without having the status of inhabitant of the country."[39] Thus the risk was that a foreign population would settle permanently in Prussia with all the rights of Prussians but without being subject to the same obligations, especially military service. Mühlen believed that every foreigner who wanted to reside in France had to request admission to residency and that everyone admitted to residency had to request naturalization ten years after admission, but as we know this was not the case.[40] At all events, to avoid creating such a class of permanent and privileged foreign residents, Mühlen proposed to return to the principle of domicile, by virtue of which naturalization would be automatic.[41] But he did not convince his colleagues, who rejected his proposal to send the text back to the administration.[42] After ten years of legal vicissitudes the bill on Prussian nationality was definitively adopted on 27 April 1842, and the new law was promulgated on 31 December 1842.[43] From that point on, one was Prussian if born to a Prussian father, and a foreigner could become Prussian only through naturalization.

Neither Racism nor Nationalism: The Jurists Rule

At this stage of the analysis, two observations need to be made: France and Prussia undertook to codify their nationality laws according to very similar rules, and ethnicity was not a factor in the use of jus sanguinis to define Prussian or French persons.

In France jus sanguinis was imposed as a law of the nation understood as a family, in contrast to jus soli, a symbol of "feudal allegiance." In Prussia jus sanguinis, which originally included Poles and Jews, imported the legal technique of naturalization from France the better to exclude "undesirable" immigrants, most often non-Prussian Germans.[44] In the context of birthplace, the work "foreigner" was used to refer to someone from another German state.[45]

Far from reflecting a particular conception of the Prussian or German nation, the Prussian code was therefore developed in an effort to compare and harmonize legislations—the German word used by the reviewer was *Angleichung*—and it referred more to French than to Austrian law.[46] However, in the mid-nineteenth-century context, Prussian nationality law could have been written under the influence of the "historicist" legal school of thought; under the inspiration of its founder, Friedrich Karl von Savigny, this school tended to defend a specifically German legislation, a blend of classical Roman law, old laws from the Holy Roman Empire, and provincial and local customs.[47] The historicist school had in fact been created and developed in opposition to the French system of universalist or philosophical codification based on natural law.[48] Savigny was a member of the Council of State when the king of Prussia launched the process of developing legislation that would define a subject; in March 1942 he was named minister of justice and president of the commission for reviewing laws.[49] In a well-known treatise on Roman law, he observed that in the legal realm, "authors' opinions and court judgments offer us the most pronounced and abundant dissidence: Germans, French, English, and Americans all fight against one another." He added, however, that *"in the realm of nationality, there was a tendency toward rapprochement and reconciliation of which the science of law supplies us no other example. One might say that we have here a common good shared by all civilized nations and 'it is a matter of melding national contrasts in a community accepted by all.'"*[50]

The observation of convergence and the search for harmonization were customary among the legal scholars charged with developing nationality law, among other things; they tended to read and borrow from one another's work.

The Prussian example in fact shows—and this dimension is often forgotten or neglected—that nationality law is in the main a highly complex body of legislation most often crafted by specialized legal scholars, to whom a political or administrative leader subcontracts or delegates the task of drafting the text. This influence may be indirect, as when a politician uses a jurist to help him identify the techniques that would allow him to accomplish political goals. It can also become complete domination: we have seen how Tronchet imposed his own views as the French Civil Code was being drafted. In France all the reforms of nationality law that have come along since the Code have been prepared by jurists; magistrates of the judiciary order, from the Bureau of Seals to the Ministry of Justice, members of the Council of State (Camille Sée in 1887, 1896, and 1915), and law professors (Henry Lévy-Ullmann in 1927,[51] Jacques Maury in 1945). All these categories of jurists could also be brought together in specialized commissions (as in 1912, for preparation of the bill that led to the law of 1927, and also in 1971–73 and 1987–93).[52]

Many reviewers of nationality bills in Parliament had legal backgrounds and had worked as lawyers or law school professors: Dubost in 1889; Mallarmé, Lisbonne, and Lambert in 1927; Foyer and Mazeaud in 1973. These jurist-parliamentarians were equipped to establish the limits of what was "legally" feasible in conformity to the principles and the jurisprudence with which they were already acquainted or were becoming acquainted. They were also capable of translating into legal terms the "demands" that came from their assembly.

The domination of legal professionals over politicians, and the resulting perception of nationality as a specialized legislation independent of politics, was fundamental in the nineteenth century. From 1803 to 1880 the French Civil Code remained substantially unchanged, despite the succession of seven regimes (Consulate, Empire, Restoration, July Monarchy, Second Republic, Second Empire, Third Republic), geographical upheavals, and last but not least, pressures for change, as early as 1818. The legal historian Alan Watson has demonstrated, by studying and comparing Roman, Greek, Germanic, European, American (North and South), and African law, that political events have little influence over changes in the realm of civil law.[53] The same legal regulations could often operate, for example, in the worlds of Julius Caesar, the popes, the Middle Ages, Louis XIV, Bismarck, and the twentieth-century welfare state.[54]

Borrowings and Transfers

Borrowing from foreign provisions—as in the Prussian example—is another phenomenon that Alan Watson has observed on a broad scale. Watson has sometimes been criticized for exaggerating the degree of borrowing in the laws of nations; in response, he argues that he has not stressed borrowing enough, and that he himself is still astonished by the level that it has attained (he is similarly astonished by how much autonomy jurists have).[55] For legal scholars, borrowing represents a quasi-economic interest: a savings in time and intellectual energy. In addition, borrowing from legislation that has already proved itself elsewhere gives authority to a proposed legal novelty when this novelty must be justified; borrowing makes it possible to benefit from experience. Jurists are the artisans and technicians of these transfers; they can "certify" that they work well abroad and they can justify the historical legitimacy of imported rules. Borrowing can take many different forms: it can be partial, or it can involve an entire system of legislation. It can be carried out by analogy, by an extensive transfer of regulations that already exist on the internal level (but simply as annexes, or as part of local codes), or it can bear upon a foreign body of laws.

Like Prussian law, French law also borrowed during those two centuries, but most often to act at the borders of nationality law—to naturalize, denaturalize, or preclude the renunciation of nationality.

At the beginning of the Revolution, for example, to break with the royal prerogative of naturalization, the law of 1790 organized a system for automatic naturalization that was taken up again in the constitution of 1793. A foreigner resident in France—for five years, later just one—who acquired property or married a French woman became French automatically, whether he wanted to or not.

This jus domicili existed in Prussian law and in the legislation of many German states: the acquisition of the quality of being French by marriage to a French woman, established in 1790 and again in 1793, was a custom in Metz,[56] and also in Strasbourg.[57] However, the details of the mechanism for acquiring nationality seem to have been inspired by an edict applicable to Corsica issued by King Louis XV in June 1770 and inserted on page 125 of the second volume of the Corsican code. To "reestablish the island of Corsica in the flourishing state it formerly enjoyed, and of which its fortunate position and the fertility of its soil make it capable" and to reduce "the losses in inhabitants that it has experienced through the misfortunes that have devastated it," the king decided "to invite foreigners there and to favor their settlement." He thus declared "that the foreigners who take part in island life, either by marrying a Corsican girl, or by acquiring a house or property worth six thousand pounds, or by establishing residency there and practicing either agriculture or an active trade during six consecutive years, shall be deemed native Corsicans, reputed bourgeois and inhabitants of the place where they have settled and, so long as their said establishments last, shall be eligible to share in all the rights, privileges, and exemptions enjoyed by native Corsicans and Frenchmen, without any difference or exception."

On 6 April 1809, thus a few years after the adoption of the Civil Code and on the eve of a new war with Austria whose outcome appeared uncertain, Napoleon issued a decree ordering the return of all Frenchmen, even naturalized foreigners, who were serving a foreign power at war with France; his inspiration was a provision that had been adopted by England in 1807 with respect to all English sailors, even naturalized foreigners, serving in foreign navies.[58] In practical terms it was a matter of weakening the enemy's organization by depriving it of the French nationals who were serving in its army or administration.[59] In legal terms, however, the decree had a broader impact: it eliminated the freedom to change nationality instituted by the Civil Code, at least for anyone who resided in enemy territory.[60] Before long the senatus-consulte of 26 August 1811 suppressed that freedom everywhere. French nationals were henceforth forbidden to be naturalized in a foreign country without the emperor's consent.[61] In one stroke, as Claude Goasguen has shown, the perpetual allegiance of French nationals to France was instituted on the English model; it remained unchanged, in legal texts and in principle, until 1889.

France, in contrast, exported its own Civil Code throughout Europe insofar as nationality law was concerned. In mid-nineteenth-century Europe, when national leaders convoked their state jurists and instructed them, in sum, "Draw up a nationality code for me," the jurists did not hesitate to copy the French Civil Code.[62] Under its inspiration, the innovation of jus sanguinis became the law of modern nation-states,[63] the model gradually adopted by the various countries of continental Europe. The spread of jus sanguinis into most continental European nations was so pronounced that a great American jurist could write in 1911, in the *Columbia Law Review*: "Prior to the French Revolution the rule was almost universal in Europe, both in England and on the continent, that birth on the soil of a state made the person so born a subject (national) of that state. This was sometimes referred to as the common law of Europe. Sometimes it was referred to as a rule of public law. This rule of birth on the soil, the *jus soli*, was first seriously departed from in modern times in the Civil Code of France in 1804, which made the *jus sanguinis* the almost exclusive rule as to nationality at birth."[64] In turn Austria (1811), Belgium (1831), Spain (1837), Prussia (1842), Italy (1865), Russia (1864), the Netherlands (1888), Norway (1892), and Sweden (1894) adopted jus sanguinis as the basis for their legislation.[65] This was a period when jurists were maintaining relations among themselves on the international level, and during which comparative law was at its apogee.[66]

At the opposite pole, the "feudal" British tradition of jus soli was maintained and transplanted to the British colonies, in North America (the United States and Canada), Europe (Ireland), Africa (South Africa), and Oceania (Australia). This tradition continued to influence Portugal and Denmark until the northern European states decided to adopt a common nationality regime in the 1920s.[67]

This divergence between France and the United Kingdom, which created two types of legal regime, did not have any ethnic dimensions at the outset: for France it was a matter of simultaneously reinventing Roman tradition and breaking with the feudal tradition that the United Kingdom was maintaining, by bringing *jus familii* to the fore: the nation as opposed to the state.

Nationality Law Independent of the Concept of Nation

From nearly the same starting points, French and German nationality laws diverged as of 1889 — in France jus soli regained an important place, whereas in

Germany jus sanguinis persisted alone—until they converged once again in the German reform of 2000. How can this divergence lasting more than a century be explained? To answer that question is to follow Marc Bloch's suggestion that the comparative historian should take a "specially lively interest in the perception of differences . . . resulting from divergent developments from the same starting-point."[68]

In France the jus sanguinis inscribed in the Civil Code was soon challenged. As early as 1818 demands that children born in France to foreigners be subjected to French nationality—that is, to obligatory military service—were heard in the border regions. But owing to the prestige of the Civil Code, it was only when France became—or was clearly perceived as—a country of immigration, in 1889, that jus soli was restored to an important place in its nationality law.

In Germany, in contrast, jus sanguinis took root. Until 1871 the Prussian law of 1842 served less to define Prussians rigorously than to unify the nationality legislation of the various German states. All the more so in that in 1851 the treaty of Gotha allowed nationals from any German state to acquire the quality of subject in a different German state after five years' residency. That treaty—which was not always applied—helped open a path toward citizenship in a federal Germany. In 1866 the Germanic Confederation went one step further, by authorizing all citizens of each member state to move to any other member state and live there.[69] After the annexation of Alsace and Moselle in 1870, Germany's "little empire" was constituted, and in 1871 Prussian nationality law was extended to the entire territory, unchanged except for the elimination of the clause imposing restrictions on Jews. Each state retained its own nationality and the power to naturalize, but each adopted the slightly modified Prussian legislation.[70] The formal maintenance of the law of 1842 also made it possible, in the context of a "partial" unification of Germany, to maintain the treaty signed by Prussia with Austria after the revolution of 1848.

Could one not argue, however, that beginning in 1871, with the annexation of Alsace-Moselle, jus sanguinis took on an ethnic dimension? Not really, for to do so would mean confusing nationality law—a technique for attributing a state to an individual—with mechanisms of incorporation, mechanisms whereby a group or a collectivity is identified with the national community.

After his victory over France, Bismarck annexed Alsace, except for Belfort, and part of Lorraine. The idea was to weaken France's ability—France being the eternal enemy, in Bismarck's eyes—to "play" a major role in Europe in the future, an ability facilitated until then by Germany's division into several smaller powers. Bismarck could also use the "reattachment" of Alsace-Moselle to benefit the broader project of German unification, so that it would no longer look to the southern German states, Bavaria in particular, as if the Empire were simply annexing those states under Prussian tutelage.[71]

On the French side, the war of 1870, the transformation of northern France into a battlefield, the invasion, and finally the occupation would "maintain [and] codify a highly repulsive image" of Germany,[72] and would play a major role in the evolution of that image. Germany was no longer "that new race . . . formed of the mixture of those races" admired by the French historian Ernest Lavisse,[73] for whom Prussia, a "mosaic, patiently and intelligently composed . . . from all points in Germany and Europe dissolved in a single population," was a model of the melting pot in Europe.

The wrenching loss of Alsace-Moselle gave rise among the French to a feeling that Germany was not a normal nation like France, that it was instead a "racial" nation. In his exchange of letters with the German philosopher David Strauss, Ernest Renan observed that

> the nationalities are badly sorted out . . . Lovely French provinces are not part of France, and that is very advantageous, even for France. Slavic countries belong to Prussia. These anomalies serve civilization well. The reuniting of Alsace with France, for example, is among the phenomena that have most contributed to the propaganda of Germanism; it is through Alsace that Germany's ideas, methods, books usually pass to reach us. It is undeniable that, if one were to put the question to the Alsatian people, an immense majority would declare themselves in favor of remaining part of France. Is it worthy of Germany to attach to itself forcibly a rebellious, irritated province, one that has become irreconcilable, especially after the destruction of Strasbourg?"[74]
>
> People speak of French law, of German law. . . . Our politics is the politics of the rights of nations; yours is the politics of races; we believe that ours is better. The exaggerated division of humanity into races, beyond the fact that it is based on a scientific error, for very few countries possess a truly pure race, can only lead to wars of extermination, to zoological wars, if I may say so, analogous to those that the various species of rodents or carnivores wage against one another throughout their lives.[75]

But at the time no one in France related the "racial" concept of the nation denounced by Renan to jus sanguinis. Everyone still distinguished between nationality law (a means for attributing nationality to individuals) and the conception of the nation. Jus sanguinis was maintained in France when a debate over a reform of nationality law took place in 1872. In 1887 Camille Sée, the Council of State's reviewer for what would become the law of 1889, advocated its reinforcement in a form that would have been more radical than the one found in the Civil Code, even though Sée, a pure and fervent republican and Alsatian patriot, favored opening full French citizenship to all the French colonies in Africa, Asia, and Oceania, "to encourage the assimilation of the natives and the French," whereas the defenders of jus soli opposed this.[76]

And while Renan was invoking the right of nations to choose their destinies through the expression of a collective will ("A nation's existence is . . . a daily plebiscite, just as an individual's existence is a perpetual affirmation of life"),[77] the Senate's reviewer for the bill, Antonin Dubost (who was close to Renan),[78] was advocating for the provision of the law of 1889 that imposed French nationality on many foreigners who did not want it.

The complete opposition between the mechanism used to attribute nationality to a person and the one used to constitute the nation recalls what had already happened under the French Revolution. Between 1790 and 1795 nationality was attributed automatically to all foreigners residing in France, even against their will.[79] At the same time, the attribution of the quality of active citizen to a Frenchman presupposed the swearing of an oath on his part. There was thus, as Weiss says,[80] an antithesis between the attribution of the quality of being French to a foreigner — imposed without possibility of refusal — and the attribution of the quality of citizen to a French person: the latter in fact presupposed a formal manifestation of will. This conceptual distinction between the nation and nationality law, a total opposition that was taken for granted in the construction of both entities, thus meant that while Germany was perceived in France as an ethnic nation in 1872 and in the years that followed, no one attributed that characteristic to jus sanguinis.

The Identification of Jus Sanguinis with Racial Germany: Analysis of a Representation

Less than twenty years after the Franco-Prussian War, in 1889, under the impact of immigration, France reincorporated some elements of jus soli into its nationality law. In Germany emigration and colonization encouraged the maintenance of jus sanguinis, which allowed German subjects living abroad to transmit their nationality to their children and allowed the Prussian Empire to retain a connection with them. This emigration had grown markedly in the years following the constitution of the Empire. Although the number of foreign residents had nearly tripled between 1890 and 1910, from 430,000 to 1,260,000, the number of émigrés was considerably higher: 3.5 million Germans were living abroad. Almost as soon as it was unified, Germany was aware of becoming a country of emigration and colonization.[81] In addition, the Prussians, Bavarians, and Rhenans who lived abroad, far from the internal divisions that opposed them in Germany, were perceived—and perceived themselves—as Germans from a single country; in their compatriots' eyes, they represented the unity of a new country which, like Italy,[82] made a unifying symbol of its émigrés. The problem was that the Prussian law of 1842, incorporated into the law of the Empire, provided for the automatic loss of German nationality after ten years' residency abroad. From 1895 the Pangermanic League, supported by associations of Germans abroad, demanded reforms in the law to maintain ties to the millions of Germans who had emigrated during the nineteenth century. Interministry discussions began in 1898 and went on for fifteen years. In these discussions the partisans of an ethnic approach (the Pangermanic League and the Ministry of the Navy, with the support of Chancellor Bethmann Hollweg), who wanted German émigrés to be able to retain and transmit their German nationality unconditionally, were in effect opposed to those (the Ministry of Foreign Affairs and the Prussian ministries) who were willing to see some of those emigrants remain active in the defense of German interests abroad and keep their nationality, but only if they truly desired to do so and demonstrated real loyalty to the German Empire.[83]

The latter position was the one that triumphed. By virtue of the law of 22 July 1913, known as the Delbrück law, Germans living abroad no longer lost their nationality unless they were naturalized in their new country. Even then they could keep their German nationality, but only if they obtained explicit prior authorization from the German government, as provided in article 25, line 8, of the law of 1913. Authorization would be granted only to candidates who (if male) agreed to carry out their military service.

Needless to say, the Pangermanic League was not satisfied.[84] In concrete terms, the law of 1913 did not go nearly as far as a law adopted a year earlier in Italy. Italians living abroad remained Italian automatically if they acquired foreign nationality—Italian nationality could only be lost through a voluntary act.[85] A French jurist observed, moreover, that the earlier German legislation had been much more dangerous than the Delbrück law: "a German naturalized as French in principle retained his German nationality."[86] In addition, the ten years of residency abroad at the end of which Germans lost their nationality did not count if a German citizen was registered with a German consulate abroad, or if the stay abroad was interrupted by even a brief visit to Germany. In short, under the old legislation it had been easier for a German who became French to remain German if he wanted to than it was under the new law.[87]

However, once war broke out the adoption of that clause—the explicit right for Germans naturalized abroad to keep their German nationality—provoked very strong reactions in western countries, and contributed to the development of legislation on loss of nationality that was aimed in particular at naturalized persons of German origin.

At the outset, in 1913, reactions were fairly moderate. For example, France's ambassadors in Great Britain, Russia, and the United States were instructed by the French minister of foreign affairs to try — discreetly — to make the governments of those countries aware of the negative effects of the law. An excerpt from a speech given in the Reichstag by Baron Richthofen on 27 February 1912 was translated and distributed to the ambassadors.[88] But in Great Britain, the law of 1870 included a provision on the perpetual allegiance of English subjects naturalized abroad.[89] Russia too had "many subjects who had two nationalities."[90] It was in the United States that the Delbrück law provoked some reservations, as naturalized Americans had to give up any foreign allegiance for all time.[91] But after the onset of hostilities these reactions took on a new dimension.

In the United States, as early as July 1914 an important jurist considered that "the introduction of a quite novel provision, according to which Germans residing in foreign countries may keep their German nationality, under certain conditions, after obtaining naturalization as citizens of such countries" seemed "to carry the principle of dual nationality further than it [had] ever been carried before."[92] And when war broke out, the reactions grew stronger still. In June 1915, in an article titled "When Is an American Not an American?,"[93] the former president Theodore Roosevelt called the German law into question. On 24 June 1917, in the *New York Times*, a retired U.S. Navy rear admiral expressed his view that the German law called into question the validity of all naturalizations granted to Germans; he suggested annulling them all and refusing to grant American nationality until the Delbrück law was abrogated.[94] On 16 July 1917 a district judge refused to naturalize a German on the grounds that "any doubt about the meaning of our laws [on naturalization] must be interpreted as opposing the admission [of a German to American naturalization]."

In Great Britain, a law dated 7 August 1914 allowed the secretary of state to revoke naturalization certificates that had been obtained through false affirmations or fraud.

In France the laws of 7 April 1915 and 18 June 1917 instituted a procedure for withdrawing nationality from naturalized citizens of enemy origin.[95]

This was the context in which the connection began to be made, in France, between a "racial" nation on the German model and jus sanguinis. First, the war reactivated the French perception, commonly accepted since the forced annexation of Alsace-Moselle, that Germany was a racial nation. With the Delbrück law that perception was reinforced. And at the end of the hostilities, when some right-wing politicians relaunched the fight for jus sanguinis that had been carried out during the war (in reaction to the overly easy integration of children of immigrants into French nationality by means of jus soli under the law of 1889), the left responded that the right had a racial, German conception of nationality. A good example of this discursive displacement, this intellectual connection with a political vocation, is found in an article published in 1919 in *La Revue politique et parlementaire* by Georges Gruffy, one of the most influential jurists of the period. "La naturalisation et le préjugé de la race" is particularly interesting because Gruffy first presents the distinction between jus soli and jus sanguinis as jurists were in the habit of doing at the time, linking it to the migratory situation: Germany and Italy were inclined toward jus sanguinis because they were countries of emigration; France was inclined toward jus soli because it was a country of immigration. Later in the article, when Gruffy presented the internal French debate that opposed the left, which supported jus soli, to the partisans of jus sanguinis on the right, he called the latter into question in the following terms: "They start from a sort of dogma, namely, the existence of a French race, that some would readily characterize in the German manner as an 'elect' race."[96] In the eyes of the French public the link between Germany, with its ethnic or racial conception of the nation, and jus sanguinis was now established. To be in favor of jus sanguinis was to be racist in the German manner, and for a long time this republican discourse disqualified the French partisans of jus sanguinis — who reoriented their restrictionist or even xenophobic struggle, turning it against naturalization.

German Nationality Law in the Twentieth Century

But if jus sanguinis came to characterize German racism in the French imagination, it was only with Hitler that German law became racist, not by virtue of the law of 1913, which was maintained virtually intact, but owing to a piece of exceptional legislation.[97] The law of 14 July 1933, which was to be taken up again seven years later (in July 1940) under Vichy, provided for two types of "withdrawal" of German nationality.

The first targeted all naturalizations that had taken place between 9 November 1918, the date the Empire fell, and 30 January 1933, the date when Hitler came to power. Any naturalization that had been granted between those two dates could be revoked if it did not appear "desirable."[98] During those years the law of 1913 had remained in force[99] and been the object of an overly liberal application, as the Nazis saw it. The question whether a naturalization should be considered "undesirable" was settled according to "ethnic-national principles." The order of application of this law, issued on 26 July 1933, specified that the following groups would be "in the first place the object of an examination in view of a revocation of their naturalization: (a) Jews from the East, unless they had fought on the front during the war or had acquired special merit from the standpoint of German interests; (b) persons who had committed a serious infraction or a crime or had behaved in a way prejudicial to the health of the state and the people."[100] The second type of withdrawal targeted Germans who found themselves abroad.

In all, 38,766 persons were stripped of their German nationality by these two procedures. Then, from 25 November 1941 procedures of collective withdrawal targeted all Jews who had left the territory of the Reich. During this time hundreds of thousands of *völkisch* Germans—of "Aryan stock"—from neighboring countries had been integrated into German nationality by virtue of the Nazi legislation.

Pre-war German nationality law is not at issue here. To think this would be to suppose that Hitler would have been hindered from acting if German legislation had been structured according to different legal principles. After all, Vichy demonstrated some years later that one could apply legislation involving a racist exception while retaining jus soli and the law of 1927, one of the most liberal laws in the history of France. The techniques for attributing nationality were not in themselves racist nor, on the contrary, "open"; they always had to be interpreted according to the context and the way they were put into practice.

After the fall of the Nazis, those from whom German nationality had been withdrawn were reintegrated, but the law of 1913 was maintained unchallenged, for it provided a way to keep a connection with Germans who found themselves on the other side of the Iron Curtain. In the 1960s the Federal Republic of Germany became a country of immigration. In 1972, when for reasons of inconsistency the federal constitutional court at Karlsruhe (*Bundesverfassungsgericht*) annulled a decision of a Bavarian administrative court that had authorized the nonrenewal of a residency permit for a foreign worker who had spent more than five years in Germany, immigration into Germany became permanent as a matter of law.[101] But as long as Germany was not reunified, this fact could not be publicly acknowledged. Political priority remained with the Germans residing on the other side of the Iron Curtain, and officially Germany was not—politically it still could not yet be—a country of immigration.

After Germany's reunification in 1990 the vast majority of Germans came together on a single territory with stable borders on which jus soli could be legitimately constructed. Two reforms adopted in turn gave priority to the situation of children of immigrants.

Since 1 January 1991 any young foreigner aged sixteen to twenty-three has been able to obtain German nationality if he or she has lived in Germany for eight years, including six spent in school.[102] This innovation, brought about by Chancellor Helmut Kohl's conservative-liberal majority, was followed in 1999 by an even more important reform, approved by the new majority — Social-Democrats and Greens — joined by the liberals: the introduction of jus soli. Since 1 January 2000 every child born in Germany to a foreign parent with a residency permit is German. However, at the age of twenty-three, if a different nationality has been transmitted to him by his parents, he will have to choose between that one and German nationality.

Until very recently, the Prussian law of 1842 was compatible — assuming a few adaptations — with the context of its application in Germany, which was initially a country of emigration with uncertain borders, then a country with a divided territory and population. In parallel fashion and on the same basis, the "racial" concept of the German nation was compatible with the incorporation of specific groups and territories. This was so for the annexation of Alsace-Moselle. It was also true of the Nazi policy of incorporating into the German nation *völkisch* Aryans from Sudetenland, Bohemia, and Hungary, which had been added to German territory. After the war, moreover, by an Allied decision announced on 17 November 1949, members of those groups could keep the German nationality that Hitler's decrees had conferred on them, if they so desired, for the Führer's decree of 19 May 1943 constituted a legal basis for their nationality.[103]

These policies helped to maintain confusion outside the country, but also inside Germany itself, between nationality law and the concept of the nation. However, ten years after its reunification, a country whose nationality law was said to depend on an ethnic conception of the nation[104] adopted — relatively easily — measures allowing the integration of children of non-German immigrants into its nationality. For like France in 1889, Germany a century later had become a country of immigration in its turn and had drawn the consequences of a new perception of its situation in that regard.

Immigration and Nationality: The European Convergence

The sensitivity of nationality law to the perception of the national situation with regard to immigrants is not specific to France and Germany; this is clear from a comparative study of the legislation of the fifteen oldest countries of the European Union and of North America (Canada and the United States). All the nationality laws of these countries were dominated in the mid-nineteenth century by jus sanguinis (influenced by the French Civil Code) or jus soli (influenced by British law). As long as there was no contradiction between this legal tradition and the national perceptions with regard to immigration, the original laws were retained. In countries of immigration such as the United States and Canada, the "British" jus soli allowed children of immigrants to acquire Canadian or American nationality automatically, at birth. For the countries on the European continent that were then largely countries of emigration, the "French" jus sanguinis allowed them to prolong ties with their nationals abroad (and their children).[105] When a contradiction between nationality legislation and the national perceptions vis-à-vis immigration eventually came to light, a change ensued, not in a mechanical fashion but according to internal processes and political debates proper to each country.[106]

The most important change occurred in the countries of continental Europe with the legal tradition of jus sanguinis, when they came — like France, but much later — to perceive themselves as countries of immigration.[107] Provisions attributing nationality automatically to the grandchildren of immigrants by virtue of the "double" jus soli were adopted in the Netherlands (1953), Belgium (1992), and Spain (1982). Other provisions facilitated the acquisition of nationality by children of immigrants: in most European countries — Belgium, Denmark, Spain, Finland, the Netherlands, Sweden, and to a lesser extent Italy — they acquired the nationality of their country of residence not at birth but later, conditional upon residence or a voluntary declaration, a sign of their socialization.[108] Finally, in the "old" countries of the European Union, except for Greece and Luxembourg, birth on the national territory makes access to nationality easier than it is through naturalization procedures, thus confirming the premonitory observation of an American jurist: "No modern State which conceives of itself as having the slightest attractive power can really suffer that it can have growing up within it over several generations a body of people who do not belong to the State."[109]

The comparative history of German and French nationality law thus does not show any equivalence, any directly causal link between jus sanguinis, an ethnic conception of the nation, and Germany on the one hand, or between jus soli, a civic or elective conception of the nation, and France on the other hand. The legislation adopted in Prussia in 1842 was very close to the French legislation of the time, based on a form of jus sanguinis that had no ethnic dimensions. This was the period during which the French Civil Code influenced jurists of many continental European countries as these were developing their own nationality laws. The comparison shows, moreover, that the creation and implementation of two distinct regimes for attributing nationality at birth — jus sanguinis and jus soli — owed more in the nineteenth century to the considerable importance and autonomy of jurists than to the quite variable conceptions of each nation.

These laws, which became legal traditions or objects of belief within legal traditions, have nevertheless been widely amended whenever their implementation has placed them in conflict with national perceptions of immigration. The contradiction between jus sanguinis and the perception of having become a country of immigration affected France in 1889. In Germany and in the majority of the states in the European Union that have long been countries of emigrants or emigration, nationality law based on jus sanguinis did not open up to jus soli until after the Second World War, when those countries perceived themselves as having become countries of immigration.

We must note nevertheless that the causes of change — the kinds of demands that emerge in public debate — have evolved: in France, for example, at the end of the nineteenth century it was the demand for equality of obligation in the realm of public *duties* and security that led to the imposition of jus soli on the children of immigrants. Since 1945 there has been a growing tendency to claim jus soli — to ensure equal *rights* tied to birth on national territory. Formerly the state imposed its nationality; it embraced its subjects by instrumentalizing them. Since 1945 children of immigrants have demanded nationality and obtained it almost as a right. But French law, constructed for the exercise of power, though not inattentive to individual demands, has adapted quite well — in a technical sense — to this transformation, without having to evolve very much. The passage from an imposed jus soli to a demanded jus soli hints at the development of a "territorial" nationality, a part of the new paradigm of international law.[110] It is also translated by a historical evolution in the relations between the state and the individual, a topic to be examined in later chapters.

There is no automatic relation, moreover, between the presence of immigrants and the evolution of nationality laws. When the dominant feeling, under the effect of uncertain borders, territorial disputes, or a tradition or continuing practice of emigration, is that an important part of the constitutive population lives beyond the country's borders, the adoption of measures for the legal inclusion of children or even grandchildren of immigrants is politically very difficult. This was true of Germany for a long time. It is still true in Greece, and to some extent in Italy.

Nationality law was thus influenced at the outset by the legal tradition, then by the national perceptions with regard to immigration. Both in reality and in representations of that reality, the conception of the nation and nationality law have thus developed independently. During the twentieth century Germany and France managed to have racist or ethnic policies to which jus soli was no more an obstacle than jus sanguinis had been. On the contrary, the similarity of nationality legislation may mask very different conceptions of a nation: for example, the British and the French have very similar laws governing nationality, even though they offer somewhat different conceptions of the nation. In a country such as Canada, the same nationality law can allow very different or even opposing conceptions of the nation to coexist, in Quebec on the one hand and in the Anglophone provinces on the other.

This observation of a convergence of nationality laws in countries that have become countries of immigration—this opening to jus soli—tells us in reality just one thing: through the development of the migratory phenomenon, where the border of nationality had been closed to the children of immigrants, it has been opening up. The specific mechanisms of this border crossing still remain to be analyzed.

For depending on whether children of foreign parents are irrevocably citizens from birth or have to wait to reach the age of majority, whether they can keep or must give up their parents' nationality, laws that appear to converge toward openness will have opposite consequences in practice. Nationality legislation includes the modalities of access to nationality of immigrants and their children, but also of spouses of citizens; it includes rules for transmission of nationality but also for loss of nationality. Technically it is a matter of complex arrangements whose elements interact. No element—for example, jus soli—can be interpreted without considering its modalities of application or the other elements of a particular configuration. More important than the study of some isolated element that has no meaning in itself—jus soli, for example, or jus sanguinis—the study of the configuration in action and in comparison is most instructive where French nationality law is concerned.

A look back at the three major moments in the development of this law will make it clear that each step has been taken to the detriment of different categories of French people: women, colonized peoples, and naturalized persons in turn.

8.

Discrimination within Nationality Law

❧ Each major step in the development of French nationality law was taken to the detriment of certain categories of French people, leaving them with fewer rights or otherwise worsening their situation.

With the Civil Code in 1803, nationality became a right attached to persons. Attributed definitively at birth, it could no longer be lost by a transfer of residence outside the country, and it was transmissible through parentage, that is, through jus sanguinis. However, it was a right reserved for men; women's status was lowered, in contrast, and remained so for a long time.

The second step, that is, the law of 1889, opened French nationality to the descendants of immigrants through jus soli. If these children were born in France to a parent born in France (making them grandchildren of immigrants), French nationality was attributed automatically at birth: this was the double jus soli. If they were born in France to immigrant parents, nationality was granted at the age of majority provided that they still resided in France. This societal approach, which integrated people into French nationality in increasing numbers as one generation succeeded another, was applied to everyone in France and in Algeria, with the exception of the indigenous Algerian Muslim population. Algerian Muslims might have been formally French, their children and grandchildren might have been born in France, but they could only become fully French by a cumbersome procedure of "naturalization."

With the law of 1927 French nationality became — this was the third step in its development — an instrument of demographic policy: it was made available on a massive scale to immigrants who desired it, through naturalization. However, those naturalized immigrants were barred from exercising political rights and from being admitted into certain professions right away.

Radically innovative, then eager to embrace immigrants on a broad scale, French nationality law has sometimes created inequalities at its core, sometimes accepted and maintained inequalities over long periods.

The Status of Women in Nationality Law: Belated Equality

At the end of the nineteenth century inequality between men and women was the rule internationally where nationality was concerned. When a couple married, if the man and the woman were of different nationalities the woman took her husband's nationality and lost her own. This rule, inscribed in the French Civil Code of 1803, was not only adopted by the countries of continental Europe that had already been influenced by the Napoleonic Code as a whole but also by countries such as England and the United States.[1] In France in the mid-1920s, 150,000 women born French became foreigners because they married foreigners, even though they continued to live in France. They were thus subjected to the status of foreigners in France and to the laws of their husband's country. The law of 1927 put an end to the rule according to which nationality was automatically lost. But it was only in 1973 that women's equality and independence vis-à-vis men were definitively assured.[2]

Under the Old Regime a foreign woman could request and obtain a lettre de naturalité.[3] A French woman could marry a foreigner and keep her nationality.

During the Revolution a foreign woman could be naturalized on the same basis as a man, automatically, under the regime of the law of 1790 or the constitutions of 1791 and 1793; then, with the constitutions of 1795 and 1799, she could do so by declaring that she was establishing her domicile in France, which gave her the right to be naturalized after seven or ten years' residency. A foreign woman who married a French man and resided in France was considered French herself: this was not what the law or the constitution prescribed, but it is what can be deduced from the debates that took place on 16 October 1793 when the Convention decreed that "foreigners born subjects of governments with which the Republic is at war will be detained until peace [is established]."

At the same time, the Convention decided that "[foreign] women who have married French men . . . are not included in the present law, unless they are suspect or married to suspect men."[4] Bertrand Barère de Vieuzac specifies: "When a French man marries a foreigner, his wife becomes French at once. . . . This is a very well-known axiom, consecrated in the code of all peoples: *that the wife follows the destiny of her husband.*[5] . . . This is not an exception that I am asking you to consecrate, but a right."[6]

As for the French woman marrying a foreigner, not only did she keep her nationality but through her marriage she permitted her husband to acquire it as well. Let us recall that under the law of 30 April 1790 all foreign men established in France would "be reputed to be French . . . after five years of continuous residency in the kingdom, if they have, in addition, married French women." The same mechanism was taken up by the constitution of 1791, and the five-year waiting period was reduced to one year by the constitution of 1793.

The Civil Code: A Step Backward The promulgation of the Civil Code thus constituted a profound break not only with the Revolution but also with the Old Regime. A married woman became a dependent of her husband in terms of civil law. During the discussion of the section "On Marriage" in the Council of State, Bonaparte asserted: "A wife is the husband's property, she belongs to him as the fruit tree belongs to the gardener." This is because "nature — has made our women our slaves! The husband has the right to say to his wife: Madame, you shall not go out. Madame, you shall not go to the theater. Madame, you shall not see such and such a person! That is to say: Madame, you belong to me body and soul."[7]

A woman's dependence on her husband was also de rigueur in matters of nationality: a foreign woman who married a Frenchman became French. Similarly, a French woman who married a foreigner became a foreigner. If she became a widow, she could only recover the quality of being French if she was living in France, or if she moved back, with government authorization, and declared her intention to remain there permanently.[8] Only men transmitted nationality to their children: only a child born to a French father was French. Finally, foreign women could no longer be naturalized. Earlier naturalization had been governed by article 3 of the constitution of 1799, which provided that "foreigners [became] French citizens when, after reaching age twenty-one and having declared the intention to reside in France, they [had] resided there for ten consecutive years." The article was interpreted in a generic way and applied to women as well as men: a foreign woman could be naturalized as French upon declaring her intention to settle permanently in France.[9] But when the Civil Code was promulgated, article 7 declared that "the exercise of civil rights is independent of the quality of citizen, which is acquired and retained only in conformity with constitutional law."[10] Thus article 3 of the constitution of 1799 no longer applied to anyone but citizens exercising political rights — that is, to men. Consequently a foreign woman could no longer be naturalized.

This exclusion also applied to admission to residency. Article 13 of the Civil Code indicated an exception, however: "Foreigners who have been admitted by the authorization of the Emperor to establish residency in France will enjoy all civil rights, as long as they continue to reside there."

Having studied the practices of admission to residency in Strasbourg, Jennifer Heuer observes that during the years that preceded the Civil Code, foreign women had just as much access to residency as men. It was often a step toward acquiring the quality of being French, and their petitions mentioned their desire "to acquire the rights of citizenship after the term prescribed by the constitution."[11] A few days after this part of the Civil Code was promulgated, the mayor of Strasbourg wrote to the prefect of his department to ask him whether the previous rule—according to which "foreign women who applied for authorization to settle in France were assimilated to foreign men, in the mode of admission"[12]—remained in force under the new legislation. The response was perfectly clear: from prefect Henri Sée's standpoint, the new law was applicable only to "foreigners capable of becoming full French citizens, and in consequence, only to the masculine sex, since the exercise of political rights does not belong to women."[13]

The prefect's interpretation went well beyond what the Civil Code prescribed, since admission to residency had been created as a status independent from naturalization. But Sée's interpretation was most often followed in practice, with the consequences brought clearly to light by Heuer:[14] from September 1803 to September 1804 the register of the city of Strasbourg alone recorded nine admissions to residency involving German women. Between 1803 and 1849, for all of France only eleven of the 2,832 Germans who obtained naturalization or admission to residency were women.[15]

Transformations in the Rights of Married Women: France and the United States This regime of inferiority and dependence was slightly relaxed during the second half of the nineteenth century. The law of December 1849 reopened naturalization to foreign women. In 1891, the double jus soli, discreetly introduced in 1851 and imposed in 1889 on children "born in France to *a foreigner* who was himself born in France," was deemed by the Supreme Court to apply to children born in France to a foreign mother who had been born in France herself.[16] Until that point, according to administrative practice the term "foreigner" had been deemed to designate only the father.[17] This restriction appeared all the more shocking in that it excluded mothers who were born French and had become foreigners as a result of marrying foreigners. At the same time the French government, pressured by foreign governments, nevertheless found it "not very logical" to allow a woman born French "to transmit to her children her nationality of origin, which she had lost . . . in contracting marriage with a foreigner . . . preventing by the same token the foreign father who had transmitted his nationality to his French wife from transmitting it to his own children."[18] However, the law of 1893, adopted to rectify the Hess decision in the Supreme Court, did not reverse this provision:

a child born in France to a mother born in France was still French at birth, as the court had decided, but he or she had the right to decline the quality of being French in the year after reaching the age of majority.[19]

This equalization of the rights of men and women nevertheless touched only a very limited sphere of nationality law. At the beginning of the twentieth century, on the essential issue—the status of married women—nothing had changed since 1803.[20] Quite to the contrary, the rule appeared completely stabilized, as is attested by the decision by the U.S. Congress in 1907 to apply it to American women who married foreigners.[21] However, in 1922 in the United States and in 1927 in France, this rule was abolished. On this subject the comparison between France and the United States is particularly instructive. The vote of 1907 illustrates what would be the singular destiny of the status of married women in the area of nationality both in the United States and in France in the years that followed: it became an element on the frontier of women's struggle for equality on the one hand, and on the frontier of immigration and population policies on the other.

During the early years of the twentieth century immigration reached a level hitherto unknown in the United States: 1907 was a record year, with 1,285,349 entries.[22] The times thus lent themselves to restrictionist policies, and on 20 February 1907 Congress adopted measures along these lines—an increase in the entry fee from $2 to $4; exclusion of unaccompanied minors, persons suffering from physical or mental deficiencies, and prostitutes—while instructing a commission on immigration (the Dillingham commission, named after the senator who headed it) to look into additional measures. The commission's report, submitted in 1911, played a decisive role in the implementation of numerical limits and the ethnic selection of immigrants (provisions adopted in 1921 and tightened in 1924).[23]

A few days later, the vote on the law of 2 March 1907 seemed to correspond to the goal of "reducing the number of Americans who, in the eyes of the federal government, have compromised their status as citizens by maintaining or establishing foreign liaisons of a certain type."[24] American feminists had already won a number of victories on the road to equal rights with men; however, this provision was adopted unbeknown to them, without real debate, in the context of a bill on immigration and nationality.[25] They continued to mobilize in the years that followed and throughout the First World War, with the particular goal of extending the right to vote to all American women. They won that right in 1920 in the form of the Nineteenth Amendment to the Constitution, shortly after the war's end.[26]

In the wake of that victory American feminists militated for eliminating the clause in the law of 1907 that prescribed deprivation of nationality for an American woman marrying a foreigner: they got both the Republican and the Democratic candidates to support the principle during the presidential election campaign of 1920.[27] But their efforts did not suffice to influence the vote on the Cable Act of 22 September 1922.[28]

The decisive argument was that now that the right to vote had been won, a foreign woman marrying an American became a voter at the same time as she became an American, perhaps without being able to speak English or being familiar with American culture, whereas an American woman who married a foreigner lost the right to vote and her nationality. This argument was invoked by the feminist movement, but of course it pleased the restrictionists. The Cable Act thus disconnected marriage and nationality, and allowed American women to retain their nationality after marrying foreigners, the better to control access to nationality of foreign women marrying American men.[29]

Before 1922 a foreign woman became American automatically after her marriage to an American. Henceforth she would have to go through naturalization proceedings, which allowed for government control.[30] The racism of American restrictionists also appeared in a clause specifying that if an American woman married a foreigner who was "ineligible for naturalization" — for example, an Asian — she would be punished immediately: she would lose her American nationality for the duration of the marriage. She could recover it only by naturalization, the procedure that was henceforth imposed on foreign women.[31]

In France at the beginning of the twentieth century, women had won far fewer rights than in the United States. Feminism had developed since the late nineteenth century, but its successes were limited. A single woman had the same civil rights as a man; a married woman remained largely dependent on her husband. To be sure, the law of 1884 reestablished divorce, which had been abolished on 8 May 1816;[32] however, the causes recognized as legitimate were restricted,[33] and the law no longer allowed for divorce by mutual consent, which had been instituted by the Civil Code in 1804. In 1900 a law allowed women to practice law. As of 1907 a woman could dispose freely of her salary. But she could not conduct business without her husband's permission; without him she could not go to court, sign a contract, or sell or acquire property (even for nothing). Article 213 of the Civil Code still specified that husbands owed their wives protection, and wives owed their husbands obedience.

The First World War saw French women mobilize in the service of their country; since they could not take up arms, they devoted themselves not only to exclusively "feminine" tasks — volunteering as nurses with the Red Cross, for example — but also to all the other professional activities in which they replaced men who had gone to the front. They finished the war as heroines.[34] However, their status with regard to nationality hardly progressed at all. There was a lot of concern too about the situation of French women who had become German or Austro-Hungarian upon marrying: they sometimes remained interned with their husbands or had their property sequestered.[35] A campaign was launched by the newspaper *La Française*,[36] and on 10 February 1916 Senator Louis Martin[37] submitted a bill that would have allowed French women to keep their nationality after marrying foreigners; it came to nothing.[38]

At war's end feminists rallied to the new sacred union for motherhood and an increased birth rate. Their contribution to the victory was forgotten, and they even had to face rising antifeminism. In 1920 the law forbade distributing information about birth control, and tightened restrictions on abortion, which became a criminal offense in 1923.[39] On 21 November 1922 the Senate rejected a bill that had been adopted by the Chamber of Deputies on 20 May 1919 and that would have granted women the right to vote.[40] It was in this hostile context that Parliament was nevertheless to establish the independence of married women in a much more liberal way than in the United States: in 1922, the very year in which the French Senate rejected the right to vote for women, it approved their independence when they married foreigners. This was because the demand, relatively overlooked in writings about women, was at the frontier of women's rights and the demographic exigency.

More Than 100,000 French Women Become Foreigners Throughout the nineteenth century French women married foreigners in ever-increasing numbers. Generally speaking, only half as many foreign women married French men. With increased immigration these mixed marriages went from a few hundred to a few thousand a year, and then to several thousand: the phenomenon of the woman born French becoming a foreigner in her own country of birth and residence was amplified.

In the year 1919 alone seventeen thousand French women became foreign by marrying foreigners.[41] The more time passed, the more their numbers increased. Between 1900 and 1926 more than 190,000 French women became foreigners by marriage.[42] During the same period just under thirty thousand women regained their French nationality, most often when their husbands were naturalized, or as a result of widowhood, separation, or divorce.[43] There were probably nearly 150,000 women born French who had become foreigners at the time of the census of 7 March 1926, which counted a million foreign women. Formerly French-born women thus represented about 6.5 percent of the foreign population and 15 percent of the foreign female population.[44] This loss of "nationals" seemed absurd at a time when the populationists were interested in naturalizing foreigners.[45]

The massive scale of this phenomenon also made people aware of the unacceptable social position of French women married to foreigners, and it soon aroused mobilization and indignation well beyond feminist circles. By marrying a foreigner, a French woman changed nationality often without wanting to, and sometimes without knowing she had done so. Indeed, information about that automatic consequence of marriage played no part in the prescribed formalities surrounding the celebration of a marriage. The officer of the civil state (article 75 of the Civil Code) read documents pertaining to the state of the future spouses, asked them if a marriage contract had been made, then heard their declaration of reciprocal commitment. And that was all. Once the marriage had been pronounced, the woman changed nationality. Having become a foreigner, she was required to register at once according to the prescriptions of the decree of 2 October 1888 and the law of 8 August 1893; she had to get a foreigner's identity card in conformity with the decree of 2 April 1917, and she could even be the object of a warrant of expulsion.[46] Such women were sometimes obliged to leave France to accompany their spouses, to whom they owed obedience.

The situation was sometimes dramatic. So much so that on 2 October 1919, the minister of the interior required that mayors demand of any Chinese man desiring to marry a French woman "a certificate attesting that he had no legitimate wife." The minister had been informed by the French embassy in China that several women taken to China by their husbands, who had come to work in France during the war, had discovered that their spouses already had legitimate wives in China. "Condemned to vegetate in poverty and amid unimaginable privations, in a country whose language and customs they [did not know]" owing to the limited resources of their spouses, they could find themselves "sequestered, reduced to the subaltern situation of second wife, targets of the despotic authority of the legitimate wife."[47] A few thousand Chinese men had in fact remained in France, and in the census of 1926 there were several hundred women who had been born French but had become Chinese by marriage. Cases of French women married to Italians were more numerous, and could also pose problems.[48] These women were prevented from divorcing, for divorce was not authorized by their husbands' country of origin.[49]

All women married to foreigners lost the social subsidies reserved for French women. They also lost the right to work in positions reserved for the French, while the number of women working in public agencies such as the postal service and in law firms had multiplied: thus in 1914, among public primary school teachers 59 percent were already women, and between 1906 and 1921 the number of women employed in civil service positions went from 283 to 30,378; in 1921 half of all civil service employees were women.[50] The situation of female civil servants desiring to marry foreigners was analyzed by the commission on naturalizations after the vote on the law of 1927: "The former legislation . . . had created situations that were sometimes very cruel and gave rise to complaints that moved public opinion. Female civil servants whom foreigners wanted to marry had backed off from carrying out a union that, by making them lose their quality of being French, must as a result deprive them of their job: these renunciations, already very painful, came to be aggravated, in certain cases, by the scandal of natural motherhood. The cause of these unfortunate women, victims of an overly rigorous legislation, could not fail to create, in our Country, a current of sympathy and a desire for reparation."[51]

The Law of 1927: The Union of Feminists and Populationists As soon as the war was over, feminist movements mobilized. The congress of the National Council of French Women met in Strasbourg on 8–9 October 1919 and made the adoption of reforms a priority.[52] And Parliament acted very quickly: Senator Louis Martin had been the first to submit, in 1916, a bill[53] allowing French women to keep their nationality after marriage to a foreigner. In 1918 André Honnorat and Adolphe Landry proposed that French women marrying foreigners could keep their nationality automatically if they continued to live in France.[54] This populationist option was defeated by a coalition bringing together supporters of women's rights, who criticized it for maintaining women in a dependent position, and opponents of jus soli, who did not like the bill's territorial aspect.[55] The text finally adopted, which became part of the law of 10 August 1927, was a fusion between the proposals of the feminist senator Louis Martin and the left-wing deputy Ernest Lafont; it had the advantage of satisfying the feminists and the populationists alike.[56]

In a first phase it was decided that a French woman would keep her nationality when she married a foreigner, but that she could take her husband's nationality if she wished.[57] The National Council of French Women, meeting in 1922, looked at the adoption of this provision as "a big step taken in just a few years," but it expressed dissatisfaction with the absence of reciprocity, that is, with the maintenance of the automatic acquisition of French nationality by a foreign woman who married a French man: "There is . . . a contradiction that makes too openly visible the exclusively national sentiment that has inspired the authors."[58]

Senator Martin then submitted a new text and succeeded in getting it adopted:

this provision guaranteed the same status to foreign women, who would also have the choice between retaining their nationality and becoming French. Martin added a complementary measure:[59] women who had lost French nationality in the past through marriage to a foreigner would be able to recover it by making a declaration before a justice of the peace within one year after promulgation of the law. This guarantee that thousands of women who had lost their French nationality could get it back ensured the support of the populationists, and the law was passed.[60]

Unquestionably the law was an instrument serving demographic purposes. This is illustrated by a statement of André Mallarmé, who reviewed the bill in the Chamber of Deputies: "The reform we are proposing that the Chamber adopt will constitute major progress for feminism, not in the sense in which the most ardent feminists understand it, for we are not giving the French woman the vote, but we are guaranteeing her a means of exercising her social influence to the benefit of the future of her race, we are allowing her to retain little Frenchmen for France."[61]

The populationists had good reason to be satisfied, moreover. The provision allowing women who had lost their nationality (by marrying foreigners) to recover it by a declaration had the effect of reintegrating more than 35,000 women into French nationality. Furthermore, every year more than half the foreign women who married French men chose to become French (and that proportion continued to increase), while fewer than 5 percent of the French women who married foreigners chose to take their husband's nationality. As a result, the balance of acquisitions of French nationality, which had been negative before 1927, immediately became positive and increased regularly from then on.

It was also a victory for the feminists; their strongest supporter in Parliament, Senator Louis Martin, had helped by successfully reconciling their demands with those of the populationists and the natalists.[62] The populationist concern allied with feminism produced an exceptionally liberal text, all the more easily in that unlike in the United States, the granting of French nationality to a foreign woman did not yet entail giving her the right to vote.[63]

The end of automatic loss of nationality for French women did not have as a counterpart, as in the United States, the restriction of the right of foreign women to take their husband's nationality. In the United States from that point on, a foreign woman marrying an American had to go through the naturalization process, and her request could be rejected by the federal government. In France a foreign woman marrying a French man and a French woman marrying a foreign man now each had the choice of taking her husband's nationality, but this was

TABLE 8

Marriages between French Nationals and Foreigners, 1925–1931

	Foreign women and French men		French women and foreign men		Increase or decrease in number of French women
		Became French		Became foreign	
1925	5,880		11,181		−5,301
1926	6,282		11,556		−5,274
1927	6,314		11,539		
1928	6,137	3,076	11,639	535	+2,541
1929	6,136	3,273	11,301	563	+2,710
1930	6,490	3,482	12,100	601	+2,881
1931	6,364	3,955	10,956	553	+3,402

Source: Depoid, *Les naturalisations en France*, 56, 61.

not an obligation.[64] The woman's wishes alone produced an immediate effect, since her decision could be made in complete independence, with no intervention from the state.

A New Step Backward (1927–1973)

The regime of the law of 1927 was doubtless too liberal, too favorable to women's rights in the eyes of the French administration. The new text had scarcely been adopted when it gave rise to "reservations bordering on criticism" during a meeting of the "naturalization commission" set up by the Ministry of Justice to advise the government on naturalization policy. In its meeting of 13 October 1927[65] the commission expressed concern that "the development of households of disparate nationalities might constitute a danger or at least a source of concern for public security." It considered requiring that in each government service the marriage of a female employee to a foreigner would be subject to prior authorization (the absence of authorization could not prevent the marriage, but would of course have professional consequences). However, the commission finally decided to be more flexible: government offices that already required authorization before any marriage (such as the army) would require that the nationality of the spouse be specified; the others would have the right to submit certain categories of agents to the regime of prior declaration. Still, the failure to make a declaration could constitute a professional fault leading to a disciplinary sanction that in exceptional cases could be followed by the expulsion of the foreign spouse or a shift of the employee to a different service.[66]

At the end of the 1930s, partly owing to the economic and political crisis, certain foreign women marrying French men were suspected of doing so to regularize their situation or to protect themselves from expulsion. To combat such "fraud," a decree-law promulgated on 12 November 1939 required that a woman seeking to change her nationality upon marrying had to make an explicit declaration before the marriage took place. French nationality did not become effective for foreign women until six months later, a waiting period during which the government could oppose the acquisition, if the Council of State concurred.

Despite this restriction the law of 1927 was still too liberal for populationist legislators in 1945. Thus the provision that allowed women—foreign or French—the freedom to choose their nationality upon marrying was reconsidered. The system adopted in 1945 was entirely conceived for the purpose of ensuring that after a mixed marriage, a maximum number of women would be French. Unless she had voiced explicit reservations beforehand, a foreign woman marrying a French man received French nationality automatically. In contrast, a French woman, unless she declared before marrying that she wanted to take her husband's nationality, remained French.

Raymond Boulbès, the author of the nationality code,[67] justified this backward step as follows: "The reaction against the traditional principle appeared too harsh. In 1927, the desire was to leave women free, on the principle of the autonomy of will, to decide whether or not she wanted to follow her husband's nationality. . . . There was no need to proscribe the principle of unity of nationality which is a given of our civilization, at once Latin and Christian."[68] In reality the goal of the law was not based on the principle of unity of nationality in a couple—a principle applied only for foreign women marrying French men. A French woman marrying a foreign man remained French and would thus have a different nationality from her husband. Legal technology had never been pushed so far to make it as easy as possible for women to maintain or acquire French nationality. The Liberation, which saw the triumph of familialism over feminism,[69] was the moment when populationism was thus taken to the extreme: during the period between 1945 and 1973, demographic logic was applied at full strength.

It was only in 1973 that equal treatment of men and women was finally secured. Originally, in 1971, the government sought simply to tidy up the code of 1945. The ambition was very modest: to unify nationality law in metropolitan France and its overseas territories, and to include provisions allowing the natural child of a French mother to acquire the mother's nationality. As far as the status of married women was concerned, the government's proposal included no modifications.

But under the leadership of Jean Foyer, the reviewer designated by the National Assembly, the text took a different turn. Foyer, minister of justice from 1962 to 1967, had initiated reforms in civil law that guaranteed equality between men and women, and between natural and legitimate children in the areas of guardianship, matrimonial regimes and inheritances, parental authority, and filiation.[70] However, this equality between men and women was not yet guaranteed in nationality law, which belonged to civil law, as Foyer saw it: "The idea that the husband's nationality — in the case in point, his French nationality — has to be communicated to the foreign women he marries is no longer compatible with the principles of the new family law, principles in which the ancient predominance of the husband (and of the father where the exercise of parental authority is concerned) has been replaced by equality between the spouses (or the parents)."

"The solution of the nationality code is a wart that must be burned off," he wrote in his report.[71] Despite the insistent reservations of the Ministry of Justice,[72] Foyer got the National Assembly to adopt a total equalization of the status of men and women in nationality law.[73]

From that point on marriage between two persons of different nationalities had no automatic effect on the nationality of either: each person could retain his or her nationality of origin.[74] But the French person's spouse — man or woman — could, after the marriage, request French nationality and obtain it by a simple declaration, whether he or she resided in France or abroad.[75] Women became completely free, and for the first time so did foreign men marrying French women: they were no longer obliged to go through naturalization proceedings. Finally, if the spouses maintained different nationalities, they transmitted both to their children.

Since 1973 women have remained equal to men in matters of nationality, with regard both to marriage and to transmitting nationality to children.[76] Thanks to the alliance between the populationists and the feminists in 1922, a foreign spouse of a French person can become French by a simple declaration, whereas foreign spouses of people from other European countries or the United States have to go through a naturalization process. And thus we find that France, which invented nationality in 1803 as a personal right, to the detriment of women, and maintained it as such for more than a century, has had until recently[77] one of the most liberal nationality laws in the world with respect to women.

The Colonized People of Algeria

The law of 1889 — the second step in the development of French nationality — marked the return of jus soli. At the end of the nineteenth century France had become a country of immigration, the foremost in Europe. But children born in France to foreign parents only rarely requested nationality, although they were legally entitled to do so. For this reason, generation after generation, independently of the new migratory trend, the foreign population automatically increased, owing to jus sanguinis and the small number of naturalizations. Hence the law of 1889, which reorganized the boundary between the French and foreigners. The familial approach to nationality was supplemented by a socialization approach. The obligatory force of jus soli, based on socialization, was applied gradually, in step with the shift in generations. French nationality was attributed automatically at birth to the grandchildren of immigrants, under the effect of the double jus soli. It was granted to children born in France to immigrant parents when they reached the age of majority, if they continued to reside in France.

The law was applied in France but also in the French territory of Algeria, at the urging of the Algerian members of Parliament. Algeria was in fact the only one of France's "modern" colonies[78] that had become, by virtue of the constitution of 1848, a French territory. It was the only colony that attracted foreign residents, emigrants from metropolitan France and also from Spain, Italy, Malta, and Germany;[79] their children would thus be made French by the law of 1889. Remaining apart from this process of "integration," which had already involved Algerian Jews in 1870, were the "Muslim natives" who made up the majority of Algeria's population. Formally they were French subjects. Practically their nationality was denatured, emptied of its rights: the law of 1889 downgraded their status irremediably.

From a Closed-Door Policy to a "One-Drop-at-a-Time" Approach When the treaty of capitulation was signed by the Bey of Algeria on 5 July 1830, France made a formal commitment "not to touch the freedom of the inhabitants of all classes or their religion."[80] In practice the natives—this is what Algeria's inhabitants were called—were governed according to a special and distinct status, depending on whether they were Jews or Muslims, but they were not French. As early as 1832 the civil intendant of the regency in Algiers—the equivalent of a prefect[81]—requested on behalf of "a Moor of Algiers, one of the most important owing to his fortune and his renown," an act "that would recognize him officially as a French subject, and by this token guarantee him the protection of France in any place and in any situation in which he may find himself." And he added, speaking for himself: "France may not always remain in possession of this country. . . . If it leaves, if a Muslim power is established here, there will be no security for us, Moors of Algeria, . . . we who shall have united our interest with [France's], who shall have lent a hand to the consolidation of its authority and the introduction of European mores. For this case in particular, we need to be assured of France's protection and to have the right to claim to represent her, wherever we might seek asylum, either among our own children or among our coreligionaries of Africa and the Levant."[82]

The intendant urged the government to act quickly.[83] As soon as the annexation of Algeria was pronounced by a royal ordinance of 24 February 1834, the native Muslims and Jews were considered French subjects.[84] But they did not have full French nationality, and there was no procedure by which they could obtain it. One proposal did seek to facilitate naturalization as early as 1846 by reducing the ten-year waiting period that applied in metropolitan France at the time, but it reserved that benefit to foreigners residing in Algeria: "Naturalization of Muslims is impossible, because it could not take place without overturning their civil laws, which are at the same time religious laws. . . . The Koran is the religious code of Muslims; it is also their *civil* and political code . . . [It] indicates not only what must be believed, but what must be done in purely civil matters. There is thus in Islam such a connection between civil and religious law that it is impossible to touch one without affecting the other."

The minister of war also rejected the idea of naturalizing Jews: "One of the most serious mistakes the government could make in Algeria would be to grant Jews, a demeaned and scorned population, what we do not grant Muslims. Like the latter, the native Israelites must, in relation to ourselves, remain what they are and solely what they are, that is, French subjects; as the Koran does for the Muslims, the Talmud attributes to the Jews civil laws that we have retained for them."[85]

This bill, which did not see the light of day owing to the fall of the July Monarchy, was revived throughout the 1850s with no better success, but with the same orientation: France was ready to facilitate the naturalization of foreigners, but there was no question of "naturalizing" Muslims or Jews. Between 1851 and 1865, for example, the ministry of war strove to make an exception by naturalizing Mohamed Ben Hacem. Born 4 March 1830 in Algiers, first a lieutenant in the 1st regiment of Algerian sharpshooters, he fought in the African and Italian campaigns, then became a student at the agricultural school in Grignon: "Mr. Mohamed ben Hacem, who has excellent principles, also possesses in his intelligence and his education a notable superiority over most of the native officers."[86] On 25 July 1864 he was finally admitted to residency as "of Moorish origin," and the ministry of war requested his exceptional naturalization at once, by virtue of article 2 of the law of 3 December 1849, which provided for reducing the waiting period from ten years to one for a foreigner who had rendered important services to France. But the Council of State did not agree, and it was through the senatus-consulte of 14 July 1865 that ben Hacem became, several months later, one of the first Algerian Muslims to be "naturalized" as French.[87]

Inspired by Ismaël Urbain, that senatus-consulte was promulgated by Napoleon III in the context of his "Arab kingdom" policy.[88] It allowed Muslim and Israelite natives to ask to "enjoy the rights of French citizens"; a foreigner who had lived in Algeria for three years could benefit from the same procedure. The request was investigated, and if all went well the "quality of French citizen" was bestowed through a decree issued by the Council of State. For the first time full nationality was opened to native Jews and Muslims. The three categories of Algerian inhabitants who were not fully French — 30,000 Jews, 3,000,000 Muslims, and 250,000 foreigners — were dealt with separately but on almost the same basis, in this ad hoc nationality law that was applied henceforth in Algeria. The formal equality among the three categories of "not fully French" people was quickly shattered as of 1870, when the status of Jews was modified.

The Crémieux Decree and the "Naturalization" of Algerian Jews On 24 October 1870 a decree of the National Defense government that had been set up after the defeat at Sedan in the Franco-Prussian War conferred French nationality on the indigenous Israelites of the departments of Algeria and abrogated the senatus-consulte of 14 July 1865 as far as this group was concerned.[89] For the Jews of Algeria, this was the final step in a process of assimilation that had begun at the start of the French conquest and been well received by this small minority that had been discriminated against under the regime of the beys in Algeria.[90]

As early as 1834 the French authorities took a first step in assimilating the Algerian Jews to those of metropolitan France by removing from the rabbinical court the power to pass penal judgments on conflicts between Jews (leaving it the power to act only in cases involving marriage, divorce, or religion).[91] In 1841 the rabbis lost all juridical power over their coreligionists, who were henceforth to be judged "exclusively . . . by French courts."[92] After the constitution of a bishop's seat in Algiers by a papal bull of 9 August 1838 and of a consistorial church for Protestants on 31 October 1839, the Israelite consistory of France took steps to align the Algerian Jewish community with the Napoleonic model of metropolitan France. The ordinance of 9 November 1845 created a central consistory in Algiers and provincial consistories in Oran and Constantine.[93] The law of 16 June 1851 finally submitted to French law all transmissions of property except those carried out between Muslims — thus including all those carried out by Jews.

"Collective naturalization" was soon demanded by the majority of Algerian Jews. During his trip to Algeria in May 1865, Napoleon III received a petition to this effect signed by ten thousand Jews. From 1865 to 1869 the general councils of the three Algerian provinces, on which both colonials and Muslims sat, expressed unanimous wishes each year in favor of the naturalization of the native Jews. On 9 March 1870 the deputy Léopold Le Hon, who had returned from an investigation in Algeria and become the spokesmen for the colonials,[94] intervened before the legislative body to attest to the Algerian Jews' wish to be naturalized "en masse":[95] "there is no good reason to refuse them the favor they are asking and there is a very great need not to delay this act."[96] Napoleon III had already approved the act in principle; on 8 March 1870 his government transmitted the bill for collective naturalization, and on 24 October 1870, after an investigation and a favorable opinion from the governor general Patrice de Mac-Mahon, it became one of the seven decrees inspired by Adolphe Crémieux on the subject of Algeria that were passed by the provisional government.[97]

Crémieux, minister of justice, was also president of the Universal Israelite Alliance;[98] during his seventeen trips to Algeria he had become well acquainted with his co-religionists, and he had spent twelve years fighting for collective naturalization.[99] But if the provisional government, meeting in Tours on 4 September, a few days after the defeat at Sedan and the fall of the Empire, passed several measures on the subject of Algeria at a time when the reorganization of the army, the mobilization of the population, and the reconquest of France's territory were the priorities,[100] it was because the situation in Algeria was particularly unstable. The defeat of Napoleon III, who had been perceived as partial to the natives, heartened the European community, which had welcomed the arrival of the Republic. It was feared that the Prussians would do something to destabilize the Muslim population, already on the verge of insurrection.[101] Part of the army and the administration had remained loyal to the emperor. The colonials grew impatient: they sent delegations to Tours to demand the firing of military leaders and the appointment of a civilian governor; as that appointment was delayed, the municipal council in Algiers, which was soon constituted as a defense committee, gave Romuald Vuillermoz, its recently elected mayor, the role of interim extraordinary commissioner.[102] Instability reigned. One of Crémieux's seven decrees of 24 October 1870 was thus intended to satisfy the colonials by carrying out the traditional republican program:[103] it "assimilated" Algeria administratively to metropolitan France and divided it into three departments, under the authority of a civil governor general reporting to the minister of the interior. The legal assimilation of the Algerian Jews went in the same direction: it ensured their loyalty to the new regime and brought to a French population of about 90,000 the reinforcement of 35,000 new citizens; it employed the same strategy for consolidating the Algerian situation to the benefit of the provisional government.[104]

This collective naturalization was carried out, in contrast, against the will of the colonial administration; a segment of the colonials, after approving it, came to oppose it as well. After the legislative elections of 9 July 1871, when the Algerian Jews voted overwhelmingly for Vuillermoz over the conservative candidate Auguste Warnier, on 21 July 1871 Thiers's government proposed a decree that would wholly abrogate Crémieux's decree.[105] A special commission appointed by the National Assembly proposed that the Algerian Jews could become fully French by simple declaration.[106] A compromise was finally reached between Crémieux and Admiral Louis Henri de Gueydon,[107] the new civil governor of Algeria:[108] a decree of interpretation issued on 7 October 1871 confirmed that the decree of 24 October 1870 had naturalized "the Israelites born in Algeria since the French occupation or born since that period to parents who had been established in Algeria at the time the occupation took place."[109] This decree of collective naturalization thus did not include Jews from the territories colonized after 1871, for example those from M'zab, a territory attached to France in 1882; except in cases of individual naturalization, these Jews retained the status of "native Israelite" until 1962.

Foreigners Rather than Muslims The Crémieux decree that brought about the collective naturalization of Jews might have led to a policy of access to "full nationality" for the Muslims. Among the colonials this perspective, immediately rejected in 1871, was rejected more and more strongly as the years went on. In March 1871 a massive revolt occurred in Kabylia, in the wake of the French army's defeat by Prussia and the disorganization of power in France.[110] With Napoleon III the Muslims lost a protector. They feared that the civil power re-

placing military authority and the Arab bureaus would confer unlimited freedom of action on the colonials. The suspension on 19 December 1870 of the
senatus-consulte of 1863 governing the dividing up of tribal lands increased their
fears. On 24 December 1870 the extension of civil authority to territories formerly under military protection confirmed that the Muslims were indeed in the
hands of the colonials.[111] The subsequent revolt in Kabylia lasted six months and
brought 200,000 natives and 86,000 Frenchmen into conflict. On 5 May 1871 Mohamed Mokrani, the leader of the revolt, was killed by French troops, and on 13
September Kabylia was definitively subjugated. At that point, how could anyone
envisage the collective naturalization that had been called for between 1858 and
1870? As governor de Gueydon[112] summed it up in 1872: "One would be creating
at a single stroke two million citizens amidst whom the French minority would
be stifled. What would then become of the principle and the basis for our domination?" The "new doctrine" of the Algerian colonizers was established: there
was no question of mass naturalization; the narrow door of individual naturalization that had been opened by the senatus-consulte of 1865 would have to suffice. Naturalization was often viewed unfavorably by the Muslims (who regarded
those who sought and received it as *M'tourni*, renegades), and the number of
naturalizations was low, typically twenty to seventy a year, with a peak of 137
in 1875.

In Paris, however, voices were raised in "indigenophile" circles in favor of
granting Algerian Muslims immediate or gradual access to full nationality. Paul
Leroy-Beaulieu, who founded the French society for the protection of natives
of the colonies in 1881, spoke out clearly in favor of assimilation—a gradual
assimilation, which would make it possible to merge the different elements of
the Algerian population.[113] As he saw it, supporting the Arabs' right to vote
would make it possible to "disaggregate the compact mass of each tribe, [that
is,] to prepare a fertile ground for our ideas and our laws where they could more
easily germinate and take root."[114] In Parliament collective naturalization "in
the status" was proposed in 1887 by two deputies on the left, Henri Michelin and
Guillaume Gaulier.[115] But the administration of Algeria was opposed: "Certain
Arabophiles, who would like to make Muslims happy in spite of themselves, are
asking that they be naturalized en masse. The argument most frequently invoked
is the precedent of the naturalization of the Jews. As if one could repair one
foolish mistake by committing another, an even more serious one. The measure,
which would necessarily entail obligatory military service, would have as consequences: 1° the overturning of the personal status to which the natives hold more
than to life itself; 2° the right to vote granted to ignorant, fanatic, and hostile
masses, in the middle of which the French would be drowned; 3° the arming of a

warlike race that owes its inferiority in war only to its inexperience in the current strategic conditions and to its lack of cohesion."[116]

With a view to making the transitions easier, a bill proposed by Alfred Martineau in 1890 anticipated "granting French naturalization gradually to all the Muslim natives of Algeria."[117] First, only those living in communes where "the French population [was] more numerous than the Muslim population" would be involved. In the other communes Martineau proposed to grant naturalization to (1) all children born after promulgation of the law, (2) the natives who had served under the French flag or had held administrative positions, and (3) those who had benefited from an adequate education as confirmed by a certificate of primary studies. This project got a good deal of support. Some legal scholars, such as André Weiss, joined the cause.[118] But it came up against a parliamentary majority easily mobilized by the representatives of the French in Algeria. A powerful colonial group was in fact formed in the Chamber of Deputies; a few weeks after its creation on 15 June 1892 it brought together ninety-one deputies "seated on the most diverse benches, but all united by the desire to ensure the power and greatness of external, colonial France."[119] This colonial group quickly became, along with the agricultural group, one of the strongest in Parliament. It counted 120 members in the Chamber elected in 1893, nearly 200 in 1902, and 250 in the Chamber elected in 1936.[120]

In reality the elected representatives of the French colonials in Parliament were energized at that time by a cause other than that of the Muslims. The senatus-consulte of 1865 had not had the anticipated effects on the foreigners living in Algeria (Spaniards, Italians, and so on). Despite the low cost and the rapidity of the procedure,[121] between 1865 and 1881 there had been only 4,428 naturalizations, an average of 276 a year. The foreign population had grown so much that it exceeded the French population. Hence Governor Louis Tirman's observation: "Since we no longer have the hope of increasing the French population by means of official colonization, we must seek the remedy in the naturalization of foreigners."[122] On 30 September 1884 Tirman submitted to the government a bill developed by the law school in Algiers that would have conferred French nationality on anyone born in Algeria to foreign parents (unless the person decided to retain his or her original nationality in the year after reaching the age of majority).[123] But the government, attached to the principle that "nationality results from blood ties," rejected a provision that would have consecrated jus soli.[124] On 23 May 1885 Tirman tried again, proposing a special law for Algeria; this too was rejected.[125] An opportunity finally arose when the full text of the nationality law (adopted in 1889) came up for discussion in the Chamber. The deputies from the Nord and the border departments wanted to see jus soli return in order to impose equality of obligations, in particular military service, on the children of immigrants. Support from the representatives from Algeria, who won the application of jus soli for their territory, undoubtedly contributed to the adoption of the law of 1889.[126] Henceforth, children born in Algeria to a parent born in Algeria were French at birth, just like children born in France to a parent born in France.[127] As for parents born abroad, the children would be French upon reaching the age of majority, unless they renounced French nationality during the year that followed. Applied to a foreign population that had been present in many cases for two generations, the law had immediate effects. In 1890 the number of military conscriptions rose from 2,631 to 4,740, and remained at the higher level in subsequent years.[128] In the census of 1891 there were 267,672 French persons as opposed to 215,793 foreigners; in 1896 the gap had increased (331,137 versus 211,580). In 1898 Governor Edward Laferrière estimated that among the 384,000 French people in Algeria, 275,000 were French "by origin" and 109,000 were "naturalized" (including 53,000 Jews). The law of 1889 was indeed "the birth certificate of the European people of Algeria."[129]

The Inferior Status of Indigenous Muslims At the request of the representatives from Algeria, the law of 1889 thus did not apply to the indigenous Muslims. To become fully French, they were governed by the senatus-consulte of 1865. Remaining subjects, they had a special status. In 1830 such a status might have looked like a privilege granted by the victor to the vanquished:[130] the right of self-government. But that privilege evaporated very quickly, and Muslims found themselves subjected to an exceptional status of inferiority.

With the signing of the surrender in 1830, the conditions of purchase or forced sales of real property in Algiers were already in violation of the terms of capitulation.[131] This was the first act of a policy of expropriation that punctuated the several stages in the long, hard conquest of Algeria. It preceded the confiscation of the beylik's lands and the transfer to state ownership of religious goods (*habous*) — properties donated to religious entities such as holy cities or mosques.[132]

Two types of lands remained: private properties and collective tribal lands; the latter, on which members occupied the plots they worked, could neither be transferred nor rented.[133] After the massacre of the Europeans from the Mitidja Plain by Abd el-Kader's troops in 1839, the lands of the Sahel and Mitidja tribes were confiscated. Then, after ordinances adopted in 1844 and 1846, uncultivated lands — the rich tribal lands around Algiers, Bône (now Annaba), and Oran in particular — and those to which no tribe could present regular property titles were declared ownerless and became state property. Abd el-Kader's surrender in

1847, then the definitive conquest of Kabylia in 1857, made it possible, owing to the practice of "cantonment," to take a further step toward agricultural colonization: the bulk of the lands that had been occupied by the vanquished tribes were considered to have become the property of the French state, with the natives occupying them only as usufructuaries. These usage rights were exchanged for property rights, but only for the least fertile lands.[134] With the repression of the insurrection in Kabylia in 1871, the insurgents and their tribes[135] saw 446,000 hectares (1,102,100 acres) of their best lands confiscated. Finally, the Warnier law of 26 July 1873 brought an end to the regime of the senatus-consulte of 1863, which had acknowledged the "cantoned" tribes'[136] right to ownership of the territories of which they had had "traditional and permanent enjoyment on any basis whatsoever."[137] Formally intended to give individual property to the Arabs, the Warnier law made it possible to eliminate the traditional practice of joint ownership. Any European owner of even a tiny part of a jointly owned property could request the elimination of joint ownership. For the natives, a sale in such cases most often led to financial ruin and the loss of their property.[138]

Sequestration was in fact one of the three specific penalties that could be applied to the indigenous Muslims for "infractions peculiar to the native population not provided for by French law."[139] Codified in 1881, the special infractions gradually came to constitute a veritable "native code."[140] A list of twenty-seven infractions specific to the native population was established in 1874. The list was augmented in 1876 and again in 1877. In 1881 it included the following infractions among others: leaving the territory of the commune without a travel permit; committing a disrespectful act; making an offensive statement about an agent of the authority even unrelated to his functions; making a complaint or a demand that was known to be inaccurate or that was repeated to the same authority after it had been resolved according to regulations.[141] In addition to sequestration, the native could be punished by a fine or a prison sentence. These individual penalties could be supplemented by collective fines inflicted on the tribes or the douars (Arab tent villages), in the case of forest fires.[142] In autonomous communes (communes in which full authority was vested in the mayor), the justice of the peace had the power to judge and decide on penalties. In mixed communes (those in which some Europeans resided), the administrator of the commune played the role of judge.

It goes without saying that the exercise of public freedoms was extremely limited (the ban on public meetings and travel was total between 1862 to 1890, then slightly relaxed).[143] Furthermore, the representation of Muslims in elective political bodies in Algeria diminished after 1870: the decree of 7 April 1884 reduced to one fourth (rather than one third) the number of municipal councilors who could be elected by the Muslims to each council in an autonomous commune, and there could never be more than six, even in the municipal council of Algiers, which had forty members. Finally, Muslim councilors could no longer participate in mayoral elections.

In the aftermath of the anti-Semitic disturbances of 1897–98, when the colonials obtained the creation of a sixty-nine-member assembly that could establish Algeria's budget under the control of the governor and Parliament, the composition of this assembly—called "the financial delegations"—reflected the unjust status of the indigenous population: forty-eight Europeans (twenty-four elected by the colonial farming community, twenty-four by non-colonials, representing 630,000 people) as opposed to twenty-one Muslim delegates who represented no fewer than 3.6 million people.[144] The same disparity was found in taxation: in 1907 the taxes paid by Muslims represented 45 percent of Algeria's total budgetary receipts, whereas only 4–8 percent of the expenses—and the percentage was particularly low for expenditures on schools—went to the Muslims.[145]

Nationality Denatured To escape indigenous status, an Algerian Muslim could ask to become fully French. Although he was already formally French, he had to submit to an even more restrictive naturalization procedure than the one reserved for foreigners residing in France.

When efforts are made to explain the very low number of Algerian Muslims who sought access to full nationality, the reason most often given is the desire of a large majority of the population to keep the personal status dictated by the Koran. It was true that the senatus-consulte of 1865 did not oblige Algerian Muslims to renounce their religion—they could retain it as a moral code and a collection of religious prescriptions—but it did oblige them to respect the French Civil Code, that is, to refrain henceforth from practicing the five customs that were incompatible with that code: polygamy; the right of *djebr*, which allowed a Muslim father to marry off his child until a certain age; the right of a husband to break the conjugal bond at his own discretion; the theory of the "sleeping child," which made it possible to recognize the legitimate filiation of a child born more than ten months and as long as five years after the dissolution of a marriage; and finally, the male privilege in matters of inheritance.[146]

It would have been possible to naturalize Algerian Muslims "in the status," that is, to declare them fully French while allowing them to retain their personal status in conformity with the Koran's prescriptions. For reasons of convenience rather than principle, this was not envisaged. Naturalization "in the status" was already present in French colonial law: the inhabitants of the four French communes in Senegal had been made French by the combination of the law of 24

April 1833 and the abolition of slavery in 1848; the law of 29 September 1916 had later confirmed their standing, along with that of their descendants, as French citizens.[147] By the decree of 5 April 1848, the natives of the five French cities of India had also been granted the right to vote independently of their personal status.[148] They were French and citizens independently of any individual naturalization, enrolled on the same electoral lists as other French citizens for the election of a deputy to the Chamber, even if the exercise of their political rights was limited to the territory of the colony.

It must not be supposed either that the mere fact of renouncing the personal status of the Muslim[149] (that is, the customs incompatible with the Civil Code) sufficed for acquiring full nationality in Algeria.[150] Proof of this is found in André Bonnichon's study of Muslims converted to Catholicism.[151] In the 1920s, depending on who was doing the estimating, there were several hundred or a few thousand such cases.[152] Most were naturalized, but not all, sometimes for reasons of age: converts younger than twenty-one did not yet have access to naturalization. In these cases the non-naturalized convert was still viewed as a Muslim subject to the "native code," to the penal and police regime, to the repressive indigenous courts, and also, where there was one, to the court of the *cadi* (a Muslim judge with jurisdiction over civil, legal, and religious matters). To justify that practice, the court of appeals in Algiers ruled in 1903 that the meaning of the term "Muslim" was not "purely confessional, but that it [designated] on the contrary the entire body of individuals of Muslim origin who, not having been granted full nationality rights, necessarily retained their Muslim personal status, without there being any need to distinguish whether they [belonged][153] to the Mahometan cult or not."

This imputation of an ethnic or religious origin, which maintained the converted Muslim in the indigenous status as long as he had not gone through naturalization (a procedure that required a decision by the public authority), reveals the ethnico-political — and not merely civil or religious — character of this status. Muslims could exit from indigenous status only if they asked to do so and if the state accepted the request, after an investigation, as in a classic naturalization proceeding. The senatus-consulte of 1865 did not use the term "naturalization," since Algerian Muslims were presumed to be French. Nevertheless, legal doctrine, the Supreme Court, and the administration called and continued to call this procedure by its true name, naturalization — a naturalization handled in the Ministry of Justice according to the same modalities and by the same services as the naturalization of foreigners. In 1987 Professor Paul Lagarde characterized contrasting approaches to the attribution of nationality as follows: "What the legislator [takes] into consideration is the intensity of the bonds that unite an individual to his population. If these bonds are very strong, then nationality will be attributed to that person without anyone asking him his opinion. Individual desire will play no role. In contrast, if the bonds are real but not sufficiently strong, then an appeal may be made to the interested party's affirmative desire to reinforce the bonds that in themselves alone would not have been sufficient."[154]

He could have added that if these bonds are contestable, the appeal is made not only to the person's desire but also to state control.

In the French settlements in India, the natives had obtained individual rights to full nationality: by the decree of 21 September 1881, to become fully French they had only to renounce their personal status by a voluntary act and declare that they were placing themselves under the empire of French law.[155] No discretionary decision by the government was involved: all natives of India of both sexes over the age of twenty-one could make that declaration at the moment of marriage, or before an officer of the civil state or a justice of the peace in their place of legal residence.

For Algerian Muslims the choice had thus been made to maintain naturalization, the most difficult and most controlled procedure of all. And the procedure was not made easy. Applicants encountered obstacles at every turn. A dossier had to include eight separate documents, including a certificate of good conduct and good morals; a candidate had to appear in person before the mayor (decree of 21 April 1866) or the administrative authority and "declare that he had abandoned his personal status to be governed by French civil and political laws";[156] an administrative investigation was made into the candidates' morality, their antecedents, and especially their family situation; finally, the dossier was transmitted along with the opinions of the prefect and the governor to the Ministry of Justice and then to the Council of State, before a decree was signed by the president of the Republic.[157]

The naturalization procedure was all the more difficult in that the local administration proved exceptionally uncooperative. All the testimony points in the same direction.

Jules Ferry, who went to Algeria in 1892 as the head of a delegation of seven senators, noted that "the administrators [were] systematically opposed to naturalization."[158] Albin Rozet[159] attested for his part that on 23 December 1913 in the Chamber of Deputies, "a Native came to find an administrator, a village mayor, and said to him: 'I want to be naturalized.' The administrator or the mayor answered him: 'What do you need to be naturalized for? You will have trouble in your family, your wife is probably not enthusiastic, your son-in-law will quarrel with you.'"[160] This testimony was confirmed in 1919 by the Socialist deputy Doizy[161] and then by the former governor Maurice Viollette,[162] who wrote in 1931:

"Naturalizations would be infinitely more numerous if the administration made them easier."[163] André Bonnichon also pointed out the lack of eagerness to welcome naturalization requests: "We have been told about the case of a justice of the peace in Kabylia where seventy-two dossiers had lingered for two, three, and four years."[164]

The result: in fifty years (1865 to 1915), 2,396 Algerian Muslims became French through naturalization. The majority were military men, civil servants, or Catholic converts. Until 1899 the number of requests rejected was very small. From 1899 it grew markedly, reaching one third, one half, or even three fifths of the requests;[165] the administration justified this by asserting that "the applicants' qualifications are examined with severity and with a concern for granting the quality of being French only to those who have given unequivocal proof of their attachment to France."[166]

To characterize the situation of French subjects, thus of Algerian Muslims, reference is often made to a decision of the court of appeals in Indochina in 1910: "an intermediate situation between that of French citizens and that of foreigners; in their nationality, they resemble citizens; in their personal status, they resemble foreigners."[167]

As for the Algerians, one could say that in their nationality, they resembled foreigners without being entirely their equals, and that in their personal status they were inferior to foreigners. Like newly arrived foreigners in France, Algerians were subjected to the procedure of naturalization to become fully French. However, descendants of foreigners automatically became French, while descendants of Muslim Algerians, who were also born on French soil, still had to go through naturalization proceedings. In addition, foreigners in France benefited from the same civil rights as French nationals, and were subject to the same penal laws; finally, they were protected by their own state as represented in France (including in Algiers) by consuls. Muslims, for their part, were subject to the "native code" unilaterally decreed and administered by France. Theoretically a Muslim abroad was under the protection of a French consul; but the protection was purely theoretical in that Muslims did not have the right to leave their villages without authorization.

The naturalization procedure to which the Algerian Muslims were subjected — despite being legally French — thus constituted, to use Zouhir Boushaba's terms, a "denaturing of the notion of nationality."[168] The nationality of the Algerian Muslim, emptied of its rights and its meaning, could in fact only become "full" through a procedure reserved in French law for the least "assimilated" foreigner. Algerian Muslims were thus de facto part of the most "undesirable" foreign origin, a group whose members were accepted only in very small numbers.

The Failed Reform of 1919 At the turn of the century the situation seemed to be evolving. The emergence of the "Young Algerian" movement, inspired by the Young Turks, involved a few hundred "advanced" graduates of French schools, primary school teachers, businessmen, and industrialists; they had relaunched a movement seeking rights for Algerians. In 1872 Jules Ferry had already met with educated and politicized young Muslims who "talked to him about the problems of naturalization or the representation of Muslims."[169] In 1908 and 1909, when opening military service to Algerian Muslims was being discussed in metropolitan France, the "Young Algerian" movement was in favor, for it hoped to be able to obtain, in exchange, gradual equality of public freedoms and citizens' rights.[170]

At the same time, in 1911 in Paris *La Revue indigène* published the opinion of several law professors who called for "naturalization in the status"; according to the journal's editor Paul Bourdarie, this had become "an ineluctable necessity."[171] This special issue of *La Revue indigène* inaugurated a movement that gained traction with the decrees of 17 January and 3 February 1912 extending military recruitment to Muslims. In June 1912 nine Young Algerian delegates went to Paris, and under the leadership of Albin Rozet were variously received by Raymond Poincaré, Théodore Steeg (minister of the interior), and Georges Clemenceau. The delegates submitted what came to be known as the "Young Algerian" Manifesto of 1912. In it they demanded the end of the "indigenate" regime, equality with respect to taxation,[172] a better representation of Muslims in the assemblies in Algeria and in metropolitan France, and the right to be naturalized "in the status" through simple declaration, for those who had satisfied their military service obligations.

When the First World War was declared, the Algerian Muslims supplied 173,000 soldiers and 119,000 workers; they had been requisitioned to replace the workforce that had been mobilized in metropolitan France. On 25 November 1915 Georges Clemenceau and Georges Leygues, presidents of the commissions on foreign affairs in the Senate and the Chamber, asked for "the admission of natives to the benefit of a new regime of naturalization not implying the renunciation of personal status." When Clemenceau became president of the Council of State in November 1917, the process started up again. The Socialist deputy Marius Moutet[173] put together several bills submitted during the war,[174] and in the name of the Chamber's commission on foreign affairs he proposed to make access to full nationality easier: according to his proposal, any Algerian Muslim more than twenty-five years old could become a French citizen upon a simple request to the civil tribunal where he or she had legal residence, if at least one of the following conditions was fulfilled: the applicant had served in the French army or had a son who had taken part in a campaign during the war; was a landowner or farmer, or was registered on the tax rolls; held or had held a position in the civil service, a mandate by election, or a decoration; or was married to or born to a native who had become a French citizen.[175] What is more, respect for the French Civil Code meant renouncing one's personal status only for the future. Thus a polygamist could become fully French under the new law; he would only have to abstain from increasing his polygamy.

The colonials' elected representatives to the "financial delegations" immediately mobilized against what looked to them like the "tomb of French supremacy in Algeria."[176] They adopted several motions, drawing the attention of the government and of Parliament especially "to the certain danger there would be, in maintaining their past personal status, in allowing thousands of natives to exercise the rights of French citizens, to participate in making laws to which they would not be subjected, and one day to submerge under their votes those of the French people of Algeria."[177] Clemenceau then asked Governor Charles Jonnart to find a compromise, and on the question of personal status the government yielded.[178] The law of 4 February 1919 did create a new procedure of access to full nationality,[179] but it set such conditions that it appeared in certain respects more restrictive than the senatus-consulte of 1865. In addition to monogamy or celibacy, two years' residency in the same commune was required. The public prosecutor or the governor could also oppose a request "on grounds of unworthiness" — in other words, as Charles-Robert Ageron has said, "owing to unsuitability."[180] The effect of the law was thus weak. Here again the procedure deterred those who might benefit from it. Candidates frequently had trouble supplying the necessary documents. In the absence of a valid birth certificate, for example, an *acte de notoriété* established by six witnesses was required, which implied paying the witnesses' travel expenses and compensating them for a day's lost wages.[181] Many people did not have the means. Between 1919 and 1930, 1,204 Muslims were naturalized, out of 1,547 requests. An additional 760 were naturalized through the procedure established by the senatus-consulte of 1865, which had been maintained at the suggestion of the Moutet report against the advice of the Algerian administration; this procedure primarily allowed people in military service, residents of metropolitan France, or young people under the age of twenty-five to escape from local control or from the restrictions of the procedure of 1919.[182]

The law of 1919 was the last attempt to improve Muslims' rights by the attribution of French nationality. Owing to this law's restrictive nature, demands made after 1919 focused on obtaining real rights for subjects who had not had them—abolishing the "native code," establishing fiscal equality, ensuring the right to vote—*without the attribution of full French nationality*.

From 1920 to 1962: Rights without Full Nationality With the failure of the provision for access to full nationality, the other element of the law of 4 February 1919—the right of elected Muslim representatives to participate in the mayoral elections in municipal councils—first became important.

According to one provision of the law, Muslim council members—who could constitute one third of the municipal council rather than one fifth, as before—would participate in the election of the mayor.[183] The elected representatives of the colonials on the financial delegations rose up vigorously against granting Muslims the right to participate in electing the mayor, and adopted several motions: "This innovation seems to us extremely serious. . . . The French majority [*sic*] cannot agree that its will should be dominated by that of natives who have not wanted the rights of citizens"; "It would be inopportune, premature, and dangerous to allow the indigenous municipal council members to participate in the election of the French mayors and adjuncts."[184] Hubert Lyautey, who followed the session of the financial delegations closely, wrote to a friend: "I believe the situation is hopeless. The French agricultural colonials have a pure Boche mentality, with the same theories on inferior races destined to be exploited mercilessly. Among them there is neither humanity nor intelligence."[185]

But while the colonials succeeded in getting "naturalization in the status" withdrawn, the government and Parliament did not yield on the right of elected Muslim council members to participate in mayoral elections. Another important aspect of the law of 1919 law is that access to the right to vote was extended. There were 100,000 voters instead of 5,000 for the general councils and the financial delegations, or 10.5 percent of the Muslims aged twenty-five and above; more than 425,000, or 43 percent, for the municipal councils in autonomous communes and the tribal assemblies of the *douars* reconstituted as autonomous communes in 1918.[186] This in effect created a Muslim electoral body exempt from the "native code," which the "advanced" Muslims—the leaders, but also an agricultural middle class that was coming into existence[187]—would keep alive independently of Paris, where it was still not represented in Parliament.[188] The elections of November 1919 thus saw voter participation of 75 percent, an electoral campaign, and an opposition victory: those opposed to the colonial administration won between 32 percent and 42 percent of the seats in the general councils and the financial delegations.

The times had changed: the First World War had internationalized the right of nations to dispose of their own lands and had allowed various Algerian political organizations to take root.

A descendant of emir Abd el-Kader, emir Khaled, founded Ikdam ("resolve, audacity") in March 1919, and in May 1919 he asked President Woodrow Wilson to recognize the claims of Algerian Muslims. In metropolitan France, where immigration had developed since 1919 (Algerian Muslims no longer needed travel permits),[189] the North African Star party (L'Étoile nord-africaine, ENA), founded in 1926 by Messali Hadj, advocated Algerian independence. In Algeria in 1927 Ferhat Abbas and Dr. Ben Djelloul founded the Federation of Elected Native Representatives and renewed the demand of the "young Muslims" for equal rights. At the same time, a movement was developing among the *oulemas*, reformist theologians who were defending Algeria's "cultural" identity with the formula "Arabic is my language, Algeria is my country, Islam is my religion."[190]

In 1936 Léon Blum's government, inspired by Algeria's former governor Maurice Viollette, proposed that a small group of Muslims, some 24,000, be granted the right to vote alongside the 200,000 French voters, independently of their personal status, which they would be able to keep.[191] Compared to the naturalization "in the status" proposed in the Moutet report of 1919, this new proposal was very modest. But it was supported in Algeria only by the oulemas' movement and by Ferhat Abbas. The Algerian People's party (Parti du peuple algérien, PPA), created in 1937 after dissolution of the ENA, favored independence and opposed Viollette's proposal. Above all, the project spurred a revolt among the colonists' elected representatives, who rejected the transgression of the principle on which the colonization of Algeria rested: the distinction between French citizens and Muslim subjects.[192] They feared not so much the effect of enlarging the electoral body on the election of deputies (they proposed, moreover, to have the Muslims vote in a separate electoral college to elect ten deputies and three senators) as the effect on the election of mayors.

The law of 1919 had in fact already stirred up in the little commune of Mekla what these representatives feared in other communes: the possibility that "Muslims" could be a majority in a municipal council. Mekla, a mixed commune, was a special case: the very small population that was fully French was principally made up of naturalized Muslims, who had thus elected five municipal councilors of Muslim origin in the college of ten councilors reserved for Frenchmen with full rights. The five other members of the municipal council were natives, and in all, the ten "Muslims" had helped elect a mayor, who was moreover a "European" Frenchman. In his memoirs in 1931, Maurice Viollette recalled that at the request of the governor general of Algeria, the council of the prefecture (today the administrative tribunal) had annulled the election of the mayor and his adjunct, because they had been elected with a majority of "native" votes. The considerations were the following: "The newly elected council includes five French members and five natives who are naturalized French and five non-naturalized natives, that is, ten natives versus five Frenchmen. . . . At no time did the legislature imagine allowing these native councilors, non-naturalized, generally illiterate, elected by restricted suffrage, allying themselves notably with a minority and sometimes with elements of disorder, to arbitrate and distort the electoral manifestations in the communes; . . . it would in fact be unconstitutional to continue to allow these native councilors, elected by restricted suffrage, to arbitrate and distort the will clearly expressed by universal French suffrage and to bring, within the Algerian communes, currently undergoing rapid changes, troubles of an administrative and economic order of exceptional seriousness, of such a nature in particular as to abolish any principle of national sovereignty there."[193]

The proposal of Blum and Viollette multiplied by a factor of four or five the number of Muslims in the first college, and thus the "risk" that the situation in Mekla would be reproduced. As the elected representatives of the colonists did not want to see this happen at any price, they ensured that the proposal would fail.

Later on, the Second World War and Liberation made possible advances that would have been inconceivable a few years earlier. The ordinance of 7 March 1944 eliminated the penal status of natives and subjected the Muslims to the same courts and the same laws as all the French. In addition, it naturalized 60,000 Muslims in their personal status, and these thus became electors in the first college, while all male Muslims aged twenty-one or older, 1,210,000 persons, became electors of a second college. The ordinance of 17 August 1945 introduced parity of representation between the Muslim college and the college of common law; each was henceforth represented by twenty-two members of Parliament: fifteen deputies and seven senators. The Lamine Gueye law of 17 May 1946 recognized the citizenship of all French nationals. Finally, the statute of 20 September 1947 established the principles of political and civic equality and of equal access for all to public service positions.

Beginning in 1956, in the framework of the policy of "integration," all the institutions elected by the double college were gradually dissolved.[194] The ordinances of 15 November 1958 gave Algerian Muslims (men and women) a proportional representation that better reflected their importance in the Algerian population: forty-six deputies out of sixty-seven, and twenty-two senators out of thirty-one.[195]

But on the political and military levels, a process was already under way that led in 1962 to Algeria's independence. At that time only some ten thousand Muslims were fully French, either because they themselves had been naturalized or because one of their parents had been. Some remained in Algeria and were granted the new Algerian nationality; others were in metropolitan France or went to live there with their French nationality.[196] As for the vast majority of Algerian Muslims, they could remain French, but on condition that before 22 March 1967 in France (that is, in metropolitan France or the overseas departments) they sign a declaration recognizing their French nationality and have the declaration formally recorded by the minister in charge of naturalizations.[197]

By a sort of historical irony, from 1962 the double jus soli that applied in metropolitan France allowed all children born in France to a parent born in Algeria to be French from birth, without distinction of origin. As for the status of their children, all the former inhabitants of Algeria—French nationals, Jewish or Muslim subjects—were equal, retroactively.

The Legal Limitations on Naturalized Persons

The third stage in the development of French nationality began in 1927. The law of 10 August 1927 opened naturalization on a vast scale to recent immigrants in France. The minimum period of residency in France was reduced from ten years to three, and the effect was immediate: naturalizations doubled, from an annual average of 10,000 adults in 1925–26 to 22,500 in 1928 and 1929. In all, between 1928 and 1933, 125,000 adults and 155,000 children were naturalized.[198] And it was in 1934 that naturalized persons lost the right to hold civil service positions or to practice law for the same waiting period—ten years—as the waiting period prescribed by the law of 1927 for holding elective office. Since 1814 the political rights of naturalized persons had been limited. With the law of 1934 this limitation crossed a new threshold.

The Traditional Inferiority of Naturalized Persons By an ordinance of 14 June 1814, King Louis XVIII declared: "In conformity with the former French Constitutions, no foreigner may sit, from this day forward, either in the Chamber of Peers or in the Chamber of Deputies, unless, through important services rendered to the State, he has obtained from us letters of naturalization verified by the two Chambers." This signified that only what was henceforth called "grand naturalization" allowed someone to serve in Parliament; simple naturalization no longer sufficed. Grand naturalization was subject to no prior conditions. It was a private law affecting solely the person to whom it applied. André Masséna was the first. After him, until 1848 only twenty-one naturalized persons benefited from the right to be elected to Parliament.[199] The provisional government's decree of 5 March 1848, which declared that all French people twenty-five years of age or above would be eligible, implicitly abrogated that distinction. But the law of 3 December 1849 reestablished it, at the request—as we have seen—of the Republican left. Jules Favre argued in favor of granting the National Assembly the exclusive power to naturalize. Eugène Rouher, minister of justice under Louis-Napoleon Bonaparte, argued for the power of the president of the Republic and the administration. The debate was settled by a compromise: the administration definitively retained the power to naturalize,[200] and the left, which feared that the executive power would naturalize en masse for electoral ends, got a provision passed according to which a naturalized person's right of eligibility could be conferred only by the National Assembly. That ineligibility, eliminated in 1867,[201] was reestablished once again in 1889, at a time when the legislature was eliminating admission to legal residency as an autonomous status and cracking open the door to naturalization: naturalized persons were ineligible for ten years, unless the Parliament reduced this waiting period by a special law.[202]

Professional Ineligibility: The Counterweight to Offset Mass Naturalizations? The law of 1927 inaugurated another period: that of the broadening of temporary interdictions, which became the explicit counterpart of the demographic (and instrumental) approach to naturalization. The law of 1927 extended the ten-year period of ineligibility to all elective functions and mandates, including not just political but also professional mandates (for example, being a delegate elected by the employees of a company).[203]

The law of 19 July 1934 added to ineligibility for election that of appointment to public positions remunerated by the state, enrollment at a bar, or titular appointment to a ministerial office ("unless the military obligations of active service in the French army have been fulfilled").[204] Lawyers concerned about Jewish refugees from Germany and Austria arriving in France with law degrees pushed to get this provision adopted by Parliament. With the support of jurist colleagues in Parliament they succeeded easily, extending the restriction to all civil service positions.[205]

There was strong pressure at the time to challenge the law of 1927; it was viewed by restrictionists—who were often racists—as too liberal. But the law remained intact, and naturalizations proceeded. The idea was then clearly expressed that the new ineligibilities for naturalized persons were the counterweight to maintaining the new openness: "The quality of being French may sometimes be granted to foreigners, who are moreover quite worthy of this favor, and whom France may have an interest in admitting to the number of its citizens without further delay, without waiting until the assimilation of the individuals concerned is perfect on the day of their naturalization. It is therefore entirely natural to provide a sort of intermediate period during which the naturalized person, even while possessing French nationality, is temporarily kept out of certain positions that require, more than others, a complete assimilation of the ideas, habits, and language of our country."[206]

To the limitations on rights that already affected naturalized persons — ineligibility for or impossibility of access to certain public functions during a ten-year period — the decree of 12 November 1938 added ineligibility to vote for five years. The ordinance of 1945 maintained the ineligibility to hold elective office for a period of ten years and the ineligibility to vote, to hold a civil service position, or to practice law, for five years (article 81). The law of 28 April 1952 instituted an ineligibility period of five years for holding a civil service position at the municipal level.[207]

This entire set of provisions, adopted in 1927 and confirmed after the war when the demographic logic of nationality policy was at its highest level, prevented many French people from pursuing the career of their choice. Some left France to put their talents to use in other countries.[208] This discrimination against "skilled" naturalized persons reflected one of the new characteristics of French immigration and nationality policy that Mauco was defending in the 1930s, 1940s, and 1950s: immigrants were made to hold the "low-level" jobs in French society that the French no longer wanted to do. At that point France was practicing explicitly — and until recently has often practiced implicitly — discrimination against prospective immigrants from elite groups.

After the Second World War, with the development of human rights legislation, such discrimination quickly began to appear intolerable. Thus on 17 July 1978 Parliament eliminated the five-year period of ineligibility related to employment and voting. The ten-year period of ineligibility for election to public office remained in place; it was eliminated by the laws of 8 and 20 December 1983.

Only then did discrimination among French people disappear from nationality law. All French nationals were henceforth equal under the law. But who, concretely, becomes French? How does one become or remain French, when one can claim to be French by parentage, by birth on French territory, by marriage, or by naturalization? The study of nationality law as it is practiced today will be the subject of the final chapter.

How Does One Become or Remain French?

French Nationality in Practice

The noblest title on earth is that of being born a Frenchman; it is a title con-
ferred by Heaven, and which no individual on earth should have the power to
withdraw. For my part, I wish that every man of French origin, though he were
a foreigner in the tenth generation, should still be a Frenchmen, if he wishes to
claim the title. Were he to present himself on the other bank of the Rhine, saying,
I wish to be a Frenchman, I would have his voice to be more powerful than the
law; the barriers should fall before him, and he should return triumphant to the
bosom of our common mother. — COUNT DE LAS CASES, Memoirs of the Life,
Exile, and Conversations of the Emperor Napoleon, *vol. 2 (London: Henry*
Colburn, 1836), 325

‣ All French people are henceforth equal before the law. But how
does one acquire French nationality when one does not have it from birth? The
law provides that children born in France to foreign parents can easily become
French. It also provides that foreign residents in France can ask to be naturalized, and that spouses of French nationals can become French by simple declaration. But between the law and its application there is often considerable distance.
The goal of this final chapter is thus to study the *practice* of French nationality:
How, concretely, can it be acquired by someone who does not possess it? How
can it be retained or transmitted by someone who acquires a foreign nationality,
or who lives abroad? French law today, as we shall see, tends very broadly to
embrace or to retain as French nationals those who find themselves at its borders.
This openness is fostered by a traditional indifference to dual nationality, which
has nevertheless as its constitutive counterpart the prerogative of withdrawal of
nationality, a reserve of sovereignty for use in exceptional cases.[1]

Two Relatively Open Procedures: Birth and Residency in France . . .

Children born in France to two foreign parents not born in France become French at the age of eighteen, provided that they have lived in France for five years since the age of eleven—this verifies that they have been educated in the French social context. The five years of residency may be continuous or discontinuous; they can thus be easily proved by school certificates. Young people can avoid waiting to turn eighteen by voluntarily acquiring French nationality through a declaration procedure, beginning at the age of thirteen. Between the ages of thirteen and sixteen, such acquisition requires the consent of the child's parents and a five-year period of residency from the age of eight on. Between the ages of sixteen and eighteen, children can acquire nationality independently of their parents if they have lived in France for five years since the age of eleven.[2]

If, on the contrary, a young person does not want French nationality at the age of eighteen, he or she can decline it between the ages of seventeen and a half and nineteen.[3] In 2005, 27,258 young people between the ages of thirteen and eighteen chose to acquire French nationality before the age of eighteen.[4] Some 2,966 acquired it at the age of eighteen.[5] That same year, eleven young people between the ages of seventeen and a half and nineteen declined French nationality. Let us recall that in 1993, the last year this procedure was in effect (before its interruption between 1994 and 1998), 1,611 young people had refused French nationality in that way.[6]

It can thus be said that virtually all children born in France to foreign parents acquire French nationality if they are in France during their adolescence, and the majority do so voluntarily.

. . . and Marriage

Following the French Civil Code, in the nineteenth century most countries included provisions in their laws that required a woman to take her husband's nationality. In the interest of ensuring equal treatment for men and women, all the European countries have eliminated those provisions. Most now oblige foreign spouses of their citizens to request naturalization if they wish to acquire their spouse's nationality.[7] Often, the minimum period of obligatory residence is reduced in relation to common-law naturalization (three years as opposed to five in the United States, the Netherlands, and the United Kingdom).[8] But most countries also require the spouses of nationals to reside on their national territory. This is not true of France.

Until 2003 a foreign spouse of a French citizen could acquire French nationality by a simple declaration made in France or abroad after one year of marriage. With the laws of 26 November 2003 and 24 July 2006, the required length of marriage has been extended in two phases, to two years, then four, and even five if "the foreigner, at the time of his or her declaration, cannot demonstrate at least three years of uninterrupted residency in France counting from the date of marriage," or if the French spouse, living abroad, is not registered on the French Consulate rolls. In addition, if the marriage took place abroad it must have been officially registered in France. Nationality is acquired one year after the declaration has been registered, if the government has not denied the registration or has opposed the attribution of nationality. The impact of these legislative modifications has been considerable. In 2004, 33,131 foreign spouses of French citizens acquired French nationality by declaration; in 2005, 20,714 did so — of these, 2,042 (9.9 percent) were living abroad at the time.[9]

In 2005, for 20,690 declarations registered, 2,472 were rejected — 10.7 percent of the total number of decisions — owing to the absence of one of the legal conditions required to make the marriage valid: lack of a common household (37.8 percent of the decisions) or annulment of the marriage, for example. In addition, twenty-one decrees of opposition were signed by the government.[10] When a decree of opposition is issued, the declaration is admissible, but the administration notes either lack of assimilation (90 percent of the cases) or unworthiness (10 percent);[11] 89 percent of the declarations recorded thus take effect one year after they have been made.

Of the spouses of French people who fulfill the increasingly strict conditions regarding the length of marriage and who request French nationality, 90 percent obtain it. As for naturalization, a procedure principally applicable to foreigners born abroad who have come to live in France, more than 70 percent of the requests receive a favorable response, but the wait involved — both the required period of residency and the time required for the procedure itself — is particularly long.

The Contradictions of Naturalization

Although it comes from discretionary power, naturalization in France is subject to numerous legal and jurisprudential constraints. The common-law waiting period of five years is applied without regard to the candidate's status in the preceding years; in the United States, in contrast, the same five-year period is counted only from the time the candidate obtained a green card, that is, the status of permanent resident.[12] The five-year wait is not required (and has not been since 1973) for people coming from a territory or country in which French is the official language (or one of the official languages):[13] Belgium, Benin, Burkina-Faso, Cameroon, Canada, the Central African Republic, Chad, the Comoros, Congo, Djibouti, Gabon, Haiti, Ivory Coast, Lebanon, Louisiana, Luxembourg, Mali, Monaco, Niger, Rwanda, Senegal, the Seychelles, Switzerland, Togo, Val d'Aosta, Vanuatu, Zaire.

No waiting period was required either for people who came from—or who had once been residents in—one of the territories or states over which France has exercised sovereignty, a protectorate, a mandate, or guardianship, until 2006. This little-known provision—little known because the administration seems to have been instructed not to apply it[14]—was introduced by the law of 22 December 1961. Marcel Prélot, who reviewed the bill for the Senate, had pointed out in 1961 that "to every citizen of a formerly French country who for many long years had maintained the French traditions and culture acquired under the fleur de lys or the tricolor flag . . . France, a generous mother, must, when that individual asks for French nationality, grant the favor that is put before you."[15] He argued so well for the maintenance of this symbolic bond with all the countries over which the French flag had once flown that the Senate, soon followed by the National Assembly, eliminated all time limits. Thus this provision applied to all the territories over which France, at any moment of its history, has exercised "either sovereignty, a protectorate, a mandate, or guardianship." It involved some of the Francophone countries already included in the earlier list— for example, Belgium, Senegal, and Haiti—but also many states and territories of the Caribbean,[16] much of Canada (not only Quebec but also Newfoundland, Prince Edward Island, Nova Scotia, New Brunswick, parts of Ontario, Manitoba, and the Northwest Territories), twenty states in the United States in addition to Louisiana,[17] Indochina and the southern part of the Indian peninsula, Algeria, Tunisia, and Morocco, Malta, the Ionian islands, the Illyrian provinces, the Netherlands, the parts of Germany and Italy that were attached to France during the Revolution and under the Empire,[18] some Swiss cantons, and finally Catalonia.[19] After the author of this book explained in an article in the *New York Times* how this law could apply to the incumbent president of the United States Bill Clinton, as a former resident of Arkansas, once part of French Louisiana,[20] this unknown provision became famous and was eliminated in the law of 24 July 2006.

Yet no waiting period is now required of refugees or stateless persons protected by the Geneva Convention or of those whose naturalization presents an exceptional interest for France. The waiting period is two years for foreigners who have had two years of higher education in France and have earned a degree from a university or one of the Grandes Écoles.

But between theory and practice there is a big gap: 2 percent of the applicants obtained their naturalization in 2005 after less than two years' residency in France, and over all 10.6 percent obtained it with less than five years' residency. In fact, the average length of stay in France at the time of naturalization is fifteen years and seven months.[21]

How can such a delay be explained? First, according to consistent decisions by the Council of State, the residency of a foreigner who requests naturalization must be current and must have a stable and permanent character that coincides with the center of his or her family ties (the candidate's family — spouse and children — have to live in France) and professional activities. Apart from exceptional cases — high-level athletes, artists, categories that have been singled out for priority treatment, and so on — a request for naturalization is not examined favorably if the candidate does not have at least three years' residency.

In addition, naturalization is not particularly encouraged in France. The administration considers that it must result first of all from a voluntary act on the applicant's part.[22] As a general rule, it is only when a foreigner makes an active inquiry that the necessary information is provided. Sometimes applicants are overtly dissuaded: one prefecture devotes only two hours a week to accepting dossiers. In another, the waiting period for an appointment at which a candidate could submit a completed file was — in late 2004 — fifteen months![23] Moreover, once the file has been submitted, the average time for it to be processed in a prefecture is seven months. But the prefectures often "cheat," by dating the start of the procedure not from the moment the file was submitted but from the time the assimilation interview took place and its transcript was prepared.[24]

This drift in the treatment of naturalization probably explains why the rate of immigrants — that is, persons born foreigners abroad — who have become French was, according to the census of 2004, only 40 percent (two million out of five million immigrants), and a considerable number of these cases involved nationality acquired by declaration after marriage.[25] This rate of naturalization is much lower than, for example, Canada's: the high Canadian level — 69.5 percent in 1991 — is explained, according to Irene Bloemraad's comparative study, by the Canadian authorities' institutional efforts to make naturalization a decisive element in the process of integration.[26] In France the great majority of applications submitted still receive a positive response, once the administrative obstacles are overcome. French legislation presents naturalization as a favor to the applicant. But the broad freedom of action, the kingly power the public authorities are thought to have at their command, is more theoretical than real. Reforms in the procedure for handling applications introduced in 2003 in the Naturalization Bureau (Sous-direction des naturalisations, Rezé, Loire-Atlantique) brought the average waiting period down from sixteen months[27] in 2002 to three months at the end of 2004.

The Itinerary of a Naturalization Application

Naturalization requests are submitted individually to offices in prefectures or subprefectures. In the file a candidate must supply various bits of information: civil status, proof of length of residency in France. However, most of the information about the candidate is gathered by inquiries addressed to the national and local police and to city hall. The departmental office of social action is consulted about the family situation. A doctor supplies a health certificate. The investigation must also reveal the precise nature of the candidate's professional activity. Finally, an assimilation report is prepared, and a report from the prefect is attached: this report summarizes the content of the file and includes a judgment as to its acceptability. Once complete the file is transmitted to the Naturalization Bureau at the Ministry of Social Affairs, which is responsible for ruling on all requests.

Until 2003 files were initially examined and analyzed by at least two people. A "drafter" filled out an "investigation sheet," proposed a favorable or unfavorable decision, and indicated the elements on which that judgment was based. Next a "reviewer" studied the dossier; if he or she confirmed the drafter's proposal, the decision was implemented. If there was a difference of opinion the file was transmitted to the head of the unit, and if necessary to the head of the bureau. Since 2003 only problematic files have been examined by both a drafter and a reviewer. The others, handled directly by drafters, are subject to regular verification by sampling. For delicate cases, the assistant director, the director of population and migrations, or the minister's cabinet can make decisions as a last resort. This centralization has an advantage: similar dossiers are treated in the same way. All decisions are made according to criteria defined by the Nationality Code, which has been included since 1993 in the Civil Code, in conformity with various ministerial memoranda and directives. Since 1993, in addition, rejections have to be justified—that is, the elements of fact and law on which they are based have to be spelled out. Finally, the evolution of the complex jurisprudence of the Council of State has to be followed with close attention. Administrative jurisprudence has developed significantly since 1981—applicants whose requests were turned down have been informed of their right to appeal.

The candidate's file must first of all be declared "admissible," then his naturalization must be judged "opportune." Non-admissibility can be established only for reasons of nonconformity with the requirements of the law. The first criterion of admissibility is residence. To be naturalized the candidate must have his or her habitual residence in France at the time of the request, and must be living in France at the time the naturalization decree appears. Residency must be effective and customary (Supreme Court, decision of 9 January 1957); and it must coincide with the center of family ties and professional preoccupations (Supreme Court, decision of 12 November 1957), which must be established in a stable manner (Council of State, 28 February 1986, Akhras decision).

Under the impetus of the Council of State,[28] these conditions have nevertheless evolved in a liberal direction. The Council of State now takes family ties and professional interests into account case by case. It attributes importance to the applicant's length of stay in France, to his or her financial situation, and to the familial, professional, and political motives that might lead to a return to the country of origin or, on the contrary, might constitute an obstacle to return.

Administrative legislation has also brought about a perceptible evolution in the administrative practice that refused to view a student as a resident. The administrative court of appeals in Nantes, for example, has ruled that "the absence of a potential long term residence in France cannot be 'deduced from the mere circumstance that the individual is authorized to stay in France only to earn his or her university degree.'" By failing to take into account other circumstances having to do with the applicant's personal situation, the administration would be committing a legal error in declaring the request not admissible (Nantes administrative court of appeals, 14 April 2000, Ajomiwe decision). Earlier the Council of State had considered as admissible, for example, a request made by a young woman who had arrived in France in 1972 as a student and was working half time when she submitted her request, even though some of her resources came from her parents (Perahia decision, 1982). The same decision was made in the case of a student working as a hostess and earning a salary of 3,000 francs a month (Gamska decision, 11 July 1986).[29] In fact, the administration examines students' applications case by case, and it is supposed to apply the same criteria as for other applications: stability of residence and resources in France.

Every candidate must also demonstrate "his or her assimilation to the French community, in particular by a sufficient knowledge, according to his or her condition, of the French language" (articles 21–24). If a candidate knows no French, or so little that he or she cannot take care of "the necessities of daily life," the request will be declared non-admissible; this reason accounts for 40 percent of the cases of non-admissibility. The other possible reasons included in the Code are invoked less often: to be naturalized, candidates must be of "of good conduct and morals" (Civil Code, articles 21–23); for example, they must not have been subjected to major condemnations (Civil Code, articles 21–27).

Once the conditions of admissibility have been verified, each request is evaluated to determine whether it satisfies a certain number of criteria of "opportuneness," which are supposed to be the expression of a political will determined by the government.

First of all, certain cases have priority: refugees and stateless persons, applicants who have served with the French Foreign Legion (around a thousand a year), and applicants for whom access to nationality is a condition for professional advancement—for example, someone who needs to be naturalized to be eligible for a job in public administration. Favorable treatment is also granted to applicants from states in which France "has exercised responsibilities" when they belong to "certain communities that have maintained or currently maintain close relations with our country":[30] these would be Christians from Lebanon, Syria, or Egypt, or Jews from the Maghreb.[31] In each case the administration examines the stability of the applicant's residence and resources in France, behavior, and degree of assimilation to the French community.

When the public authority has doubts about an applicant's loyalty, it can ask for supplementary information or opinions from state security agencies (Renseignements généraux, Direction de la surveillance du territoire, Direction générale de la sécurité extérieure)—or, if lack of compliance with tax regulations is suspected, the internal revenue service (Direction générale des impôts). In the past membership in a union or a political party could constitute a negative element in the dossier or even justify a negative decision. This has not been true of union activity since 1976, and of political activity since 1982. However, the Council of State has confirmed that belonging to a federation involving extremist movements that advocated the "rejection of the essential values of French society" could justify a refusal.[32]

The Council of State has, in contrast, challenged what had become an administrative custom—the requirement of family unity: if a naturalization request came from only one partner in a couple, it led to a negative evaluation. Since 1986 (decision of 26 September 1986, Ministry of Social Affairs v. Spouse Vo Ngoc Que), the Council of State has judged that a request cannot be declared nonadmissible on the pretext that a spouse is not associated with it; moreover, the Council has pointed out that access to nationality is recognized for individuals and not for couples or families. A request for naturalization may thus be made by a single member of the family. In practice, however, the absence of the spouse in the request, or the impossibility of naturalizing the spouse, is often a reason for the administration to reject or defer the request.

Before an administrative judge intervened in this area, the administration also liberalized its approach to requests from elderly persons. Until 1981 such requests were most often rejected on the grounds that the national collectivity should not provide financial support to the increased number of people who would benefit from the minimum income allotted to elderly citizens. Since 1982 the request must be denied only if it is visibly motivated by the desire to receive that minimum income, in the absence of a sufficient work history in France to justify it. Today one can no longer say that age is an obstacle to naturalization; on the contrary, it may even encourage a liberal interpretation of the other criteria. If there is an involuntary deficiency in assimilation, for example, owing to "the candidate's advanced age," this is no longer considered an obstacle to naturalization.[33] A lengthy period of residency in France — twenty years, for example — has also become a positive element of appreciation that can counterbalance an involuntary deficiency in assimilation.

The power of the administration in the area of naturalizations — a regal power, juridically speaking, and on the order of a favor, as the Council of State has confirmed on several occasions[34] — has become, societally speaking, as much a power to grant as to deny. All in all, the constraints that weigh upon the public authority are more and more numerous. Since 1998, owing to the new orientations adopted by the government, the number of decisions and the proportion of positive decisions have been increasing: 67 percent of the 55,385 decisions were positive in 1998, 72 percent of 67,368 in 1999, 79 percent of 84,137 in 2003, 72 percent of 63992 in 2005.[35] In 2005, 41.1 percent of the nonfavorable decisions were made for reasons of nonadmissibility, 2.7 percent were rejections, and 54.6 percent were decisions to defer. In 2005, 68,784 foreigners became French by decree, while 33,001 children benefited from the collective effect attached to the naturalization of a parent: 101,785 persons in all.

An investigation carried out by CREDOC (Research Center for the Study and Observation of Living Conditions) in 1998[36] on the basis of a sample of 2,907 files that had been the object of positive decisions during the years 1992, 1994, and 1995 makes it possible to discern the typical profile of a naturalized French citizen. One element stands out right away: the applicant's youth. While no request can be made before the age of eighteen, more than 50 percent of the candidates are under the age of thirty-five; what is more, nearly 30 percent of the persons naturalized arrived in France before the age of ten and more than 15 percent before the age of five. They often requested French nationality while they were still students: twice as many students can be counted among naturalized persons as among the French population at large (16.4 percent versus 8.3 percent). This student presence helps make naturalized French citizens a more educated population than foreigners resident in France, on average, but also more than the overall French population, on average: 14 percent of France's naturalized citizens have some higher education. Three groups stand out for the high level of their education: Lebanese, Africans from outside the Maghreb, and Europeans from outside the European Union. Those with the fewest diplomas come from Turkey, Portugal, and Southeast Asia. For the rest, the majority of the naturalized population is made up of people in the workforce (70 percent). In fact, the middle classes are underrepresented in the naturalized population, since the majority are salaried employees practicing trades demanding fewer qualifications than those practiced by the French population at large (44 percent blue-collar workers), while employees at the managerial level are slightly underrepresented — and artisans, businessmen, and company heads are more so.[37]

Acceptance of Dual Nationality

By birth and residence in France, by marriage, or by naturalization, 155,000 foreigners became French in 2005.[38] Foreigners' access to French nationality is also facilitated by France's traditional indifference to dual nationality. Formally, by signing the convention of the Council of Europe that eliminates cases of dual nationality among member states, France has endorsed the classic conception according to which one must belong to a single nationality.[39] In practice, however, like Great Britain, France has always allowed people taking on French nationality to retain their former nationality as well.

The French position on dual nationality was developed around the time of the First World War, in reaction to article 25 of the German law of 22 July 1913 — known as the Delbrück law — allowing Germans naturalized abroad to retain their original nationality. In a first phase, France refused to limit the state's power to attribute French nationality to the children of immigrants, on the pretext that foreign states were counting such children as their own nationals. In a second phase, Parliament refused to withdraw French nationality from all naturalized persons of enemy origin on the pretext that they had kept their original nationality. Finally, in 1927 a policy of massive naturalization was adopted: the legislature was not concerned at that point with whether new French persons kept their original nationality or not. At most it was willing to make permanent a procedure for revoking nationality that had been introduced temporarily for the period of the war, a step whose significance we shall see shortly.

Since then France has accepted dual nationality and has never required newly naturalized persons to give up their nationality of origin. In practice, that indifference has probably contributed to the smooth integration of a large number of immigrants, for when nationality of origin has no practical impact it is gradually lost in succeeding generations. In contrast, Germany's practice of requiring naturalized persons to renounce their original nationality fosters a certain vigilance about maintaining identifications that are often artificial or imaginary.

During the past quarter-century dual nationality has spread widely — in France and among the large democratic countries as a group — as a consequence of the equality that men and women acquired in matters of nationality in 1973.[40] A woman no longer loses her nationality by marrying a man of another nationality; she transmits it to her children just as her husband does his. This new situation has destabilized the most conservative legislation and called into question the European convention of 1963 that was adopted for the purpose of avoiding dual nationality.

Jus sanguinis ad vitam aeternam! Dual nationality has also developed abroad, as France allows its nationals living outside the country to acquire a foreign nationality without losing their French nationality, which they are able to transmit without any time limit or generational limit. This is a recent development in the status of French nationals abroad, who were formerly subjected to strict limitations on their rights.

With the Civil Code in 1803 French nationals had already regained the right to settle in a foreign country without the risk of losing the quality of being French, or even of being declared dead in civil terms, as they had under the Old Regime and the Revolution. But while they were free to be naturalized abroad, they would lose their French nationality in the process.[41] By a decree of 6 April 1809, the French quickly lost the freedom to be naturalized, moreover: on the eve of a new war with Austria, Napoleon ordered the return of all French nationals — even those who had been naturalized into other nationalities — who were serving a power at war with France. Legally, for those who resided in enemy territory the decree eliminated the freedom to change nationality that had been instituted by the Civil Code. A senatus-consulte of 26 August 1811 extended that interdiction everywhere.[42] From that point on, no French person had the right to be naturalized in a foreign country without the emperor's permission. The perpetual allegiance of the French to France was instituted; in the text and as a principle, it would remain in force until 1889.[43]

The law of 1889 restored the right of French persons to acquire a foreign nationality, but they would then lose their French nationality, unless they were men still of an age to bear arms: in that case they had to request authorization from the government. The point was to make sure that no Frenchman acquired another nationality to avoid military service, at a time when such service had become obligatory. This provision remained in force in various forms until 1945.[44] The ordinance of 19 October 1945 thus provided that men must still request authorization to acquire a foreign nationality until the age of fifty (article 9).

The law of 9 April 1954 confirmed again that every man under the age of fifty who was naturalized abroad lost French nationality only if the step was authorized by the French government. But the goal had changed: earlier the idea was to make sure that French men did not avoid military service; in 1954 "it [was] essential that French nationals who [held] positions abroad through which they could spread French culture or France's moral or economic influence be allowed to keep their French nationality, even though they voluntarily acquired the nationality of the country in which they exercised their professions, that acquisition often being a condition for the exercise of certain functions."[45] This was a response, moreover, to a desire expressed by the High Council of French Nationals Abroad dating from September 1950. But the result was paradoxical. Legally a man who took a foreign nationality, unless he obtained government authorization — and in practice he did not request it — kept his French nationality. A woman, in contrast, lost her French nationality if she took a foreign nationality. The law of 1973 that ensured the equality of men and women in all areas put an end to what women experienced as "bullying and discrimination."[46]

Since then acquiring a foreign nationality, even voluntarily, no longer causes either men or women to lose their French nationality. That happens only in response to an explicit individual request.[47] The dual nationality of French people abroad is thus fully recognized. French men and women abroad can transmit their French nationality to their descendants, generation after generation, in an extraordinarily liberal fashion — the administration can oppose this transmission only in cases where the ascendant left France more than fifty years earlier.

Revocation: A Counterweight to Liberalism

This liberal acceptance of dual nationality is counter-balanced by the maintenance in contemporary legislation of clauses providing for revoking French nationality. I am not speaking here of withdrawing nationality for fraud:[48] provisions for this have been included in legislation in the United States since 1906,[49] in the United Kingdom since 1914, and in France since 1938. At soon as naturalization becomes official, the state supposes that all legal conditions have been satisfied.[50] If at some later time this turns out not to have been so, the naturalization is annulled and viewed as if it has never existed.

At issue here is the fact that *today* any person who has acquired French nationality and who possesses another nationality may have his or her French nationality revoked. At the time it was definitively adopted in French legislation in 1927, revocation of nationality was sometimes denounced as foreign to a legal tradition — it had actually been a tradition in private and not public law — according to which something cannot be given and withheld at the same time.[51] The circumstances of its introduction (at a moment when the French legislature was choosing to open the door to widespread naturalization and to accept dual nationality), its survival in French law, but also in British and American law, leads me to see revocation as not at all alien to liberal nationality law but rather constitutive of it.

Although a law adopted in 1906 in the United States already allowed revocation for fraud or illegality (which in concrete terms led to the annulment of more than fifteen thousand naturalizations between 1906 and 1940),[52] French law was modeled rather on British law, in a process that stretched from 1914 to 1927.[53]

Article 7 of the British law of 7 August 1914[54] allowed the secretary of state to revoke naturalization certificates obtained on the basis of false statements or fraud. A new act promulgated on 8 August 1918 authorized the withdrawal of naturalization for a whole series of new infractions: failure to reside in the British Empire (staying away for more than seven years); lack of loyalty toward the sovereign or connivance with the enemy during a war; condemnation to penalties including deprivation of liberty for twelve months or more, or to fines of at least one hundred pounds. A provision of the law of 1918 — specifically included in reaction to article 25 of the German law of 22 July 1913, the so-called Delbrück law — authorized the revocation of a person's naturalization if, by virtue of the law of a state at war with His Majesty, he or she remained a subject of that state.[55]

In France the right of Germans naturalized abroad to keep their original nationality provoked very strong reactions as soon as the First World War broke out. A lively debate took place in Parliament. The monarchist Catholic deputy Jules Delahaye proposed to "divest German immigrants as a group of their quality of being French."[56] But Parliament did not follow his proposal for collective denaturalization; it adopted the law of 7 April 1915, which provided that naturalized persons of enemy origin who had borne arms against France, left French territory to avoid a military obligation, or "retained the nationality of their country of origin" could have their French nationality revoked — after a ruling by the Council of State.[57] Since the administration had difficulty bringing tangible proof,[58] Parliament adopted a new law (promulgated on 18 June 1917) spelling out "the circumstances apt to lead to the presumption that the naturalized person had kept his or her original nationality" and vesting the power of revocation in the courts.[59] By the end of the war, 549 naturalized persons of German, Austro-Hungarian, and Turkish origin[60] had had their French nationality revoked in application of these two laws.[61] The majority of the 473 men — often veterans of the Foreign Legion — lost their French nationality owing to insubordination.

When the war was over, things changed even more. The Treaty of Versailles made it easy for Germans who had emigrated to Alsace-Moselle — before or during its attachment to France — to obtain French nationality if they continued to live in Alsace-Moselle, which had become French once again. Questions were raised about their loyalty, all the more so because the Delbrück law, still in force, allowed a German who became French to keep his original nationality. It was at this precise moment, thanks to close cooperation between the Ministry of Justice and Senator Frédéric Eccard, professor at the law school in Strasbourg, that the "republican" doctrine of revocation was developed with reference to the question of dual nationality.

On 14 January 1915 the deputy Jean Lerolle had already proposed to add a provision to the law of 1889 requiring a foreigner seeking naturalization to demonstrate that "the acquisition of French nationality would make him lose his original nationality."[62] The legislation committee of the Ministry of Justice — made up of law professors and legal specialists from the various ministries — had then rejected any measure taken against persons who acquired full French nationality automatically, children born in France to foreign parents, or foreign wives of French men, "the attribution of French nationality abroad" being inspired by "imperative considerations of such value in the eyes of the French legislature that they must not be sacrificed to the desire, however legitimate it may be, to avoid conflicts with foreign arrangements": "our law cannot bow before foreign legislation and give up viewing as French those individuals upon whom it has deemed it appropriate and in our interest to confer this title every time it pleases foreign law to keep them in bonds of allegiance."[63] In contrast, the committee suggested denying naturalization to any applicant whose country of origin allowed the retention of his or her own nationality.

This was not at all the direction in which Parliament chose to go in 1922. It decided in fact not to prevent Germans from becoming French, even if they kept their original nationality: "To withdraw French nationality from naturalized persons, it must not suffice to seek to know whether they remain attached to their old fatherland. One must acknowledge, in the absence of proof to the contrary, that a person who has acquired French nationality *is in no way suspect and dangerous owing simply to the fact that he or she still has moral and financial interests in the country left behind*. . . . In order for suspicion to take on substance, the naturalized person must have given an *external manifestation* of lack of loyalty and faithfulness to his or her adopted country. Such persons must have engaged in acts incompatible with the quality of being French. Their unworthiness must result from their actions, their words, their writings."[64]

A naturalized person could thus indeed possess another nationality: as long as this possession did not lead to an attack on the authority and security of the French state, France was not concerned.[65] The person's dual identity was a matter for the private sphere; the state did not need to be concerned. This acceptance of dual nationality had a limit, however: the situation in which the person acted in a way that the state could not sanction. If the state was not to call its own existence into question, a dual French-German national who fought against France in 1914 could not remain French. The state thus imposed its sovereignty, symbolized here by the power to revoke nationality. The power to take exceptional measures allows the liberal regime that accepts dual nationality—in France and the United Kingdom, unlike in Germany—to maintain its full authority. Foreigners who wish to become German while keeping their original nationality do not have the right to do so; revocation is consequently absent from German nationality law. Great Britain and France have never paid attention to dual nationality; they do not require renunciation of one's nationality of origin.[66] The right to dual nationality for someone who wants to become French or British consequently has a counterweight in revocation, a reserve of sovereignty that the state can use in exceptional circumstances.

Articles 9 and 10 of the law of 1927 thus provided that those who had requested and acquired French nationality could have it revoked for one of three reasons: (1) having carried out acts inimical to the internal or external security of the French state; (2) having committed acts beneficial to a foreign state but incompatible with being a French citizen and inimical to France's interests; (3) having avoided the obligations resulting from the laws of recruitment. However, the decision to revoke could be made only during the ten-year period following naturalization. Revocation under the law of 1927 was, as in 1917, a legal procedure and thus oppositional; it obliged the administration to go to court, where the judge would allow the naturalized person to defend his or her cause; in addition, it was open to appeal.[67]

Ten years later, the decree-law of 12 November 1938 restored the responsibility for revocation procedures to the Council of State, and it specifically extended revocation to another category of naturalized persons. Beyond lack of loyalty, "unworthiness" was added as a reason for revocation: the term applied to persons who had committed, in France or abroad, after their naturalization, a crime or an offense leading to a prison sentence of more than one year.[68] The context was the application of the law of 1927, which had led to massive naturalizations; on the right, there was pressure to change the law or to reduce the number of naturalizations. Since the interest of the French state is perceived to lie in increasing its population, the number of naturalizations did not go down, but rather went up. In exchange, a clause was introduced (one already present in British law) that made it possible to revoke the nationality of someone who had committed a crime or an offense. The Ministry of Justice had viewed the law of 1927 as a break with the prevailing approach to naturalization itself. When there was a long waiting period of ten years, "legal assimilation ratified actual assimilation." With the shift to three years, "predictions" were substituted for "yesterday's diagnostics."[69] The inclusion of a revocation clause transformed naturalization into a sort of ten-year contract considered broken or invalidated, even a posteriori, if a crime or offense had been committed. Quite minor offenses could justify revocation. But between 1928 and 1939 French nationality was revoked in only sixteen cases, while 261,000 adults were naturalized.[70]

With Vichy denaturalizations were of a different nature — of the opposite nature, one might say, for revocation and thus exclusion became not the exception but the rule. It was no longer a matter of instituting a liberal policy but of reversing its effects. It was no longer a matter of punishing a fault, a crime, an offense, or disloyal behavior of a person toward the state, after allowing him or her the possibility of making a case before independent magistrates. All the naturalizations that had taken place since 1927 could be annulled as the state saw fit, without recourse and independently of any infraction. As a result, between 1940 and 1944 just under 2,000 adults were naturalized, while 15,154 denaturalizations were imposed.[71]

In fact it was only after the Second World War that the procedure of revocation, introduced in 1927 and modified in 1938 and then again in 1945, functioned to its full capacity: there were 279 revocations between 1947 and 1953, while paradoxically, the field open to the procedure was narrowing. In the 1930s the case that received the most attention was that of Thomas Olszanski.[72] A militant syndicalist and communist miner, he was secretary of a miners' union, responsible for propaganda among immigrant Polish workers. His activism and his charisma made him subject to expulsion for political reasons in the early 1930s, as was true of numerous other immigrant activists.[73] But Olszanski had been naturalized in 1922, and for him to be expelled, his French nationality had to be revoked. On 7 August 1931 the administration thus brought charges in the Douai court, based on articles that Olszanski had published in *L'Enchaîné*, a biweekly communist publication from the Nord department, and sought revocation of his nationality for "acts contrary to the internal and external security of the French state." The court delivered its sentence on 22 July 1932; the sentence was ratified on 7 December by the court of appeals in the same city, and on 7 March 1933 by the Supreme Court.[74] André Malraux, Paul Signac, Jean Guéhenno, Élie Faure, René Crevel, Bernard Lecache, and Paul Nizan appealed to the minister of justice in support of Olszanski's request to have his nationality restored. Nothing worked: on 17 October 1934 Olszanski was taken to the Belgian frontier and never saw France again.[75]

In December 1948 — at the beginning of the cold war — the Ministry of the Interior asked the Ministry of Justice to assess the possibility of initiating a procedure for revoking the nationality "of naturalized foreigners guilty of violence or acts of sabotage during strikes."[76] But the government initiated only a small number of revocation procedures against naturalized communist militants, targeting some who had returned after the war to a country of origin that had become communist — Poland, Bulgaria, or Czechoslovakia. The great majority of the 722 procedures set in motion by the administration and of the 479 that actually led to revocation[77] involved naturalized persons — often of German or Italian origin — who had collaborated with the occupying power (by serving in the Waffen ss or other German or Italian groups, working voluntarily in Germany, denouncing resisters; most had been condemned by the Liberation courts).[78] Moreover, in seventy-three cases revocation was imposed for insubordination, and in forty-six cases — just under 10 percent — for a crime that had led to a prison sentence of at least five years (the minimum sentence required by the Nationality Code of 1945 for instituting a revocation procedure).[79]

Since the late 1950s revocation for disloyalty — which can be applied in principle to any French person who also maintains a foreign nationality[80] — has fallen into disuse. Today there is at most one case a year (the last was in 2003), and revocation is applied only to persons sentenced for a crime to five years of prison or more. But the procedure remains as a reserve of sovereignty that allows the state to intervene in exceptional cases. At the very basis of the liberalism of French nationality law, the revocation clause represents a sort of latent deterrent.

How Can One Prove French Nationality?

By birth or marriage to a French person, by birth or residency on French soil, access to or retention of French nationality is relatively easy today. Earlier the state imposed its nationality most notably on young men born in France who sought to avoid the draft. Now individuals seek nationality, and the state grants it readily, but the certification procedure that has been instituted has paradoxical consequences.

Whatever the path through which they have obtained nationality, all French persons are equal. All national legislation recognizes the members of the national community as equals no matter how they acquired membership — through jus sanguinis, jus soli, marriage, and so on. Often, however, one path takes precedence over another. In the United States jus sanguinis is only a complement to the predominant jus soli: in a symbolic manifestation of that predominance, only an American citizen born in the United States can become president. The paradox of French law is that filiation is in theory the predominant principle, since nationality is transmitted through birth to a French parent beginning with the first generation, while it is acquired through birth on French territory only after two generations. In practice, being French by the double jus soli or by marriage or naturalization is immensely advantageous whenever one needs to supply proof of French nationality or to obtain a certificate of nationality. The birth of two generations on French soil can be proved by two birth certificates. Declarations by marriage and naturalizations are officially registered, and even published in the *Journal officiel*. In contrast, for someone who is a descendant of a French person but was not born in France to a parent born in France, it is not easy to obtain a certificate of nationality; such a person may have to seek a court decision to have his or her status as a French national confirmed.

The Certificate of Nationality The certificate of nationality is a recent creation. Until the Second World War, when one needed to prove one's status as a French national to obtain a pension, social benefits, or a job, mayors — or police commissioners, in some cities — delivered certificates that attested to a person's French nationality. These were taken at face value as long as they were not subject to any serious challenge. The Ministry of Justice was consulted only in exceptional cases. When the ministry could not reach a decision, it suggested that the matter be referred to the courts.[81] During the First World War, a first campaign was mounted for the creation of a certificate of nationality. Senator André Honnorat noted how seriously the certificates produced by foreign states were taken —

they allowed foreign nationals in France to avoid conscription—and proposed that proof of nationality be supplied by an annotated birth certificate, that is, a document that would include a mention of French nationality. He also suggested that justices of the peace—the equivalent of today's small claims court judges—should be responsible for delivering these certificates.[82] The Ministry of Justice was opposed to this, arguing that the matter was too delicate to be entrusted to such a low-level judge. On one point, however, the ministry agreed with Honnorat: it declared that regional civil courts should have the exclusive power to settle questions of nationality.[83]

But no proposal came to fruition in the period between the wars, despite the efforts of law professors,[84] for two questions remained: Who should be granted the power to deliver the certificates, and what should be done for French people who were not born in France? In the context of preparations for the law of 1927, the jurist Georges Gruffy believed he had found the solution to the second problem: "for persons born outside of France, there must be a fictitious birthplace in France." He thus proposed a city in the very center of France ("for fear of invasions and the destruction of archives"): Riom, Limoges, or Vichy, according to preference.[85]

It was in fact in 1941 under the Vichy regime, with the goal of "harmonizing . . . the strictness of the conditions for delivery of these certificates with the importance of the quality of being French," that the minister of justice Joseph Barthélemy decided to grant to justices of the peace the exclusive power to deliver the certificates, under the control of the public prosecutor's office.[86] Given the distinctions made by the Vichy regime between French people and foreigners, between Jews and non-Jews, but also between French nationals born to a French father—for whom public-sector positions at the highest level were reserved—and French nationals of foreign origin,[87] the Ministry of Justice prescribed that in cases where the candidate's parents had not always been French, the justice of the peace had to abstain from ruling and had to consult the Chancellery. The number of consultations, which had been negligeable until that point, reached 12,973 in 1942, and 18,966 in 1943.

After the Liberation a memorandum of 10 November 1944 gave judges increased power to deliver certificates without involving the Ministry of Justice.[88] The ordinance of 1945 instituted the regime of proof and litigation that is still in force today. In cases where a question of nationality is contested, the civil jurisdiction of common law, here the *tribunal de grande instance*, is the *only* one competent to rule. The ordinance also instituted a certificate of nationality that only a justice of the peace is qualified to deliver.[89] The responsibility for supplying proof lies with the person who is claiming to be or not to be French.[90] The advantage of the certificate is that it is taken at face value as long as it is not the object of a serious challenge. For those who were born in France to a parent born in France, were naturalized, or registered a declaration to be French after marrying a French person, proof can be easy to produce, by means of two birth certificates, an excerpt from the *Journal officiel*, or the declaration recorded by an officer of the court. In contrast, someone born to a French parent abroad has to use a path other than simple filiation to prove that one parent was French. If that is impossible, the applicant has to go farther back through the generations along the paternal line. And if that too proves impossible, the applicant must resort to a special judicial procedure pertaining to the status of French national (*la possession d'état de Français*).

Inhabitants of Alsace-Moselle and the Possession of French Status After the war, certificates of nationality were not legally mandatory.[91] Little by little, successive administrations came to require them as proof of nationality, thus creating special difficulties for people such as those originally from Alsace-Moselle.

Let us imagine the case of Mr. X, born in Paris in 1947 to a father born in Alsace-Moselle — that is, in one of the current departments of Bas-Rhin, Haut-Rhin, and Moselle — in 1917.[92] It is 1971, and Mr. X wants to prove that he is French in order to take an examination for an administrative position. Now he cannot prove this by showing that he was born in France to a person born in France, since in 1917 Alsace-Moselle belonged to Germany. Moreover, his father may be a descendant of a native of Alsace-Moselle, or the son of a German immigrant who had been in Alsace-Moselle since 1871, or the product of a mixed marriage (one parent from Alsace-Moselle, one from Germany), or finally, the son of a foreigner.[93] If his father was born in Alsace-Moselle, the Treaty of Versailles of 1919 restored his French nationality with full legal rights, although it obliged him to add his name to the register of the commune in Alsace-Moselle where he had his legal residence.[94] In 1971, then, the son has to provide an extract from the communal register on which his grandfather had had to record the reintegration of his own father into French nationality in 1919. This is impossible, as the register was lost or destroyed during the Second World War. He must then prove that he is the descendant of a man from Alsace-Moselle, a man who had been French before 1871, and go back up the chain of his ancestors. His grandfather was born in 1895. His great-grandfather was born in 1870. His great-great-grandfather was born in 1850. It is the application of the law of 1889 (which attributed French nationality to a child born in France to a father born in France) to these two ancestors that will prove the French nationality of their descendant, Mr. X, born in 1947.

The descendants of people from Alsace-Moselle found it unacceptable to be subjected to administrative demands like these in 1971, which they saw as "harassment and unjustifiable discrimination."[95] The law of 22 December 1961, modified by the law of 29 June 1971, allowed people born in Alsace-Moselle before 1918 to prove their French nationality by "simple" possession of a French status (that is, a status concerning only the interested party himself or herself).

The possession of a status is a notion found in the Family Code and imported into the area of nationality. Article 311.2 of the Civil Code defines the possession of a status as the will of an individual confirmed by "public say-so." A child who bears the name of his natural father, and who is recognized as his father's son by his father and by third parties, possesses the status of natural child. The fact of declaring oneself French, even if the declaration is ratified by the belief of third parties, is nevertheless insufficient to establish possession of the status of French national. Since nationality is a bond of public law between an individual and the state, it requires that the state recognize the individual as a member of its national community. The possession of a status, applied to nationality, is thus a set of facts "that translate the appearance of the bond of nationality uniting a person to the French state."[96] The applicant must have behaved as a French person would have behaved, but above all he or she must have been viewed by the state and its administrators as French: he or she will have received a passport or a voting card, if a man he will have fulfilled his national service obligation, and so on.[97] After all this, a decision will be made in court to recognize the applicant as having French nationality,[98] given the concordant indices that make it possible to prejudge the status of French national.

Since the laws of 1961 and 1971 indicated that the possession of a status would be used only "subsidiarily," many civil court judges still require that descendants of people from Alsace-Moselle try to establish proof by filiation before they agree to use the procedure of possession of a status to obtain a certificate of nationality.[99] The subsidiary character of that mode of proof was finally eliminated in 1998; since then, for inhabitants of Alsace-Moselle possession of a status has been "the proof par excellence of French nationality."[100]

Residents of Alsace-Moselle have been joined in recent years by a large number of French people born abroad themselves or born to parents born abroad: when people in these groups need to obtain certificates of nationality, they have a very hard time establishing proof.[101] In 1994 the administration decided to replace the old paper national identity card with a plasticized card reputed to be "unfalsifiable."[102] To be certain that the claim to French nationality was valid, it required a certificate of nationality from all French persons born abroad or born to foreign parents.[103] "Quarrels proliferated at the window between persons under the jurisdiction of the court and civil servants not well versed in the subtleties of nationality law:"[104] in a memorandum of 21 February 1996, the Ministry of the Interior ordered the services involved to stop systematically requiring certificates of nationality from such persons and to allow them instead to prove their French nationality by producing their own national identity card plus that of a parent.[105] The difficulty of supplying proof of one's nationality, when one can prove it only by filiation, is the only inequality that remains in French nationality law.

All contemporary nationality legislation combines elements of jus sanguinis, jus soli, and rights based on marriage or residency. French nationality has the peculiarity of combining these approaches in such a way that they are very broadly encompassing. French law thus cannot be identified with any varying configurations. Paradoxically, in fact, since the Revolution the French tendency to centralize has—unlike in Germany—resulted in legislation that retained at each stage quite diverse modes of attribution of nationality, often borrowed from the provinces or from abroad, *without abandoning any of them.* When one of them became the dominant principle, the others were not given up, and could thus be reactivated if legislative adaptations proved necessary.

Conclusion

▶ A few weeks before his death on 8 March 1872, Francis Lieber, a professor at Columbia University, wrote to Charles Sumner, a senator from Massachusetts, the leader of the radical Republicans in the Senate, and a fervent abolitionist.[1] Lieber had been writing to Sumner almost weekly for twenty-seven years.

A Prussian refugee who had come to the United States in 1827, Francis Lieber[2] founded the systematic study of governments, a discipline that became known in America as political science; in 1858 Lieber was awarded the first chair devoted to that discipline at Columbia University.[3] Lieber was Sumner's closest friend, though the two often disagreed on political and intellectual issues. Sumner was a long-standing Francophile, while Lieber had a reawakened pride in his origins and rejoiced in the victory of Bismarck's Prussia over the France of Napoleon III in the war of 1870. On that occasion Lieber held public meetings of support for Germany in Central Park in New York, bringing together Americans of German origin. Here is what Lieber wrote to his friend Sumner a few months after the Prussian victory and the foundation of the German Empire:[4]

> I have received this day from Berlin, a call to collect money among the Germans in America for a Bismarck Foundation in the University of Strasburg! I shall send some money and be done with, I suppose.
>
> The Germ. Government is evidently bent on making Strasburg a first rate university, which means something. The French neglected it shamefully. But they neglected and neglect everything except Paris. And here again I come to my old question: What is it that makes the French the only people who can convert conquered people? They receive no benefit from France. Yet they speak for France. Germans, English, Americans, none can do it. What is it?
>
> Ever Yours F. L.

Sumner had already answered that question, in a way, by fighting through-out the 1860s for the introduction of the following provision into the American Constitution: "All persons are equal before the law, so that no person can hold another as a slave." According to his biographer, the American historian David Donald, he had borrowed the expression "equal before the law" from the French Declaration of the Rights of Man and the Citizen, and he wanted to be the first to introduce it into the American constitution and American jurisprudence.[5] When he proposed this amendment to the U.S. Senate, his colleague, Senator Howard, begged him "to dismiss all reference to French Constitutions or French codes and go back to the good old Anglo-Saxon language employed by our fathers in the [Northwest] ordinance of 1787."[6] Sumner believed that the conservatives opposed it because the concept of equality did not come from England, "for the idea itself finds little favor in that hierarchical kingdom."[7]

The principle of equality at the heart of the French Revolution was not foreign to the Old Regime in France. David Hume had already suggested in 1777 that one of the successes of absolutist governments lay in the absence of difference between old and new subjects: "Compare the *pais conquis* of France with Ireland, and you will be convinced of this."[8]

What made a citizen of Strasbourg feel so attached to France was that when France ruled Alsace, he was on equal footing with all other citizens throughout the country. In contrast, after 1872, when Alsace became a colonial territory of the new German Empire, the same citizen could only feel inferior to the Prussians,[9] just as a Scotsman or an Irishman could only feel inferior to an Englishman. This concept of equality — among territories under the Old Regime, and among individuals since the Revolution — is at the heart of the success that Francis Lieber was questioning. But what does the identification with France — favored by the equality from which inhabitants of conquered or integrated provinces benefited — mean when individual access to nationality is in question?

We have seen that French nationality law is made up of an accumulation of provisions adopted under various influences: it has been modified over time, for example, to take into account the emancipation of the individual with respect to the state, to protect the interest of the state where demographic concerns were at issue, and to ensure the equality of women and men. Thus we have seen that nationality has its own particular history, and that it has by no means been an exact reflection of some stereotypical concept of the nation.

It is easy to imagine that keeping a group of foreigners who reside on national territory from acquiring nationality over long periods can contribute — even if the group is ultimately admitted — to a situation in which feelings of discrimination and inequality are perpetuated. Fortunately, French nationality policy has had a different outcome. Today the French are French by virtue of jus sanguinis, jus soli, marriage, or residence: all these approaches have been incorporated into French nationality law, and all are now in widespread use.

A person who is not French by birth can cross the boundary of nationality fairly readily, as long he or she can prove a tie to France by birth on French territory, residency in France, or — especially — marriage. Such crossings are facilitated by France's openness to dual nationality. In addition, French citizens easily transmit their nationality to descendants born abroad.

Today all French people are equal: children born in France to foreign parents are French from birth, unconditionally. In contrast, children born in Germany to foreign parents are German from birth, but their nationality is provisional: at the age of twenty-three they can lose it if they choose to keep the nationality that was transmitted to them by their parents. French people are thus equal in terms of nationality, in all but one respect: some can provide proof of nationality more easily than others. As Philippe Bernard notes, "the profound trauma caused to hundreds of thousands of persons suspected of fraud because they were born abroad" when difficulties arise over the attribution of a nationality certificate "cannot be measured."[10]

If this trauma — which lasts only until a nationality certificate is awarded — "cannot be measured," what can be said about the past discrimination and resulting trauma that affected French Jews during the Second World War, or women, colonized peoples, and naturalized persons for much longer periods?[11]

The Jews whose full French nationality was withdrawn in 1940 in Algeria, or those who were denaturalized or subject to the threat of denaturalization in metropolitan France, experienced a trauma that time has not eradicated either for them — as Jacques Derrida attests[12] — or for their children. At least they have had the possibility of retaining an identification with the Republic, which reestablished the Crémieux decree in Algeria in 1943 (although not without difficulty), and annulled the denaturalizations of Jews in metropolitan France in 1944.

Can as much be said about women? Between 1803 and 1927 French women who married foreigners lost their nationality and had to accept the status of "foreigner" in France. The provision affected a few hundred women each year throughout the nineteenth century. After it began operating on a large scale at the beginning of the twentieth century and even more so after the First World War, the law of 1927 quickly enabled French women to keep their nationality or to recover it if they had lost it. This trauma, which must have deeply affected the women involved, seems to have disappeared from collective memory.

Naturalized persons, for their part, were subjected—between 1927 and 1984— to restrictions in the arenas of suffrage and professional opportunity. Many new citizens were thus prevented from practicing their chosen trades. However, these limitations were temporary; they were removed at the end of a waiting period lasting five to ten years.

The situation with respect to the colonized people of Algeria is rather different in a crucial sense. During the entire period of French presence in Algeria, from 1830 to 1962, Algerian Muslims were held in a position of inferiority that was reflected in their legal status. Formally they were French nationals, but theirs was a denatured nationality, emptied of its rights; to become fully French they had to apply for and complete the naturalization procedure that was in principle reserved for foreign immigrants.

After Algeria became independent, the children of Algerian Muslim immigrants born in France became equals of the children born in France to European or Jewish parents from Algeria. They were French at birth through the effect of the double jus soli, because they were born in France to parents born in France (i.e. in Algeria before 1962).

In the early 1980s, however, the "Algerian debate" was revived. The political right demanded that children of Algerians manifest their "desire" to be French. The issue was presented as a matter of legal technicalities and therefore as a subject of legitimate debate. For the descendants of Algerian Muslims, though, the inability to become fully French could easily be perceived symbolically as a return to the inferior status that their parents had already suffered in Algeria. They could in fact not become fully French without making a formal request. Those on the left who sometimes responded by proposing to grant citizenship to immigrants without nationality were paradoxically closing the circle, unwittingly regressing to an earlier inegalitarian position: citizenship without full nationality was what Blum and Viollette had proposed to Algerian Muslims in the 1930s when granting full nationality had become impossible. The debate that had already taken place in Algeria was thus transferred, as Benjamin Stora ably shows,[13] from the former colony to metropolitan France. But while the same struggle took place, its outcome in contemporary France was the inverse of the outcome in Algeria: equality of rights finally triumphed over difference and inferiority.

Today the children of Algerians born in France are fully French. But the trauma transmitted by previous generations and repeatedly reactivated in the recent debates will not simply disappear with the granting of equal rights. Perhaps our deeper knowledge of the history of French nationality legislation will facilitate the twofold task of (re)cognition that lies ahead. The French of metropolitan France need to understand the extent to which, in colonial Algeria more than anywhere else, France pushed to the extreme the confusion between the words of the law and the realities of lived experience, emptying the very terms "nationality" and "equality" of their content. Given that background, it is important to understand that shifting from the status of subject without rights to the status of a full French national is much more complex than the transition from being a foreigner to becoming French. For Algerian Muslims and their children, the story told here ought to help make it possible to distinguish between facts and stereotypical representations. France is not — France is no longer — Algeria; the terms of French law mean what they say and apply to all. And these two centuries in the history of French nationality can be read as a progressive opening up to foreigners, a conquest of equality, and finally a series of victories over discrimination. In this history, they have become full participants in every respect.

GLOSSARY

Allegiance (and nationality)

"Allegiance must not be confused with nationality. The term 'French allegiance' is still often used in France, especially in administrative language. 'Allegiance' is a word from Old French that has been adopted in a large number of countries, particularly Anglo-Saxon countries, where it is still in use. Allegiance is the personal bond between a suzerain and a vassal; in France, as we shall see, it was the bond that united the king to his subjects. It is a bond of the feudal order. The word 'allegiance' recalls the liegeman, linked to his lord by the strongest possible bond. The bond of allegiance disappeared with the French Revolution. It was replaced by the bond of nationality. [In France, it] is no longer a bond of subjection involving a personal relationship between the sovereign and a subject but rather an abstract legal bond between the state and an individual, while in some countries, on the contrary—for example, in England—not only the expression but the institution of allegiance can still be found. Indeed, there is no British nationality, strictly speaking; there are only personal relations between the sovereign of Great Britain and each of his subjects. Furthermore, one does not speak of English citizens, but rather of British subjects." Henry Lévy-Ullmann, *Droit international privé* (Paris: Les Cours de Droit, 1932–33), 304.

Allegiance (liberation from the bond of)

A French person who has another nationality may petition the government to "lose" his or her French nationality. The request must be addressed to the minister in charge of naturalizations through the intermediary of the prefect of the candidate's legal residence in France, or from the French consul for candidates living abroad; authorization is generally granted only in the latter case. See Paul Lagarde, *La nationalité française*, 3rd edn. (Paris: Dalloz, 1997), 156–58.

Certificate of nationality

The ordinance of 19 October 1945 instituted the certificate of nationality that only a justice of the peace — today a chief clerk of a *tribunal d'instance* — is authorized to deliver.[1] The candidate who claims to be or not to be French is responsible for supplying proof. The advantage of the certificate is that it has legal value as long as it is not the object of a successful legal challenge. It is delivered on the basis of proofs that the candidate must provide to demonstrate his or her French nationality.

Civil Code and Nationality Code

Nationality law is as much a border law as a law governing borders. Depending on the authors and the periods, it is private law or public law, internal law or international law.[2] Uncertainty about its place has been translated by shifting categorizations.

Beginning in 1791, the modalities by which French nationality was attributed and acquired were defined in the successive constitutions adopted under the Revolution.

On 18 March 1803, when the section of the Civil Code pertaining to the enjoyment of civil rights went into effect, these modalities ceased to be defined by the constitution and were henceforth governed by the Civil Code.

The law of 10 August 1927 "removed" nationality from the Civil Code and made nationality legislation autonomous. The ordinance of 19 October 1945 created a Nationality Code whose provisions were reintegrated into the Civil Code in 1973, following a proposal by Pierre Mazeaud.

Declaration (acquisition of nationality by)

The procedure for acquiring nationality by declaration implies a voluntary act and weak control on the part of the public authority. Since 1803 it has been used for children born in France to foreign parents; as of 1927 spouses of French nationals can also acquire nationality by declaration. The same procedure is used by people seeking to renounce or to regain ("reintegrate") their French nationality.

Double jus soli

The laws of 22 and 29 January and 7 February 1851 instituted a system for attributing French nationality on the basis of two sequential births in France. Children born in France to a foreign father or — as of 1891 — to a foreign mother born in France were themselves French. A person in this situation could most readily prove French nationality by producing his or her own birth certificate and that of a parent.

Escheat, right of

Until the 1750s the right of escheat was construed both as an ineligibility to inherit or bequeath and as the king's right to seize the property of foreigners who died without a French heir. When the National Assembly abolished this right in 1790, it also ruled, in separate deliberations, on the eligibility of foreigners to inherit. When the right of escheat was reintroduced in 1803, restrictions on inheritance were restored, but the state did not regain the right to seize foreigners' property.[3]

Jus sanguinis and jus soli

These terms appeared only in the late nineteenth century, several years after the first occurrences of the word "nationality." They were not used in the debates over the Civil Code, or in discussions of nationality policy during the fifty years that followed. Charles Demolombe did not use these terms either, but in 1845 in his *Cours de Code civil* he wrote that "today it is origin, it is *blood* alone and no longer the bond, the natal territory, that makes a person French by birth."[4]

Camille Sée did not yet use *jus soli* or *jus sanguinis* in his report on nationality in 1885, but on 7 November 1887 Antonin Dubost, reviewing Sée's report for the Chamber of Deputies, wrote: "Admitting as a principle, almost as a dogma, that the fact of birth within the territory could not create a right, rejecting absolutely the *jus soli* of the old legislation that still remains in the legislation of several European states, most notably England, and permitting itself to go much further in that respect than the authors of the Code, the Council of State proclaims that nationality can result only from filiation, *jus sanguinis*."[5] After the vote on the law of 1889, when birth on French soil could permit attribution of French nationality at birth, the use of the two terms began to spread. One possible interpretation: the attribution of French nationality by birth on French soil or through filiation remained legally dependent on residency both under the the Old Regime and under the Revolution. Only from 1803 was nationality attributed irrevocably at birth by the bond of paternal filiation, and from 1851 by a "double birth" in France (unless the person involved renounced French nationality upon reaching majority, an option that remained open until 1889). Only as of these dates can one speak of attribution of nationality at birth by *jus sanguinis* or by double *jus soli*.

Jus sanguinis, jus soli, and Roman law

A Roman citizen who left his city-state transmitted his citizenship to his descendants; the latter were thus attached to Roman territory regardless of their birthplace. One's attachment to a *place of origin* subsisted independently of birthplace and was transmitted to one's posterity. In the thirteenth century this right of origin shifted toward the development of *jus soli*, first by limiting ascendency to the ancestor's generation and then by allowing the acquisition of citizenship on the simple grounds of birth within the territory of the city-state. To justify the transmission of the quality of being French by filiation, eighteenth-century jurists borrowed from Roman tradition chiefly the transmission of citizenship by filiation without regard to place of birth.[6] *Jus soli* and *jus sanguinis* each originated in a transformation of Roman law; thus two distinct regimes based on Roman law were produced in two different periods.[7]

Legal residency (admission to)

Instituted by article 13 of the 1803 Civil Code, this status became obsolete in 1889 and disappeared in 1927. Like naturalization, admission to legal residency was the object of a decision by the head of state. In support of a request for this status, a foreigner had to produce a birth certificate that made it possible to prove his or her origin (i.e. birthplace) and age, the passport on the basis of which he or she entered France, the proof of a state or profession ensuring that the candidate would not be a burden on the commune where he or she sought to establish legal residency, and finally, testimonials to good past and future behavior. Moreover, this was an independent status, distinct from naturalization until 1889. Persons admitted to legal residency enjoyed all the civil rights reserved to French nationals so long as they continued to live in France. In contrast, unlike French nationals, men with the status of legal resident were not subject to obligatory military service: this explains the great success of this status between 1803 and 1889, and its elimination in 1889.

Mixed marriage

In this book, marriage between two persons of different nationalities. In contemporary France, the term is sometimes used to characterize a marriage between two persons of different religious or ethnic backgrounds.

Nationality

The word appeared toward the beginning of the nineteenth century in a literary context: according to Gérard Noiriel,[8] Madame de Staël used it for the first time in *Corinne ou l'Italie*.[9] But it also appeared around the same time in legal and administrative vocabulary: although the expression *qualité de Français* was most commonly used to refer to the bond that linked the individual to the state, the word *nationalité* (nationality) was noted by Walther von Warburg in 1808.[10]

On 11 August 1821, in a report to the departmental review council, the mayor of Bastia noted that "among the inhabitants of Bastia we have a considerable number of foreigners, dock workers, tradesmen, farm laborers, and porters, most of them from Genoa, who have contracted marriage, acquired real property, and set up businesses. Where enjoying the privileges attached to the quality of being French is concerned, no one questions the *French nationality* of these persons."[11] The use of the term spread under the July monarchy, even though in the parliamentary debate over the reform of military service in 1831, it was only used by an army officer, Colonel Lamy. Benoît Guiguet shows that the Supreme Court first used the term in 1834.[12] It appeared for the first time in the 1835 edition of the *Dictionnaire de l'Académie française*. It was frequently used by J.-F. Taullier in *Théorie raisonnée du Code civil* (1840), by Valette in 1842 in his commentary on the *Traité sur l'état des personnes et sur le titre préliminaire du Code civil*,[13] by Mailher de Chassat in *Traité des statuts (lois personnelles, lois réelles) d'après le droit ancien et le droit moderne, ou du Droit international privé* . . . , more deliberately by Jean-Jacques-Gaspard Foelix in his *Traité de droit international privé*,[14] and by Demolombe in 1845 in his *Cours de Code civil*. It was thus during the 1840s that the term was adopted as a synonym for "quality of being French" in discussions of nationality policy. Starting with the Turin treaty of 24 March 1860, the treaties on annexation (2 February 1861 between France and Monaco, 8 December 1862 between France and Switzerland), and the treaty in which the French Republic yielded territories to the German Empire (Frankfurt, 10 May 1871), the term "nationality" came into routine use.[15] The law of 16 December 1874 mentioned "nationality of origin" for the first time. The term "French nationality" first appeared in the law of 30 December 1880 that ratified the annexation of Tahiti and the Windward Islands, specifying that "French nationality is acquired by full right by all the former subjects of the King." At the recommendation of Camille Sée, the law proposed by Senator Batbie and submitted to the Council of State for its review was titled *De la nationalité*; it became the law of 1889.

Naturalization

Naturalization is *the granting by a state* of the nationality of that state to a foreigner who *requests* it. Naturalization thus differs from other procedures for acquiring nationality (by declaration, or as a benefit awarded automatically by law) by virtue of the deciding role played by the state. The word *naturaliser* (to naturalize) has existed in French since 1471, and the word *naturalisation* appeared in 1566. Under the Old Regime, from the sixteenth century on, the French king had the prerogative of naturalizing, or granting lettres de naturalité. Under the Revolution, between 1790 and 1795, naturalization became automatic, as soon as the conditions specified in the law of 30 April–2 May 1790 or in the constitution of 1793 (especially conditions of residence) were met. From 1795 a foreigner could achieve naturalization by declaring his intent to settle in France, after a waiting period of seven years (constitution of 1795) or later ten years (constitution of 1799). As of 1809, at the end of the ten-year waiting period, naturalization required a decision by the emperor. Since then no naturalization has taken place without a decision by the executive power.

Parliamentary procedure under the Third Republic

The parliamentary procedure of the Third Republic was very different from the procedures in effect in the Fifth Republic today. There were no specialized commissions, except for that governing the budget. The parliamentarians were divided among bureaus (eleven in the Chamber, nine in the Senate) whose membership was chosen by lot and renewed monthly. Every month four temporary commissions were designated; these included the commission on parliamentary initiatives, which had two representatives from each bureau, thus twenty-two members in the Chamber and eighteen in the Senate. These commissions studied the texts of bills and selected the ones that would be presented to the full assemblies. If their selection of a given bill was confirmed, the bill was sent back to the bureaus or to a commission specially charged with examining the bill; the commission could continue to function with its membership intact throughout the examination of the different versions of the bill and until the final version was adopted or rejected.[16]

Possession of the status of French

Possession of a status is a notion imported from the Family Code—with slight transformations—into the realm of nationality. Article 311.2 of the Civil Code defines the possession of a status as the will of the individual corroborated by "what people say." A boy or a girl who bears the name of his natural father, and who is recognized as that father's child by that father and by third parties, possesses the status of natural child. The fact of declaring oneself French, even if that declaration is supported by the belief of third parties, is nevertheless insufficient to establish possession of the status of French national. Since nationality is a bond of public law between an individual and a state, it requires that the state recognize the individual as one of its nationals. The possession of a status, applied to nationality, is thus a set of facts "that translate the appearance of a bond of nationality linking a person to the French state." The concerned party must have behaved as a French person would have behaved, but above all must have been viewed by the state and by public administrations as a French person: he or she will have often been issued a passport or a voter's card, will have carried out military service if a male, and so on.

Reintegration

The procedure of reintegration allows a person to recover French nationality after he or she has lost it. For a long time it concerned French women who from 1804 to 1927 automatically lost their French nationality when they married foreigners. Under the law of 14 October 1814, which was in effect until 1849, it also concerned people from countries that had been integrated into France during the Revolution or the Empire. After 1918 it concerned people from Alsace-Moselle and in the post-colonial period it concerned those from the former French colonies.

Seals (Bureau of)

The Service of Seals originated in the Old Regime.[17] The king's decision to naturalize went into effect definitively only after a letter patent had been reviewed and sealed by the chancellor.[18] The Revolution interrupted the system of seals, which was reestablished by Napoleon in Year X. At the outset the Council of Title Seals (1808) and its successor, the Seal Commission (1814), were independent from the minister of justice; they were headed first by the arch-chancellor, then by the chancellor of France. The commission ruled on the legitimacy of letters of nobility, letters patent conferring or confirming titles, letters of "grand" naturalization, and lettres de naturalité. Six specialized public auditors were charged by the commission with investigating such matters; they replaced the lawyers on the Council of State. The Seal Commission was incorporated into the Ministry of Justice under Louis-Philippe by the order of 31 October 1830; from 1832 the Service of Seals, from then on part of the civil branch (*Direction civile*) of the Ministry of Justice, exercised these powers, retaining them until 1945: among other things the Service of Seals was in charge of certifying name changes, marriage dispensations, titles, laws, letters patent, diplomas, and finally admissions to legal residency, naturalizations, reintegrations, and authorizations to serve abroad along with the regulation of the seal rights pertaining to these matters. The *référendaires* (special auditors) were eliminated by attrition by a decree of 11 June 1892, and disappeared altogether in 1927. In 1945 responsibility for investigating naturalization requests was transferred to the Ministry of Population.

Seals (keeper of the)

"The head of Justice formerly — and, with interruptions, up to 1848 — held the fine title of Chancellor of France. Currently, the Chancellery is no longer headed by a 'Chancellor,' but by a Keeper of the Seals. This title is official . . . It comes from pre-1789 terminology. The chancellor was normally responsible for keeping the seals. He was a high officer of the Crown, and could not be dismissed. Thus the king could not revoke his charge. But experience had led to the discovery of a way to get rid of a chancellor without revoking his charge. The king would send him off to some country residence and require him to remain there; the seals would be confiscated and entrusted to someone who did not have the title of chancellor, someone who was merely 'the keeper of the seals.'

"The possession of the seals once had an importance that is difficult to imagine today. A particular value was attached to the external force of the written title. The material authenticity of a title was proved by the apposition of a cachet which was known to be in the hands of a single responsible person. This preoccupation persisted during the Revolution. The original text of laws was inscribed on a parchment; this parchment passed under the seal of the state and was deposited in the archives of the Ministry of Justice. . . .

"The Old Regime had two categories of seals: the personal *cachet* of the king, which was used for certain individual acts, such as the famous *lettres de cachet*, and the great seal of France, without the apposition of which a legislative measure or order was not valid. Now, the 'great seal of France' could only be apposited by the person to whom it was entrusted. It sometimes happened that this person took upon himself the right to judge whether the act that he was being asked to seal was worthy. The chancellor of France thus gave himself the right to refuse to seal orders of which he disapproved. It remained to the king either to bow to that decision or to remove the seals from the recalcitrant chancellor and entrust them to a 'keeper.' This explains why, on several occasions, the king, upon naming a chancellor, specified that he himself would keep the seals. History also retains the memory of chancellors whose authority was somewhat diminished, as the king was 'keeping the seals.'"[19]

NOTES

Introduction

1. Valéry Giscard d'Estaing, "Immigration ou invasion?," *Le Figaro Magazine*, 21 September 1991.

2. Decision 93-321 DC, 20 July 1993, *JO*, 23 July 1993, 10391.

3. See Alain Finkielkraut, *Être Français aujourd'hui et demain*, vol. 1 (Paris: Union Générale d'Éditeurs, 1988), 595–601 (a hearing before the Nationality Commission, 16 October 1987), and Finkielkraut, "Sur un vers de Racine," *Le Monde*, 29 October 1987.

4. Rogers Brubaker, *Citizenship and Nationhood in France and Germany* (Cambridge: Harvard University Press, 1992); Miriam Feldblum, *Reconstructing Citizenship: The Politics of Nationality Reform and Immigration in Contemporary France* (Albany, N.Y.: SUNY Press, 1999); Gérard Noiriel, *The French Melting Pot: Immigration, Citizenship, and National Identity*, trans. Geoffroy de Laforcade (Minneapolis: University of Minnesota Press, 1996); Noiriel, *La tyrannie du national: le droit d'asile en Europe, 1793–1993* (Paris: Calmann-Lévy, 1991); Peter Sahlins, *Unnaturally French: Foreign Citizens in the Old Regime and After* (Ithaca: Cornell University Press, 2004). See also Jean-Charles Bonnet, *Les pouvoirs publics français et l'immigration dans l'entre-deux-guerres* (Lyon: Éditions de l'Université de Lyon II, 1976); Bernard Laguerre, "Les dénaturalisés de Vichy, 1940–1944," *Vingtième Siècle*, no. 20 (October–December 1988), 3–15; Danièle Lochak, *Étrangers de quel droit?* (Paris: Presses Universitaires de France, 1985); Hélène Morère, "La loi du 10 août 1927 sur la nationalité" (master's thesis, University of Paris I, 1985–86); Claude Goasguen, "Les Français au service de l'étranger sous le Premier Empire: législation et pratique" (LL.D. diss., University of Paris II, 1976); Cécile Mondonico, "La loi du 26 juin 1889 sur la nationalité" (master's thesis, University of Paris I, 1990).

5. See the glossary.

6. See Jean-Paulin Niboyet, *Traité de droit international privé français*, vol. 1, *Sources, nationalité, domicile* (Paris: Sirey, 1938), 110.

7. For a defense of the argument that the two are related, see Dominique Schnapper, *Community of Citizens: On the Modern Idea of Nationality*, trans. Séverine Rosée (New Brunswick, N.J.: Transaction, 1988); on the conception of the nation-state see Gil Delannoi, *Sociologie de la nation* (Paris: Armand Colin, 1999).

8. On the history of citizenship see Pierre Rosanvallon, *Le sacre du citoyen: histoire du suffrage universel en France* (Paris: Gallimard, 1992). On contemporary developments see Fred Constant, *La citoyenneté* (Paris: Montchrestien, 2000).

Chapter 1: From the Old Regime to the Civil Code

1. In 820 the word *aubain* designated a foreigner in relation to the Carolingian Empire. Later, until the mid-thirteenth century, it designated a person born outside a given seigneury; the lord (*seigneur*) was thus the one who exercised the right of escheat. Little by little, the king appropriated this right for himself. See Jean-François Dubost, "Étrangers en France," *Dictionnaire de l'Ancien Régime*, ed. Lucien Bély (Paris: Presses Universitaires de France, 1996), 518–22. The correspondence between foreigners residing in the kingdom and aubains was far from complete: certain foreigners were exempt from the right of escheat and certain French nationals were aubains because they were born outside of marriage or outside the kingdom; see Jean-François Dubost and Peter Sahlins, *"Et si l'on faisait payer les étrangers": Louis XIV, les immigrés et quelques autres* (Paris: Flammarion, 1999), 65–66.

2. Unless he was exempt from the right of escheat. On the *droit d'aubaine* in the modern period see Dubost and Sahlins, *"Et si l'on faisait payer les étrangers,"* chapter 3.

3. On the body of law governing nationality under the Old Regime and the history of the right of escheat until its abolition in 1819, see Peter Sahlins, *Unnaturally French: Foreign Citizens in the Old Regime and After* (Ithaca: Cornell University Press, 2004).

4. As opposed to simply maintaining a home there.

5. See Marguerite Vanel, *Histoire de la nationalité française d'origine: évolution historique de la notion de Français d'origine du XVIᵉ siècle au Code civil*, preface by Jean-Pierre Niboyet (Paris: Ancienne Imprimerie de la cour d'appel, 1946), 8, and Dubost and Sahlins, *"Et si l'on faisait payer les étrangers,"* 66.

6. This jurisprudence triumphed only gradually, however. For example, a judgment issued by the Rouen parlement on 21 August 1670 required the parents' marriage

to have been contracted in France. See Vanel, *Histoire de la nationalité française d'origine*, 9.

7. Ibid., 50.

8. At the beginning of the same century, French kings had granted members of their own families who had married foreign princes or sovereigns the favor of considering their descendants, and even those of their retinue who accompanied them abroad, as French. In May 1576 King Henri III issued an edict according to which the children of French nationals who had been expatriated during the wars of religion were to be considered French even though they had been born abroad. These precedents facilitated the evolution of the jurisprudence in question. See Vanel, *Histoire de la nationalité française d'origine*, 50, and Vanel, "Le Français d'origine dans l'ancien droit français (XVe–XVIIIe siècle)," *RCDIP* 35 (1940–46), 220–31.

9. The application of jus sanguinis suffered from political measures taken against French nationals who had emigrated for religious reasons. After the revocation of the Edict of Nantes in 1685 and until the adoption of the Edict of Tolerance in 1787, the king was supposed to grant letters of naturalization only to Catholics. Peter Sahlins shows that the actual practice was more liberal, as letters were granted without that condition, in the interest of the kingdom or its subjects, to Protestants and even, after 1760, to Jews. See Peter Sahlins, "Fictions of a Catholic France: The Naturalization of Foreigners in Ancient Regime France," *Representations* 37 (1994), 85–110.

10. It was also under François I that the power to *naturalize* devolved once again exclusively to the king. Acquired in principle by the monarchy in the fourteenth century, the power had continued to be contested at the initiative of princes or even governors: under François I it was imposed definitively and replaced letters of municipal affiliation (*lettres de bourgeoisie*). See Dubost, "Étrangers en France."

11. Peter Sahlins, "La nationalité avant la lettre: les pratiques de naturalisation en France sous l'Ancien Régime," *Annales HHS*, no. 5 (September–October 2000), 1081–1108; Sahlins, *Unnaturally French*.

12. Legally such letters or declarations of naturalization were not always necessary; they were precautionary measures "sought in order to provide protection against other petitioners, against royal taxation, or against rival candidates for a monastic charge." These declarations acknowledged that the petitioner had held the status of French national before the issuance of the letter; this was not so for the letters of naturalization that transformed foreigners into French nationals. See Dubost, "Étrangers en France," and Sahlins, "Nationalité avant la lettre."

13. "Among the majority of the Constituents . . . , there was a will to break with the past. . . . Everything that has anything at all to do with feudalism had to disappear": Jean-Louis Halpérin, characterizing the state of mind of the members of

the Constituent Assembly regarding civil legislation, in *L'impossible Code civil*, preface by Pierre Chaunu (Paris: Presses Universitaires de France, 1992), 87–88.

14. See Marcel Garaud, *Histoire générale du droit privé français: la Révolution et l'égalité civile*, foreword by Georges Lefebre (Paris: Sirey, 1953).

15. In 1789 there were still 1,500,000 serfs in France. Personal servitude was abolished in principle on 4 August 1789, but it was abolished in fact by the decree of 15 March 1790. See Jacques Godechot, *Les institutions de la France sous la Révolution et l'Empire* (Paris: Presses Universitaires de France, 1951), 8.

16. The integration of the Jews came about in two stages. Those Jews known in France as Portuguese, Spanish, and Avignonnais Jews were accepted through a decree issued on 28 January 1790; finally, on 27 September 1791 the National Assembly "revoked all the adjournments, reservations and exceptions inserted in preceding decrees regarding Jewish individuals who swear the civic oath." See Philippe Sagnac, *La législation civile de la Révolution française (1789–1804): essai d'histoire sociale* (Paris: Hachette, 1898), 252–58.

17. See Laurent Dubois, *A Colony of Citizens: Revolution and Slave Emancipation in the French Caribbean, 1787–1804* (Chapel Hill: University of North Carolina Press, 2004).

18. Pierre Rosanvallon notes, however, that the constitution of 1791 granted the right to vote to nearly four and a half million of the six million men who were at least twenty-five years old at the time and thus old enough to vote. At this point France had twenty-six million inhabitants. See Pierre Rosanvallon, *Le sacre du citoyen: histoire du suffrage universel en France* (Paris: Gallimard, 1992).

19. This decree spelled out the conditions that foreigners had to meet to become French citizens (*AP*, vol. 15, 30 April 1790, 340).

20. Peter Sahlins demonstrates that a certain number of individual naturalizations were signed by the king as late as July 1790. In an irony of history, the decree of 30 April–2 May 1790 was published in the form of a letter patent, that is, a royal letter of naturalization. This decree can thus be seen as the last act of naturalization promulgated under the Old Regime monarchy and as the first one of the new regime. Sahlins, *Unnaturally French*, chapter 1.

21. Jean-Jacques-Gaspard Foelix, "De la naturalisation collective et de la perte collective de la qualité de Français: Examen d'un arrêt de la Cour de cassation du 13 janvier 1845," *Revue de droit français et étranger* 2 (1845), 321–47.

22. Some of the bilateral agreements on abolishing the right of escheat had specified that 10 percent of all the legacies in question would be reserved for the state of residence; this was called the right of detraction. See J.-G. Locré, *Esprit du code Napoléon, 1805–1808*, vol. 1 (Paris: Imprimerie impériale, 1814), 281.

23. Scotland, the United Provinces, the Catholic Swiss cantons.

24. These particular privileges applied to the foreign merchants who traded at the Lyon fairs; they applied to foreigners who worked or resided in a part of the territory where the law of escheat did not apply, or, at various times, to foreigners who worked or resided in certain provinces or cities (Bordeaux from 1474 on, Metz from 1552, Dunquerque from 1662, Marseille from 1669). In addition, foreigners who had been born in a territory claimed by France could become French simply by establishing their residence on French territory (according to the borders that existed at the time residency was established). The stakes here were political: if the state had exercised the right of escheat on such people, it would have been implicitly acknowledging that it had no rights over the territory in question. Thus an inhabitant born in Flanders or in the Milan region who had come to live in France would receive a letter of naturalization (which was a declaration on the part of the state). The beneficiary was viewed as having always been French.

25. Spain and Denmark in 1742, Holland in 1773, Russia in 1787.

26. The exemption was made in exchange for a right of detraction equivalent to 10 percent of the right of escheat. Agreements were signed with Austria (1766), Poland (1777), the United States of America, Portugal (1778), Bavaria (1778), and many German states.

27. While there must have been some uncertainty about the meaning of this provision, the debate that took place a few months later on 9 August 1791, at the time the statement was included in the constitution, leaves no room for doubt: one deputy, Garat (the elder), supported by Tronchet, proposed to delete the phrase "for religious reasons" so as not to limit the right of return to the quality of being French "to the descendants of Protestants alone, but to extend it to all descendants of French people." Le Chapelier opposed this, with majority support in the Assembly: he asked that "these words be retained as reparation for a persecution that was carried out under the government of Louis XIV and that we all deplore." AP, vol. 29, 302–3.

28. On 6 June 1791, during the debate over the draft of the Penal Code, the National Assembly asked the constitution committee — which was made up of a representative of each of the Assembly committees charged on 23 September 1790 with the task of drawing up a draft of the first constitution — to address the "question of what makes a Frenchman, how one becomes French, and how one ceases to be French." Charles de Lameth, AP, vol. 27, 6 June 1791, 1.

29. The provision in question is title II, article 2. The draft constitution was presented on 5 August 1791, and the discussions of articles 2, 3, and 4 took place on 9 and 10 August 1791 before the National Assembly. AP, vol. 29, 321–35.

30. Under the Old Regime, the criteria for attributing the quality of being French were sometimes applied differently depending on the territories under the control of the various parlements.

31. Marie-Joseph Chénier (1764–1811), brother of the poet André Chénier, had established his reputation by composing hymns and two plays (*Charles IX* and *Caius Gracchus*) in the service of the Revolution, when he was elected deputy to the Convention from Seine-et-Oise. He voted for the death of the king; he was a republican and an anti-Robespierrist. Chénier outlived his brother, who died on the scaffold; he was reelected to the legislative body and served in the upper parliamentary chamber, the Council of Elders (Conseil des Anciens). He accepted the coup d'état of 9 November but quickly shifted to the opposition. See "Chénier" in Auguste Kuscinski, *Dictionnaire des conventionnels* (Paris: Rieder, 1917), 135–36.

32. François Furet and Denis Richet, *La révolution française* (Paris: Hachette-Pluriel, 1963), 153.

33. Jean Tulard, Jean-François Fayard, and Albert Fierro, *Histoire et dictionnaire de la Révolution* (Paris: Robert Laffont, 1987), 606.

34. A part of Lorraine incorporated into the Kingdom of France in 1678, Longwy was fortified by Vauban on the order of Louis XIV.

35. Some were opposed to adopting this text (Lasource and Basire) or had reservations about it (Thuriot). AP, vol. 48, 688–91.

36. The names in italics did not appear in Chénier's propositions; instead Chénier had proposed two Englishmen (Horne Tooch and William Bolts), an Irishman (Naper-Tandi), and a Pole (Malakouski). See Albert Mathiez, *Révolution et les étrangers: cosmopolitisme et défense nationale* (Paris: Corbeil, 1918), 15–16; see also Karin Dietrich-Chénel and Marie-Hélène Varnier, "Intégration d'étrangers en France par naturalisation ou admission à domicile de 1790/1814 au 10 mai 1871," vol. 6 (Ph.D. diss., Université d'Aix-Marseille I, 1994), 219–20. The American historian Robert R. Palmer, wondering why Hamilton had been awarded honorary French citizenship but Jefferson, who was much better known in France, had not, hypothesized that Jefferson's friendship with Lafayette might have worked against him; the National Assembly must have thought that Hamilton was more favorable to revolution than Jefferson. See Robert R. Palmer, *The Age of the Democratic Revolution: A Political History of Europe and America, 1760–1800*, vol. 2 (Princeton: Princeton University Press, 1964), 55.

37. Only three other such decrees were to be issued later by the National Convention: for the American Joel Barlow, on 17 February 1793 (he is praised in the record of the session held on that date; Barlow was to be the American ambassador to Paris during the first Empire), the Italian Philippe Buonarroti, on 27 May 1793 (Buonarroti, who headed Corsica's administrative offices, had made his request on

9 September 1791), and the Belgian Pierre Plouvier, on 10 June 1793. See Dietrich-Chénel and Varnier, "Intégration d'étrangers en France," vol. 6, 215–33.

38. In 1784 Maryland's legislative body had adopted "An Act to naturalize major-general the marquis de Lafayette and his heirs male for ever." Lafayette's "citizenship" was thus transferred to the United States in 1788 when the Federation was proclaimed. More recently, honorary citizenship was granted to Winston Churchill by the U.S. Congress in 1963. See Pub. L. no, 88-6, 77 Stat. 75: "That the President of the United States is hereby authorized and directed to declare by proclamation that Sir Winston Churchill shall be an honorary citizen of the United States of America."

39. The conditions for exercising this honorary citizenship were evoked in the observations of the Supreme Court justice James Iredell in Talbot v. Jansen, 3 U.S. (3 Dallas) 133, 164–65 (1795), when Iredell compared the conditions applying to Americans who had been made French citizens with Lafayette's legal situation: "Did any man suppose, when the rights of citizenship were so freely and honorably bestowed on the unfortunate Marquis de Lafayette, that that absolved him, as a subject or citizen of his own country? It had only this effect, that whenever he came into this country, and chose to reside here, he was ipso facto to be deemed a citizen, without any thing farther. The same consequence, I think, would follow in respect to rights of citizenship, conferred by the French Republic, upon some illustrious characters, in our own, and other countries. . . . Some disagreeable dilemmas, may be occasioned by this double citizenship, but the principles, as I have stated them, appear to me to be warranted by law and reason, and if any difficulties arise, they show more strongly the importance of a law, regulating the exercise of the right in question."

40. In *The Social Contract*, evoking "the man who dares to undertake the establishment of a people," Rousseau writes that this person "must deprive man of his own strength so as to give him strength from outside, which he cannot use without the help of others." Then, after insisting on the extraordinary character of the legislator within the state — "he who controls the laws ought not to control men" — Rousseau indicates that it was customary in most Greek cities to entrust the establishment of their laws to foreigners: "The modern Italian republics have often imitated this habit; the republic of Geneva did the same and did well" (Jean-Jacques Rousseau, *Discourse on Political Economy* and *The Social Contract*, trans. Christopher Betts (Oxford: Oxford University Press, 1994), book 2, chapter 7, 76–77). Cf. Bonnie Honig, *No Place like Home: Democracy and the Place of Foreigners* (Princeton: Princeton University Press, forthcoming). See also Jean Carbonnier, "A beau mentir qui vient de loin ou le mythe du législateur," *Essai sur les lois* (Paris: Répertoire du Notariat Defrénois, 1979), 227–38.

41. On 31 August 1791 Claude-Bernard Navier (1756–93) was elected deputy from Côte-d'Or to the Legislative Assembly, where he sat among the moderates. At the end of the Legislative Assembly's mandate he was appointed to the High Court of Appeals.

42. AN, BB11/2. Navier had put forward two other considerations in his report on the requests submitted by Philippe Buonarroti, Priestley (the younger), and Conrad de Laube (Buonarroti alone would be made a French citizen, on 27 May 1793): (1) "It is always important for a State to increase its population by adding to the number of its citizens"; (2) "it would amount to violating the Principles of Our Constitution, as it were, to reject foreigners who ask to live under our empire. Since the Declaration of Rights that is its foundation has made it, so to speak, the property of all men."

43. See Sophie Wahnich, *L'impossible citoyen: l'étranger dans le discours de la Révolution française* (Paris: Albin Michel, 1997), book 2.

44. *AP*, vol. 76, 641.

45. *AP*, vol. 88, 545.

46. Jean-Jacques-Gaspard Foelix, *Traité de droit international privé*, 4th edn. (Paris: Marescq aîné, 1866 [1847]), 322.

47. Philippe-Antoine Merlin (1754–1838) was a deputy from Douai to the Estates General and to the Constituent Assembly, then to the Convention: he played an important role in the committee on legislation. He was minister of police and justice in 1795, and a member of the executive directorate from 5 September 1798 to 18 June 1799; he was named solicitor general (*procureur général*) on the Supreme Court in 1801. In 1784–85 Merlin had been part of the team of legal advisors, practitioners, and attorneys working with Joseph-Nicolas Guyot, a former magistrate who published the *Répertoire universel et raisonné de jurisprudence en matière civile, criminelle, canonique et bénéficiale*, 1st edn., 17 vols. (Paris: Visse, 1784–85). From 1812 Merlin published his own *Répertoire universel et raisonné de jurisprudence*, 3rd edn., 17 vols. (Paris: Garnery, 1812–25). See Louis Gruffy, *La vie et l'oeuvre juridique de Merlin de Douai (1754–1838)* (Paris: Duchemin, 1934), Jean-Louis Halpérin, *Le Tribunal de cassation et les pouvoirs sous la révolution (1790–1799)* (Paris: LGDJ, 1987), and Hervé Leuwers, *Merlin de Douai, un juriste en politique (1754–1838)* (Amiens: Artois Presses Université, 1996).

48. Merlin had concluded along these lines on 22 March 1806, before the Supreme Court (Cour de Cassation); but while the court went along and declared valid a divorce pronounced at Mac-Mahon's spouse's request, it was on the basis of a different argument. See Merlin, *Répertoire universel et raisonné de jurisprudence*, "Divorce, Sect. IV, §X," 3rd edn., 1813, vol. 4, 789–90. It was only in a decision by the Supreme Court on 27 April 1819, confirming a decision by the royal court of Paris

dated 25 April 1818, that Merlin's approach was confirmed: "given that the law of 2 May 1790, distinguishes between foreigners who must be deemed French and those who wish to be admitted to the exercise of the rights of active citizens; that it imposes on the former two conditions, 1° having maintained legal residence continuously in the kingdom for five years; 2° having either acquired real property, or married a French women, or set up a business . . . ; that for the latter it requires the same conditions and in addition the swearing of the civic oath; that it follows from this that [the civic oath required of the foreigner who wanted to exercise the political rights of an active citizen was not required of the one who simply wanted to be deemed French]." Ibid., 4th edn., 1825, vol. 17, addendum, 217–18. This specific case concerned the Prince d'Hénin, who had married a Frenchwoman in 1766 and lived in France until he died, in 1794; since the two conditions specified above had been fulfilled, he was declared to have died a Frenchman.

49. This interpretation by Merlin of the constitution of 1791, which comes up in his conclusions under the Mac-Mahon decision of 1806, was followed in later court decisions. See Cour de Paris, 18 March 1823 (Dal. 1823.2.150); Rennes, 13 February 1824 (Dal. 1824.2.92); Riom, 7 April 1835 (Dal. 1836.2.57); Douai, 19 May 1835 (Dal. 1836.2.66); Nîmes, 22 December 1825 (Sir. 1825.2.164).

50. The article gave rise to little discussion. Only one amendment was adopted, at Thuriot's suggestion, replacing the reviewer's term *réside* (resides) by *est domicilié* (is domiciled): "I think that the state of the individual must be determined, for a rich man could occupy a large number of workers or servants to vote in his favor, and you must prevent this abuse. I ask that the word '[is] domiciled' be substituted for 'resides'; for in order to be 'domiciled,' one must have *rented the apartment or have bought the house where one is living*." *AP*, vol. 66, 283.

51. Decision of the Colmar court on 13 October 1829 (Dal. 1830.2.25).

52. Lyon court, 10 November 1827 (Dal. 1828.2.14), Colmar court, 13 October 1829 (Dal. 1830.2.25); Orléans court, 25 June 1830 (Sir. 1830.2.461); Douai court, formal hearing, decision of 23 November 1840 (Dal. 1841.2.162; Lyon court, decision of 26 November 1841 (Dal. 1843.2.8); imperial court, Aix, formal hearing, 18 August 1858 (Sir. 158.2.519); *a contrario*, a decision of the Montpellier court, 22 June 1826 (Sir. 1827.2.94) does not take the constitution of 1793 into account in judging whether a foreigner who had been living in France since 1789 had the quality of being French.

53. Excerpt from the decision of the Douai court; among the courts cited above, only the Orléans court deemed it necessary for the foreigner to express the wish to acquire the quality of being French.

54. Excerpt from the decision of the Colmar court, 13 October 1829 (Dal. 1830.2.25).

55. Aix court, formal audience, 18 August 1858 (Sir. 1858.2.519).

56. The law of 1790 irrevocably naturalized, until 2 September 1791, all foreigners who had been living in France since at least 1786. Foreigners who had arrived in France between 1786 and 1788 became French between 1791 and 1793 only if they manifested their wish to do so. But if they were still legally resident in France when the constitution of 1793 was promulgated, on 10 August 1793, they automatically became French nationals at that point. The same thing held true for foreigners who had been legally resident in France for at least one year between 10 August 1793 and 22 September 1795, the eve of the implementation of the constitution of 1795.

57. The mayor of Bastia alluded to these rules, asking for their reinstatement, in a statement to the departmental review council on 11 August 1821 (AN, F9/170); the prefect of the Nord department did the same thing in a letter to the minister of the interior (AN, F9/227).

58. In addition, this new constitution no longer retained the honorary naturalization that was formerly attributed by the legislative body—naturalization-reward, Hermann called it in the debate, asking in vain for its reinstatement. Lanjuinais responded that to bring back honorary naturalization "would open a door to intrigue, we have too cruelly experienced this," and Hermann's suggestion was rejected. The debates over the articles of the constitution of 1795 are reproduced in their entirety in *Esprit de la Constitution ou Recueil exact et complet de la Discussion qui a eu lieu à cet égard dans la Convention, depuis le 16 messidor jusqu'au 23 fructidor, an III de la République*, vol. 1 (Paris: Dupont), 184–95.

59. This new procedure, proposed by Pierre-François Daunou, was adopted after a spirited discussion. Several members of the Convention found the conditions set for the acquisition of the "title of French citizen" too easy to meet. Like Lakanal, Mailhe considered the waiting period worth "very little": the British government "will within a period of seven years and at very little expense be able to populate France with ferments always ready to shake up, tear apart, dissolve your social state." Daunou replied that it was "difficult for an enemy power to maintain a foreign agent for seven years before he could exercise his rights as a citizen." He recalled that "residence under the age of twenty-one counts for nothing, that one must be twenty-one years old to declare one's intention with respect to residence" before the seven-year waiting period began, and the article was thereupon adopted.

60. Dietrich-Chénel and Varnier, *Intégration d'étrangers en France*, vol. 1, 20.

61. Subsequently the active citizen, as a member of the sovereign political body, had to fulfill supplementary conditions: to be a French male at least twenty-five years old, and to pay a direct contribution at least equal to three days' work.

62. The only confusion had to do with the conditions under which the quality of being

French could be lost. In article 6 of title 2, the motif of losing the quality of being French (for example, by being naturalized in a foreign country) was intertwined with that of simply losing the quality of being a political citizen (through condemnation to penalties entailing civic degradation or judgment in absentia).

63. The Jacobin members of the Constituent Assembly of June 1793 had not taken into account the reservations expressed in April 1793 by Lanjuinais, who criticized Condorcet's draft constitution because it confused the two senses of the word "citizen": "rigorously speaking, it signifies only those who are admitted to the exercise of political rights . . . in a word, the *members of the sovereign* . . . ; in ordinary usage," to be a "citizen of a country, a member governed by the general laws of its inhabitants, independently of age, sex, and reason . . . it suffices not to be foreign, not to have become foreign, and not to have suffered civil death." *AP*, vol. 63, 563–64.

64. Earlier, article 4 of the constitutional act of 24 June 1793 declared, for example, that "every man born and having his legal residence in France who has reached the age of twenty-one . . . is admitted to the exercise of the rights of a French citizen"; article 8 of the constitution of 1795 provided that "every man born and residing [rather than "being domiciled," or having his legal residence] in France who, having reached the age of twenty-one, has had his name recorded on the civic register of his canton, who has lived since that time for a year in the territory of the Republic, and who pays a direct personal or property-based contribution, is a French citizen." Article 2 of the constitution of 1799 provides that "every man born and residing in France who, having reached the age of twenty-one, has had his name entered into the civic register of his communal district and who has lived since that time for a year in the territory of the Republic is a French citizen."

65. For a defense of this interpretation see for example Michel Borgetto, "Être français sous la Révolution," *Crises*, no. 2 (1994), 80–88, and Michel Troper, "La notion de citoyen sous la Révolution française," *Études en l'honneur de Georges Dupuis: Droit public*, preface by Georges Vedel (Paris: L.G.D.J., 1997), 301–22.

66. Vida Azimi, "Le suffrage 'universaliste,' les étrangers et le droit électoral de 1793," *La constitution du 24 juin 1793, l'utopie dans le droit public français?*, Proceedings of a colloquium held in Dijon, 16–17 September 1993, ed. Jean Bart, Jean-Jacques Clère, and Michel Verpeaux (Dijon: University of Dijon, 1997), 204–39.

67. Pierre-Antoine Fenet, *Recueil complet des travaux préparatoires du Code civil* (Paris: Videcoq, 1836), vol. 7, 3.

68. Tronchet justified this disjunction, for "the former legislation confused civil rights and political rights, and attached the exercise of both to the same conditions" (Fenet, *Recueil complet*, vol. 7, 32–33). Was the break with jus soli that Tronchet sought the cause of this disconnection with the constitution? The fact remains

that the legislature worked, for example, between 1793 and 1796 on three drafts of the Civil Code, all reported by Cambacérès, during very different phases of the Revolution. In none of these three drafts did Cambacérès and his colleagues deem it necessary to define French persons, since for them this was covered by the successive constitutions. Fenet, *Recueil complet*, vol. 1, 99ff.; Cambacérès, *Mémoires inédits*, vol. 1 (Paris: Perrin, 1999), 162–80, 377–79; Halpérin, *L'impossible Code civil*, 233.

69. Decision of 29 November 1849 (Sir. 1851.2.34), 21 April 1880 (Sir. 1881.2.119). The court in Aix — which in a case in 1858, concerning the grandson of a foreigner who had established legal residence and taken a wife in France at the time of the constitution of 1793, had declared that the grandson was French — added that "in the absence" of the grandfather, the father would have transmitted his nationality, for he "would have held his quality of being French by law, as being born in France [28 September 1799] to a foreigner who had established residency there before the publication of the Napoleonic Code, which modified the old principles in this respect." Imperial Court of Aix, formal hearing, 18 August 1858, (Sir.1858.2.519).

70. The same evolution occurred with article 3 of this constitution, which specified that "a foreigner becomes a French citizen after having reached the age of twenty-one, having declared his intention to settle in France, and having resided there during ten consecutive years." Jennifer Ngaire Heuer, *The Family and the Nation: Gender and Citizenship in Revolutionary France, 1789–1830* (Ithaca: Cornell University Press, 2005), 129. From 1803 this article governing the naturalization procedure was valid only for those who could obtain political rights, that is, men; by the same token, foreign women, to whom it applied between 1799 and 1803, could no longer be naturalized from 1803 on (ibid., 170–71).

71. On 19 May 1789 Emmanuel Sieyès (1748–1836) was elected deputy to the Estates General from the Third Estate; Sieyès, a priest, had published the celebrated brochure *Qu'est-ce que le Tiers État?* (What Is the Third Estate?) in January of the same year. A member of the constitutional committee under the Constituent Assembly, he was elected to the Convention and then in Year IV to the Council of the Five Hundred (Conseil des Cinq-Cents); he maintained a low profile during the difficult periods of the Revolution. He facilitated Bonaparte's rise to power; Bonaparte had him appointed consul, then distanced him from power by naming him to the Constitutional Court (the Sénat Conservateur).

72. AN, Archives Sieyès, 284AP/5.

73. This meeting took place in Bonaparte's quarters in late 1799, bringing together fifteen people: the five members of the constitutional sections of the Council of Elders (Garat, Laussat, Lemercier, Lenoir-Laroche, and Regnier), seven from the Council of the Five Hundred (Lucien Bonaparte, Daunou, Boulay [de la Meurthe],

Chazal, Chénier, Chabaud-du-Gard, and Cabanis), and the three consuls. See Jean Bourdon, *La Constitution de l'An VIII* (Rodez: Carrère, 1942), 13–37.

74. François Piétri, *Napoléon et le Parlement ou la dictature enchaînée* (Paris: Fayard, 1955), 42, 54.

75. Jean-Jacques Cambacérès (1753–1824), from a family in Montpellier belonging to the *noblesse de robe*, was a magistrate with the *cour des comptes* in Montpellier in 1774; he became president of the Hérault criminal court before being elected deputy from that department. A moderate (he voted to suspend Louis XVI's death sentence), he devoted himself to the work of the parliamentary committee on legislation, which he headed. On 20 July 1799 he was appointed minister of justice, a position he kept after the coup d'état of 9 November. He became consul under the constitution of 1799, pressed for the proclamation of the Consulat for Life, and supported the Empire, which made him arch-chancellor on 18 May 1804 and awarded him many honors.

76. The first draft, in the context of the adoption of the Montagnard constitution of June 1793, was presented to the Convention on 9 August in the name of the committee on legislation; it was abandoned on 3 November 1793. The second was presented to the Convention on 9 September 1794 in the name of a commission on the classification of laws and decrees, when the Thermidorian reaction was at its height. The third draft was taken up again under the Directorate, by the same commission, between January and June 1796, and is dated 4 June 1796. After the coup d'état of 18 Brumaire, a draft was also developed by the deputy Jacqueminot. This draft did not contain a definition of French persons either. See Fenet, *Recueil complet*, vol. 1, and Jean-Louis Halpérin, "Code civil," in Albert Soboul, Jean-René Suratteau, and François Gendron, eds., *Dictionnaire historique de la Révolution française* (Paris: Presses Universitaires de France, 1989), 243–44.

77. From 1676 the Conseil des prises handled all legal matters arising from the wartime capture of ships at sea.

78. Félix Bigot de Préameneu (1747–1825) was a lawyer in the Paris Parlement before the Revolution. Elected to the Legislative Assembly, he was part of the moderate faction; he went into hiding during the Terror and reappeared only after 18 Brumaire. Bonaparte made him commissioner to the Supreme Court and a member of the Council of State. Jacques Maleville (1741–1824) was a lawyer in Bordeaux before the Revolution. A partisan of the new ideas, he was president of the Directorate of the Dordogne department in 1790, and in 1791 he joined the High Court of Appeals. Elected deputy from Dordogne to the Council of Elders in 1796 and reelected in 1799, he was recalled to the Supreme Court after 18 Brumaire, and he headed the civil section after Tronchet left. Jean-Étienne Portalis (1745–1807), an attorney at the bar of Aix in 1765, was elected in 1796 and sat alongside his

brother-in-law Siméon in the ranks of the counterrevolutionary opposition to the Directorate. A royalist, he had to go into hiding after the coup d'état of 18 Fructidor (4 September 1797); he returned to France only after 9 November 1799.

79. Las Cases, *Mémorial de Sainte-Hélène*, vol. 1 (Paris: Gallimard–La Pléiade, 1977 [1823]), 593–94.

80. This election took place on 22 April 1800: Tronchet received 31 of 38 votes cast; see M. de Royer, Procurer General to the Cour de cassation, "Discours sur la vie et les travaux de M. Tronchet, ancien président du Tribunal de cassation," a transcript of the opening session of the Cour de cassation held on 3 November 1853.

81. Antoine Boulay (de la Meurthe) (1761–1840), son of a plowman, became a lawyer at the bar of Nancy in 1785 and a judge at the tribunal of Meurthe in 1792; he was dismissed as a moderate in 1793. After 27 July 1794 (9 Thermidor, when the Reign of Terror ended) he became president of the civil tribunal of Nancy, then in 1795 served in the Council of the Five Hundred, where he joined the moderate republicans. He participated in the conspiracy of 18 Brumaire and presided over the interim commission of the Five Hundred, but he refused an offer to be minister of police. Boulay was appointed to the Council of State, where he headed the section of civil and criminal legislation; he served until 1814.

82. Fenet, *Recueil complet*, vol. 7, 4. Tronchet was not a member of the Council of State, but the decree naming the commission of 12 August 1800 had provided (in article 7) that Tronchet, Bigot de Préameneu, and Portalis would attend the Council sessions in which the Civil Code was to be discussed.

83. Ibid., 6.

84. "Notice d'arrêts, sur la question quand le Français retiré en pays étranger a perdu ou conservé le droit de cité," Consultations de François-Denis Tronchet (1748–Year VIII), Bibliothèque de la Cour de cassation, consultations 1418 and 1783.

85. On the jurisprudence of the Old Regime see Vanel, *Histoire de la nationalité française d'origine*; Sahlins, *Unnaturally French*; and Dubost and Sahlins, *"Et si l'on faisait payer les étrangers."*

86. See Anne Lefebvre-Teillard, "Jus sanguinis: l'émergence d'un principe (Éléments d'histoire de la nationalité française)," RCDIP 82, no. 2 (April–June 1993), 223–50.

87. Consultations de François-Denis Tronchet (1748–Year VIII), consultations 1441 and 1783. On the *origo* in Roman law see Yan Thomas, "Le droit d'origine à Rome: contribution à l'étude de la citoyenneté," RCDIP 84, no. 2 (April–June 1995), 253–90.

88. Fenet, *Recueil complet*, vol. 7, 69–76.

89. Tronchet had suggested adding "and who shall continue to reside"; the article finally approved reads as follows: "The foreigner who has been admitted to de-

clare that he wishes to settle in France in order to become a citizen and who has resided in France for a year since making that declaration will enjoy all his civil rights, as long as he continues to reside there."

90. He added: "The children of the abdicant were always able to regain the quality of being French; they were even allowed to share, with the children that the abdicant had left in France, the inheritances that became available to their profit. They held this right owing to the favor of their origin, and they enjoyed it independently of treaties made with the nation in which they were born. However, they were allowed to exercise this right only when they committed themselves to remaining in France and when they satisfied this commitment." Fenet, *Recueil complet*, vol. 7, 26.

91. Ibid., vol. 7, 9.

92. François Richer, *Traité de la mort civile, tant celle qui résulte des condamnations pour cause de crime, que celle qui résulte des vœux en religion* (Paris: Desaint et Saillant, 1755).

93. Tronchet, who as commission president should have introduced the bill, was known for having a particularly inaudible voice. Mirabeau said of him that "he doesn't have as much voice as enlightenment."

94. Prosper Duvergier de Hauranne, *Histoire du gouvernement parlementaire en France*, vol. 1 (Paris: Michel Lévy Frères, 1857), 495.

95. Fenet, *Recueil complet*, vol. 7, 166.

96. On 18 December 1891 the reviewer, Thiessé, spoke out against the inhumanity of this punishment: "The dissolution of marriage is the abandonment of the spouse, the misery of the children, the despair of all: these are sacrifices that must be made to the irrevocable decision of nature. But a dissolution against nature, a dissolution of two living beings who had joined themselves together until the last breath by the most sacred of all ties; what power can hope for this? Where is its right? Where is the necessity? . . . From that moment on, his spouse, who has not left him, will be called a widow by the law. That widow, who does not know if she is such, finds herself in a position that has no name: she is the widow of her husband, and yet she cannot marry another. She will have children, and unlike other children it will not be known when they are born whether they are legitimate or bastards." Ibid., 184–87.

97. Ibid., 590.

98. Pierre-Claude-François Daunou (1761–1840), elected deputy to the Convention from Pas-de-Calais, opposed the decision to execute Louis XVI. Imprisoned between 3 October 1793 and 24 July 1794, he rejoined the Thermidorian convention after his release. The chief author of the constitution of 1795, he joined the Tribunate after 1799 and was named its president. But as an opponent of despotism he

became part of the first fifth eliminated by the Sénat Conservateur at the suggestion of Cambacérès with Tronchet's complicity. Later Daunou became conservator of the Pantheon library, archivist of the Empire, and professor at the Collège de France. See Auguste Kuscinski, "Daunou," *Dictionnaire des Conventionnels* (Paris: Rieder, 1917), 178–79, and A. H. Taillandier, *Documents biographiques sur P. C. F. Daunou* (Paris: Firmin-Didot, 1841).

99. Stanislas Girardin, *Journal et souvenirs, discours et opinions*, vol. 3 (Paris: Moutardier, 1828), 246–48.

100. Cited in ibid., 258.

101. Fenet, *Recueil complet*, vol. 7, 591.

102. See Cambacérès, *Mémoires inédits*, 600–601.

103. Cambacérès summarized his reasons for urging Napoleon to nominate Tronchet as follows: "Tronchet's opinions had always been moderate. He had neither hesitated to defend the King, nor refused the deputation to the Legislative Body under the regime of the Constitution of Year III [1795]. . . . Tronchet had always treated me well while I was a practicing attorney. The relations I had with him at the time had added to the feeling of veneration that was inspired by his talents and his integrity." He concludes: "Tronchet was appointed and was very useful to us." See ibid., 546.

104. On 7 January 1802 Cambacérès got the Council of State to discuss and approve this idea, and he brought it before the Sénat Conservateur. See Maurice Vitrac, ed., *Journal du Comte P. L. Roederer* (Paris: Daragon, 1909), 104–5. A few days later, on 18 January, Napoleon wrote to Cambacérès: "I beg you to make sure we are rid of exactly twenty and of sixty bad members that we have in the constituted authorities . . ." Godechot, *Les institutions de la France*, 492.

105. Minutes of the sessions of 12 and 13 March 1802 (21 and 22 Ventôse, Year X) of the Republic, Archives of the Sénat Conservateur (French Senate Library). The Sénat Conservateur decided to publish a senatus-consulte without including justifications.

106. Earlier, in the session of 9 March 1802, the Sénat Conservateur had designated the new members of the Tribunate who were to replace the outgoing ones; these incoming members included Lucien Bonaparte, Daru, who was general secretary of the Ministry of War, Carnot, and Thouret (minutes of the sessions of the Sénat Conservateur).

107. Halpérin, *L'impossible Code Civil*, 274–75.

108. It was Cambacérès who played the key role in setting up this arrangement, which seems to have taken place between Tronchet and Bonaparte.

109. By a judgment of 8 April 1802, the Tribunate had been reorganized into three sections. Earlier, the Tribunate lacked the power to amend the text and had been

obliged only to pronounce a positive or negative opinion; henceforth, "if the government were to deem it useful," the draft of a proposed law under deliberation in the Council of State could be communicated to one of the three sections, and conferences — something like mixed commissions — could be set up, headed by a consul and composed of members of these sections and Council of State members. Fenel, *Recueil complet*, vol. 1, xvi.

110. "A child is born in France to foreign parents: the latter have just arrived. A few days later, they return to their own country; their child goes with them. The child himself may never reappear in France during his entire lifetime. One wonders on what basis such an individual may be French. No bond attaches him to France. He is linked neither by feudalism, since feudalism does not exist in the territory of the republic, nor by intention, since the child cannot have any opinion, nor by reality, since he does not remain in France and his parents had only an ephemeral residence there." Ibid., vol. 7, 592–93.

111. This remark was made by M. de Royer, solicitor general to the Supreme Court, in a "speech about the life and works of M. Tronchet, a former president of the Cour de Cassation," in Cour de cassation, *Audience de rentrée du 3 novembre 1853* (Paris: Ch. Lahure, Imprimeur de la Cour de cassation, 1853), 2.

112. Fenet, *Recueil complet*, vol. 7, 6–7, 621.

113. The first discussion of the section of the Civil Code concerning the legal attribution of Frenchness had taken place in the general assembly of the Council of State on 25 July 1801. It was definitively adopted on 6 March 1803.

Chapter 2: The Triumph of Jus soli

1. Émile Boutmy, "Les rapports et les limites des études juridiques et des études politiques," *Revue Internationale de l'Enseignement* 17, no. 1 (1889), 222.

2. On the history of the word "nationality," see the glossary.

3. Article 10, §1, of the Civil Code provides that "every child born to a Frenchman in a foreign country is French" and does not mention the status of children born in France. There was general agreement that the article should be read as follows: "Every child born to a Frenchman *even* in a foreign country is French." See Lucien Gérardin, *De l'acquisition de la qualité de Français par voie de déclaration, étude sur le bienfait de la loi* (Paris: Larose, 1896), 1.

4. He would also lose it if he accepted a public position in a foreign country without authorization from the French government, or if he settled abroad "without the intent to return" (Civil Code, article 17). For the authors of the Code, French nationality was an advantage, an honor, even a privilege, and thus few Frenchmen abroad were expected to give it up. Moreover, every Frenchman who had settled

abroad was presumed to have maintained a desire to return. This was the rule under the old law (Robert Joseph Pothier, *Traité des personnes*, 8 vols. (Paris: La veuve Desant, 1776–78), part 1, vol. 2, section 4, no. 62), and it was confirmed by a decision of the Supreme Court on 13 June 1811. See Isidore Alauzet, *De la qualité de Français, de la naturalisation et du statut personnel des étrangers* (Paris: Imprimerie et librairie générale de jurisprudence, 1880), 60–61.

5.   See chapter 8; see also Claude Goasguen, "Les Français au service de l'étranger sous le Premier Empire: législation et pratique," 2 vols. (Ph.D. diss., Université de Paris II, 1976).

6.   In all, between 14 April 1812 and 13 January 1814 only thirty-nine letters authorizing naturalizations were signed and sealed (including twenty for the German Grand-Duchys and nine for the United States); 1,668 letters of authorization for service abroad were signed by the emperor or the empress, including 1,600 unsealed letters, the majority of which concerned the kingdom of Naples (866), Westphalia (235), or Spain (374). See ibid., 342–44.

7.   During the discussion of the Civil Code in the Council of State (on 22 August 1801), the Council member Roederer had already pointed out that it was a "flaw in the Constitution that it did not authorize the granting of lettres de naturalité . . . Men of rare merit, such as Franklin, for example, could never become French because they would be too old to hope to complete their political internship." See Philippe-Antoine Merlin, "Naturalisation," *Répertoire universel et raisonné de jurisprudence*, 5th edn., vol. 21 (Brussels: Tarlier, 1825–28).

8.   Fundamental ("organic") senatus-consulte of 4 September 1802.

9.   Decree of 17 March 1809.

10.   With the law of 3 December 1849, for the first time since the Revolution naturalizations were to be governed by a legal text bringing together all the provisions having to do with foreigners, from naturalization to expulsion, that had formerly been governed by article 7 of the law of 19 October 1797. On this point see Charles P. Gomès, "Les limites de la souveraineté, les juges dans le cadre de l'immigration en France et aux États-Unis" (Ph.D. diss., Instituto Universitário de Pesquisas do Rio do Janeiro, 2001).

11.   See Patrick Weil, preface to Bruce Ackerman, *Au nom du peuple: les fondements de la démocratie américaine* (Paris: Calmann-Lévy, 1998), 9–25.

12.   National Legislative Assembly, minutes of the session of 28 November 1849, 666. By seeking to attribute the power to naturalize to the National Assembly, Favre was following the Belgian or Dutch example.

13.   Between 1804 and the last trimester of 1814, fewer than twenty of these decisions made by decree were published in the *Bulletin des lois*. See Karin Dietrich-Chénel and Marie-Hélène Varnier, "Intégration d'étrangers en France par naturalisation

ou admission à domicile de 1790/1814 au 10 mai 1871," vol. 1 (Ph.D. diss., Université d'Aix-Marseille I, 1994), 34.

14. AN, BB11/4.

15. AN, BB11/3.

16. This was one of the formulas conventionally used in requesting admission to residency.

17. AN, BB11/77.

18. Merlin, *Répertoire universel et raisonné de jurisprudence*, vol. 21 (Paris: Garnery, 1812–25), 1, Walsh-Serrant decision of 27 July 1803 (Supreme Court).

19. The Supreme Court issued a decision on 2 July 1822 according to which "a foreigner may have a de facto legal residence and a home in France even though, according to article 13 of the Civil Code, he cannot have a legal residence there without government authorization." Supreme Court, civil section, Sir.1822.1.346.

20. Memorandum from the prefect to the vice-prefects and mayors of the department (Colmar, 13 August 1817). Cited in Sibylle Panke, "L'immigration à Mulhouse au XIXe siècle" (master's thesis, Université des sciences humaines, Strasbourg, 1993), 55.

21. This "droit d'aubaine" included only the incapacity to inherit from a French native and not the state's right to confiscate the estate, nor even the capacity to make a will or to transmit a succession. See Peter Sahlins, *Unnaturally French: Foreign Citizens in the Old Regime and After* (Ithaca: Cornell University Press, 2004), 300.

22. As the Tribunate member Gary indicated in his report to the legislative body (session of 4 March 1794): "It is a policing and security measure as much as a legislative provision. The government will use it to combat vice, and to welcome virtuous men exclusively, those who will offer guarantees to their adoptive family." Pierre-Antoine Fenet, *Recueil complet des travaux préparatoires du Code civil*, vol. 7 (Paris: Videcoq, 1836), p. 649.

23. See Charles L'Ébraly, *De l'admission à domicile et des droits qu'elle confère à l'étranger qui l'obtient* (Paris: Larose, 1898), 29.

24. See Georges Levasseur, *La détermination du domicile en droit international privé* (Paris: Rousseau, 1931), 298–306.

25. See Panke, "L'immigration à Mulhouse," 53.

26. AN, BB11/77–80.

27. These last two files are found in AN, BB11/79.

28. AN, BB11/80.

29. AN, BB11/79.

30. AN, BB11/80. On mixed marriages in Mulhouse see Panke, "L'immigration à Mulhouse," 58–59.

31. Jennifer Heuer, *The Family and the Nation: Gender and Citizenship in Revolutionary France, 1789–1830* (Ithaca: Cornell University Press, 2005), 175.

32. See map, pp. 376–77.

33. Presentation of the reasons for the bill on naturalizations made in the Chambre des Pairs on 9 August 1814, Impressions no. 12 (Archives PP DB 301).

34. The validity of this law was extended after the Hundred Days by the law of 5 June 1816 and another on 29 October 1817.

35. Dietrich-Chénel and Varnier, "Intégration d'étrangers en France," vol. 1, 86–96.

36. See André Weiss, *Traité théorique et pratique de droit international privé*, 2nd edn., vol. 1 (Paris: Librairie Larose et Tenin, 1907), 614. Regulations issued by the Council of State on 17 May 1823 and 22 June 1836 (D.A., vol. 18, see *Droits Civils*, p. 55, no. 2, 104 and 105). Cass. May 4, 1836 (Sir. 1836.1.860); Nancy, formal hearing, 21 August 1845 (Garnier, jurisprudence de Nancy, see *étranger*); Paris, 11 December 1847 (Sir. 1848.2.49; D. P. 1848.2.49).

37. Cass., 14 April 1818 (Sir. 1819.1.193; Sir. Chronique); Paris, August 24, 1844 (Sir. 1844.2.568). Under the Old Regime wives and children benefited from the declaration only if they were explicitly named in the text.

38. Dietrich-Chénel and Varnier, "Intégration d'étrangers en France," vol. 1.

39. These two departments came right after the Seine on the list of departments with the highest number of recorded naturalizations: Seine, 745 (10.89%); Moselle, 553 (8.08%); Ardennes, 470 (6.87%), Nord, 276 (4.03%), Bouches-du-Rhône, 271 (3.96%).

40. See Serge Slama, *Le privilège du national: étude historique de la condition civique des étrangers en France* (Nanterre: Université de Paris X, 2003).

41. Decree of 28 March 1848 (*Le Moniteur universel — Journal officiel de la République française*, 30 March 1848, 717).

42. ADN, M 495–9.

43. *La Liberté, Journal de Lyon*, 5 April 1848.

44. According to M. Rouher, Minister of Justice, 2,475 naturalizations were granted (*jo*, parliamentary debates, National Legislative Assembly, session of 28 November 1849, 669). But the Ministry of Justice statistics include only 1,580 decisions in 1848 and 617 in 1849, making 2,197 for the two years combined. These figures are from the Compte général de l'Administration de la justice civile, cited in Pierre Depoid, *Les naturalisations en France (1870–1940)*, Ministère des Finances, Service national des statistiques, Direction de la statistique générale, Études demographiques no. 3 (Paris: Imprimerie Nationale, 1942).

45. This becomes apparent, for example, from the dossiers transmitted by the prefectures of Bas-Rhin (ADBR, SM27) or Isère (ADI, 128M3).

46. See Gérard Noiriel, *La tyrannie du national: le droit d'asile en Europe, 1793–1993*

(Paris: Calmann-Lévy, 1991), and Cécile Mondonico, "La loi du 26 juin 1889 sur la nationalité" (master's thesis, Université de Paris I, 1990), 12.

47. According to Jacques Grandjonc, the events of 1848 emptied France most notably of its large German colony; cited in Yves Lequin, ed., *Histoire des étrangers et de l'immigration en France* (Paris: Larousse, 1992), 323.

48. Session of 28 November 1849, 670.

49. Pierre-Jacques Derainne, "Le travail, les migrations et les conflits en France: représentations et attitudes sociales sous la Monarchie de Juillet et la Seconde République" (Ph.D. diss., Université de Bourgogne, 1998–99), 363ff.

50. Ibid., 290–92.

51. An opinion of the Council of State, rendered on 7 June 1803 and approved on 9 June by the government, made the application of article 3 of the constitution subject to article 13 of the Civil Code: "in all cases in which a foreigner wishes to settle in France he is required to obtain the authorization of the government." However, this opinion was not included in the *Bulletin des Lois*, so it never had the force of law and was in fact never applied; the practice of making the ten-year wait begin at the time of the simple declaration of intent registered at city hall continued until 1848. See Déc. min. Justice, 16 February 1825 and 14 August 1830, and Jean-Jacques-Gaspard Foelix, *Traité de droit international privé*, 4th edn. (Paris: Marescq aîné, 1866), 7.

52. At the time of the July Monarchy, these amounted to 175 francs, or the equivalent of three months' salary for a mill worker; mill workers in Mulhouse made 2 to 3 francs a day. Moreover, on top of the basic charge, the candidate had to pay 22 francs in registration fees and 8 francs for publication. See Panke, "L'immigration à Mulhouse," 54.

53. ADN, M 495–9.

54. Decision of the Supreme Court, 23 July 1855. Dal. 1855.1.353; Sir. 1856.1.148. Bordeaux court, 14 July 1845; Dal. 1846.2.163; Sir. 1846.2.394.

55. They kept it after the beneficiary's death; their only obligation was to continue to live in France. See Alexandre Duranton, *Cours de droit français suivant le Code civil*, 3rd edn., vol. 1 (Paris: Alex-Gobelet, 1834), 5.

56. "Two years of experience demonstrated that voluntary commitments could not suffice to maintain the weak corps that circumstances allowed us to keep in the armed forces." AP, t.s. 20, session of 7 January 1818, 213, cited in Annie Crépin, *La conscription en débat ou le triple apprentissage de la Nation, de la Citoyenneté, de la République (1798–1889)* (Arras: Artois Presses Université, 1998), 9.

57. See Crépin, *La conscription en débat*, chapter 2.

58. See Bernard Schnapper, *Le remplacement militaire en France: quelques aspects politiques, économiques et sociaux du recrutement au XIXᵉ siècle* (Paris: SEVPEN, 1968).

59. Crépin, *La conscription en débat*, 12.

60. AN, F9/227, Nord, dossier 10, letter from the prefect to the minister of the interior, 24 November 1818, cited in ibid., 140.

61. AN, F9/227, Nord.

62. Peter Sahlins cites a note from the Pyrénées-Orientales prefect indicating that "the entire district of the French Cerdagne [a part of Catalonia that became part of France under the Treaty of the Pyrenees in 1659] 'wants to follow attentively French or Spanish laws, according to which ones will exempt them from personal obligations.'" *Boundaries: The Making of France and Spain in the Pyrenees* (Berkeley: University of California Press, 1989), 225.

63. Copy of the memorandum addressed by the mayor of the city of Bastia to the review council on 11 August 1821 (AN, F9/170).

64. Not until half a century later, on 24 March 1881 and 20 October 1888, were memoranda issued by the Ministry of the Interior, one mandating that registers be kept in every municipality and the other inviting mayors to transmit a copy of the registrations to the Ministry of Justice. These two memoranda produced few results. Gérardin, *De l'acquisition de la qualité de Français*, 188.

65. See chapter 8.

66. Adrien-Théodore Benoît-Champy (1805–72), an attorney at the Paris bar, was elected representative from Côte-d'Or to the Legislative Assembly on 13 May 1849. He was part of the conservative majority in the Assembly and supported the coup d'état of 2 December 1851. See Adolphe Robert, Edgar Bourloton, and Gaston Cougny, eds., *Dictionnaire des parlementaires français* (Paris: Bourloton, 1891).

67. A report by Benoît-Champy on behalf of the commission charged with examining the proposal made by Raulin and Benoît-Champy concerning the status of children born in France to foreigners who had themselves been born in France. National Legislative Assembly, agenda for 6 January 1851, *Le Moniteur universel: Journal officiel de la République française*, 6 January 1851, 41–42.

68. Charles Séruzier, *Précis historique sur les Codes français* (Paris: Videcoq père et fils, 1845), 32–33.

69. Henri-Jean-Baptiste Dard, *Code civil des Français avec des notes indicatives des lois romaines, coutumes, ordonnances, édits et déclarations, qui ont rapport à chaque article* (Paris: J. A. Commaille, 1807), 2. The law of 3 September 1807 substitutes the title "Code Napoléon" for "Code civil des Français," which was, according to Bigot de Préameneu, no longer suitable for a code that was already viewed as the common law of Europe.

70. M. du Coetlosquet, "Rapport no 702 fait au nom de la 5ᵉ commission d'initiative

parlementaire, sur la proposition de MM. Raulin et Benoît-Champy, relative à l'état des enfants nés en France d'étrangers qui eux-mêmes y seraient nés." National Legislative Assembly, session of 9 January 1850, 8.

71.   Antonin Dubost, "Rapport sur la nationalité," Chamber of Deputies, no. 2083, November 7, 1887, 4. Dubost (1844–1921), after a career as a prefect, was elected deputy from Isère in 1880, then senator from the same department in 1897; he was president of the Senate from 1906 to 1920. A committed republican, he published two works on Danton, *Danton et la politique contemporaine* (Versailles: Imprimerie de Cerf, 1877) and *Danton et les massacres de Septembre* (Paris: Librairie générale de vulgarisation, 1885).

72.   On this topic see Centre de recherches d'histoire nord-américaine, Université de Paris I, *L'émigration française, études de cas: Algérie, Canada, États-Unis* (Paris: Publications de la Sorbonne, 1985) [international series no. 24]; Camille Maire, *En route pour l'Amérique: l'odyssée des émigrants en France au XIXᵉ siècle* (Nancy: Presses Universitaires de Nancy, 1993); Nancy Green et François Weil, *Citoyenneté et émigration: Les politiques du départ* (Paris, EHESS, 2007).

73.   Anselme-Polycarpe Batbie (1828–87) won the post of auditor at the Council of State through a competition in 1849, became a doctor of law in 1850, and was excluded from the Council of State in 1852. He was then appointed to direct a course in administrative law at the law school in Dijon in 1852, in Toulouse in January 1853, and then in Paris in January 1857. The author of *Traité théorique et pratique du droit public et administratif*, 4 vols. (Paris: Cotillon, 1861–63) and an Orleanist, he was elected as a representative from Gers in the National Assembly on 8 February 1871, and then elected senator from the same department on 30 January 1876. Batbie was minister of public instruction and religion in the Broglie government that was appointed by President Mac-Mahon after Thiers resigned. After the elections of 14 October 1877 he supported Mac-Mahon in his attempts to resist the republican majority in the Chamber of Deputies. See Robert, *Dictionnaire des parlementaires français*, and Roger Vidal, *Batbie, homme politique, économique, juriste* (Paris: LGDJ, 1950).

74.   Batbie thus achieved a goal that he had already set for himself in 1881 during the debate over the law passed on 14 January 1882. This law facilitated the acquisition of French nationality by children of naturalized citizens who formerly would have had to reach the age of eighteen to become French; the object of the reform was to allow them to join the army or take school entrance exams. See Mondonico, "La loi du 26 juin 1889," 43.

75.   Born on 10 March 1847 in Colmar, Camille Sée earned his law degree in Strasbourg; on 10 September 1870, at twenty-three, he became secretary general to the

minister of the interior. Vice-prefect of Saint-Denis in 1872, he served as deputy from that department from 1876 to 1881, in the ranks of the republican left. Sée was the author of the law of 21 December 1880 that established secondary education for girls. After losing in the elections of 4 September 1881, he was appointed to the Council of State, where he served until his death on 20 January 1919. See Françoise Mayeur, *L'enseignement secondaire des jeunes filles, sous la troisième République* (Paris: Presses de la Fondation nationale des sciences politiques, 1977); Mona Ozouf, *L'École, l'Église, et la République, 1871–1914* (Paris: Le Seuil, 1992), 243–44.

76. The fundamental ("organic") law of 24 May 1872, which limited the powers that the Council of State had acquired under the Empire, nevertheless specified that it could be asked for advice on "projects initiated by Parliament that the National Assembly deemed appropriate to refer to it" (article 8, §4).

77. A child born in France could become French if the parents made a declaration in his or her name; a foreigner who had married a French woman could be naturalized after one year of authorized residency; finally, admission to residency would lose its effects for foreigners who failed to seek naturalization within three years after being granted admission.

78. "Rapport sur la nationalité," Chamber of Deputies, no. 2083, 1887, 4.

79. In twenty-five years the increase was slow, since foreigners were counted for the first time in 1851; at that time they numbered 379,289, or 1.05% of the total population.

80. Source: Ministry of Commerce. The figure is 1,115,214 according to the statistics provided by the Ministry of the Interior, corresponding to the information supplied by the decree of 2 October 1888.

81. Bimetalism tied the value of currency to two standards, gold and silver. See Marc Flandreau, *The Glitter of Gold: France, Bimetallism, and the Emergence of the International Gold Standard, 1848–1873* (Oxford: Oxford University Press, 2004).

82. Mondonico, "La loi du 26 juin 1889," 39–40.

83. In addition, the war had brought about the death of 138,871 people, of whom 17,000 were prisoners; 137,626 more were wounded.

84. Dubost, "Rapport sur la nationalité," Chamber of Deputies, no. 2083, 1887, 233.

85. Mondonico, "La loi du 26 juin 1889," 8.

86. See Jean-Jacques Becker and Stéphane Audoin-Rouzeau, *La France, la nation, la guerre: 1850–1920* (Paris: Sedes, 1995), 90–91.

87. Born on 1 March 1846 in Bavai (Nord), Maxime Lecomte earned his doctorate in law in Douai in 1870 and came out of the war of 1870 with the rank of lieutenant, after taking part in battles of the northern army led by Faidherbe. An attorney at

the bar of Amiens in 1876, he was elected deputy from the Nord department in 1884 and belonged to the Republican Union. Defeated in the elections of 1885, he was returned to office in 1887. He represented the Nord department in the Senate from 1891 until his death on 10 June 1914.

88. Rogers Brubaker, *Citizenship and Nationhood in France and Germany* (Cambridge: Harvard University Press, 1992), 105.

89. The entirety of the speech delivered by Lecomte on 2 June 1885 in the Chamber of Deputies is reproduced in Maxime Lecomte, *Paroles d'un militant, 1869–1909* (Paris: Félix Juven, 1909), 71–81. In the debate over the law of 1889, Lecomte gave the same speech almost word for word. See *JO*, beginning of the session of Parliament of 16 March 1889, 594.

90. Bill concerning the nationality of sons of foreigners born in France, presented by Maxime Lecomte, 25 June 1885, no. 3904, Doc. Parl., vol. 2, 302.

91. Ibid.

92. *RA*, 1885, vol. 1, 21.

93. Cited in Weiss, *Traité théorique et pratique*, vol. 1, *La nationalité* (Paris: Sirey, 1907), 436–37.

94. Lecomte mentioned this fact in speaking to the Chamber of Deputies on 16 March 1889 (595).

95. On 6 June 1889 according to a report by Jean-Jacques Delsol, a senator from Aveyron. See Jean-Jacques Delsol, *Rapports et discours parlementaires, 1871–1882* (Paris: P. Mouillot, 1893), 264–98.

96. *JO*, Doc. Parl. 1887, annex no. 2083, 236.

97. From 1891 the parent could be either the mother or the father.

98. *JO*, Doc. Parl. 1887, annex no. 2083, 236.

99. In the text of this law, naturalization once again took on the restricted sense that it still has of "sovereign and discretionary act of the public authority by virtue of which a foreign subject acquires the title and the rights of a citizen." See Weiss, cited in René Vincent in *Le Droit*, 3, 3 and 4 February 1890, "De la condition des mineurs dont les parents acquièrent ou recouvrent la qualité de Français." Until that point the doctrine held that "naturalization" was the admission of foreigners to the number of nationals of a given state. See George Cogordan, *Droit des gens: la nationalité du point de vue des rapports internationaux*, 2nd edn. (Paris: Larose, 1879), 117, and Daniel de Folleville, *Traité théorique et pratique de la naturalisation: études de droit international privé*, 3 (Paris: A. Marescq aîné, 1880); see also the jurisprudence (Supreme Court of Douai, 16 April 1889).

100. Chamber of Deputies, bill no. 773; its goal was to modify article 1 of the law on naturalization of 29 June 1867.

101. M. de la Batut listed these rights: "the right to gather firewood, the right to teach, the right to adopt or to be adopted, the benefit of the transfer of property, exemption from the *judicatum solvi* deposit [required of a party who applies in one country for recognition or enforcement of a judgment given in another country] before the courts."

102. See chapter 8.

103. This proposal grew out of the Sée report (Projet de loi sur la nationalité, rapport de M. Camille Sée, Conseil d'État, n°44 113, 1ère annexe au rapport n°428, Sénat, 25 April 1883, 94–95), but it had been suggested by the Bureau of Seals within the Ministry of Justice (AMJ).

104. These proposals were aimed at taxing either all foreigners (M. Pradon), only foreign employees and workers exercising their profession in France (M. J. Thiessé), or else the employers who recruited foreign employees and workers (M. Steenackers); see the discussion of the reasons for Steenackers's bill no. 1973 "intended to establish a tax on those who employ foreigners" (Chamber of Deputies, appendix to the minutes of the session of 12 July 1887). They were justified by a concern for reestablishing equality between French nationals and foreigners or for putting an end to the "privileged situation" of foreigners in France; however, liberal economists such as Paul Leroy-Beaulieu fought against these proposals. See M. J. Thiessé, Chamber of Deputies, Report no. 400, on the laws proposed by Thiessé and Chardon, appendices to the minutes of the session of February 4, 1886; and Paul Leroy-Beaulieu, "La question des étrangers en France au point de vue économique," *JDIP* 15, nos. 3–4 (1888), 169–79.

105. Decree dated 2 October 1888.

106. Gustave Dallier, *La police des étrangers à Paris et dans le département de la Seine* (Paris: Arthur Rousseau, 1914).

107. See Gérard Noiriel, *The French Melting Pot: Immigration, Citizenship, and National Identity* (Minneapolis: University of Minnesota Press, 1996), 79, and Marcel Lachaze, *Du statut juridique de l'étranger au regard du droit public français* (Paris: Dalloz, 1928). The rights related to working conditions remained in place without discrimination: specifically, legislation limiting work hours for children and women, modified in 1892 and 1900; and the law of 1898 on work-related accidents, although it limited indemnification of families of immigrants to those who resided in France.

108. Becker and Audoin-Rouzeau, *La France, la nation, la guerre*, 115–20.

109. Gérardin, *De l'acquisition de la qualité de Français*, 3.

Chapter 3: To the Aid of the Nation

1. Alphonse Bard, "Rapport sur l'application pendant l'année 1890, de la loi du 26 juin 1889 relative à la nationalité, présenté à M. le garde des Sceaux," *JORF* (1891), 1160.

2. From 1803 French women who married foreigners lost their French nationality and took that of their husband (see chapter 8). Thus they often regained French nationality when their husbands acquired it (in 1890, 3,372 women were reintegrated out of 4,174 reintegrations in all—the men reintegrated were mainly from Alsace and Moselle).

3. In the Isère department, for example, all those who requested admission to residency in 1888 were redirected toward naturalization in 1890 (ADI, 128 M 6).

4. The application of the ruling of 7 December 1891 (see note 16, below) had also led to recognizing the quality of being French in persons who had requested it earlier through naturalization or declaration. Between 8 November 1892 and 5 May 1893 the Ministry of Justice counted 572 cases of this type (428 naturalizations) and thus estimated the number of persons affected by the ruling for 1892 as a whole at 1,100 (including 850 naturalizations).

5. Cf. Peter Sahlins, *Unnaturally French: Foreign Citizens in the Old Regime and After* (Ithaca: Cornell University Press, 2004): 304–5.

6. Memorandum no. 1, 16 January 1827.

7. Ségolène de Dainville-Barbiche, "Les archives du Sceau, naturalisations, mariages, changements de nom, titres," *La Gazette des archives* 160–61 (1993), 127–51.

8. Georges Tessier, "L'audience du Sceau," *Bibliothèque de l'École des chartes* 109 (1951), 51–95.

9. According to Camille Jordan in "Examen des pouvoirs de la chancellerie en matière de naturalisation," *Bulletin de la Société de législation comparée* 47 (1918), 313–47.

10. Under the old legal system, naturalization was granted by the king without local intermediaries. Legitimization at the local level was instituted by the Revolution. See Sophie Wahnich, *L'impossible citoyen: l'étranger dans le discours de la Révolution française* (Paris: Albin Michel, 1997), 80–90.

11. When Napoleon reestablished state power over the naturalization of foreigners by a decree issued on 17 March 1809, the same formalities that had already been instituted by the Civil Code for the procedure of admission to legal residency were prescribed for naturalization.

12. ADN, M495–9.

13. Memorandum no. 5805-93.

14. Georges Gruffy, "Naturalisation et francisation," *JDIP* (1916), 1120.

15. Jordan, "Examen des pouvoirs." In "Une réforme législative nécessaire, la preuve de la nationalité à organiser," *RDIP* (1919), 234–61, Joseph Champcommunal speaks of a "centralizing Office of Nationality."

16. On 7 December 1891 a Supreme Court ruling had interpreted the new article 8, paragraph 3, of the Civil Code — "every individual born in France to a foreigner who was born in France" — as concerning also the mother: "given that nothing in the text of the law indicates that this individual's parents both have to have been born in France or that the father rather than the mother has to fulfill this condition." See Affaire Hess, Sir. 92.1.81 and the note by Antoine-Louis Pillet; Pandect. franç. 92.1.129 and the note by André Weiss. See also Lucien Gérardin, *De l'acquisition de la qualité de Français par voie de déclaration: étude sur le bienfait de la loi* (Paris: Larose, 1896), 20. Article 1 of a law passed on 22 July 1893 stated that a person born in France to a mother born in France could renounce the French nationality that had been attributed at birth.

17. The originator of the expression was R. Fabre de Parrel in a speech at the formal hearing at the opening session of the Supreme Court in 1901. See *La Loi*, 6–7 October and 30–31 October 1901. Cited in Gruffy, "Naturalisation et francisation," 12 n. 1.

18. Civil Code, article 8, paragraph 4.

19. Civil Code, new article 12, paragraph 3. The same right to renounce was available to a minor child of a father who had regained French nationality (article 18 of the same law).

20. Decree of 1888 (*JO*, 1890, 862).

21. Article 3, law dated 22 July 1893.

22. André Weiss, "Loi du 16 juin 1889 sur la nationalité," *Annuaire de législation française* (Paris: Cotillon, 1890), 128. Janine Ponty notes that after the Second World War, young Poles who declared their intention to claim nationality were able to obtain scholarships from the School of Mines, for which French nationality was required, or to enter the national teacher-training school. "Le problème des naturalisations," *Revue du Nord* 7 (1992), 104 [special issue].

23. Jacques Wolgensinger, *André Citroën* (Paris: Flammarion, 1991).

24. Senate, supplementary report no. 19, prepared by Anselme-Polycarpe Batbie on behalf of the commission charged with examining the naturalization bill (extraordinary session, 1886, annex to the minutes of the meeting of 4 November 1886).

25. Gaston Cluzel, *De la nationalité des enfants mineurs d'étrangers dans la législation française* (Paris: Arthur Rousseau, 1901), 141. Nevertheless, as Cluzel notes, unity of nationality was not guaranteed in families where some of the minor children

had not been born in France. They could become French only when their father was naturalized, and at that point they had the option of repudiating their French nationality.

26. Copies of this document printed by the Ministry of Justice are available in the Isère departmental archives, for example.

27. Re Valz, 26 July 1905, Dal. 1906.1.25.

28. See Frantz Despagnet, "Du rôle du Conseil d'État dans la naturalisation d'après la loi du 22 juillet 1893," *RDP* (1894), 101–14.

29. I am grateful to Anne Simonin for supplying me with this figure, which came from her own research.

30. See Pierre Depoid, *Les naturalisations en France 1870–1940*, Ministère des Finances, Service national des statistiques, Direction de la statistique générale, Études démographiques no. 3 (Paris: Imprimerie Nationale, 1942), 41, 59.

31. Several hundred among them (610 were counted on 17 June 1916, including 170 Italians, 89 Spaniards, 86 Belgians, and 83 Swiss) were naturalized by virtue of article 3 of a law passed on 5 August 1914: these men had committed themselves to military service for the duration of the war (CAC 1995065/11).

32. Jean-Claude Farcy, *Les camps de concentration français de la Première Guerre Mondiale (1914–1920)* (Paris: Anthropos-Economica, 1995).

33. Confidential letter from the Ministry of War to André Honnorat, 18 June 1916 (AN, 50 AP 27).

34. Report of the legislation committee of the Chancellery, May 1915 (CAC 1995065/11).

35. Cf. Dominique Decherf, *Bainville: l'intelligence de l'Histoire* (Paris: Bartillat, 2000).

36. Jacques Bainville, *La guerre démocratique: journal 1914–1915* (Paris: Bartillat, 2000), 166 (15 November 1914). See also his chronicles from 23 January and 1 April 1915.

37. Jean Lerolle (1873–1962), a lawyer, was vice-president of the Catholic Association of French Youth before becoming deputy of the 7th arrondissement in Paris in 1912; he was reelected deputy in 1914 and again in 1928 and 1932.

38. Chamber of Deputies, 11th legislature, annex no. 511 to the minutes of the session of 14 January 1915, a law intended to modify the conditions of naturalization, proposed by the deputy Jean Lerolle.

39. Article 7 of the English law dated 7 August 1914 allowed the secretary of state to revoke certificates of naturalization that had been obtained through fraud or false assertions.

40. Cf. "Questions de nationalité pendant la guerre," *RDIP* (1917), 379–81.

41. Cf. Depoid, *Les naturalisations en France*, 42–43. Under the 1915 law 123 persons were stripped of their nationality, as were 426 under the 1917 law. At the Senate's request, the law of 7 April 1915 also provided for the review of 758 naturalizations granted after 1 January 1913; 94 of the 123 withdrawals of nationality imposed under the 1915 law corresponded to that review. See Maurice Bernard, annex 2291, Doc. Parl.-Ch., session of 7 July 1916, 1057 n. 1.

42. Cf. Georges Gruffy, "La naturalisation et le préjugé de la race," *RPP* 100 (July–September 1919), 40 n. 3. For partial information about these withdrawals see also AD, CAC, no. 324.

43. Memorandum of 15 September 1918 from the Ministry of the Interior, Directorate of the National Police, ADI 127 M 1.

44. This concern about "German methods" was also expressed for example in Henri Hauser, *Les méthodes allemandes d'expansion économique* (Paris: Armand Colin, 1916).

45. The entire report is found in CAC 19950165/10.

46. Presentation of the reasons for bill no. 4497 concerning withdrawal of the quality of being French, Chamber of Deputies, session of 21 March 1918.

47. *JO*, Déb. parl., Senate, 11 October 1919, 1625–26.

48. André Pairault, *L'immigration organisée et l'emploi de main-d'oeuvre étrangère en France* (Paris: Presses Universitaires de France, 1926).

49. See chapter 8.

50. Adolphe Landry (1874–1956), a graduate of the École normale supérieure, agrégé in philosophy, Ph.D. 1901, chair holder at the École Pratique des Hautes Études, was a deputy (from 1910) and later a senator from Corsica until his death. A populationist, very concerned about the declining birth rate, he published *La révolution démographique* in 1934 and *Traité de démographie* in 1945; he was president of the board of directors of the National Institute for Demographic Studies (of which the first director was Alfred Sauvy).

51. AN, 50 AP 27.

52. Many jurists, for example Gruffy and Lévy-Ullmann, sensitive to the examples of fraud reported during the war, advocated that control be returned to the Council of State and that decisions be published. See Henry Lévy-Ullmann, "Rapport sur le projet de loi portant refonte des textes relatifs à l'acquisition et à la perte de la nationalité française," excerpt from *Bulletin de la Société d'études législatives* (Paris: Rousseau, 1918).

53. Report by the deputy Félix Liouville, annex no. 7303, 13 March 1924 (*JO*, Doc.-Parl.-Ch., 1924, 567–68).

54. Jean-Charles Bonnet, *Les pouvoirs publics français et l'immigration dans l'entre-deux-guerres* (Lyon: Éditions de l'Université de Lyon II, 1976), 153.

55. Bureau du Sceau, "Étude sur le problème de l'assimilation des étrangers en France," 1924 (CAC, 95065/11).

56. Hervé Le Bras, *Marianne et les lapins: l'obsession démographique* (Paris: Olivier Orban, 1991), 177.

57. Note for the keeper of the seals (CAC, 95065/11).

58. For naturalization the fees amounted to 1,300 francs, or approximately two months' salary for a print-shop worker or an elementary school teacher; see Bonnet, *Les pouvoirs publics*, 152–53. The naturalization dossiers from the Rhône department studied by Bonnet show that the monthly income of most candidates was between 750 and 1,000 francs. Admission to residency cost 500 francs. See André Weiss, *Traité théorique et pratique du droit international privé* (Paris: Larose et Tenin, 1907–13), 371.

59. On 24 September 1925 the minister of justice wrote to all the prefects that it had been brought to his attention "that candidates for naturalization had given up on their requests because of the high Seal fees required of them . . . and because they found it impossible to pay such sums" (ADI 127 M 1.).

60. See *JO*, Chamber of Deputies, 1926, 631, question no. 6738 addressed by Roger Lafagette to the minister of justice.

61. From 1820 (memorandum no. 616, B4), the *référendaires* became official intermediaries for the formulation of requests for letters of naturalization. The decree of 11 June 1892 led to the elimination of this body through attrition. There were still eleven référendaires at the time, all living in Paris; they had replaced the former royal secretaries.

62. AN, 50AP63.

63. Decree of 6 December 1923 (*JO*, 21 December 1923).

64. On the Foyer français see AN, 50AP63, and Bonnet, *Les pouvoirs publics*, 77–79.

65. Cf. a note from R. A. Olchanski, vice president of the Foyer français, to André Honnorat: "The Ministry of Justice has asked us kindly to receive foreigners who need information, on behalf of the Bureau of Naturalizations. These foreigners come twice a week to the rue du Banquier and are received by a delegate from the Ministry of Justice who has been graciously placed at our disposal." This "delegation of functions" was discontinued in 1934 (AN, 50AP63).

66. Note for the keeper of the seals (CAC, 95065/11).

67. Louis Barthou (1862–1934), a lawyer at the bar of Pau, was elected in 1889, at the age of twenty-seven, as Republican deputy from Oloron-Sainte-Marie. He became a minister (of public works) in 1894, at thirty-two, and president of the Council of State in 1913; he was responsible for the passage of the law extending military service to three years. Close to Poincaré, he became minister of defense after the war, then served several terms as keeper of the seals. He was Doumergue's minister of

foreign affairs in 1934. Barthou died from wounds received in the attack that killed the king of Yugoslavia in Marseille on 9 October 1934. See Rosemonde Samson's biographical notice in Jean-François Sirinelli, ed., *Dictionnaire historique de la vie politique française au XXᵉ siècle* (Paris: Presses Universitaires de France, 1986), 89–90. Cf. Michel Papy, ed., *Barthou: un homme, une époque* (Pau: J & D, 1986); Robert J. Young, *Power and Pleasure: Louis Barthou and the Third Republic* (London: McGill-Queen's University Press, 1991). See also, in Jean-Baptiste Duroselle, *La décadence 1932–1939, politique étrangère de la France, 1871–1969* (Paris: Imprimerie Nationale, 1985), chapter 3, "L'ère Barthou" (1934), 87–121.

68. Archives Honnorat, 50AP63. André Honnorat (1868–1950), a journalist and then a civil servant in the Ministry of the Navy, was elected deputy from the Basses-Alpes department in 1910 (as a member of the Radical Left group). From 20 January 1920 to 13 January 1921 he was minister of public education and fine arts. He was elected to the Senate in 1921 and reelected regularly to 1940, where he was among the eighty members of Parliament who refused to vote in favor of granting plenary powers to Marshal Pétain. The founder of the Cité Internationale for foreign students in Paris, Honnorat also introduced daylight saving time in France, ordered the transfer of Gambetta's heart to the Pantheon, and arranged for the burial of an "unknown soldier" under the Arc de Triomphe.

69. Charles Lambert (1883–1972), a lawyer at the court of appeals in Lyon, served in the Chamber from 1924 to 1932 and was an active member of the League of the Rights of Man. Named high commissioner for immigration in 1926 by Herriot, he withdrew from political life after 1932.

70. The commission consisted of six deputies, six senators, three high-ranking civil servants from the Ministry of Justice, a representative from the Ministry of Foreign Affairs, Paul Lefebvre-Dibon (president of the National Alliance for Population Growth), and R. A. Olchanski (vice-president of the Foyer français).

71. Charles Lambert, *La France et les étrangers (Dépopulation-Immigration-Naturalisation)*, preface by Édouard Herriot (Paris: Delagrave, 1928), 132–34.

72. Report presented by the deputy Charles Lambert to the keeper of the seals in the name of the commission charged with studying questions of nationality and naturalization (Archives Honnorat, 50AP63).

73. The head of civil affairs and seals intervened directly in the debates of the commission on civil and criminal legislation when it met on 4 November 1925. See Hélène Morère, "La loi du 10 août 1927 sur la nationalité" (master's thesis, University of Paris I, 1985–86), 76.

74. Senate, session of 20 November 1925 (*JO*, 1624).

75. *JO*, Doc. Parl., Chamber of Deputies, special session, 25 October 1925, annex 1991, 1–2.

76. Ministry of Justice, Direction des Affaires Civiles et du Sceau, "Commentaire de la loi du 10 août 1927 sur la nationalité" (Paris, 14 August 1927), 3.

77. Rémy Estournet, *La pratique de la naturalisation française depuis la loi du 10 août 1927* (Montpellier: Imprimerie de la presse, 1937), 73.

78. Bureau du Sceau, "Étude sur le problème de l'assimilation des étrangers en France," 1925 (CAC 95065/11).

79. Charles Lambert in *Le Radical*, 4 June 1926, cited in Ralph Schor, *L'opinion publique et les étrangers en France, 1919–1939* (Paris: Publications de la Sorbonne, 1985), 532.

80. *JO*, Déb. Ch., first session, 7 April 1927, 1221. Earlier in the discussion, Barthou had made a very clear pronouncement: "This is a necessary guarantee; if you do not write it into the law, the law falls, and in that case, I for my part would not have sufficient authority to ask the Senate to vote in favor of a law from which the guarantees indispensable to national security had been dropped" (ibid., 1217).

81. Senate, 20 November 1925 (*JO*, 1623).

82. Chamber of Deputies, first session, 31 March 1927 (*JO*, 1127).

83. On the way Parliament worked during this period, and on the construction of parliamentary majorities, see Nicolas Roussellier, *Le Parlement de l'éloquence: la souveraineté de la délibération au lendemain de la Grande Guerre* (Paris: Presses de Sciences Po, 1997), 275–78.

84. *Le Temps*, 13 November 1926.

85. Excerpt from a letter addressed by Lambert to Jean-Charles Bonnet, 9 March 1970, in Bonnet, *Les pouvoirs publics*, 81.

86. Lambert, *La France et les étrangers*, 131.

87. André Honnorat was one of the first to be concerned — from 1923 on — about the danger of the German militarist and nationalist movement and the successes in Bavaria of the "racist movement of Hitler and Ludendorff." See André Honnorat, *Un des problèmes de la paix: le désarmement de l'Allemagne, textes et documents* (Paris: Alfred Costes, 1924), 145. On the earliest appearances of the notions of "racist" and "racism" see Pierre-André Taguieff, *La force du préjugé: essai sur le racisme et ses doubles* (Paris: La Découverte, 1988), 130–33.

88. Marie de Roux in *L'Action française*, 17 October 1926.

89. "La France aux autres," *Le Figaro*, 23 August 1927, 1.

90. In 1912 Walter Rathenau had declared: "Three hundred men, each of whom knows all the others, control the destinies of the European continent, and choose their successors from those around them." This declaration was later distorted by Urbain Gohier (who wrote many of Coty's articles) and by Louis-Ferdinand Céline, who did not fail to include a truncated quotation from Rathenau in *Bagatelles pour un massacre* (Paris: Denoël, 1937): "The entire world is controlled by

300 Israelites whom I know." See Pierre-André Taguieff, *Les Protocoles des Sages de Sion*, vol. 1, *Introduction à l'étude des Protocoles, un faux et ses usages dans le siècle* (Paris: Berg International, 1992), 91 n. 100. On Urbain Gohier see Grégoire Kaufmann, "Urbain Gohier," in *L'antisémitisme de plume, 1940–1944: études et documents*, ed. Pierre-André Taguieff (Paris: Berg International, 1999), 412–18.

91. After letting Léon Daudet go to prison for insulting the police, Barthou was the target of pamphlets by Maurras and Daudet.

92. Depoid, *Les naturalisations en France*, 24, 25.

93. Ibid., 55.

94. What were called *francisations* at the time included naturalizations, reintegrations (including of the minor children of reintegrated adults), and acquisitions of nationality through declaration by minors born in France and by spouses of Frenchmen.

95. Among them were 808,000 Italians, 508,000 Poles, 352,000 Spaniards, and 254,000 Belgians.

96. Marie-Claude Blanc-Chaléard, *Les Italiens dans l'est parisien: une histoire d'intégration, 1880–1960* (Rome: École française de Rome, 2000), 406.

97. Ministry of Justice, Bureau of Seals, 2 November 1932 (AMJ).

98. ADN, 5Z19.

99. 18 January 1915.

100. See Gruffy, "La naturalisation et le préjugé de la race."

101. Jean-Paulin Niboyet, "La nationalité d'après les traités de paix qui ont mis fin à la guerre de 1914–1918," *Revue de droit international et de législation comparée*, nos. 3–4 (1921), 288–319. The decree of 11 January 1920 allows certain categories of nondescendants of people from Alsace-Moselle to claim French nationality: Germans who made their home in Alsace-Moselle before 1870; non-German foreigners who became citizens of Alsace-Moselle before 3 August 1914; spouses of anyone reintegrated automatically. The Germans who were residents before 1914 and after 1918 had to go through the naturalization process.

102. Léon Baréty (1883–1971), a graduate of the École Libre des Sciences Politiques with a doctorate in law, was elected deputy from Alpes-Maritimes in November 1919.

103. Chamber of Deputies, 1st session, 31 March 1927, 1104.

104. See the abundant correspondence between Gruffy and Honnorat in AN, 50AP27.

105. See Patrick Weil, "La politique d'immigration de la France et des États-Unis à l'égard des réfugiés d'Europe centrale à la veille de la Seconde Guerre mondiale," *Les Cahiers de la Shoah*, no. 2 (November 1995), 51–84.

106. See Patrick Weil, "Races at the Gate: A Century of Racial Distinction in American

Immigration Policy (1865–1965)," *Georgetown Immigration Law Journal* 15, no. 4 (summer 2001), 625–48.

107. See Lambert, *La France et les étrangers*. None of the active participants in the debate was totally xenophobic: no one was opposed to the naturalization of foreigners in itself, and no one advocated a policy of zero naturalizations.

108. Robert A. Divine, *American Immigration Policy, 1924–1952* (New Haven: Yale University Press, 1957), 5.

109. On René Martial (1873–1955) see William H. Schneider, *Quality and Quantity: The Quest for Biological Regeneration in Twentieth-Century France* (Cambridge: Cambridge University Press, 1990), 231–55; Pierre-André Taguieff, "Catégoriser les inassimilables: immigrés, métis, juifs, la sélection ethnoraciale selon le docteur Martial," *Recherches sociologiques*, no. 2 (1997), 57–83; Taguieff, "La 'science' du Docteur Martial," *L'antisémitisme de plume 1940–1944*, 306.

110. In 1909, as the first director of the Bureau of Hygiene in Douai, René Martial had the opportunity to see and treat many immigrant workers who were employed in nearby mines or were in transit toward other destinations. During the war he organized the health services of a camp in Castres that housed and employed six thousand Vietnamese workers; he then set up a bureau of health control for Spanish migrants who had come to work in the Pyrénées-Orientales. After the war he spent three years as director of health services in the Moroccan city of Fez. Later, during trips to Poland, Czechoslovakia (1931), and Latin America, he continued to observe migrants.

111. *Traité de l'immigration et de la greffe inter-raciale* (Paris: Larose, 1931) and *La race française* (Paris: Mercure de France, 1934).

112. Schneider, *Quality and Quantity*, 231–55.

113. René Martial, "Le problème de l'immigration: examen sanitaire et logement des immigrants," *RPP* 129 (1926), 391.

114. The law enacted in 1924 did not go into effect in the United States until 1928, moreover; it took time to calculate the quotas.

115. René Martial, "Le problème de l'immigration," *Mercure de France*, 15 April 1935, 267–94.

116. Taguieff, "La 'science' du Docteur Martial," 306.

117. Martial made his calculations based on the work of Ludwig and Anna Hirszfeld, "Essai d'application des méthodes sérologiques au problème des races," *L'Anthropologie* 29 (1918–19), 507–37. Cf. Schneider, *Quality and Quantity*, 248, and Taguieff, "La 'science' du Docteur Martial," 311.

118. Taguieff, "La 'science' du Docteur Martial," 313.

119. Martial, *La race française*, 306–7.

120. Martial, "Le problème de l'immigration," 287–88.

121. On William Oualid see Georges Wormser, *Français Israélites: une doctrine, une tradition, une époque* (Paris: Minuit, 1963), 143–48.

122. See William Oualid, *Législation industrielle* (Paris: Les Cours du droit, 1936–37), 360–62.

123. See Patrick Weil, "Georges Mauco: un itinéraire camouflé, ethnoracisme pratique et antisémitisme fielleux," *L'antisémitisme de plume, 1940–1944*, ed. Pierre-André Taguieff, 267–76; Élisabeth Roudinesco, "Georges Mauco (1899–1988): un psychanalyste au service de Vichy: de l'antisémitisme à la psychopédagogie," *L'Infini*, fall 1995, 73–84.

124. See Georges Mauco, *Les étrangers en France: étude géographique sur leur rôle dans l'activité économique* (Paris: Armand Colin, 1932).

125. Mauco took up this study of Pairault's thesis; ibid., 188–89.

126. See Patrick Weil, "Racisme et discriminations dans la politique française de l'immigration, 1938–1945/1974–1995," *Vingtième Siècle*, July–September 1995, 74–99.

127. Jouvenel died shortly afterward, and the committee with him, but Landry then set up a French Committee on Population, which included most notably Fernand Boverat, president of the Alliance against Depopulation, Michel Huber, director of statistics, and Albert Demangeon; Georges Mauco became its secretary general. After Landry was elected to the presidency of the International Scientific Union on Population, Mauco became president of the Committee on Population and served in that role until 1953.

128. "Conférence permanente des Hautes études internationales," French mission text no. 3, dealing with the assimilation of foreigners in France (Paris: League of Nations, April 1937, 577AP2).

129. It was in part along the lines Mauco was advocating that Philippe Serre sought to establish an immigration policy, and failed. One project would have created a commission on naturalizations: at the level of the Bureau of Seals it could have verified the ethnic origin and professional qualifications of new immigrants, examined appeals to the decisions to reject applicants, and unified the jurisprudence in the area. The Ministry of Justice, concerned with retaining its prerogatives, was strongly opposed (note dated 3 March 1938, CAC 19950165/11).

130. Janine Ponty, "Une intégration difficile: les Polonais en France dans le XXᵉ siècle," *Vingtième Siècle*, July–September 1985, 51–70.

131. Janine Ponty, "Le problème des naturalisations," *Revue du Nord*, no. 7 (1992), 104 [special issue].

132. Weil, "La politique d'immigration de la France et des États-Unis," 51–84.

133. Schor, *L'opinion française et les étrangers*, 284.

134. Martial, *La race française*, 234, cited in Taguieff, "La 'science' du Docteur Martial," 320.

135. Between 1935 and 1938 many Polish Jews fled from the anti-Semitism that was then in a critical phase in Poland. See Janine Ponty, *Polonais méconnus: histoire des travailleurs immigrés en France dans l'entre-deux guerres* (Paris: La Sorbonne, 1988), 136.

136. Nicolas Kossovitch and Ferdinand Benoit, "Contributions à l'étude anthropologique et sérologique (groupes sanguins) des Juifs modernes," *Revue anthropologique* 42 (April–June 1932), 99–125, cited in Taguieff, "La 'science' du Docteur Martial," 325.

137. René Martial, *Les métis: nouvelle étude sur les migrations, le mélange des races, la retrempe de la race française, et la révision du code de la famille* (Paris: Flammarion, 1942), 225, cited in Taguieff, "La 'science' du Docteur Martial," 326.

138. Created to report to the head of government by a decree issued on 23 February 1939, the High Committee was charged with "coordinating the efforts and following the implementation of measures taken by the various ministerial services concerning the development of the birth rate, rural population, urban deconcentration, policy related to foreigners' penetration, length of stay, establishment on French territory, and integration into the French population" (article 1 of the decree). The commission's members were Georges Pernot (senator), X. Adolphe Landry (deputy), Philippe Serre (deputy, former minister), Fernand Boverat (president of the Alliance against Depopulation), and Frédéric Roujou (*maître des requêtes* in the Council of State). The secretary was Jacques Doublet, auditor for the Council of State and member of the head of government's staff.

139. Weil, "La politique d'immigration de la France et des États-Unis," 51–84.

140. AN, Cote F60/493.

141. Bonnet, *Les pouvoirs publics*, 217.

142. Rémy Estournet, *La pratique de la naturalisation depuis la loi du 10 août 1927* (Montpellier: Imprimerie de la presse, 1937), 5.

143. Other provisions included not allowing the naturalized person to be elected to office or to vote for a period of five years.

144. In December 1938, in response to a proposal by the Seine department's counselor general Louis Darquier de Pellepoix to annul all naturalizations granted since 11 November 1918 and to promulgate a special status for Jews governing their right to vote and their eligibility to hold public office, the prefect of the Seine department supplied the following information about naturalization requests:

145. See Chamber of Deputies, second session, 16 March 1939, written question no. 8531 submitted by Raymond Gornez; 29,426 names were listed in the decrees (including spouses), 5,417 dossiers were rejected, and 17,308 were tabled.

TABLE 9

Disposition of Requests for Naturalization, 1924–1935

	Requests filed with the Prefecture of Police	Dossiers transmitted to the Chancellery	Naturalizations
1924	4,614	3,002	1,516
1931	15,195	4,767	2,959
1932	21,774	6,934	3,051
1933	18,184	6,477	3,792
1934	19,151	4,870	2,142
1935	19,587	3,566	1,577

Source: APP, DA 430.

146. Depoid, *Les naturalisations en France*, 44–56.

147. Bonnet, *Les pouvoirs publics*, 254–55.

148. Blanc-Chaléard, *Les Italiens dans l'est parisien*, 400.

149. The twenty-three naturalization dossiers studied by Marie-Claude Blanc-Chaléard (ibid., 401–2) show that these criteria—being the spouse of a Frenchwoman or father of a minor child or children—were in reality decisive.

150. Jean-Louis Crémieux-Brilhac, *Les Français de l'an 40*, vol. 1, *La guerre oui ou non?* (Paris: Gallimard, 1990), 488–89.

151. On 13 July 1939, after the government had been informed that the Fascist authorities might be inciting some Italian nationals to take French nationality the better to serve their mission, the minister of justice warned the prefects against requests from Italians who had "important positions, for example industrialists, businessmen, or artisans; it is appropriate to respond with precision to the question 'Does he still have ties to the country whose nationality he possesses and the foreign countries where he has lived? Are there still interests and family ties?'" (CAC 19950165, art. 12).

152. See Senate, 7 December 1939, parliamentary questioning on naturalizations; *JO*, Déb. Parl., Senate, 692–700.

153. Decree issued 22 October 1939, and BB 30/1741.

154. On this High Committee and the context of Georges Mauco's intervention see Rhama Harouni, "Le débat autour du statut des étrangers dans les années 1930," *Le Mouvement social* no. 188 (July–September 1999), 61–75.

155. AN, Cote F60 494, minutes of the meeting of 28 March 1939 of the High Committee on Population.

156. See Laurent Joly, "Darquier de Pellepoix, 'champion' des antisémites français (1936–1939)," *Revue d'histoire de la Shoah*, no. 173 (2001), 35–61.

Chapter 4: Vichy

1. The law of 7 October 1940 abrogated the Crémieux decree (24 October 1870), which had naturalized all Algerian Jews. See chapter 8.

2. See chapter 7. The legislation that the French Revolution applied to émigrés was modeled on the treatment inflicted by Louis XIV on the Protestants; it also probably inspired Raphaël Alibert, the first keeper of the seals under the new regime and a member of Action Française.

3. The Vichy regime's legislation imposing racist and political exclusion can be consulted in its entirety on a CD-ROM, *La persécution des Juifs de France, 1940–1944, et le rétablissement de la légalité républicaine: Recueil des textes officiels, 1940–1944* (Paris: La Documentation Française, 2000).

4. On 10 September withdrawal was extended to French nationals who had left the overseas territories, and finally, on 8 March 1941, to every French citizen who "as of 1 December 1940 [had] left or [would] leave for a dissident zone."

5. The order governing the application of the law dated 26 July 1933 specifies: "The question whether a naturalization must be considered as undesirable will be determined according to national-ethnic principles. Racial, political, and cultural motives will be considered in the first instance to decide whether an increase in the German population—by means of naturalization—would be in keeping with the interests of the Reich and the people. . . . [The following categories] will thus be in the first instance the object of an examination in view of revoking their naturalization: a) Jews from the East, unless they fought on the front during the First World War or have acquired special merits with regard to German interests; b) persons who have committed a grave infraction or crime or who have behaved in a manner prejudicial to the health of the State and the people." Maurice Ruby, *L'évolution de la nationalité allemande d'après les textes (1842 à 1953)* (Baden-Baden: Wervereis, 1954, 515).

6. "The criterion of radical unassimilability of a defined category of the population is the least contestable criterion of a racist vision . . . racist thought or vision tends to render absolute the differences between certain human groups, then to define

norms on the basis of these absolutizing operations (excluding for example the 'undesirables,' that is, the unassimilables, those who, by nature, could not embody French identity)." Pierre-André Taguieff, "L'identité française," *Regards sur l'actualité*, nos. 209–10 (March–April 1995), 17.

7. AMJ.

8. ACE, dossier no. 224-643. Louis Canet, born 18 July 1883, was a member of the Council of State until 1953 and remained an advisor to the Ministry of Foreign Affairs on religious matters until late 1946. Canet sat regularly on the Council of State, on the commission responsible for all questions concerning the status of Jews. See Bruno Neveu, "Louis Canet et le service du conseiller technique pour les Affaires religieuses au ministère des Affaires étrangères," *Revue d'histoire diplomatique* 82 (1968), 134–80.

9. While it is true that the Council of State was not consulted on the drafting of the laws of 22 and 23 July 1940 or on the status of Jews, it is inaccurate to say that the Council was not invited to give its opinion on all the proposed exclusionary laws. Jean Massot, "Le Conseil d'État et le régime de Vichy," *Vingtième Siècle*, no. 58 (April–June 1998), 88. The Council of State was consulted on the proposed exclusionary nationality law and participated actively in the drafting process.

10. On the decree of 16 July 1941 see Robert Badinter, *Un antisémitisme ordinaire: Vichy et les avocats juifs (1940–1944)* (Paris: Fayard, 1997).

11. AD, Papiers Louis Canet, art. 27.

12. To "prepare" these reports, Louis Canet got personal information about the people making requests (Claude Lévi-Strauss, for example) from one of his colleagues in the Ministry of Foreign Affairs.

13. ACE, commission responsible for all questions concerning the status of Jews, dossier no. 229,733, session of 26 November 1941 (in preparation for the decree of 14 January 1942), reviewed by Canet.

14. Canet also had reservations about the proposed decree aimed at controlling Jews' access to farming and related professions. In his report on the decree he noted the following in particular: "it appears certain that by giving Jews access to the agricultural profession, which the Germans view as constituting a peasant nobility, France would be degraded in the eyes of the occupying power, dropping below the high standing with which the author of *Mein Kampf* had credited it at a time when he was treating the inhabitants of southern Italy, central Europe, and Japan with great severity." This part of Canet's report was not included in the note approved by the Council of State (ACE, dossier 229,744).

15. Leo Strauss, *Persecution and the Art of Writing* (Glencoe, Ill.: Free Press, 1952), 24–26.

16. Born in 1889, Paul Didier was named head of the 3rd bureau, "Seals, Naturalization, and Nationalities," of the Direction of Civil Affairs and Seals on 5 August 1937. He was replaced by Henry Corvisy on 22 September 1940 and appointed judge at the *tribunal de première instance* of the Seine department by a ruling on 4 October 1940. He refused to take an oath at the opening session of the Seine tribunal in September 1941. Questioned about the motives for this refusal, Didier indicated that "he did not want to swear an oath of allegiance to the Head of State." He was forced to interrupt his professional activity at once and was relieved of his functions. Marc-Olivier Baruch, *Servir l'État français: l'administration en France de 1940 à 1944* (Paris: Fayard, 1997), 312. Didier regained his position as magistrate and was appointed president of the chamber at the court of appeals in Paris on 17 October 1944.

17. In July 1940 Corvisy (1893–1968) was assigned to organize the Ministry of Justice in Paris, and on 22 September of that year he took on the title of assistant director of the Bureau of Seals. He remained in his new position only three months, time enough to set up the denaturalization commission; on 30 December 1940 he became director of criminal affairs and pardons. He was replaced as head of the Bureau of Seals by André Levadoux, who became assistant director of seals on 26 July 1941. Corvisy was named to the Supreme Court by a special provision on 21 February 1944, but his appointment was revoked on 17 March 1945, without a pension. The revocation was annulled on 15 July 1957, and he was reintegrated for a few days in 1958 before he retired.

18. Raphaël Alibert (1887–1963), a doctor of law, was received in the *auditorat* of the Council of State in 1910; he resigned in 1924 to go into the private sector. After the Liberation he was tried in absentia (he had fled the country) and on 7 March 1947 he was sentenced to death, national degradation, and the confiscation of his property. He was granted amnesty by decree on 26 February 1959.

19. AMJ, note from the Ministry of Justice, 31 July 1940, 4.

20. Reduced waiting periods were provided, however, for particular categories: five years for candidates under the age of thirty-five, three years for veterans and for parents or spouses of French nationals.

21. Only requests for which the ministry thought naturalization could be granted were forwarded to the Council of State.

22. At that point it was still optional for the administration to submit bills to the Council of State for its opinion; this became obligatory only on 18 December 1940. See Jean Marcou, "Le Conseil d'État sous Vichy: 1940–1944" (LL.D. diss., University of Grenoble II, 1984), 67–78.

23. On 14 August the minister of foreign affairs had transmitted his views on the bill

to the Council of State: he came out against linking the right of residency to access to nationality, and he found too long the proposed ten-year waiting period for naturalization. Instead he proposed that the keeper of the seals have the power to oppose automatic access to nationality on the part of children born in France to foreign parents; his opinion was followed on this point alone.

24. ACE, Council of State, excerpt from the record of deliberations, no. 233,768, session of 16 August 1940, Armand Guillon reviewing, 2.

25. She would not be subject to the new ten-year waiting period, however, provided that her request for naturalization had been made before the marriage took place. Council of State, excerpt from the record of deliberations, no. 223,768, session of 14 November 1940, 4.

26. Armand Guillon (1889–1968), doctor of law, a graduate of the École Libre des Sciences Politiques, and an attorney at the court of appeals in Rennes, was appointed prefect of the Tarn department in 1926, of Haute-Garonne in 1929, and of Nord in 1934, then was named resident general of Tunisia in 1936 before being appointed in 1938 to the Council of State from outside the Council, where he served until he retired in 1950.

27. Letter GR/JL dated 16 January 1941 from Georges Dayras. Dayras, assisted by Charles Germain, a magistrate from the Bureau of Seals detached to work with him in Vichy, did not turn out to be the most liberal member of the group drafting the proposal for the Vichy ministry and answering the objections of the Council of State.

28. Joseph Barthélemy (1874–1945), a lawyer and then a professor of law at the law school in Paris and the École Libre de Sciences Politiques, was a deputy from the Gers department (representing the center-right) from 1919 to 1928. He was the author of many books on constitutional law and parliamentary law and was named minister of justice on 27 January 1941. Arrested in August 1944, incarcerated, and then released owing to the state of his health, he died in May 1945 before he could appear before the High Court of Justice.

29. Military archives, dossier 3R 598/2.

30. Letter YC/PJ, Ministry of the Interior, from the Admiral of the Fleet, minister, and secretary of state within the Ministry of the Interior, to the keeper of the seals (AMJ). The Ministry of the Interior requested in addition that decisions denying access to nationality through open or tacit means be carried out according to the terms of its proposal.

31. Note dated 22 April 1941 from the Bureau of Seals to the Ministry of Justice on the establishment of quotas for naturalization on the basis of race or nationality of origin (AMJ).

32. AMJ.

33. Notes from 17 December 1941 and 8 March 1942 from the admiral of the fleet, minister of foreign affairs, Direction of Political and Commercial Affairs, Department of Chancelleries and Litigation, no. 243, AN BB30/1711.

34. The deputy director for Europe in October 1937, Charles Rochat (1892–1975), had become director of political affairs in the Ministry of Foreign Affairs on 5 July 1940, just when Lagarde and Bressy, diplomats who "had stood out for the pessimism of their remarks during the final months of the 'phony war,'" were taking over as director and deputy director for Europe. Jean Baillau, ed., *Histoire de l'administration française: les Affaires étrangères et le Corps diplomatique français*, vol. 2, *1870–1980* (Paris: CNRS, 1984), 542–43. Rochat was the head of Darlan's cabinet when Darlan succeeded Laval, and he served as secretary general at the Quai d'Orsay from 1942 to 1944, a job that he had actually taken over upon Charles-Roux's departure on 1 November 1940.

35. AMJ. This note signed by Rochat seems to have been inspired by Pierre Bressy, deputy director for Europe at the Ministry of Foreign Affairs. Very active in immigration issues, on 2 April 1941 Bressy had written directly to Florian Chardon, the head of Barthélemy's cabinet, using the same terms and the same arguments as those developed in Rochat's letter. Bressy was forced to retire after the Liberation, but he was reintegrated in 1951 by a decision of the Council of State.

36. ACE, dossier 223,768.

37. Ibid.

38. AN BB 30/1711.

39. From 23 February 1941 to 18 April 1942, the date of his departure, Darlan combined the functions of head of government with those of minister of the interior and minister of foreign affairs. Laval, when he returned to power, did the same.

40. AN BB 30/1411.

41. 31 August 1942, letter no. 1238 to the Ministry of Justice; vice-presidency of the Council, note on the creation of a High Council on Foreigners, 29 March 1941 (AMJ).

42. Maurice Gabolde (1891–1972), a lawyer and then a judge, was general prosecutor at Chambéry when the Second World War broke out. After 1940 he joined the Collaboration group, a Germanophile organization created by Alphonse de Châteaubriant. In early 1942 he was appointed by Pétain to be general prosecutor at the Supreme Court of Riom. He left with Pétain in August 1944 for Sigmarigen, then fled to Spain. Condemned to death in absentia in March 1946, he died in Barcelona in January 1972.

43. AMJ.

44. The proposed legislation finally set up as legal conditions of acceptability what had formerly been optional factors: morality, loyalty, degree of assimilation, health.

45. This had been the practice from 1849 to 1889, but at the time there were only a few hundred applications for naturalization each year, compared with several thousand a year during the 1930s.

46. All the provisions of the Vichy laws that made nationality of origin a prerequisite for gaining access to public office and to the exercise of the professions of lawyer, doctor, pharmacist, dentist, and veterinarian were finally incorporated into the new legislation.

47. Marshal Pétain had both his residence and his offices in the Hôtel du Parc in Vichy. People referred to "le Parc" then the way they would refer now to the White House in the United States.

48. BB 30/1713. From September 1940 on Vichy submitted a large number of the texts applicable in the occupied zone to the German authorities. Baruch, *Servir l'État français*, 71.

49. Joseph Barthélemy, *Ministre de la Justice, Vichy, 1941–1943*, preface by Jean-Baptiste Duroselle (Paris: Pygmalion/Gérard Watelet, 1989), 361.

50. The entire correspondence between the German authorities can be found in the National Archives under the call number AJ 40/547.

51. For a description of these authorities see Michael R. Marrus and Robert O. Paxton, *Vichy France and the Jews* (New York: Basic Books, 1981), 77–83.

52. This opinion was expressed by SS-Hauptsturmführer Dr. Peters (AJ 40/547).

53. "Wissenschaftliche Vorbereitung wichtiger Arbeiten von ma gebenden Staats- und Parteistellen."

54. An indication given in a letter from Höhn on 1 December 1939, "kriegsbeordert" (Berlin, Humboldt University Archives, university personnel dossiers, Höhn dossier, 133, 149).

55. Berlin, Humboldt University Archives, Institut für Staatsforschung dossier UK 827/, 31.

56. In 1940 the institute had six permanent employees paid by the university: the director Höhn, the chief assistant Hofmann, three staff members, and a laborer. In addition, nine scientific assistants (*wissenschaftliche Hilfskräfte*) were paid from research funds contributed principally by the Ministry of Foreign Affairs (*Auswärtiges Amt*), the Ministry of Propaganda (Goebbels), and the SS (Berlin, Humboldt University Archives, Institut für Staatsforschung Assistenten dossier UK 828/, November 1935–February 1946).

57. Membership no. 2175900. For biographical information see Robert S. Wistrich, *Who's Who in Nazi Germany* (London: Routledge, 1995 [1982]), 125–26; see also

Bernd Rüthers, *Carl Schmitt im Dritten Reich: Wissenschaft als Zeitgeistverstärkung*, 21st edn. (Munich: C. H. Beck, 1990), 85ff, 90ff.; and Berlin, Humboldt University Archives, university personnel dossiers, Höhn dossier.

58. Contacts among members of this group persisted: Hofmann's note about the Vichy proposal was addressed to Ohlendorf, for example; Six became one of Höhn's collaborators again after the war, at Höhn's management school in Bad Harzburg.

59. Joseph W. Bendersky, *Carl Schmitt, Theorist for the Reich* (Princeton: Princeton University Press, 1983), 232ff.

60. On this subject see Anna-Maria Gräfin von Lösche, *Der nackte Geist: die juristische Fakultät der Berliner Universität im Umbruch von 1933* (Tübingen: Mohr Siebeck, 1999), 418–26. See also Heinz Höhne, *The Order of the Death's Head: The Story of Hitler's S.S.*, trans. Richard Barry (New York: Coward-McCann, 1970), 236.

61. Reinhard Höhn (1904–2000) was forty years old when the war ended. After being declared missing for some time, he reappeared as head of an academy for business leaders which he had founded in Bad Harzburg in 1956, and where he developed the very successful "Bad Harzburg model" for managerial training. Several of his former contacts turned up in the academy, for example Franz Six, who had been condemned to twenty years in prison at the Nuremburg trials. The Bad Harzburg school became one of the best-known postwar schools for managers and remained so until 1971, when the press, in particular the Social Democratic party (SPD) newspaper *Vorwärts*, discovered Höhn's past. Höhn published a second edition of a treatise on business law, on limited-liability corporations, in 1995. He granted my assistant Franz Mayer a telephone interview on 12 April 1996.

62. Hofmann was Gerichtsassesor (which means that he had completed his legal training with a second state examination) and Diplom-Volkswirt (he had a degree in economics). Alongside his activities at the institute, Hofmann was working on a doctoral thesis titled "Die preussische Verwaltung in der Kritik von Wissenschaft und Praxis um die Jahrhundertwende" (the Prussian administration in the critique of research and practice at the end of the century).

63. Berlin, Humboldt University archives, dossier Institut für Staatsforschung Assistenten dossier UK 828, November 1935–February 1946.

64. In addition to his own work, Hofmann assisted Höhn by supervising the other collaborators in the institute. According to Höhn, Hofmann's clear ideological line—"klare weltanschauliche Linie"—was very useful in that position. His traces fade after 1945. However, in a telephone interview on 12 April 1996, Höhn mentioned that Hofmann had become a lawyer in Heidelberg after the war.

65. Hofmann may well have taken over Höhn's responsibilities: Höhn was absent from Berlin that day, since he was on vacation from 10 to 21 October. It is quite possible that other people worked on the document signed by Hofmann. But Hof-

mann had already worked on a closely related subject himself, in "Questions of Nationality in the General Government" (Poland); this document dealt with the problem created by the many Poles who were trying to escape from the German authorities by declaring that they also held American nationality. This suggests that he himself drafted or supervised the specialists' report (Berlin, Humboldt University Archives, university personnel dossiers, Höhn dossier, 149–50).

66. Höhn-Mayer interview, 12 April 1996.

67. See Ulrich Herbert, *Best: Biographische Studien über Radikalismus Weltanschaung und Wernunft, 1903–1989* (Bonn: Dietz, 1996).

68. At the end of the war there were thought to be 50,000 to 75,000 children in that situation. See Philippe Burin, *La France à l'heure allemande* (Paris: Le Seuil, 1995), 213.

69. As a result, between June 1940 and August 1944 the vast majority of foreigners who acquired French nationality were children born to foreigners in France.

70. Jean-Armand Camboulives (1893–1983) was director of civil affairs and seals from 6 September 1940 to 23 November 1942, when he was appointed to the Supreme Court by Joseph Barthélemy. Jean Nectoux, the former head of Barthélemy's cabinet, succeeded him; see Barthélemy, *Ministre de la Justice*, 613.

71. Declarations formerly recorded at the Ministry of Justice were shifted to the prosecutors of the courts of appeal by the decree of 25 August 1937.

72. Memorandum CG/GM dated 1 July 1941, to the prosecutors of the Republic. The matter had been called to the attention of the keeper of the seals by a letter dated 28 May 1941 from the prosecutor of the Republic in Marseille.

73. On 26 September 1944 François de Menthon, keeper of the seals, ordered the prosecutors to proceed with the recording of declarations indicated in the memorandum of 1 July 1941.

74. A request submitted on 30 July 1942, for example, was registered on 9 October 1944.

75. Suspension of a request made 1 July 1943.

76. AD, Guerre 1939–45, Vichy Europe, series C, vol. 199.

77. Ibid.

78. And not the Direction of Consular and Administrative Affairs, which was traditionally in charge of these matters within the Ministry of Foreign Affairs.

79. Report of an interministry meeting held at the Ministry of the Interior on 5 September 1941 (CAC, 19950165, art. 11).

80. AD, Guerre 1939–45, Vichy Europe, series C, vol. 199, item 65. For the Italians the same caution was not required. The occupying authorities seem to have intervened in mid-1942 to ensure the interdiction of any naturalization of persons of

German origin, but the French administration continued to make exceptions for some legionnaires' dossiers.

81. In 1941 thirty-three German and thirty-one Italian legionnaires requested naturalization; in 1942 the numbers were twenty-nine and 341; finally, in 1943, eight and 375 (AD, Guerre 1939–45, Vichy Europe, series C, vol. 199, item 115).

82. Report of an interministry meeting held at the Ministry of the Interior on 5 September 1941 (CAC, 19950165, art. 11).

83. The dossiers handled directly in Vichy were numbered starting with VX, as opposed to X for those handled according to normal procedures.

84. See above, pp. 61–62.

85. In his letter to Vallat dated 27 June 1941, Barthélemy also proposed that a representative from the Commissariat-Général on Jewish Affairs sit permanently from then on with the Commission for the Review of Naturalizations.

86. See Patrick Weil, "Georges Mauco: un itinéraire camouflé, ethnoracisme pratique et antisémitisme fielleux," *L'antisémitisme de plume 1940–1944, études et documents*, ed. Pierre-André Taguieff, 267–76.

87. See Taguieff, "L'identité française."

88. CAC 19950165, art. 11.

89. Note AI/LP from the Bureau of Seals, 28 June 1943, for the director of civil affairs and seals (CAC 19950165, art. 11).

90. AN, 2 AG 528. This letter also follows up on requests from the Central Committee of Armenian Refugees and the Franco-Armenian Union asking that the Armenians established in France be the object of an authentic status. See a note from the Bureau of Seals for the cabinet (M. de Peretti), CG/CM undated, and a note dated 20 December 1940, CAC 19950165, art. 11.

91. The priority granted volunteer recruits — except those who were stateless persons subject to military obligations by virtue of article 3 of the law of 31 March 1928 on recruitment and who had been drafted or automatically mobilized — clearly originated in a letter sent from Vichy on 22 February 1941 by the keeper of the seals to the minister of war (SHAT, dossier 3R 598/2).

92. Formerly their requests had been transmitted with a favorable opinion only when the concerned parties had at least ten years of military service. In a letter dated 15 February 1941 the secretary of state for war declared that foreign legionnaires could henceforth prepare and transmit requests for naturalization as soon as they had fulfilled the legal conditions, that is, three years of service (SHAT, dossier 3R, 598/2).

93. This analysis is derived from an analysis of the original decrees preserved in the archives of the Naturalization Bureau (Sous-direction des naturalisations).

94. See Bernard Laguerre's pioneering article "Les dénaturalisés de Vichy, 1940–1944," *Vingtième Siècle*, no. 20 (October–December 1988), 3–15.

95. As early as 1890 the Supreme Court had judged that even in the absence of explicit legislation the federal government could take someone of foreign origin to court with the goal of having his or her naturalization annulled in the case of fraud.

96. John L. Cable, *Loss of Citizenship, Denaturalization, the Alien in Wartime* (Washington: National Law Book, 1943).

97. See chapter 3, pp. 61–62, and chapter 9, p. 240.

98. See Robert Kiefe, *La nationalité des personnes dans l'Empire britannique* (Paris: Arthur Rousseau, 1926), 69–80.

99. See chapter 9.

100. Beyond the waiting period of ten years after the naturalization decree—established by the law of 1927—or ten years after an infraction—established by the decree of 1938—the Vichy law provided that all acquisitions granted since 1927 could be contested.

101. The comparison between the provisions of 1927 and those of 1940 was an object of dispute within the Bureau of Seals. Raymond Boulbès was inspired by Jacques Maury, who used mockery and subversive rhetorical inversion to criticize the new legislation on the status of Jews, naturalized French citizens, and children of foreigners. *La Semaine juridique, Études doctrinales*, no. 165, 10.40 (October 1940), and no. 169, 11.40 (November 1940). Rather than emphasize the downgrading of status, he pointed to "the privileged situation of certain people who are French by birth" and were not subject to it. In a communication internal to the Ministry of Justice comparing Republican and Vichy legislation on the withdrawal of nationality, Boulbès indicated that the Vichy legislation concerned "all French people except those who are French by birth and on condition that the acquisition of their French nationality occurred after the promulgation of the law of 1927," while withdrawal under the law of 1927 "applied only to individuals of foreign origin who had become French at their own request." He also stressed the differences in motivation, procedure, and possibilities of recourse. Charles Germain, a magistrate who had been detached from the Bureau of Seals to serve under Dayras in Vichy and was close to the new regime, responded with a note dated 17 December 1940 that emphasized the continuity between the laws of 1927 and 1940.

102. Laguerre, "Les dénaturalisés de Vichy," 9.

103. Jean-Marie Roussel, born in 1878, was a doctor of law; he joined the Council of State on 1 January 1903. In 1923 he directed the legal services of the High Commission of the French Republic in the Rhine provinces; he rejoined the Council in 1928. In 1940 Roussel presided over the fourth committee of the litigation section,

and he became president of the section on 27 July 1942. He was forced to retire on 15 November 1944 by the Council of State's purification commission.

104. Minutes of the meeting of 21 September 1940 (AD).

105. "Un premier et important décret portant retrait de naturalisation," Cote BB 30/1711.

106. The decree of 1 November 1940, signed by Raphaël Alibert, involved 442 people (JO, 7 November 1940).

107. After some hesitation it consulted the Ministry of Justice on this point and obtained its agreement (note CG/MA, 16 December 1940, AMJ).

108. In the Spaziermann ruling of 23 December 1942 the Council of State accepted this expanded interpretation of the law of 22 July 1940; Recueil des arrêts du Conseil d'État, vol. 112, 2nd series (Paris: Sirey, 1943). M. and Mme Spaziermann's daughters had become French by declaration before the law of 1927 was passed and before their parents were naturalized. Cited in Laguerre, "Les dénaturalisés de Vichy," 5.

109. Statistics transmitted by the Naturalization Bureau to the investigating commission (3w46). I myself examined three thousand dossiers of persons naturalized between 1927 and 1940: all had been checked by the commission.

110. In addition there were two plenary meetings of the commission each week and meetings of a special subcommittee involving the presidents of the regular subcommittees.

111. This is Bernard Laguerre's hypothesis in "Les dénaturalisés de Vichy."

112. Le fichier juif, report of the commission led by René Rémond (Paris: Plon, 1996), 2.

113. The census of Jews in the southern zone was ordered on 2 June 1941, the day the second statute on Jews appeared (Le fichier juif, 65).

114. This selection by "index" is indirectly confirmed by the account of a meeting between Brinon, Gabolde, and Dayras on 2 August 1943: "It is estimated that about a third of these dossiers concern Jews, but the categorization is rather difficult, for during the periods being examined civil records contained no mention relative to race" (message 205 from Brinon to Laval and Pétain; note attached to Dayras dossier 3w144).

115. See note CG/GM of the Bureau of Seals for the keeper of the seals, 3 December 1941 (AMJ).

116. The model of a letter found in some fifty denaturalization dossiers concerning Jews, consulted in the archives of the Prefecture of Police in Paris.

117. Journal officiel, 23 July 1941.

118. BB30/1741, Dautet report, 13.

119. Naturalization service, note for the director of civil affairs and seals. At the suggestion of M. Colomies, head of the naturalization service, Jews who had requested naturalization — including some who were on the verge of receiving a favorable verdict — were the object of a decision made "in harmony with the viewpoint of the review commission," that is, a decision to postpone or to reject the application.

120. BB18/3366.

121. In "Vichy et la tradition de l'étatisation de la justice: histoire d'un demi-succès," *Serviteurs de l'État: une histoire politique de l'administration française 1875–1945*, ed. Marc-Olivier Baruch and Vincent Duclert (Paris: La Découverte, 2000), 215, Alain Bancaud reminds us that it was a matter of "reactivating" instructions that had already been issued in 1929 and 1938 in another context. See chapter 9.

122. For example, Giuliano A., naturalized in 1939, wrote a letter to the Ministry of Justice in July 1940: "Excellency, having found a very interesting job in Italy, our country of origin, we have decided, my wife, my children, and I, to renounce our French naturalization in order to become Italians again. We thus come to beg you, Excellency, to be so kind as to send to the city hall of Roquebrune (Var) our removal [from the register] so as to permit us to move back to Italy as soon as possible. Please accept, Excellency, the expression of our profound respect." He was denaturalized with his wife and three children in November 1941. At the time of Liberation his dossier was the object of a request for a thorough investigation. After a favorable judgment from the French consul general in Rome, because he had participated in the Resistance in Italy he was not subjected to a withdrawal procedure, by a decision dated 13 June 1946.

123. It should be made clear that the note with the proposal from the Bureau of Seals staff is dated 11 June 1943 (note RB/SP from the keeper of the seals to the head of government), while the decision of the head of government is dated 2 August 1943, a few weeks after the Allies — and Mussolini — landed in Sicily (AN F60 499).

124. I have found no non-Jews naturalized according to the procedure of inquiry initiated by the commission and sent directly to the prefectures. In contrast, Jews were sometimes denaturalized by the procedure of identification.

125. See BB30/1741.

126. Ibid., Dautet report.

127. Angelo Tasca (1892–1960), born in Moretta (Italy) into very modest circumstances, was one of the founders of the Italian Communist party, from which he was excluded in 1929 on Stalin's orders. He headed for Paris, where he gradually rose through the ranks of the Italian Socialist Party. Anti-Munich and close to Léon Blum, he was put in charge of Italian-language broadcasts on the French

national radio in 1937. His double rejection of communism and fascism led him to support the Vichy regime; he saw certain of its elements as necessary supports for France's recovery. As of February 1941 he was in contact with a Belgian network of informants. He was thus at the same time a Vichy supporter and a member of the Resistance. Arrested in Vichy on 3 September 1944, he was quickly liberated and became a historian of communism. See the biographical notice by Denis Peschanski in Jean Maitron and Claude Pennetier, eds., *Dictionnaire biographique du mouvement ouvrier français* (Paris: Éditions Ouvrières, 1992), vol. 42, 47–51.

128. Marc Rucart (1893–1964), a Radical deputy from the Vosges department from 1928, was minister of justice and then minister of public health in successive administrations between 4 June 1936 and 20 March 1940. On 27 May 1946 he participated in the first meeting of the National Resistance Council. Pierre Viénot (1897–1944), a deputy from the Ardennes department between 1932 and 1942, and undersecretary of state in Léon Blum's first administration from 4 June 1936 to 22 June 1937, reached London on 17 April 1943.

129. Tasca dossier, 19770889, art. 165.

130. For a biography of Montandon see Marc Knobel, "George Montandon et l'ethnoracisme," *L'antisémitisme de plume*, ed. Taguieff, 277–93. Montandon, publisher of the journal *L'Ethnie française*, was a chaired professor of ethnology at the School of Anthropology from 1933 on; he was one of the leaders of the French racist school, in the tradition of Vacher de Lapouge. A friend of the German anthropologist Hans Günther, he was Xavier Vallat's ethnoracial expert on the Commission on Jewish Affairs in 1941; in 1943 he became director of the Institute for the Study of Jewish and Ethnoracial Questions. He specialized in the recognition of "Jewish types" and worked in the Drancy camp with the Nazis' consent. He was executed by the Resistance in 1944.

131. He had published *La race, les races, mise au point d'ethnologie* in 1933 (Paris: Payot) and was editor of *L'Ethnie française* in 1935.

132. *La Lumière* (a newspaper), 26 April 1940, CD JC, XCV-114, cited in Knobel, "George Montandon et l'ethnoracisme," 283.

133. On Céline and his ties to Montandon in particular see Annick Duraffour, "Céline, un antijuif fanatique," in Taguieff, ed., *L'antisémitisme de plume*, 147–97.

134. *JO*, 4 April 1941. Along the same lines, the Duffieux commission that was set up to implement the law of 23 July 1940 issued at least one decree reversing a decree of withdrawal: on 12 February 1943 the decree of 30 April 1941 withdrawing French nationality from M. André Kahn was overturned (CAC 19770904/133).

135. Chiarazzo ruling, CE, 6 March 1942.

136. Excerpt from a text published in the newspaper *France-Soir* on 14 May 1948.

137. Secret report from the commission president to Dayras (AMJ).

138. Laguerre, "Les dénaturalisés de Vichy," 7, 8.

139. According to a law dealing with foreigners of the Jewish race (*JO*, 18 October 1940), and a law dealing with the situation in which there were too many foreigners in the economy (*JO*, 1 October 1940).

140. See the text from *France-Soir* cited above, n. 36.

141. Message 205 from Brinon to Laval and Pétain, 2 August 1943, account of a conversation between Brinon, Gabolde, and Dayras (note attached to Dayras dossier, 3w144): "It is estimated that about a third of these dossiers concern Jews, but the categorization is rather difficult, for during the periods being examined civil records contained no mention related to race. Out of 539,280 dossiers checked, 16,508 have been examined [by the commission] of which 6,307 concern Jews."

142. 19 April 1945, excerpt from the report on Dautet's defense, inspector of judiciary services under the keeper of the seals, BB20/1741.

143. The last decree reversing a decree of withdrawal of French nationality concerning Jews dates from 26 August 1942. As of September 1942 these decrees concern only persons who had been erroneously denaturalized when they were already dead.

144. CDJC archives, XLVI, folder XYZ.

145. The first decrees of renaturalization, issued on 22 March or 29 July 1941 and published in the *Journal officiel* on 3 August 1941, did not provoke reactions from the occupying authorities at the time. In contrast, they gave rise to "Marche arrière," a virulent article published on 14 August 1941 in the newspaper *La Gerbe*, on the pretext that of the forty-two decisions, eleven concerned Jews:

> The national revolution resembles a wheel that Vichy likes to turn in one direction or another—one turn ahead, two turns back. Only watch out, it may kill us. In the 1 November 1940 *Journal officiel*, the names of eleven Jews were struck from the French community. On 3 August 1941, these same newspapers printed the reintegration of these eleven products of Europe, or rather of a *race* that they have not rejected, for their part, as they are going to show us with full impunity this time.
>
> We can't have it both ways! Either there was a mistake made last year and the new judges are as good as the old ones; or—what is more certain—this reintegration is a victory for our "little pals." When one observes that eight naturalizations out of eleven were from *1936*, one can no longer doubt the direction in which the Wheel has turned yet again.

146. The commission added that D., forbidden to practice medicine, was entrusted with a job in a French company and carried out his duties to his employer's satisfaction; that once mobilized as an auxiliary doctor during the hostilities, he ac-

quitted himself with a great deal of devotion; and that above all, on 16 and 17 June 1940 he was tireless in caring for the wounded during the air strikes.

147. Born in 1916 in Bordeaux, French by declaration as of 25 June 1934, denaturalized on 1 November 1940, this woman identified herself as a Catholic. She was in fact baptized in 1930; she had been born in France and had received a French education. In 1933 she married a native-born Frenchman with whom she had two children.

148. All this information had been collected in the archives of the Ministry of Justice.

149. Marrus and Paxton, *Vichy France and the Jews*, 324.

150. CDJC, XXVII-24 and XXVII-26; Lucien Steinberg, *Les autorités allemandes en France occupée* (Paris: Centre de documentation juive contemporaine, 1966), 148, 149.

151. See Serge Klarsfeld, *Le calendrier de la persécution des juifs en France* (Paris: Fils et filles des déportés juifs de France / Beate Klarsfeld Foundation, 1993), 853–54.

152. CDJC, XXVII-39, Steinberg, *Les autorités allemandes en France occupée*, 152.

153. Marrus and Paxton, *Vichy France and the Jews*, 326.

154. F60/1485. In a letter to Brinon dated 8 September 1943, Georges Dayras drew up a statement containing rough statistical information about the number of Jews whose dossiers had been or were about to be examined by the review commission. "The result is that the total number of naturalizations of Jews between 1927 and 1940 reached 23,640 persons. 9,039 have already come before the commission and 7,055 have been the object of a decision to withdraw nationality. Thus the cases of 14,601 Jews remain to be examined." Of the Jews who came before the commission, 78 percent had thus been subject to denaturalization.

155. This recalls Xavier Vallat's attitude when the anti-Semitic legislation was enacted and the Commissariat-Général for Jewish Affairs was set up. See Laurent Joly, *Xavier Vallat: du nationalisme chrétien à l'antisémitisme d'État* (Paris: Grasset, 2001), 247–48.

156. CDJC, XXVII-35, in Marrus and Paxton, *Vichy France and the Jews*, 325, and Steinberg, *Les autorités allemandes en France occupée*, 151. According to Marrus and Paxton, this refusal marked the only point on which not only Pétain but also Laval drew the line: at the time the number of naturalized Jews was overestimated, so the leaders had reason to think that their refusal might save the lives of several thousand French Jews.

157. AN, F60 1480/2.

158. See Roussel's deposition at the fourteenth session of the Pétain trial on 7 August 1945; Roussel declared on this occasion that he had seen Pétain twice: on 24 March 1942 and 28 August 1943.

159. "In the course of my investigation, I personally observed the usefulness of this

special review. . . . This is why one of the surveys dealing with fifteen dossiers from the year 1937 showed that five of them had not yet been presented to the Commission on 20 February 1944, and remained in the general classification" (Dautet report, 9, BB30/1741).

160. For the third quarter of 1943 the figure is 1,808; for the fourth quarter, 334; for the first quarter of 1944, 477; finally, for the second quarter of 1942, 448.

161. F60/1485.

162. BB/30/1741, Dautet report, 43. Moreover, on 31 July 1941 the keeper of the seals had the Council of State approve a provision that would make it possible to extend the possibility of withdrawal beyond naturalized citizens to all persons who had acquired French nationality after birth, that is, to children of the second generation.

163. Klarsfeld, *Le calendrier*, 868.

164. 388 measures were rescinded. One ruling favorable to maintenance of nationality was issued by the commission for 651,440 persons, making a total of 666,594 cases examined definitively. These statistics were transmitted by the Naturalization Bureau to the investigating committee.

165. Bernard Laguerre looked closely into the situation of the 183 denaturalized Jews from Salonika. Of the thirty-eight who were deported, seventeen were taken before 1 September 1943 and after the withdrawal of their French nationality, at a time when that nationality offered relative protection against deportation. "Les dénaturalisés de Vichy," 13–14.

166. The Ministry of Foreign Affairs played an unusually important role in nationality politics during this period.

Chapter 5: Difficult Reestablishment

1. On the first steps taken by the Free France administration in Carlton Gardens, see Jean-Louis Crémieux-Brilhac, *La France Libre: de l'appel du 18 juin à la Libération* (Paris: Gallimard, 1998), 171–89.

2. René Cassin, *Les hommes partis de rien* (Paris: Plon, 1974), 138.

3. René Cassin (1887–1976), a law professor, was France's representative to the League of Nations from 1924 to 1938. A supporter of Free France, he joined General de Gaulle in London on 23 June 1940 and became de Gaulle's legal advisor, then president of the Legal Committee (August 1943–July 1945). He served as vice-president of the Council of State from November 1944 to 1960.

4. AN, Papiers René Cassin, 382AP74. François Marion, born in 1912 in Sèvres (92), a doctor of law, joined Free France in London in the summer of 1940. Assigned to Free France's legal service in January 1941, he became chief of staff in the sec-

retariat general of the French Committee for National Liberation in August 1943, then a member of the Legal Committee in April 1944. He was appointed master of requests for the Council of State in 1944 and became a member of the Council in 1962.

5. ASDN.

6. On 6 January 1942, for the first time, a request was registered outside Great Britain, at the French Consulate in Damas (no. 88); on 15 January 1943 the same thing happened in Beirut, at the Free France delegation to the Middle East. All such requests were later transmitted to London.

7. Article 8 of the decree of 10 August 1927, modified by the decree of November 1938.

8. Also in conformity with the internal note dated 23 August 1940, regarding marriage by FFL volunteers in England.

9. ASDN.

10. Constituted on 3 June 1943 in Algiers, initially headed by de Gaulle and Giraud as co-presidents, it was under the sole presidency of Charles de Gaulle as of 9 November 1943.

11. François de Menthon (1900–1984), a law school professor, was a municipal councilor before the war under the banner of the Popular Democratic party. Serving as captain in 1940, he was taken prisoner. After he escaped he made contact with law professors who refused to accept the defeat—Teitgen, Coste-Floret, Capitant, and René Courtin—and with them launched the clandestine newspaper *Liberté* in November 1940. In November 1941 their group merged with Henri Frenay's national liberation movement; Frenay and Menthon jointly published the movement's newspaper, *Combat*. Frenay was behind the founding of a study commission that sought to reflect on the general directions that the country might take after its liberation. He was called to Algiers and there on 7 September 1943 replaced Dr. Abadie, who had been appointed commissioner of justice in Giraud's contingent.

12. It was published in the *Journal officiel* on 26 August 1944. The GPRF replaced the CFLN as of 3 June 1944.

13. AN, 382, AP74.

14. He was forced to retire on 30 October 1944.

15. Louis Bodard, born in 1894, was a lawyer in Metz when he was expelled from the city by the Germans after the armistice of 1940. Appointed counselor to the Supreme Court in Algiers on 31 December 1940, he headed the civil affairs office in the Commissariat à la Justice in Algiers as of 23 July 1943, and then became general director of civil affairs on 2 October 1943.

16. On 4 October 1944 the Paris administration of the Ministry of Justice was charged

with putting in proper form a decree prepared in Algiers. After a subsequent de-cree was issued on 14 November 1944 and published in the *Journal officiel* on 23 November, the files examined in Algiers (a number of decisions concerning residents of Oran) were merged with those examined in metropolitan France during the last months of the Vichy regime.

17. It was then completed by complementary provisions. On 10 September revocation was extended to French nationals who had left the overseas territories. On 23 February 1941 it was applied to any Frenchman who "outside the metropolitan territory, betrayed by his acts, speeches, or writings the duties incumbent on him as a member of the national community"; finally, on 8 March 1941, revocation was extended to any Frenchman who "as of 1 December 1940 had entered or would enter a dissident zone."

18. Ordinance of the French high command, published in *Journal officiel*, no. 17, 22 April 1943.

19. By an ordinance dated 14 March 1943, Giraud had declared null and void all the actions taken by Vichy after 22 July 1940. Formally, the abrogation of the Crémieux decree dating from 7 October 1940 was annulled. Through another ordinance, also dated 14 March 1943, Giraud had again abolished the Crémieux decree. This group of ordinances can be consulted on the CD-ROM *La persécution des Juifs de France, 1940–1944, et le rétablissement de la légalité républicaine: recueil des textes officiels, 1940–1999* (Paris: Documentation Française, 2000).

20. See Michael R. Marrus and Robert O. Paxton, *Vichy France and the Jews* (New York: Basic Books, 1981), 195.

21. Michel Ansky, *Les Juifs d'Algérie du décret Crémieux à la Libération* (Paris: Centre de Documentation Juive Contemporaine, 1950), 298.

22. Ibid., 318–19. Since this reestablishment raised the question of the inferior status of Muslims once again, the declaration left open the possibility of settling, in the future, "in a definitive way, not only the status of the Israelites indigenous to Algeria but also that of the other categories of Algeria's indigenous population." See chapter 8.

23. See Jean-Pierre Le Crom, "L'avenir des lois de Vichy," *Le droit sous Vichy*, ed. Bernard Durand, Jean-Pierre Le Crom, and Alessandro Somma (Frankfurt am Main: Klostermann, 2006), 453–78.

24. A report on the subject prepared by Bodard also proposed the alternative solution of abrogation.

25. Council of State, archives of the Legal Committee, 9912/1.

26. Created by decree on 6 August 1943, the Legal Committee initially consisted of René Cassin, Pierre Tissier, René Rodière, Paul Coste-Floret, and M. Groslière,

president of the bar in Algiers. It was charged with issuing legal opinions on the texts of bills proposed by the provisional government.

27. This document is in the file of the Legal Committee, archives du Comité juridique, ACE, 9912/1.

28. Minutes of the 42nd meeting of the Legal Committee, ACE.

29. ACE, archives du Comité juridique, 9938/2.

30. Article 2 1°/ of the ordinance of 24 May 1944 (published in the *Journal officiel* of the French Republic, no. 45, on 1 June 1944).

31. Regarding the decree of 9 September 1939, which provided that French nationals who had behaved "like citizens of a foreign power" could have their French nationality withdrawn by decree issued with the approval of the Council of State, it posed a particular problem: it had been applied to the Communists and in particular to Maurice Thorez, whom some sought to reintegrate into the national community. An ordinance of 27 September 1945 thus provided for the abrogation of the decree of 9 September 1939 and made it possible to revoke the measures of withdrawal applied under that decree by a simple decree, without prior approval from the Council of State. Similarly, the withdrawal procedure seemed to have been initiated against naturalized citizens—especially those of German origin—who had collaborated with the occupier (Fla 3255).

32. See chapter 9.

33. A note intended for the magistrates of the Seal of France, 29 October 1944 (ASDN).

34. It was only in case of overwork, "if the situation arose," that the keeper of the seals asked them to give priority to certain dossiers: to the list of naturalizations he had already established he added candidates who had fought with the Allied armies, prisoners of war, and others who had acquired indisputable rights to the country's gratitude—veterans of the war of 1914–18, and people who had rendered important civil services. In addition, candidates who were of clear value to the nation by virtue of their family situation, in other words parents of children born in France, had priority once again.

35. A decree published in the *Journal officiel* on 10 April 1945.

36. Its composition was established by a ruling of 18 April 1945 (*JO*, 19 April 1945). Its members included Maxime Blocq-Mascart, a member of the National Resistance Council and a delegate to the Provisional Advisory Assembly; Fernand Boverat, vice-president of the National Alliance against Depopulation; Mme Collet, president of a Mutual Aid Committee; Prof. Robert Debré, of the Academy of Medicine; Mme Marcelle Delabit, a member of the administrative commission of the Confédération Générale du Travail; Jacques Doublet, master of requests in the

Council of State; Adolphe Landry, a former minister; Dr. Monsaingeon, president of the National Center for the Coordination of Family Activities; Robert Prigent, delegate to the Provisional Advisory Assembly. Georges Mauco, doctor of letters, advisor to the general secretary of the government, was appointed secretary of the High Committee. Landry and Boverat were already members of the ephemeral High Committee on Population, created within the presidency of the Council by a decree of 23 February 1939; responsibility for the secretariat fell to Jacques Doublet.

37. Georges Mauco (1899–1988), a geographer, defended a doctoral thesis on 13 February 1932 that was published as *Les étrangers en France: étude géographique sur leur rôle dans l'activité économique* (Paris: Armand Colin, 1932). Soon viewed as the leading expert on immigration questions, he joined the cabinet of the undersecretary of state responsible for immigration and foreigners under the Council president Camille Chautemps, from 18 January to 10 March 1938. He was appointed secretary of the High Advisory Committee on Population and the Family, he remained in that position until 1970. Mauco was interested in psychoanalysis, and he founded the Claude Bernard psychopedagogical centers. He was the author of several books on immigration, psychoanalysis, and childhood education, as well as an autobiography, *Vécu, 1899–1982* (Paris: Émile-Paul, 1982). See Patrick Weil, "Georges Mauco: un itinéraire camouflé, ethnoracisme pratique et antisémitisme fielleux," *L'antisémitisme de plume, 1940–1944, études et documents*, ed. Pierre-André Taguieff (Paris: Berg International, 1999), 267–76.

38. AN, Fonds Mauco AP577/5; published in *L'Ethnie française* 6 (March 1942), 6–15.

39. AN, 2W/66.

40. Mauco, "Révolution 1940," 6.

41. Ibid., 1.

42. Ibid.

43. Ibid., 4. After the war, because of this article the author had to justify himself before the investigating commission of the Ministry of Education. He did so with the help of testimony by Maurice Grandazzi, secretary of the Annales de Géographie; Mauco transcribed and corrected the testimony himself (AP 577/5). On Mauco and psychoanalysis see Élisabeth Roudinesco, "Georges Mauco (1899–1988): un psychanalyste au service de Vichy. De l'antisémitisme à la psychopédagogie," *L'Infini*, fall 1995, 73–84.

44. This proposal converges with reflections that had been articulated in Algiers in 1944 within an "Intercommissarial Committee for the Preservation and Development of the Population," which met with State Commissioner François Billoux to define an immigration and naturalization policy (AD, Papiers 1940, Bureau d'études Chauvel, vol. 5).

45.　Louis Joxe (1901–91) was secretary of the CFLN from 3 June 1943, then secretary general; he attended meetings of the committee, and later of the government, from 2 October 1943 until 1946. Secretary general of the Ministry of Foreign Affairs (1956–59), he was a minister under General de Gaulle from 1959 to 1968, then a member of the Constitutional Council from 1977 to 1989. See Jean Massot, "L'installation du Gouvernement d'unanimité nationale du 9 septembre et de l'Assemblée consultative provisoire," in Fondation Charles de Gaulle, *Le rétablissement de la légalité républicaine, 1944* (Brussels: Complexe, 1996), 389–417. Cf. Roselyne Py, *Notes et études documentaires: le Secrétariat général du Gouvernement* (Paris: Documentation Française, 1985).

46.　For his evocative descriptions see Louis Joxe, *Victoires sur la nuit, mémoire, 1940–1946* (Paris: Flammarion, 1981), 13–16.

47.　On the connection between this general delegation and the Commissariat au Plan see Henry Rousso, ed., *De Monnet à Massé: enjeux politiques et objectifs économiques dans le cadre des quatre premiers plans* (Paris: CNRS, 1986).

48.　In its report on its activities in 1943 the French Foundation for the Study of Human Problems noted this collaboration: "Immigration questions have given rise moreover to exchanges between the Regent and the Director of Immigration Services in the Ministry of National Equipment; finally, a note was drafted for National Equipment on the contributions that contemporary anthropological science can make to the development of a doctrine of directed immigration in France." *Cahier 2 de la Fondation* (1944), 26–27. In a private letter written around the same time, Alexis Carrel expressed an opinion about the effects of immigration on French society (or at least on Lyon): "The solidity of Lyon's middle-class inhabitants is truly astonishing. Because of their lack of ambition, their moderate wealth, their puritanism and the wisdom of their marriages, they have not degenerated. Or at least a certain number of them are more or less like their eighteenth-century ancestors. We are cousins of more or less all the *bourgeois* of Lyon and the lesser aristocracy of the region. In the Journel family there was an Irish ancestor seven generations ago. But his unfortunate influence disappeared after three generations. In these old families, there has never been any Protestant, Jewish, or foreign infiltration except for that one Irishman. No Italian infiltration" (letter dated 13 May 1944, Fonds Alexis Carrel, box 81, Georgetown University).

49.　Louis Chevalier (1911–2001), *agrégé* in history and geography and professor in the École Libre des Sciences Politiques in 1941, served as *chargé de mission* with the General Delegation for National Equipment, then was a researcher at the National Institute for Demographic Studies (Institut National des Études Démographiques, INED) from 1945 to 1974. From 1974 he occupied a chair in the "history and social structures of Paris" at the Collège de France. This report and those of Robert Gessain and Robert Sanson were published by the INED in *Documents sur l'immigration*, coll. Travaux et Documents (Paris: Presses Universitaires de France, 1947). The reports by Gessain and Sanson were published in their entirety and without alterations. Chevalier's text, in contrast, was modified by its author. The term "racial," which appeared several times in the Vichy version, was changed to "human" with the Liberation. Most significantly, Chevalier eliminated from the 1945 text the detailed indication of priorities according to ethnic origin and his own negative evaluation of the continuing immigration of North Africans and Poles ("as for the Poles, they must be considered unsuited for massive immigration in the French ethnic group"), along with his favorable assessment of political refugees.

50. In an almost material proof of this transfer of "expertise," the original dossier relating to these studies and the meetings held at the Delegation on National Equipment was kept not in the archives of that institution but rather in those of the High Committee on Population (CAC 860269/0007), under the heading "Ministry of the National Economy, 'L'introduction et le statut des Étrangers en France, essai de définition d'une politique d'immigration.'" Some of these documents may also be found in AD, unions internationales, 1st installment no. 277.

51. CAC 770 623–68, projet d'instruction, 6 June 1945.

52. In a letter to René Bousquet, manager of Foreigners and Administrative Conventions, Mauco wrote: "I see no major criticisms to make in . . . the report you sent me. . . . Still, I would note: 1) that there is no question about the attitude to take toward refugees who can continue to flow into France as they have done in the past" (letter dated 3 April 1945, AN, Cote F60/493).

53. Note from G. de Longevialle, who headed the study of immigration problems for the General Delegation on National Equipment, April 1944, 8. The report of the General Delegation on Equipment had also shown an interest in the debates over immigration policy that agitated the Vichy government; criticizing the final version of the project inspired by the minister of justice, it indicated moreover that "the text does not take into account the fundamental distinction that we want to introduce between foreigners whose assimilation is viewed as desirable and the others."

54. All these documents are in CAC 19860269 art. 3.

55. Undated note to the attention of Louis Joxe (CAC 19860629 art. 3).

56. Mauco thus chose decree no. 33 of 2 July 1945 to communicate the following to Louis Joxe: "Nearly three quarters of those naturalized are Mediterraneans and Orientals (Italians, Spaniards, Armenians). Many are city-dwellers, and the professions of the Armenians are especially those of shopkeepers, shop assistants, and filmmakers." Examination of the decree shows in fact that of the nine Armenians

there was one coal merchant, one camera operator, one worker in the shoe business, two shoemakers plus one spouse, one office worker, one tradesman, and one clockmaker.

57. CAC 19860269 art. 3.

58. Teitgen, born in Rennes on 29 May 1908, was a lawyer who later became a law professor. A prisoner of war in 1940, he escaped and participated in the Resistance within the Combat movement. At Liberation he took part in founding the Republican Popular Movement (Mouvement républicain populaire, MRP), which he headed from 1952 to 1956. He became minister of information on 9 September 1944 and remained minister of justice until 16 December 1948.

59. The passages from Mauco's text that were not included in de Gaulle's letter appear in italics within square brackets.

60. The letter was received by de Gaulle or his cabinet manager, who passed it along to Jean Donnedieu de Vabres with the note "Donnedieu to discuss with M. Palewski" (Archives Donnedieu de Vabres, AN, 539AP2).

61. AMJ.

62. Pagès had been a member of the Resistance. In September 1940, when he was assistant director of the Ministry of Labor, he informed his director, Alexandre Parodi, that the Feldkommandantur of Deux-Sèvres had repatriated 724 Spanish refugees without first consulting the French authorities (CAC 19770603/0068). On 24 November 1947 Pagès testified at the High Court trial of Frédéric Roujou, secretary general of the Ministry of Labor (AN 3W344). "M. Roujou had opposed my appointment as director of staff. I do not think that M. Roujou knew at that time that I belonged to the Resistance. But M. Roujou certainly knew my real opinions regarding the Vichy government and the occupiers." It was on 23 November 1944 that Émile Laffon, general secretary of the Ministry of the Interior, proposed his nomination to Adrien Tixier, who approved it and added the following handwritten note: "I have known M. Pagès for 10 years. He was transferred to Labor as part of a purification effort" (AD, Papiers d'Agents, Laffon, I).

63. Minutes of the meeting of the Commission Interministerielle des Naturalisations, (CIN), 20 April 1945 (AMJ).

64. A graduate of the École Polytechnique, Alfred Sauvy began working at the General Statistics administration in 1922; this office was responsible for producing statistics in France, census figures in particular. In 1938 he served in the cabinet of Paul Reynaud, minister of finance. He took an early interest in questions of population and immigration; in 1927 he published "La population étrangère en France et les naturalisations," *Journal de la Société de statistique de Paris*, no. 2 (February 1927), 60–72, and no. 3 (March 1927), 89–97. In January 1943 he published *Richesse et population* (Paris: Payot), and in 1946, in collaboration with Robert

Debré, *Des Français pour la France* (Paris: Gallimard). Upon the Liberation, on 4 April 1945, he became general secretary for family and population in the Ministry of Public Health and Population; in this capacity he coordinated the activity of various agencies in charge of immigration. He sat on the commission as the representative of the Ministry of the National Economy.

65. Minutes of the meeting of the CIN, 4 May 1945 (AMJ).

66. All these remarks were made during the meeting of the CIN on April 20; minutes of the meeting of the CIN, 4 May 1945 (AMJ).

67. Minutes of the meeting of the CIN, 11 May 2000.

68. It was the Ministry of Justice, supported by Pagès, that proposed to maintain naturalization as a reward, as a matter of urgent priority (minutes of the meeting of the CIN, 25 May 1945).

69. Ibid.

70. Ibid. The commission had weighed the effect that divulging the ranking by nationalities might have; it was aware that it would be impossible to keep secret the instructions given to the prefects, "that they would be immediately known by foreign governments which could use them to carry out a certain propaganda among their citizens in France."

71. CAC 19860129 art. 3.

72. Note from the minister of the interior to the secretary general of the government, 2 October 1945 (AN, F60 493).

73. This decision was made when the proposed ordinance was submitted on 8 October 1945 to the Interministry Commission on Population and the Family, meeting under the presidency of Jules Jeanneney. The members present were Teitgen, Parodi, and Billoux; Pleven, Tixier, and Tanguy-Prigent were absent (AN, F60 493).

74. AN, BB/30/1741.

75. To give a sense of the scope of the task, 2,381 requests for consultation were addressed to the Nationality Bureau of the Ministry of Justice in 1999 and 3,348 in 1998. See Ministères de la Justice et de l'Emploi et de la Solidarité, "Les acquisitions de la nationalité française en 1999," © Justice, 2000.

76. CAC, personnel files, Levadoux.

77. In the reference work *Répertoire de droit international*, published in 1929 in 15 volumes by Albert Geoffre de Lapradelle and Jean-Paulin Niboyet (Paris: Librairie du Recueil Sirey), Maury wrote the volume on nationality (*Théorie générale et droit français*). In his inaugural address to the French Academy, Professor Georges Vedel referred to Jacques Maury as "the unsurpassable model" (Université Panthéon-Assas Paris II, "Remise de l'épée d'Académicien au Doyen Vedel," 13 March 1999). "Jacques Maury was the professor who influenced me the most . . .

He had the most solid legal culture (one that cuts through technicalities to arrive at general ideas)" (letter from Georges Vedel to the author, 29 September 1998).

78. *La Semaine juridique*, Études doctrinales no. 165, 10.40, and no. 169, 11.0.

79. See Danièle Lochak, "La doctrine sous Vichy ou les mésaventures du positivisme," in Centre universitaire de recherches administratives et politiques de Picardie, *Les usages sociaux du droit* (Paris: Presses Universitaires de France, 1989), 252–85.

80. Professor Maury's courage is noted by Richard Weisberg in *Vichy Law and the Holocaust in France* (New York: New York University Press, 1996), 54–55. See also the preface by Danièle Lochak in the French edition, *Vichy, la Justice, et les Juifs*, (Amsterdam: Édition des Archives Contemporaines, 1998), 15, 16.

81. "The various laws I have just listed are retroactive. Normally, by virtue of the principle of non-retroactivity of laws (art. 2 of the Civil Code), they should have come into play only for the future, should only apply to access to jobs or professions *acquired* later than the date [these laws] went into effect; they should not have touched those who already had such jobs or practiced such professions. . . . There is no need to insist on the exceptional character and on the seriousness of such measures, which deprive those they affect of the possibility of earning their living as they had been prepared to do, and, sometimes, of all or nearly all of their resources." Jacques Maury, *Droit international privé*, 3rd year, faculté de droit de Toulouse, 1942–43, 60–64.

82. The Council of State is divided into six sections.

83. Instituted by a decision of 14 June 1945, the commission met fifteen times between 23 June and 30 July 1945. Other members included a former magistrate from the Bureau of Seals, M. Suzanne, counselor at the Paris Supreme Court, and Boulbès's hierarchical superior, Louis Bodard, director of civil affairs and seals.

84. Maury, *Droit international privé*, 1946–47. Testimony of Mme Thin, daughter of M. Aymond, a magistrate with the Bureau of Seals from 1945: "My father used to say that Boulbès had seven children, the six that he had with his wife and the Nationality Code" (interview, 30 April 1997).

85. Raymond Boulbès, *Commentaire du Code de la nationalité française (ordonnance du 19 octobre 1945)* (Paris: Sirey, 1946), 5.

86. Jean Foyer, "Rapport fait au nom de la commission des lois sur le projet de loi adopté par le Sénat complétant et modifiant le code de la nationalité française et relatif à certaines dispositions concernant la nationalité française" (AN, quatrième législature, première session ordinaire de 1972–73, no. 2545, 29 September 1972, 6).

87. The desire for control was manifested also in the provision that a child born in France to foreign parents could easily acquire French nationality on reaching the

age of majority but—and this was new—on condition that he or she had resided in France during the preceding five years. Thus the idea of an assimilation phase, already adopted in cases of acquisition through naturalization, was introduced for children born in France to foreign parents not born in France; according to the commission, "the stability of establishment on French soil, for the son of a foreigner born in France, [is] the guarantee of his effective assimilation" (report on the work of the nationality commission, AMJ).

88. AN, FIA 3255.

89. Formerly the responsibility for "population" was attached to the Ministry of Health, headed by the Communist François Billoux. Prigent remained minister of population until 16 December 1946. After a one-month interim, covered by the Socialist Pierre Ségelle (SFIO), the Communist Georges Marrane took over the portfolio of health and population on 22 January 1947 and kept this position in Ramadier's government until the Communist ministers left on 4 May 1947. Robert Prigent (1910–95), MRP deputy from the Nord department and a former CFTC union activist, became minister of health and population again on 9 May 1947. Germaine Poinso-Chapuis (1901–81) took over as minister of health and population from 24 November 1947 to 26 July 1948.

90. AN, Fonds Jean Donnedieu de Vabres, 539 API.

91. Ibid., subdossier "Réunions Joxe," 30 November 1945 to 18 January 1946. Minutes of the meeting of 10 December 1945.

92. AN, Fonds Mauco, 577 AP 3. Mauco continued to fight during the ensuing years for the unification of children's services and their attachment to the Ministry of Population (19860269/art. 8).

93. BB30/1741.

94. Maury, *Droit international privé*, 1946–47, 23.

95. Council of State, commission meetings, 12 and 14 December; general assembly meeting, 17 December 1945 (AN, Cote AL4570, dossier 237 804).

96. Minutes of the meeting of the parliamentary group MRP, Archives Sciences Po, MRPS 50.

97. Janine Ponty, "Les rapatriements d'ouvriers polonais" (1945–48), *Les ouvriers en France pendant la Seconde Guerre mondiale*, ed. Denis Peschanski and Jean-Louis Robert (Paris: IHTP, 1992), supplement to cahier no. 20, 71–80.

98. See Jacques Mérot, "Les orientations de la politique des naturalisations 1945–1973" (DEA thesis, University of Nantes, Centre d'information et de documentation de la DPM, October 1992).

99. Janine Ponty, "Le problème des naturalisations," *Revue du Nord*, no. 7, coll. Histoire (1992), 99–113 [special issue].

100. This criterion disappeared from the decree of application relating to the law of

1973. The decision to remove it was made during an interministry meeting on 8 March 1973 (AMJ).

101. *La défaite des vainqueurs* was the title of a work by Louis Rougier published in 1947 (Geneva: Cheval Ailé), proclaiming "Hitler's demographic victory." In *The New York Times Magazine* of 18 August 1946, Lord Beveridge, the founder of Social Security in Britain, had already compared the losses that the various European states (not including Great Britain) had incurred owing to the Second World War, concluding that all the states had seen their populations decrease except for Germany, which ended the war with an increased population. C. L. Sulzberger confirmed this in the *New York Times* on 15 January 1947: "Germany won a great demographic victory by assuring an increase of the German population and radically reducing the population of neighboring states in line with a carefully conceived program designed to achieve just this end" (13). And it is true that the birth rate had remained high in Germany compared to France. Furthermore, the German population had been increased when ethnic Germans were given German nationality with Allied approval.

102. Alexandre Glasberg, Centre d'orientation sociale des étrangers, *À la recherche d'une patrie: la France devant l'immigration* (Paris: Réalités, 1946), 250–52.

103. Memorandum of 2 April 1946.

104. Note by Prigent, 20 September 1947, cited in Mérot, "Les orientations de la politique des naturalisations 1945–1973," 53.

105. Ibid.

106. Ibid., 51.

107. This rate is an index of the administrative treatment of requests rather than of the attractiveness of naturalization. See Alexis Spire and Suzanne Thave, "Les acquisitions de nationalité depuis 1945," *Synthèses: regards sur l'immigration depuis 1945* (Paris: INSEE, no. 30, October 1999), 33–57.

108. Other statistical sources confirm that from the standpoint of the hierarchy of ethnicities, later developments did not reflect the preferences expressed by Mauco and taken up by the CIN: a ranking done in 1948, 1949, and 1950 of the proportion of naturalized citizens in relation to the presence of their groups of origin on French territory put Armenians, Turks, and Bulgarians in first place; the Nordics came in last.

109. Regarding the very weak percentage of rejections in 1947, Maurice Loisel, head of the legal service of the Naturalization Bureau, commented that "this last percentage is particularly instructive: it shows how the priority given in 1947 to the examination of the dossiers of foreigners especially useful to our economy (mine workers, metallurgical workers, etc.) postponed the need to reject or defer the least interesting requests to the following years." "La politique française en

matière de naturalisation depuis la Libération," *Revue de défense nationale* 15 (July 1952), 303–9.

110. 1st Constituent Assembly, 1945, doc. I-458; 2nd Constituent Assembly, 1945, doc. Parl. II-77. AN, 1946, doc. parlementaire no. 166 / 1951, doc. parlementaire no. 51.

111. 2/AG/450. As a member of the National Council of Vichy, Bardoux had drafted a bill providing most notably (title III, article 3) that French nationality would be attributed "in the full sense" only to legitimate children born to French fathers. A legitimate child born to a foreign father and a French mother would be French only if he or she "resided in France and exercised a profession there at the age of legal majority." Finally, naturalization could be requested only after fifteen years of residency.

112. Mérot, "Les orientations de la politique des naturalisations 1945–1973," 51.

113. Ribeyre added: "Requests by citizens of far-away countries and especially those made by foreigners from exotic countries must be greeted with the greatest reserve." Mérot, ibid., 59–60. A conservative deputy from Ardèche from 1945 to 1958, then senator from the same department from 1959 to 1981, Paul Ribeyre (1906–88) was undersecretary of state in Bidault's government in 1949 and minister of justice between 1953 and 1954. As president of the Parliamentary Association for Freedom of Education, he played a critical role in the release from prison of Xavier Vallat, the former commissioner for Jewish affairs. See Laurent Joly, *Xavier Vallat: du nationalisme chrétien à l'antisémitisme d'État* (Paris: Grasset, 2001), 320.

114. Source: "Évolution du taux de naturalisations" in Spire and Thave, "Les acquisitions de nationalité depuis 1945," 51.

115. Excerpt from the instruction of 22 November 1953, cited in Mérot, "Les orientations de la politique des naturalisations 1945–1973," 60.

116. Ibid., 66.

117. Earlier, in 1961, a law had disconnected nationality law from the law governing residency. The law of 1938 required that a foreigner hold a residency permit for three years prior to naturalization. The ordinance of 1945 demanded only that the rules governing residency be respected (meaning that a one-year residency permit sufficed). From 1967 on, no residency permit was required.

118. Mérot, "Les orientations de la politique des naturalisations 1945–1973," 70.

119. See Spire and Thave, "Les acquisitions de nationalité depuis 1945," 35–57.

120. Paul Lagarde, *La nationalité française*, 3rd edn. (Paris: Dalloz, 1997), 84–88.

121. On this law see chapter 9.

122. Jean Foyer (born 27 April 1921 in Contigné, Maine-et-Loire) was a doctor of law

and served as technical adviser under René Capitant and then under Pierre Gia-cobbi, successively ministers of education from 1944 to 1946. He practiced law in Paris, earned his *agrégation*, and went on to teach in law schools in Lille (1955), Nanterre (1968), and Paris II (1972). Elected in 1958 as a deputy (UNR) from Maine-et-Loire, he served as secretary of state and then minister of cooperation in Michel Debré's government from 1960. He was minister of justice from 1962 to 1967, and he headed the National Assembly's commission on laws from 1968 to 1972 and from 1973 to 1981.

123. On the various reforms see Jean Carbonnier, *Essai sur les lois*, 2nd edn. (Paris: Répertoire du Notariat Defrénois, 1995).

124. On the status of women in nationality policy see chapter 8.

125. Interview with Jean Foyer on 4 December 2000. These pressures were confirmed by Mme Odile Pichat, who was division head for the commission on laws (interviewed on 14 December 2000).

126. On the history of this reform and its content see Paul Lagarde, "La rénovation du Code de la nationalité par la loi du 9 janvier 1973," *RCDIP* (1973), 431–69.

127. Unless she expressed a contrary desire before marriage.

128. In the first year after marriage, the government could oppose this acquisition for specific reasons.

129. Children born to a single French parent were French at birth, but if born abroad they could renounce their French nationality; if they were born in France to two foreign parents, one of whom had been born in France, they were French at birth, but they could also renounce their French nationality upon reaching the age of majority.

130. Foyer, "Rapport fait au nom de la commission des lois."

Chapter 6: The Algerian Crisis

1. A primary school teacher and militant socialist, Adrien Tixier was director of the International Labor Office before the Second World War. He joined Free France in 1940 and was its representative in Washington between 1941 and 1943. He served as national commissioner of labor, then as minister of labor and social planning in the provisional government of the French Republic (7 June 1943 to 9 September 1944); he became minister of the interior on 9 September 1944 and served until 16 January 1946.

2. Alexandre Parodi (1901–79) joined the Council of State in 1926. From August 1938 he served as advisor in the labor minister's cabinet; in January 1939 he was appointed director general of labor and the workforce in the same ministry. In this position he oversaw the status of foreign workers and represented his ministry

on the High Council on Population, created in 1939. Removed from his positions in 1940, he returned to the Council of State and became one of the leaders of the Resistance. From September 1944 to November 1945 he was minister of labor and social security in General de Gaulle's government.

3. The permanent commission of the Council of State met on 22 and 24 October with the representatives of the ministries concerned to produce the definitive version. René Cassin, Tissier, and Parodi, members of the Council of State and the Gaullist Resistance from the start, were able to work together apart from the presence of the "experts" on the High Committee on Population (see the letter of 11 November 1945 from Pierre Tissier to the Ministry of Justice, Archives du Ministère de la Justice, Direction des Affaires Criminelles et des Grâces, Service Législatif, dossier 1086-2). Cf. Patrick Weil, "Racisme et discriminations dans la politique française de l'immigration: 1938–1945 / 1974–1995," *Vingtième Siècle*, July–September 1995, 74–99.

4. This episode in the history of immigration policy is explored in Patrick Weil, *La France et ses étrangers: l'aventure d'une politique de l'immigration, 1938–1991* (Paris: Gallimard-Folio, 2005), chapter 5, "Les lois du retour (avril 1977-mai 1981)," 144–92. At the end of the negotiation with Algeria, on 18 December 1979 at the Élysée Palace, Valéry Giscard d'Estaing presided over a restricted Council of Ministers; the goal set by a decision of the council at that stage was to send back thirty thousand adult Algerians a year for five years. The president annotated the minutes of this meeting with the phrase "Avoid speaking about quotas for children." The turning point in the negotiation came a few weeks later, in January 1980. In contradiction with the conclusions of the meeting of 18 December 1979, Prime Minister Raymond Barre announced to the Algerian minister of foreign affairs, M. Benyahia, who was on an official visit to Paris, that France had given up its goal of forced returns.

5. Danièle Lochak, *Étrangers de quel droit?* (Paris: Presses Universitaires de France, 1985), 168; Weil, *La France et ses étrangers*, 287–318.

6. Children born in France to a foreign parent not born in France (but rather, for example, in Morocco or Portugal) could renounce French nationality in the six months preceding their majority. Children born in France to a parent born in Algeria before 1962 were irremediably French by virtue of the system of double jus soli.

7. In 1983, out of 758 requests for liberation from bonds of allegiance, 544 were rejected. The government's traditional policy was to refuse to free a person from bonds of allegiance when that person resided in France. In 1984, 2,506 rejections were issued out of 2,949 requests; in 1985, 732 out of 1,034; in 1986, 385 out of 872.

Source: André Lebon, cited in Rogers Brubaker, *Citizenship and Nationhood in France and Germany* (Cambridge: Harvard University Press, 1992), 219.

8. Martin Schain, "Immigration and Changes in the French Party System," *European Journal of Political Research* 16 (1998), 603–9; David S. Blatt, "Immigration Politics and Immigrant Collective Action in France, 1968–1993" (Ph.D. diss., Cornell University, 1996).

9. See Club de l'Horloge, *L'identité de la France* (Paris: Albatros, 1995). See also Pierre-André Taguieff, "L'identité nationale: un débat français," *Regards sur l'actualité*, nos. 209–10 (March–April 1995), 13–28.

10. Paris: Plon, 1984. As Rogers Brubaker notes, the bill that Alain Mayoud had submitted a year earlier, in 1983, had not had the same impact. *Citizenship and Nationhood in France and Germany*, 245.

11. See Jean-Yves Le Gallou and Jean-François Jalkh, *Être français, cela se mérite* (Paris: Albatros, 1987).

12. See Yvan Gastaut, *L'immigration et l'opinion en France sous la Ve République* (Paris: Le Seuil, 2000), 546–47.

13. In an address to the 65th congress of the League of the Rights of Man, 20 April 1985.

14. A survey conducted by BVA-*Paris-Match* on 12 and 13 August 1981 showed that 58 percent of French people were opposed to this measure, with 35 percent in favor. *Le Monde*, 21 August 1981. Cf. Weil, *La France et ses étrangers*, chapter 6.

15. A bill intended to reform the Nationality Code, no. 183 (4 June 1986). Cf. Le Pen, no. 82 (21 April 1986), and Mayoud, no. 70 (23 April 1986).

16. These three stages have been very well described by Miriam Feldblum in *Reconstructing Citizenship: The Politics of Nationality Reform and Immigration in Contemporary France* (Albany: SUNY Press, 1999), 78–128.

17. See chapter 8.

18. See chapter 9.

19. Letter from Charles Pasqua to the minister of justice, 14 August 1986 (CAC 200 001 145/21).

20. Press conference by Albin Chalandon, 24 July 1996 (CAC 200 002 145/23).

21. Article 23 of the law of 1973 was the one that applied double jus soli to children born in France "to a parent born on a territory that had, at the moment of that parent's birth, the status of colony or overseas territory of the French Republic." In 1984 the minister of social affairs had already proposed eliminating that article along with another provision according to which foreign parents could no longer declare their children born in France before they were ten years old. See Patrick Weil, "La politique française d'immigration (entre 1974 et 1986) et

la citoyenneté," *La citoyenneté*, ed. Catherine Wihtol de Wenden (Paris: Edilig, 1988), 191–200.

22. A note considered and adopted at the session of 29 October 1986, excerpted from the register of deliberations, published by *Libération* on 5 November 1986.

23. See *Libération*, 5 November 1986.

24. Article 1 of the proposed law reforming the French nationality code, National Assembly, no. 444, 12 November 1986.

25. Brubaker, *Citizenship and Nationhood*, 236.

26. Ibid., 237–38.

27. Interview with Albin Chalandon, 25 January 2001.

28. Feldblum, *Reconstructing Citizenship*, 101.

29. See Gastaut, *L'immigration et l'opinion*, 556–69.

30. Interview in *L'Express*, 30 October 1986.

31. Cf. Feldblum, *Reconstructing Citizenship*, 114.

32. *Être Français aujourd'hui et demain*, report of the prime minister's commission on nationality (Paris: Union Générale d'Éditions, 1988), vol. 2, p. 245.

33. The law of 7 May 1984 — adopted by a Parliament with a left-wing majority — had already obliged the foreign spouse of a French person who wanted to become French by declaration to wait until six months after the marriage, whereas previously the declaration could be made immediately after the marriage.

34. *Le Monde*, 9 January 1988.

35. *Libération*, 22 October 1987 and 17 February 1988.

36. *Le Monde*, 9 January 1988.

37. Ibid.

38. *Libération*, January 1988.

39. Pierre Mazeaud presented the various provisions of the Long commission report in the form of amendments to the bill on the conditions of entry and sojourn for foreigners in France, the "Joxe law," on 3 June 1989; the amendments had been prepared with de Bresson's help (*JO*, Déb. Parl., AN 1989, 1684–1701, and interview with Pierre Mazeaud, 9 October 2001).

40. Beyond the similarity to the National Front's proposals, Valéry Giscard d'Estaing's project borrowed from a bill that had been introduced by his grandfather, Jacques Bardoux, senator from Puy-de-Dôme, under the Vichy regime, and reintroduced systematically at the beginning of each legislative session under the Fourth Republic.

41. Interview with Pierre Mazeaud, 9 October 2001. The Senate had adopted the bill on 21 June 1990 (see *Le Monde*, 22 June 1990).

42. This proposal had already been put forward by Pierre Mazeaud on 2 December 1986 during an interview with Albin Chalandon (CAC 200 00145/23).

43. The Long report proposed one year.

44. The consequences of this provision were not merely symbolic, moreover: it posed problems of proof for all children born on or after 1 January 1994 when they reached adulthood and had to prove their nationality.

45. *Le Monde*, 23 July 1993.

46. Report of the nationality commission, *Être Français aujourd'hui et demain*, vol. 1, 115.

47. See Pierre Milza, *Voyage en Ritalie* (Paris: Plon, 1993).

48. In *Affaiblissement du lien social: enfermement dans les particularismes et intégration dans la cité*, report by the High Council on Integration (Paris: Documentation Française, 1997).

49. Abdelmalek Sayad, *La double absence: des illusions de l'émigré aux souffrances de l'immigré*, preface by Pierre Bourdieu (Paris: Le Seuil, 1999), 352.

50. Patrick Weil, *Rapports au Premier ministre sur les législations de la nationalité et de l'immigration* (Paris: Documentation Française, 1997).

51. See Hugues Fulchiron, ed., *Être Français aujourd'hui: premier bilan de la mise en oeuvre du nouveau droit de la nationalité* (Lyon: Presses Universitaires de Lyon, 1996), 8.

52. *Cahiers de l'Observatoire régional de l'intégration et de la ville*, Région Alsace, 1997.

53. See for example Cécile Prieur, "Les mésaventures de Nadia, empêchée de devenir française," *Le Monde*, 31 July 1997.

54. The reestablishment of this provision, or of a provision that would have granted nationality simply by virtue of birth on French territory, was rejected by a vote of 74–54 in favor of a provision that allowed young people born in France to foreign parents to acquire French nationality by declaration beginning at the age of thirteen; see *Le Monde*, 14 November 1997.

55. The new law corrected the legislation of 1993 on another point: the waiting period imposed before spouses of French nationals could become French by declaration was lowered from two years to one.

Conclusion to Parts One and Two

1. Hervé Le Bras, *Le sol et le sang* (La Tour d'Aigues: L'Aube, 1994).

2. Jean Leca made the following remark about Renan and his "incredible declaration" in the preface to *L'avenir de la science*: "the non-existence of God and the inequality of the races are henceforth scientifically proved." In Jean Leca, *Pour(quoi) la philosophie politique: petit traité de science politique*, vol. 1 (Paris: Presses de Sciences Po, 2001), 54.

3. To avoid granting to the "double jus soli" the character of a fundamental principle recognized by the laws of the Republic in matters of nationality, the Constitutional Council retained in its justifications in 1993 the fact that "jus soli was introduced into French nationality law only in 1889 primarily to respond to the demands of conscription." Referring to that decision, Georges Vedel, dean of the Law School in Paris, said later that "the Council must be prudent when . . . it invokes situations of fact in support of justifications for its decisions. It is ill equipped to know them." Georges Vedel, "Excès de pouvoir législatif et excès de pouvoir administratif," *Les Cahiers du Conseil constitutionnel*, no. 2 (1997), 87.

Chapter 7: Jus Soli versus Jus Sanguinis

1. Fritz Redlich, "Towards Comparative Historiography: Background and Problems," *Kyklos* 9, fasc. 3 (1958), 380, 382.

2. After the Congress of Vienna in 1815, the Germanic Confederation was made up of thirty-nine sovereign states connected by a fairly loose confederal bond but increasingly unified by an increasingly integrated economy. Rogers Brubaker, *Citizenship and Nationhood in France and Germany* (Cambridge: Harvard University Press, 1992), 53.

3. Before 1829 seven German states adopted laws on state citizenship; eight more followed between 1830 and 1835 and another five between 1836 and 1848. See Andreas Fahrmeir, *Citizens and Aliens, Foreigners and the Law in Britain and the German States, 1789–1870* (London: Berghahn, 2000), p. 57 n. 30.

4. If the liberal nationalist movement had carried the day in 1848, the history of Germany would probably have turned out to be different from what actually happened: the recuperation of nationalism and the small-scale reunification of Germany under the authority of Bismarckian Prussia after an unexpected victory over Austria-Hungary in which most of the member states of the *Zollverein* were Austrian allies.

5. Rolf Grawert, *Staat und Staatsangehörigkeit: Verfassungsgeschichtliche Untersuchung zur Entstehung der Staatsangehörigkeit* (Berlin: Duncker and Humblot, 1973), 124.

6. See a note from the Prussian minister of foreign affairs to the French ambassador to Prussia, Berlin, 13 June 1818 (AD, Fonds Berlin, series C, article 84).

7. According to the expression of the Council of State's reviewer, v.u.z. Mühlen GstA, I HA Rep. 80 I Druckschriften Nr. 286 Anlage V. The edict of 2 July 1812 dealing with the emigration of Prussian subjects and their naturalization by foreign states lists for the first time the reasons for the acquisition of *Angehörigkeit*: (1) birth in Prussia; (2) establishment of residency on Prussian territory; and

(3) military service or employment as a Prussian civil servant. In *Einbürgern und Ausschließen: Die Nationalisierung der Staatsangehörigkeit vom Deutschen Bund bis zur Bundesrepublik Deutschland* (Göttingen: Vandenhoeck and Ruprecht, 2001), Dieter Gosewinkel expresses some reservations about this predominance of *jus domicili* (30).

8. Note from the Prussian minister of foreign affairs to the French ambassador to Prussia, Berlin, 13 June 1818, AD, Fonds Berlin, series C, article 84.

9. Gesetzessammlung 1806/10, pp. 170/173, Nr. 6; also published in G. H. Pertz, *Das Leben des Ministers Freiherrn vom Stein*, vol. 2 (Berlin: G. Reimer, 1850), 23–27. On serfdom in Prussia and its abolition see Godefroy Cavaignac, *La formation de la Prusse contemporaine, les origines: le ministère de Stein* (Paris: Hachette, 1891).

10. With the "law on the police conditions of trade" ("Gesetz über die polizeilichen Verhältnisse der Gewerbe").

11. Gesetzessammlung 1810/11, pp. 263/280, Nr. 1.

12. Hans Heinrich Lippe, "Die preußische Heimatgesetzgebung vom 31. Dezember 1842," 2 vols. (LL.D. thesis, Göttingen, Hannover, 1947).

13. Later, in 1820, the state gave up the possibility of controlling commerce almost entirely, by abolishing the *patente* tax. Thanks to the provision of paragraph 20 of the 30 law of May 1820 "concerning the payment of a patente," even persons who were not very capable of imposing themselves in commercial competition, because they were "not very conscientious" and had neither capital nor particular capabilities, could start a business. See Gesetzessammlung 1820, pp. 147/154, Nr. 619.

14. J. E. Wappäus, *Allgemeine Bevölkerungsstatistik*, vol. 1 (Leipzig: J. C. Hinrichs'schen Buchhandlung, 1859), 100.

15. After they moved in, if they fell into poverty they obliged the commune to look after them, because the criterion of "domicile of support" (*Unterstützungswohnsitz*) was in force. The autonomy of the communes had been reinforced by the ordinance of 23 December 1808. See Cavaignac, *La formation de la Prusse contemporaine*, 415–20.

16. GstA I HA Rep. 80 I Druckschriften Nr. 286 Anlage V, p. 1/32.

17. On the possibility of determining nationality law either unilaterally or contractually by treaties see Olivier Beaud, *La puissance de l'État* (Paris: Presses Universitaires de France, 1994), 125–26.

18. Which excluded part of the population, in theory: domestic servants, farm workers, day laborers, and so on. In practice, in the southern German states, for example, this clause excluded only domestic workers, thus relatively few people.

19. The first treaty of this sort was signed between Bavaria, Würtemberg, and Baden in 1816 (it contained an invitation to the other states to join the treaty), then by the

Grand Duchy of Hesse in 1817 and the Duchy of Nassau in 1818; during the 1920s all the German states signed similar treaties.

20. Fahrmeir, *Citizens and Aliens*, 4.

21. The basic text on the law of 1842 has been Lippe, "Die preußische Heimatgesetzgebung vom 31. Dezember 1842."

22. Paragraphs 2 and 18 of the "ordinance of 20 March 1817 concerning the installation of the Council of State" provided for an examination of the ministry's draft law by the council before the king made his decision. See Hans Schneider, "Die Entstehung des preußischen Staatsrats 1806–1817: Ein Beitrag zur Verfassungsreform Preußens nach dem Zusammenbruch," *Zeitschrift für die gesamte Staatswissenschaft* 102 (May 1942).

23. GStA PK Berlin, I HA, Rep. 77 (Innenministerium), Titel 227, Nr. 4, Bd. 1.

24. Similarly, loss of the quality of subject would no longer be automatic but would require an administrative decision.

25. The state no longer had the right (as it had in the eighteenth century) to expel its own subjects in cases of civil or criminal offense.

26. These two services rapidly increased in importance in the first half of the nineteenth century and presupposed a clear definition of the quality of subject. See Hermann Rehm, "Der Erwerb von Staats — und Gemeinde — Angehörigkeit" in *Hirth's Annalen des Deutschen Reiches* (1892), 230–31.

27. Article from 13 February 1832, p. 6, in Rep 77 Mdl Titel 227, Nr. 4 vol. 1 gb.

28. Ancillon did rely explicitly on the Austrian and French codes in drafting his bill, whereas he regretted not having found anything interesting in "the recent legislation of the other German states . . . , academic writings, . . . or politico-juridical theories of legislation . . . that start from general philosophical principles and lead only to general and abstract conclusions on indigenity" (Rep. 77 [Innenministerium], Titel 117, Nr. 4, Bd. 1). However, the reviewer, von und zu Mühlen, cited the articles from the French Civil Code related to the quality of being French *in extenso* and discussed article 13 (regarding admission to residency) at length and with painstaking argumentation. It makes us suppose that that article had been invoked or evoked in the interministerial debates. This is a hypothesis formulated by Hans Heinrich Lippe ("Die preußische Heimatgesetzgebung vom 31. Dezember 1842," 160), to which I subscribe.

29. At the time there were two ministries of the interior, one led by von Brenn (interior and commerce) and the other by von Rochow (interior and police). They were recombined in 1837. The existence of two ministries of justice, led by Mühler and von Kamptz, was also justified by the need to oversee and revise the laws in the new regions won by Prussia in which the old laws, especially the "Allgemeines Landrecht," were no longer in force.

30. Von Rochow proposed these conditions for acquisition of the quality of subject by birth: (1) birth to Prussian parents; (2) marriage of a foreign woman to a Prussian man; (3) entrance into state service; (4) having real residence in Prussia; and (5) residence in the country for a specified period of time. For von Kamptz, access by decision of the public authority should be limited to foreigners recruited into public service (Rep. 77 Mdl. Ind. Tit. 227, Nr. 4, vol. 2, p. 2).

31. The Ministry of State functioned as a collective body replacing the Chancellery after Hardenberg's death. See Thomas Nipperdey, *Germany from Napoleon to Bismarck, 1800–1836* (Princeton: Princeton University Press, 1983), 292–93.

32. Rep. 80 StR. Aa. GbA B1.176, p. 4. Von Kamptz succeeded in convincing his colleagues, and came close to carrying the day with a new argument: until then all foreign seigneurial landowners had had to take an oath of allegiance to the king even though they also kept their "citizenship of origin." If the proposal remained in its present form, that oath would either be in contradiction with the new law or else would have to be eliminated, which would not be at all beneficial to the Prussian state, since in that case foreigners could become public persons in Prussia without becoming subjects of the king: "If that principle disappeared, all the Poles could buy property and move in even while remaining Polish subjects, without owing loyalty, obedience, and in general without having the duties of the King's subjects, but only the taxes and the legal rules concerning property."

33. Rep. 80 StR. Aa. GbA B1.176, p. 4.

34. In the meantime, moreover, Austria had modified its legislation: Austrian nationality was no longer granted automatically at the end of ten years, even though persons with ten years' residency had the right to request it. See Hannelore Burger, "Passwesen und Staatbürgerschaft," *Grenze und Staat: Paßwesen, Staatsbürgerschaft, Heimatrecht und Fremdengesetzgebung in der österreichischen Monarchie, 1750–1867*, ed. Waltraud Heindl and Edith Saurer (Vienna: Böhlau, 2000), 3–172.

35. Rep. 80 StR. Aa. BgA., folios 154/158, p. 4/10. This institution was conceived by Chancellor Hardenberg as the king's immediate council, working in an independent and autonomous fashion alongside the Ministry of State, with which it remained connected both because its ministers were included on the council as members with equal rights and because the Prussian chancellor headed the council. See Hans Schneider, *Der Preussische Staatsrat, 1817–1918: Ein Beitrag sur Verfassungs- und Rechtsgeschichte Preussens* (Munich: C. Beck, 1952), 51.

36. Paragraph 29 of the "Allgemeines Bürgerliches Gesetzbuch" specified the following: "Foreigners acquire Austrian citizenship by entering into public service; by entering a trade whose pursuit requires stable residency in the country; by a ten-year period of uninterrupted residency in the country, but on condition that during this time the foreigner has not been punished for any crime." Paragraph 28:

"The full enjoyment of civil rights is acquired by citizenship. Citizenship in these hereditary countries belongs to children of an Austrian citizen by birth."

37. GstA I HA Rep. 80 I Druckschriften Nr. 286 Anlage V, p. 7.

38. For the interpretation of these articles he cites Merlin, *Répertoire universel et raisonné de jurisprudence*, vol. 4, 19.

39. GstA I HA Rep. 80 I Druckschriften Nr. 286 Anlage V, p. 20, of the report with an explicit reference to the "recollections of justice minister von Kamptz."

40. See chapter 2.

41. "If there were a provision, similar to the one in French law, stating that a foreigner cannot establish a domicile in the country without naturalization . . . one could introduce the system of certificates of reception." Protocol of 17 June 1841; Rep. 80 StR. Aa. BgA., folio 269, p. 100.

42. The joint reviewers, von Meding and Eichmann, were opposed. GstA I HA Rep. 80 I Druckschriften Nr. 286 Anlage VII and VIII.

43. From 6 November 1841 to 27 April 1842 the Council of State examined the project during twenty-five plenary sessions (Rep. 80 StR. Aa. BgA., folio 287) and adopted only one significant modification: in order to conform to the treaties signed with the other German states, the Council sacrificed the parallelism between modes of acquisition and loss of the quality of being Prussian; the law provided for a system of naturalization to acquire it, but the Council approved automatic loss after ten years' absence from the country. Protocol of 27 April 1842; Rep. 80 StR. Aa. BhA., folios 324 and 325.

44. There was discrimination against foreign Jews, however: while the naturalization of a foreigner could be decided by the regional police authorities, where Jews were concerned "the prior consent of the minister of the Interior must be sought": see paragraph 5 of the law of 31 December 1842 in Maurice Ruby, *L'évolution de la nationalité allemande d'après les textes (1842 à 1953)* (Baden-Baden: Wervereis, 1953), 483.

45. Fahrmeir, *Citizens and Aliens*, 214–17. The nationalist movement's time had not yet come: the nationalists were in the opposition, struggling against the existing monarchies that were developing their own legislations.

46. Vortrag über das Gesetz wegen Entstehung und Auflösung des Preussischen Unterthanenverhältnisses, GstA HA I Rep. 80 I Nr. ad 62a, p. 50R.

47. L.-A. Warnkoenig, "De la science du droit en Allemagne depuis 1815," *Revue étrangère et française de législation, de jurisprudence et d'économie politique* 8 (1841), 25–52.

48. See Donald R. Kelley, *Historians and the Law in Postrevolutionary France* (Princeton: Princeton University Press, 1984).

49. He succeeded Baron von Kamptz.

50.   Preface to vol. 8 of his *Traité de droit romain*, trans. from German by Ch. Guenoux (Paris: Firmin-Didot, 1840–51), 1–2.

51.   On Lévy-Ullman's role see Hélène Morère, "La loi du 10 août 1927 sur la nationalité" (master's thesis, University of Paris I, Centre de recherche et d'histoire des mouvements sociaux et du syndicalisme), 79.

52.   Half the members of Marceau Long's commission were jurists, half non-jurists. On the function of the various jurists and their role in drafting the law see Géraud Geouffre de la Pradelle, "La réforme du droit de la nationalité ou la mise en forme juridique d'un virage politique," *Politix* 32 (1995), 154–71.

53.   See especially the following works by Alan Watson: *Legal Transplants* (Edinburgh: Scottish Academic Press, 1974); *Source of Law: Legal Change and Ambiguity* (Philadelphia: University of Pennsylvania Press, 1984); *Failures of the Imagination* (Philadelphia: University of Pennsylvania Press, 1988); *Legal Origins and Legal Changes* (London: Hambledon, 1991).

54.   William B. Ewald, "Comparative Jurisprudence (II): The Logic of Legal Transplants," *American Journal of Comparative Law* 43 (1995), 490.

55.   Alan Watson, "Aspects of Reception of Law," *American Journal of Comparative Law* 44 (1995), 335–51.

56.   Jean-François Dubost and Peter Sahlins, *"Et si l'on faisait payer les étrangers": Louis XIV, les immigrés et quelques autres* (Paris: Flammarion, 1999), 88.

57.   "Contrary to the jurisprudence of all peoples, it has been the woman who established the residence or domicile of her husband, since it seemed to suffice here that he [an immigrant man] marry a Strasbourgeoise or French woman in order to receive all municipal rights," Archives communales de Strasbourg, Police 48, cited in Jennifer Heuer in *The Family and the Nation: Gender and Citizenship in Revolutionary France, 1789–1830* (Ithaca: Cornell University Press, 2005), 2.

58.   See Robert Kiefe, *La nationalité des personnes dans l'Empire britannique* (Paris: Rousseau, 1926), 13.

59.   Moreover, on 24 May 1809 the emperor of Austria, to avoid desertions by the Frenchmen in his service, issued a decree providing for capital punishment if they deserted their unit.

60.   Claude Goasguen, "Les Français au service de l'étranger sous le Premier Empire: Législation et pratique" (LL.D. diss., University of Paris II, 1976), 139.

61.   Anyone who contravened this law risked the loss of his property, the loss of the right of succession, and expulsion from the Empire (ibid., 133–35).

62.   On the influence of this code see Jean Gaudemet, "Les transferts de droit," *L'Année sociologique* 27 (1976), 29–59.

63.   Ewald, after studying the period of the American Revolution, observes that while the transfer operated almost automatically in the realm of private law—there

was a direct transposition between English and American law—the situation was slightly different in the realm of public law. See William B. Ewald, "The American Revolution and the Evolution of Law," *American Journal of Comparative Law* 42 (1994), 1–14.

64. Dudley O. McGovney, "American Citizenship," *Columbia Law Review* 11, no. 3 (March 1911), 241.

65. André Weiss, *Traité théorique et pratique de droit international privé*, 2nd edn. (Paris: Larose et Tenin, 1907). During the first half of the century the French Civil Code was the direct model, while at the end of the nineteenth century German and Italian influences were more important. See Anthoine de Saint-Joseph, *Concordance entre les codes civils étrangers et le code Napoléon* (Paris: Charles Hingray 1840); Rodolfo Sacco, "Legal Formants: A Dynamic Approach to Comparative Law," *American Journal of Comparative Law* 29 (1991), 1–34.

66. Redlich, "Towards Comparative Historiography."

67. See Patrick Weil, "The Evolution of Alien Rights in the United States, Germany, and the European Union," *Citizenship Today: Global Perspectives and Practices*, ed. T. Alexander Aleinikoff and Douglas Klusmeyer (Washington: Carnegie Endowment for International Peace, 2001).

68. "A Contribution towards a Comparative History of European Societies," *Land and Work in Medieval Europe: Selected Papers by Marc Bloch*, trans. J. E. Anderson (Berkeley: University of California Press, 1967), 58.

69. Fahrmeir, *Citizens and Aliens*, 37–39.

70. Bavaria obtained a clause allowing it to be exempt from the provisions regarding freedom of residence in the territory of another German state (ibid., 69).

71. Lothar Gall, *Bismarck* (Paris: Fayard, 1984), 460–62.

72. Stéphane Audoin-Rouzeau, *1870: La France dans la Guerre*, preface by Jean-Jacques Becker (Paris: Armand Colin, 1989).

73. Ernest Lavisse, *Études sur l'histoire de Prusse*, 3rd edn. (Paris: Hachette, 1890), 279–301.

74. Ernest Renan, "Lettre à M. Strauss," *La réforme intellectuelle et morale* (Paris: Calmann-Lévy, 1871), 180–81.

75. Ernest Renan, "Nouvelle lettre à M. Strauss," *La réforme intellectuelle et morale* (Paris: Calmann-Lévy, 1871), 197–99.

76. See Conseil d'État, Assemblée générale, session of Thursday 23 April 1896; Report of Camille Sée, no. 108114, on the bill, which included a proposal for a special decree that determined the conditions under which the provisions of the nationality law of 26 June 1889 were applicable to colonies other than Guadeloupe, Martinique, and Réunion, and the forms to be used for naturalization in the colonies. Sée proposed to extend the procedure of the Algerian senatus-consulte to the

subjects of the French Polynesian islands, the French coast of Somalia, and Mada-gascar (AN, AL 2357). On Camille Sée see chapter 2 n. 75.

77. Ernest Renan, "What Is a Nation?," lecture delivered at the Sorbonne on 11 March 1882, in *Nation and Narration*, ed. Homi K. Bhabha (London: Routledge, 1990), 19.

78. In 1884 and 1885 Antonin Dubost, reviewer for the budget for public instruction, first had eliminated the funds allocated to faculties of Catholic theology. Then he supported the proposal to create a section of religious science in the École Pratique des Hautes Études. In order to "submit them to examination, compari-son, and criticism," he suggested placing Ernest Renan at the head of the section. This was done. See *JO*, Déb. Ch. 30 June 1885, 1255. Dubost, Renan, and Marcellin Berthelot dined together in Berthelot's rooms in the Academy on 22 February 1885; ADI, 1 J 940; see also Ernest Renan, *E. Renan et M. Berthelot: Correspondance, 1847–1892* (Paris: Calmann-Lévy, 1898).

79. See above, pp. 11–12.

80. Weiss, *Traité théorique et pratique de droit international privé*, vol. 1, *La nationalité*, 355.

81. Brubaker, *Citizenship and Nationhood in France and Germany*, 184. Dieter Gose-winkel has nevertheless pointed out that as of 1885 Germany's balance of migra-tion shifted for the first time away from emigration toward immigration. Gose-winkel, *Einbürgern und Ausschließen*, 185.

82. See Ada Lonni, "Histoire des migrations et identité nationale en Italie," *Revue européenne des migrations internationales* 1 (1993), 29–46. Ferruccio Pastore, "Nationality Law and International Migrations: The Italian Case," *Towards a European Nationality? Citizenship, Migration and Nationality Law in the European Union*, ed. Randall Hansen and Patrick Weil (Basingstoke: Palgrave, 2001), 95–103.

83. This passage relies on Howard Sargent's remarkable contribution in "Framing the German Citizenship Law," presented at the CEPIC conference "Droit de la nation-alité immigration et intégration en Europe," Paris, 25–27 June 1999. I thank him for authorizing me to cite his paper. A debate arose over the status of abandoned children, who were finally considered German as long as there was no proof to the contrary.

84. See Michel Korinman, *Deutschland über alles: le Pangermanisme 1890–1945* (Paris: Fayard, 1999), 46–47.

85. Italy had wanted to react to Brazil, whose constitution had decreed in 1891 that all foreigners who found themselves inside the country on the date of the proclama-tion of the republic, that is, on 15 November 1889, would automatically become Brazilian unless they declared within six months their desire to keep their original

nationality. See Gianfosto Rosoli, "La crise des relations entre l'Italie et le Brésil: la Grande Naturalisation (1889–1896)," *Revue européenne des migrations internationales*, no. 2 (1986), 69–90.

86. Alfred Weil, "Des ambiguïtés de la dénationalisation allemande," *JDIP* (1916), 69–72. This article made it possible to warn the French against their naturalized compatriots of German origin and thereby justified the measures of withdrawal of nationality that might be applied to them. See the note by the same Alfred Weil, attaché with the office of foreign legislation and international law in the Ministry of Justice (CAC 95065110).

87. Similarly, the means for keeping German nationality while becoming American through naturalization did not exist. Theodore H. Thiesing demonstrates this quite convincingly in "Dual Allegiance in the German Law of Nationality and American Citizenship," *Yale Law Journal* 27, no. 4 (February 1918), 479–508.

88. "I limit myself to recalling that in England a German merchant is admitted to the London Stock Exchange only when he has British nationality. It is certainly very painful that any German who wants to do business on the London Stock Exchange has to give up his own nationality. What is more, in the Latin countries of South America it is not easy for a German who does not have the nationality of the country to compete with those who have acquired it" (AD, series CA Contentieux, no. 354).

89. Letter from Ambassador Jules Cambon to the minister of foreign affairs, 24 November 1913 (AD, series CA Contentieux, no. 354).

90. Letter from Ambassador Delcassé to the minister of foreign affairs, 31 December 1913 (AD, series CA Contentieux, no. 354).

91. Letter from Ambassador Jules Josserand to the minister of foreign affairs, 27 December 1913 (AD, series CA Contentieux, no. 354).

92. Richard W. Flournoy Jr., "Observations on the New German Law of Nationality," *American Journal of International Law* 8, no. 3 (July 1914), 478.

93. *Metropolitan Magazine*, 15 June 1915.

94. Casper F. Goodricht, "Why Stranger in Our Gates Remains an Alien," *New York Times*, 24 June 1917.

95. Henry Lévy-Ullmann wrote, for example: "Until 1913, naturalization was understood to be definitive. The laws of 7 April 1915 and 18 June 1917 introduced the *withdrawal of naturalization* into our legislation," in "Rapport sur le projet de loi portant refonte des textes relatifs à l'acquisition et à la perte de la nationalité française," excerpt from *Bulletin de la Société d'études législatives* (Paris: Rousseau, 1918).

96. Georges Gruffy, "La naturalisation et le préjugé de la race," *RPP* (1919), 5–19, esp. 8.

97. In 1934 state nationality was eliminated.

98. This provision was applicable until 31 December 1935.

99. Each state had formerly been free to naturalize. To ensure Prussia's restrictive control over naturalizations in each of the other states, every minister of the interior of a state could henceforth veto the decision to naturalize taken by another state in the federation. There were more controls, but other provisions must also be noted: naturalizations could be requested when one was a minor; a married woman could ask to be naturalized independently of her husband, even though it was with his authorization (paragraph 7 of the law); when foreigners born in Germany requested naturalization, if they had maintained their permanent residence until the end of their twenty-first year in the federated state to which the request was addressed, and if they made that request in the two years after they reached their majority, another federated state could not veto their request (see Ruby, *L'évolution de la nationalité allemande*, 426). In Prussia alone, between 1919 and 1931 about 130,000 foreigners were naturalized (see Gosewinkel, *Einbürgern und Ausschließen*, 373).

100. See Ruby, *L'évolution de la nationalité allemande*, 87–95.

101. Daniel Kanstroom, "Wer sind wir wieder? Laws of Asylum, Immigration, and Citizenship in the Struggle for the Soul of the New Germany," *Yale Journal of International Law* 18, no. 1 (1993), 194.

102. See Simon Green, "Citizenship Policy in Germany: The Case of Ethnicity over Residence?" *Towards a European Nationality?*, ed. Hansen and Weil, 24–51. Candidates had to meet three additional conditions: four of their six years of school had to have been at the secondary level; they had to give up their original nationality; finally, they must not have committed any crimes or infractions.

103. Only the Hitlerian decisions intended to attribute German nationality forcibly to French nationals (from Alsace-Moselle) and Luxembourgers were annulled (see Ruby, *L'évolution de la nationalité allemande*, 272–84, 817).

104. See Brubaker, *Citizenship and Nationhood in France and Germany*, chapter 6. For a pertinent critique of Brubaker see Christian Joppke, *Immigration and the Nation-State: The United States, Germany and Great Britain* (Oxford: Oxford University Press, 1999), 271–76.

105. The United Kingdom and Ireland were countries of emigration with automatic jus soli. To a limited extent, to maintain ties to their nationals living abroad these two countries enacted provisions involving jus sanguinis.

106. See Patrick Weil, "Access to Citizenship: A Comparison of Twenty-Five Nationality Laws," *Citizenship Today: Global Perspectives and Practices*, ed. T. Alexander Aleinikoff and Douglas Klusmeyer (Washington: Carnegie Endowment for International Peace, 2001), 17–35.

107. A different evolution led to a certain restriction on automatic jus soli where it existed. In the United Kingdom before the Second World War, for example, jus soli extended to all the territories of the British Empire: all subjects of the Empire, whether born in India, Canada, or Jamaica, could obtain British nationality simply by going to reside in the territory of the United Kingdom. Since 1981 and the creation of British "citizenship," the territory concerned by jus soli is only that of the United Kingdom in the strict sense. In a referendum held on 11 June 2004, the Irish people approved a constitutional reform designed to limit acquisition of nationality, which had previously been granted automatically to anyone born on Irish territory.

108. On the legal conditions governing the access to nationality of children of immigrants in the various states of the European Union, see table 16, pp. 401–2.

109. John Fisscher Williams, *International Law Association*, Report of the Thirty-Third Conference, Stockholm, 1924 (London: W. Clowes and Sons, 1925), 35, cited in Paul de la Pradelle in "De la nationalité d'origine," *La nationalité dans la science sociale et dans le droit contemporain*, ed. Benjamin Akzin and Suzanne Basdevant (Paris: Sirey, 1933), 216: "No modern State which conceives itself to possess any attractive power can really suffer that it can have growing up within it over several generations a body of people who do not belong to the State, and I think also that I am right in saying that any State which has a strong general civilization, as nearly all States have, and an attractive power, assimilates within a remarkably rapid time the immigrants who come to the country and who settle there permanently."

110. Diane F. Orentlicher, "Citizenship and National Identity," *International Law and Ethnic Conflict*, ed. David Wippman (Ithaca: Cornell University Press, 1998), 296–325.

Chapter 8: Discrimination within Nationality Law

1. As of 1844 Great Britain viewed every foreign woman married to a British subject as British, and in 1855 the United States decided to follow the same principle for foreign women who married Americans. In 1870, in the interest of reciprocity, a British woman who married a foreigner became a foreigner. See Virginia Sapiro, "Women, Citizenship, and Nationality: Immigration and Naturalization Policies in the United States," *Politics and Society* 13, no. 1 (1984), 1–26.

2. Alexandre N. Makarov, "La nationalité de la femme mariée," *Recueil des cours de l'Académie de droit international* 2 (1937), 115–242.

3. Peter Sahlins, "Fictions of a Catholic France: The Naturalization of Foreigners, 1685–1787," *Representations* 47 (summer 1994), 85–110.

4. AP, vol. 76, 641.

5. AP, vol. 76, 643.

6. Bertrand Barère de Vieuzac (1755–1841), a lawyer in the Toulouse Parliament, was elected to the Estates General as a delegate from the Third Estate and sat among the moderate liberals in the Constituent Assembly. A member of the Supreme Court and then elected again to the Convention, he was a member of the Committee on Public Safety, participated in the Terror, and remained neutral on 9 Thermidor but was condemned to deportation, a penalty that was never carried out.

7. Cited in René Cassin, "L'inégalité entre l'homme et la femme dans la législation civile," *Annales de la faculté de droit d'Aix*, new series, no. 3 (Marseille, 1919), 1–28 (the excerpt is from p. 18).

8. Articles 12 and 19 of the Civil Code.

9. See chapter 2, pp. 32–33.

10. Pierre-Antoine Fenet, *Recueil complet des travaux préparatoires du Code civil* (Paris: Videcoq, 1936), vol. 7, 32–33.

11. Jennifer Heuer, *The Family and the Nation: Gender and Citizenship in Revolutionary France, 1789–1830* (Ithaca: Cornell University Press, 2005), 170; Heuer, "'Afin d'obtenir le droit de citoyen . . . en tout ce qui peut concerner une personne de son sexe': devenir ou cesser d'être femme française à l'époque napoléonienne," *CLIO* 12 (2000), 15–32.

12. ADBR 8M25, cited in Heuer, *The Family and the Nation*, 170–71.

13. Ibid., 171.

14. Heuer, *The Family and the Nation*, 171–72.

15. Karin Dietrich-Chénel and Marie-Hélène Varnier count three naturalized women and eight admitted to residency. "Intégration d'étrangers en France par naturalisation ou admission à domicile de 1790/1814 au 10 mai 1871" (Ph.D. diss., Université d'Aix-Marseille I, 1994). Exceptionally, a few foreign women were able to be naturalized or admitted to residency because they were not, or were no longer, marriageable (examples include women who had taken holy orders, and elderly widows).

16. Affaire Hess, Sir. 92.1.81, and the note by Antoine Pillet; pandect. franc. 92.1.129, and the note by André Weiss. Lucien Gérardin, *De l'acquisition de la qualité de Français par voie de déclaration, étude sur le bienfait de la loi* (Paris: Larose, 1896), 20.

17. The administration's immediate application of this ruling made unnecessary some of the requests for naturalization submitted in 1892, since they no longer had an object, and lowered the number of naturalizations granted from 5,371 (in 1891) to 4,537 (in 1892); the impact of the decision by the Supreme Court was assessed at around 1,100 for a full year. Charles Falcimaigne, director of Civil Affairs and the Seal, report to the keeper of the seals, *JO*, 11 October 1893, 5079, no. 1.

18. Excerpts from the report to the keeper of the seals regarding the application of the 1889 law for the year 1892, *JO*, 11 October 1893.

19. Article 1 of the law of 1 July 1993. Louis Le Sueur and Eugène Dreyfus stress that unlike jus sanguinis, jus soli is neutral concerning the sex of the parents and indifferent as to their nationality: lawmakers attach the virtue of conferring nationality exclusively to a material fact, and in the presence of the one unique attributive element, birth on French territory, there is no longer any need to take the parents' nationality into consideration. "De la nationalité de l'individu né en France d'une étrangère qui elle-même y est née," *Journal du droit international privé et de la jurisprudence comparée* 19 (1892), 78–103.

20. Until 1889 article 19 of the Civil Code ("a French woman who marries a foreigner will follow the condition of her husband") applied without acknowledgment that sometimes the legislation governing the husband did not allow marriage to influence nationality. A French woman who married an Englishman before 1844 lost her French nationality without acquiring British nationality. The law of 1889 added the following: "unless her marriage does not confer her husband's nationality on her."

21. Sect. 3, Act of 2 March 1907 (34 Stat. 1228).

22. See Pierre Wurtz, *La question de l'immigration aux États-Unis* (Paris: L. Dreux and M. Schneider, 1925).

23. See Lawrence H. Fuchs, "Immigration Reform in 1911 and 1981: The Role of Select Commissions," *Journal of American Ethnic History*, fall 1983, 58–89.

24. See Candice Lewis Bredbrenner, *A Nationality of Her Own: Women, Marriage and the Law of Citizenship* (Berkeley: University of California Press, 1998), 8. Carrie Chapman, future president of the National American Woman Suffrage Association, did not hesitate to propose to exchange the right to vote of naturalized men, or of men living in urban ghettos, for that of women.

25. Ibid., 63–64.

26. On 26 August 1920 Tennessee voted in favor of the amendment adopted in 1918 by the requisite two-thirds majority of the House of Representatives, becoming the thirty-sixth state to do so and thus providing the vote that made up the required three-fourths majority of states required for ratification of a constitutional amendment. See Françoise Bach, "Les droits des femmes et le suffrage aux États-Unis 1948–1920," *Encyclopédie politique et historique des femmes, Europe, Amérique du nord*, ed. Christine Fauré (Paris: Presses Universitaires de France, 1997), 505–34.

27. Chrystal MacMillan, "Nationality of Married Women: Present Tendencies," *Journal of Comparative Legislation and International Law*, 3rd series, 7 (November 1925), 142–54.

28. 42 Stat., part. I, p. 1021, chap. 411.

29. An American woman who marries a foreigner loses her American nationality only if she renounces it.

30. However, the waiting period on American territory was reduced from five years to one.

31. This clause was abrogated in 1931. In 1934 complete equality was established between men and women. First, in the transmission of nationality for children born abroad: henceforth an American mother or father would transmit nationality independently of the other parent, provided that the American parent had resided in the United States before the child's birth; and if only one of the parents was American, the child would be American only if he or she resided in the United States for five years before reaching the age of eighteen.

32. It had been made possible by the law of 20 September 1792, and this possibility had been maintained in the Civil Code.

33. (1) Adultery; (2) excesses, physical abuse, or serious injuries; (3) condemnation of one of the spouses to a sentence including loss of civil rights; (4) three years' separation.

34. See Françoise Thébaud, *La femme au temps de la guerre de 1914* (Paris: Stock / Laurence Pernoud, 1986).

35. In December 1914, in an internment camp in the Pyrenees, these women were offered their freedom: they then had either to join their husbands' families in Germany or Austria-Hungary or else rejoin their French families. Most chose to remain in the camp with their husbands. See Jean-Claude Vimont, "La population du camp d'internement de Garaison (Hautes-Pyrénées), 1914–1919," *Les malheurs de la guerre*, vol. 2, *De la guerre réglée à la guerre totale*, ed. André Corvisier and Jean Jacquart (Paris: Comité des travaux historiques et scientifiques, 1997), 93–108.

36. Elisa Camiscioli, "Intermarriage, Independent Nationality, and Individual Rights of French Women: The Law of 10 August 1927," *French Politics, Culture and Society* 17, nos. 3–4 (summer–fall 1999), 4.

37. Born 15 January 1859 in Puget-Ville (Var), Louis Martin, doctor of law and lawyer at the Paris bar, was elected deputy from the second district of Toulon on an antinationalist republican program; he joined the radical and radical-socialist democratic left. He was elected to the Senate in January 1909 and kept his seat until 1936. A member of the honorary committees of the French League for Women's Rights (Ligue française du droit des femmes, LFDF) and of the Fraternal Union of Women, he presided over meetings of the society for ameliorating the condition of women, the committee of feminist propaganda, the LFDF, and the French Union for Women's Suffrage (Union française pour le suffrage des femmes, UFSF).

He held the record for participation in suffragist meetings and from 1918 was the driving force behind the parliamentary group for women's rights. In 1936 he was elected honorary president of the LFDF. Among other works he published *Considérations générales sur la législation civile et pénale de la Révolution française, mémoire au Conseil Municipal de Paris* (Paris: Giard et Brière, 1894), and a textbook, *Droit civil* (Paris: Dunod et Vicq, 1896).

38. *JO*, DP, Senate, 1916, annex 35, 81; and *JO*, DP, Senate, 1920, annex 229, 195. Only one restrictive measure was adopted in 1917: a foreign woman who was a "subject of an enemy nation" acquired French nationality only if her marriage to a Frenchman had received prior authorization from the minister of justice (law of 18 March 1917, *JO*, 21 March 1917).

39. Françoise Thébaud and Christine Bard, "Les effets antiféministes de la Grande Guerre," *Un siècle d'antiféminisme*, ed. Christine Bard, pref. Michelle Perrot (Paris: Fayard, 1999), 154.

40. See Christine Bard, *Les filles de Marianne: histoire des féminismes, 1914–1940* (Paris: Fayard, 1995), 147–48.

41. Pierre Depoid, *Les naturalisations en France (1870–1940)* (Paris: Imprimerie nationale, 1942), 95.

42. This figure was obtained from Depoid's tables (ibid., 59–61).

43. To be precise, 29,378 (ibid., 5). One should also add the thousands of married women before 1900 and eliminate those who left France with their husbands.

44. 1,004,522 women were counted in the census as foreign; of these, 471,983 were married, 144,765 had been born in the department where they were counted, and 42,837 had been born in another department, making 18.2 percent born in France. Only 9.5 percent of the men counted as foreigners in the census were born in France. See Statistique générale de la France, *Résultats statistiques du recensement général de la population effectué le 7 mars 1926*, vol. 1, part 5, *Étrangers et naturalisés* (Paris: Imprimerie nationale, 1931). Since 1881 the census has distinguished between persons "born to French parents" — a category which later became "born French," then in 1921 "French by birth" — persons "naturalized French," and finally "foreigners." A woman born French who had become a foreigner through marriage was supposed to check two boxes. See Alexis Spire and Dominique Merllié, "La question des origines dans les statistiques en France," *Le mouvement social*, no. 188 (July–September 1999), 119–30. The questionnaire, vol. 1, part 1, *Introduction*, 1928, 11, is not very clear, and it is probable that many women born French who had become foreigners by marriage to a foreigner only checked the first box: "Are you French by birth? . . . Or naturalized French? A foreigner? . . . From what country?"

45. Marcel Sauteraud, "Du maintien de la nationalité de la femme française qui épouse un étranger," *Revue politique et parlementaire* 101 (October–December 1919), 197.

46. This obligatory registration dates only from after 1917, for the law of 1893 did not apply to French women who became foreigners by marriage. See Frantz Despagnet, *Précis de droit international privé*, 4th edn. (Paris: Société du recueil général des lois et des arrêts, 1904), 3.

47. Memorandum from the minister of the interior, 2 October 1919, *JDIP* (1920), 365–67.

48. In 1924 Italy surpassed Belgium to become the number one source of foreign men marrying French women (3,208 out of 11,363, or 28.2 percent). On the evolution of the original nationality of the foreign wives of French men see Francisco Muñoz-Perez and Michèle Tribalat, "Mariages d'étrangers et mariages mixtes en France: évolution depuis la première guerre," *Population* 3 (1984), 427–62.

49. Trinh Dinh Thao, *De l'influence du mariage sur la nationalité de la femme* (Aix-en-Provence: Paul Roubaud, 1929), 92–93.

50. Yvonne Delatour, "Le travail des femmes pendant la Première Guerre mondiale et ses conséquences sur l'évolution de leur rôle dans la société," in Institut historique allemand, *Francia, Forschungen zur westeuropäischen Geschichte*, vol. 2 (Munich: Artemis), 495. See also Madeleine Guilbert, "L'évolution des effectifs du travail féminin en France depuis 1866," *Revue française du travail*, September 1947, 754–77.

51. The commission on naturalizations was created in 1926 by Barthou and headed continuously by André Honnorat (minutes of the meeting of 13 October 1927, AD. Fonds CNT, series 38, article 372).

52. Conseil National des Femmes Françaises, *Congrès des 8 et 9 octobre 1919*, Strasbourg; Paul Smith, *Feminism and the Third Republic: Women's Political and Civil Rights in France 1918–1945* (Oxford: Clarendon, 1996), 179–81.

53. See note 38, above.

54. If she lived abroad, she could acquire her husband's nationality (*JO*, DP, Ch. Dép., 1918, Annex 4904, 2143). The government opposed the text. See AN Papiers André Honnorat, 50 SP 27.

55. See Gaston Calbairac, *Traité de la nationalité de la femme mariée* (Sirey: Paris, 1929), 32.

56. Lafont DP Ch. Dép. 1919, annex 5716, 1935.

57. Martin proposed the opposite arrangement: the French woman would take her husband's nationality unless she expressed her desire to remain French.

58. See Conseil National des Femmes Françaises, 1920–22, 29, Section de législation.

59. Bill of 6 July 1922, Doc. Parl., Sénat, sess. ordinaire, 1922, annexe 511, p. 559, incorporated by a Senate vote on 21 June 1923 (*JO*, Déb. Parl. Sénat, p. 1040, 21 June 1923).

60. The best article on the subject is Elisa Camiscioli, "Intermarriage, Independent Nationality, and the Individual Rights of French Women: The Law of 10 August 1927," *French Politics, Culture and Society* 17, nos. 3–4 (summer–fall 1999), 52–74.

61. *JO*, Doc. Parl. Ch. des Dép., 31 March 1927, first session.

62. The term dates from 1921. See Françoise Thébaud, "Le mouvement nataliste dans la France de l'entre-deux-guerres: l'Alliance nationale pour l'accroissement de la population française," *RHMC*, April–June 1985, 276–301.

63. The law adopted also prescribed that a French woman married to a foreigner, if she herself remained French, would transmit her French nationality to her children born in France. This provision thus opened a breach in the father's monopoly on transmission of nationality.

64. There were nevertheless two exceptions to this freedom of choice: for a French woman, the acquisition of her husband's foreign nationality became an obligation if she established legal residence abroad (art. 8). And a foreign woman was obliged to become French if her own national legislation prescribed that she must take her husband's nationality (this was so in particular for women from Germany, the Netherlands, Switzerland, Czechoslovakia, and—if the marriage had taken place before 9 December 1931 or between 1 June and 13 November 1938)—Spain.

65. AD, Fonds CNT, series 38, art. 372. On the commission on naturalizations see chapter 3, pp. 44–45.

66. Session of 14 November 1927 of the commission on naturalizations (Archives Honnorat, 50 AP 67). The commission submitted these proposals to the minister of justice; I do not know whether any action was taken.

67. See chapter 5.

68. Raymond Boulbès, *Commentaire du Code de la nationalité française (ordonnance du 19 octobre 1945)* (Paris: Sirey, 1946), 17 n. 1.

69. Christine Bard, "Le triomphe du familialisme," *Un siècle d'antiféminisme*, 169–92.

70. On the various reforms see Jean Carbonnier, *Essai sur les lois*, 2nd edn. (Paris: Répertoire du Notariat Defrénois, 1995).

71. Jean Foyer, report in the name of the commission on laws about the bill adopted by the Senate completing and modifying the French Nationality Code and relating to certain provisions concerning French nationality (AN fourth legislature, first ordinary session of 1972–73, no. 2545, 29 September 1972, 5). He adds: "As

for the unity of nationality between spouses, while it is convenient, it is not—or at least it is no longer—the necessary condition for their good relationship. Is it compatible, moreover, with contemporary provisions facilitating the dissolution of marriage?"

72. Interview with Jean Foyer, 4 December 2000. These pressures were confirmed by Odile Pichat, who was the division head for the commission of laws at the National Assembly (interview, 14 December 2000).

73. On the history of this reform and its content see Paul Lagarde, "La rénovation du Code de la nationalité par la loi du 9 janvier 1973," *RCDIP*, 1973, 431–69.

74. Unless one of them expressed a contrary desire before the marriage.

75. The administration then had a year to declare itself opposed; beyond that period French nationality was automatically acquired.

76. The first major country to establish total equality between spouses was the Soviet Union, through article 103 of the Family Code in 1919. See Calbairac, *Traité de la nationalité de la femme mariée*, 225.

77. See chapter 9, p. 230.

78. In French colonial history, during a first period of colonization lasting until 1815, most of the old colonies were conquered and then lost. The modern period of colonization began in Algeria in 1830 and spread into Africa and Asia until after the First World War. See Jean Meyer, Jean Tarrade, Annie Rey-Goldzeiguer, and Jacques Thobie, *Histoire de la France coloniale: des origines à 1914* (Paris: Armand Colin, 1991).

79. The nationality law of 1889 declared that it was applicable in Algeria and in the colonies of Guadeloupe, Martinique, and Réunion (article 2).

80. This marked the end of Turkish domination over the region, which had begun in 1587.

81. At the time the civil intendant was the equivalent in Algiers of the prefect in metropolitan France, except for questions of police, press, religion, and matters involving state-owned property. See Claude Collot, *Les institutions d'Algérie durant la période coloniale* (Paris: CNRS / Office des publications universitaires, 1987), 35.

82. BB30/1604, letter from Pierre Genty de Bussy, master of requests, civil intendant, regency of Algiers under the Ministry of War, 9 September 1832. Along with a career in military administration, Genty de Bussy (1793–1867) was appointed master of requests in extraordinary service with the Council of State on 13 May 1829. He served as civil intendant in Algiers from 12 May 1832 to 12 August 1834, then went on to pursue a career at the Ministry of War and later in Parliament, where he was deputy from Morbihan from 1844 to 1848.

83. He said: "to rebuff them when they declared that they wanted to be on entirely

the same footing with us; this would be to destroy the authority of our words ourselves at the outset, it would be to stifle the trust that we seek to inspire, it would be to force men to whom our appeal is addressed to submit only half-way, with fear and thus with second thoughts and to think already about how to reserve for themselves future means of reconciliation with the masters who could return to them."

84.   Order of the court of Algiers dated 24 February 1862, cited in Auguste-Raynald Werner, *Essai sur la réglementation de la nationalité dans le droit colonial français* (Toulouse: Boisseau, 1936), 144.

85.   AN, Cote BB30 1604, item 38. One official in the Ministry of War did take a stand against the excess that consisted in closing off "all access into our political and civil family." "By letting them become citizens, we would be making no commitments to them other than to protect them as such. Must one forget that a *subject* is only a rebel in reserve?"

86.   Letter from the Ministry of War to the Ministry of Justice, 28 June 1864 (AN, BB30/1604).

87.   On 30 October 1866, to be precise (AN, BB30/1604).

88.   In 1863, in a letter to Governor Aimable Pélissier, the emperor formulated the idea of an Arab kingdom: "Algeria is not a colony properly speaking, but an Arab kingdom. The natives have the same right to my protection as the colonists. I am just as much the emperor of the Arabs as of the French" (cited in Collot, *Les institutions d'Algérie durant la période coloniale*, 9).

89.   Decree no. 136, *Bulletin des Lois no 8 de la Délégation du Gouvernement de la Défense nationale hors de Paris, République Française, XIIᵉ série. Tours et Bordeaux, du 12 septembre 1870 au 18 février 1871* (Versailles: Imprimerie Nationale, June 1871), 109.

90.   See Simon Schwarzfuchs, *Les Juifs d'Algérie et la France, 1830–1855* (Jerusalem: Ben Zvi Institute, 1981), 13–20.

91.   Beginning in 1830 the Algerian Jews were organized as a "nation" whose leader was appointed by the military authority. Their religious life was organized under rabbinical authority.

92.   Doris Bensimon and Joëlle Allouche-Benayoun, *Les Juifs d'Algérie: mémoires et identités plurielles* (Paris: Stavit, 1998), 35–36.

93.   In 1843, in the wake of a report by Jacques-Isaac Altaras, president of the Israelite consistory of Marseille, and Joseph Cohen, a young lawyer in Aix who had carried out a two-month investigation in Algeria in 1842, the minister of war appointed a commission headed by Eugène Janvier, a member of the Council of State, with the task of proposing administrative regulations for the Algerian Jews. By late 1843 the Council of State was consulted; there Thomas Bugeaud proved hostile

(see Schwarzfuchs, *Les Juifs d'Algérie et la France*, 42–54). Article 1 of the order that naturalized the Jewish community was withdrawn after the Council of State issued an unfavorable opinion (BB30/1604).

94. Charles-Robert Ageron, *Les Algériens musulmans et la France (1871–1919)*, vol. 1 (Paris: Presses Universitaires de France, 1968), 44–45.

95. Only 142 Algerian Jews were naturalized between 1865 and 1870. See Laure Blévis, "Une citoyenneté française contestée: réflexion à partir d'un incident antisémite en 1938," in Association française pour l'histoire de la Justice, *La justice en Algérie, 1830–1962*, Collection histoire de la justice no. 16 (Paris: La Documentation Française, 2005), 111–22.

96. *Le Moniteur*, 9 March 1870, 355.

97. On 18 March the Council of State had asked for an investigation into the way Muslims would react to this measure. After the investigation Mac-Mahon had come out in favor of collective naturalization. It was he and not Crémieux who was responsible for the obligatory character of collective naturalization: the project of 8 March had provided that "every indigenous Israelite could have renounced the benefit of naturalization during a two-year period." Ageron, *Les Algériens musulmans et la France*, vol. 1, 14–15, and CAOM, F80 20 43.

98. Adolphe Crémieux (1796–1880), a doctor of law who had practiced in Nîmes, moved to Paris and became a deputy from Indre-et-Loire in 1842. A minister of justice under the provisional Republic from 24 February to 5 June 1848, he signed the decree abolishing slavery. He served as minister of justice in the government of National Defense from 4 September 1870 to 19 February 1871, and as a deputy from Algiers from 20 October 1872 to 14 December 1875, when he was elected senator for life. A defender of Jewish emancipation and Jewish rights, he was responsible for the creation of the Universal Israelite Alliance, which he headed from 1863 until his death.

99. Charles-André Julien, *Histoire de l'Algérie contemporaine*, vol. 1, *La conquête et les débuts de la colonisation (1827–1871)* (Paris: Presses Universitaires de France, 1964), 467.

100. See Stéphane Audoin-Rouzeau, *1870: la France dans la guerre* (Paris: Armand Colin, 1989), preface by Jean-Jacques Becker.

101. Ageron, *Les Algériens musulmans et la France*, vol. 1, 6.

102. Alain Glais-Bizoin, *Dictature de cinq mois: mémoires* (Paris: Dentu, 1873), 176.

103. On this subject see the very informative article by Philippe Darriulat, "La gauche républicaine et la conquête d'Algérie, de la prise d'Alger à la reddition d'Abd El-Kader," *RFHOM* 82, no. 307 (1995), 171–87.

104. Glais-Bizoin, *Dictature de cinq mois*, 171–87.

105. Ageron, *Les Algériens musulmans et la France*, vol. 1, 7.

106. Report by M. De Fourtou, *JO*, 4 September 1871, 3195.

107. Vice-admiral Louis-Henri de Gueydon (1809–86) was appointed by the authorities of the Republic as the first civilian governor in Algiers; he served from 25 March 1871 to 17 June 1873.

108. See Jacques Cohen, *Les Israélites de l'Algérie et le décret Crémieux* (Paris: Arthur Rousseau, 1990), 204–11.

109. See J.-B. Sialelli, "Chronique de jurisprudence française," *Journal de droit international* no. 1 (1951), 596–98.

110. See Charles-Robert Ageron, *Politiques coloniales au Maghreb* (Paris: Presses Universitaires de France, 1973).

111. See Ageron, *Les Algériens musulmans et la France*, vol. 1, 11.

112. Later, he added that with collective naturalization France would "arrive at the Arab Republic after having escaped the clutches of the Arab Kingdom" (excerpts from two reports by de Gueydon, 4 July 1871 and 3 February 1872, cited in ibid., 346).

113. Paul Leroy-Beaulieu (1843–1916), an economist and professor of economics at the École Libre des Sciences Politiques in 1872, founded the weekly *L'Économiste français*. He published numerous books, including *Le travail des femmes au XIXe siècle* (1873), *Traité de la science des finances* (1877), and *De la colonisation chez les peuples modernes* (1908); he was elected professor at the Collège de France in 1880.

114. Paul Leroy-Beaulieu, *L'Algérie et la Tunisie* (Paris: Guillaumin, 1887), 292.

115. Bill dated 16 June 1887, annex 1846 *JO*, Doc. Ch. des Dép., ordinary session of 1887. Henri Michelin was a deputy from the fourteenth arrondissement in Paris from 1885 to 1889 and from 1893 to 1898.

116. CAOM, 8H10, anonymous note on the "naturalization of the natives," 1887.

117. Proposed law, 21 July 1890, annex 857, session of 1890, *JO*, Ch. des Dép. doc. parl. Alfred Martineau, who was elected as a Boulangist deputy from the nineteenth arrondissement in Paris in 1889, was a director with the Ministry of Colonies; later he was elected professor at the Collège de France.

118. André Weiss, *Traité théorique et pratique de droit international privé*, 2nd edn., vol. 1, *La nationalité* (Paris: Sirey, 1907), 465.

119. *Bulletin du Comité de l'Afrique française*, cited in Charles-Robert Ageron, *France colonial ou parti colonial* (Paris: Presses Universitaires de France, 1978).

120. Ageron, *France colonial ou parti colonial*.

121. The seal rights, which cost 175.25 francs in metropolitan France at the time, were set at one franc in Algeria by article 20 of the decree of 21 April 1866.

122. Speech given on 20 November 1884 to the high council of Algeria, cited in Weiss, *Traité théorique et pratique*, 436–37. The census of 1886 supports his analysis, re-

porting 219,627 French persons in Algeria and 202,212 foreigners, without counting the 17,445 Moroccans.

124. Letter from the minister of justice to the governor of Algeria, 6 December 1884, CAOM F80 2043.

125. Letter from Tirman to the president of the Council of State (who was also minister of justice), 23 May 1885, CAOM F80 2043.

126. See chapter 2.

127. Article 2 of the law of 1889.

128. See Jean Olier, "Les résultats de la législation sur la nationalité en Algérie," *RPP*, 1897, 551–60. The question of mixed-race children born to Muslim mothers and non-Muslim but unknown fathers also arose. Article 8 of the law of 26 June 1889 was supposed to attribute the mother's status to the child. Until 1921, according to Bonnichon, such children belonged to Muslim society and were brought up by their father. In 1921 mixed-race children were taken in by the rural orphanage run by the Pères Blancs in El Goa. On 2 April 1926 Viollette, governor of Algeria, declared in a memorandum that these children would be recorded on civil registers as born to unknown parents and would benefit from article 58 and accessorily article 8 of the Civil Code, thus inaugurating a period in which mixed-race children were included in French nationality. See André Bonnichon, *La conversion au christianisme de l'indigène musulman algérien et ses effets juridiques (un cas de conflit colonial)* (Paris: Sirey, 1931).

129. Charles-Robert Ageron, *Histoire de l'Algérie contemporaine, 1871–1954*, vol. 2, *De l'insurrection de 1871 au déclenchement de la guerre de libération* (Paris: Presses Universitaires de France, 1979), 118.

130. Werner, *Essai sur la réglementation de la nationalité*.

131. Charles-André Julien, *Histoire de l'Afrique du Nord, Tunisie, Algérie, Maroc* (Paris: Payot, 1931), preface by Stéphane Gsell, 646.

132. Julien situates this appropriation of religious goods in 1843; it seems to have begun as early as 8 September 1830 (ibid., 658).

133. Ibid.

134. When "cantonment" was interrupted in 1863 because of excesses, the sixteen tribes that had been "cantoned" through administrative measures saw their territories reduced from 343,000 to 282,000 hectares; the 61,000 hectares remaining, the most fertile, were by and large abandoned to private speculators. Ageron, *Histoire de l'Algérie contemporaine*, vol. 2, 11–12.

135. Julien, *Histoire de l'Algérie contemporaine*, vol. 1, 492. The financial penalties imposed on the 800,000 people involved amounted to 65 million francs.

136. Benjamin Stora, *Histoire de l'Algérie coloniale (1830–1954)* (Paris: La Découverte, 1991), 26.

137. Julien, *Histoire de l'Afrique du Nord*, 668.

138. Yves Lacoste, André Nouschi, and André Prenant, *L'Algérie, passé et présent: le cadre et les étapes de la constitution de l'Algérie actuelle* (Paris: Éditions Sociales, 1960), 379–80; Julien, *Histoire de l'Afrique du Nord*, 674–75.

139. Ageron, *Histoire de l'Algérie contemporaine*, vol. 1, 171.

140. Jean-Claude Vatin, *L'Algérie politique: histoire et société* (Paris: Fondation Nationale des Sciences Politiques, 1978), 133.

141. Ageron, *Histoire de l'Algérie contemporaine*, vol. 1, 175.

142. Collot, *Les institutions d'Algérie*, 193.

143. Ibid., 296–98.

144. The financial delegations were instituted by a decree of 23 August 1898. See ibid., 218–29.

145. Ibid., 224–27.

146. Report prepared in the name of the commission on external affairs, protectorates, and colonies, by Marius Moutet, annex 4383, session of 1 March 1918, *JO*, Doc. Parl. Ch., 314–63, especially 330. This document will be referred to in subsequent notes as the "Moutet report."

147. The four communes were Dakar, Saint-Louis, Gorée, and Rufisque. The law of 24 April 1833 included the following provision in article 1: "Every person born free, or having legally acquired freedom, enjoys in the French colonies: 1° civil rights, 2° political rights, under the conditions prescribed by the laws." The abolition of slavery in 1848 was supposed to have attributed full citizenship to the former slaves of these four communes. But in the wake of contradictory measures taken from 1858 to 1910 in relation to the personal status of the natives of Senegal, the doctrine deduced that the natives of the colonies, who had been citizens until the decree of 20 May 1857, had become subjects again. The law of 29 September 1916 indicates clearly and definitively that "the natives of the four autonomous communes of Senegal and their descendants remain French citizens, subject to the military obligations prescribed by the law of 19 October 1915." Later, the decree of 20 November 1932 recognized, in the context of their citizenship, a "reserved civil status," including the state of persons, marriage, successions, donations, and wills" applicable by Muslim or common civil courts. Werner, *Essai sur la réglementation de la nationalité*, 133–40.

148. Under the terms of a local order dating from 6 January 1819, they had retained the right to be judged according to the laws, usages, and customs of their caste, which constituted a personal status for them. Weiss, *Traité théorique et pratique*, 474–77.

149. See Christian Bruschi, "Droit de la nationalité et égalité des droits de 1789 à la fin

du XIXe siècle," in Smaïn Laacher, *Questions de nationalité: histoire et enjeux d'un code* (Paris: Centre d'Information et d'Études sur les Migrations-L'Harmattan, 1987), 58–79.

150. This was the term used by Paul Bourdarie in his introduction to the special issue of *La Revue indigène* devoted to "the naturalization of Muslims in their status." *Revue indigène*, nos. 63–64 (July–August 1911), 403.

151. Bonnichon, *La conversion au christianisme de l'indigène musulman algérien*. See also on this subject Émile Larcher, "Des effets juridiques du changement de religion en Algérie," *RA*, 1910, 1–34.

152. Bonnichon estimates that there were seven hundred of them in Kabylia, and he mentions the presence of a certain number of them in metropolitan France (*La conversion au christianisme de l'indigène musulman algérien*, 12). Jean Bastier gives the figure of two thousand in 1910, in "Le droit colonial et la conversion au christianisme des arabes d'Algérie (1830–1962)," *Annales de l'université des sciences sociales de Toulouse*, 1990, 33–104.

153. Algiers, 5 November 1903, *RA*, 1904, 2.25.

154. Report of the Nationality Commission, *Être Français aujourd'hui et demain*, ed. Marceau Long et al. (Paris: Union Générale d'Éditions, 1988), 115.

155. Werner, *Essai sur la réglementation de la nationalité*, 111–19.

156. Moutet report, 334.

157. One of the seven Crémieux decrees of 24 October 1870 had modified the procedure established by the 1865 senatus-consulte for the Muslims. Decisions on naturalization were made by the governor from then on without any intervention from the central government. But article 3 of the decree required the prior opinion of a consultative committee before the governor declared his position. Since the consultative committee had been eliminated by a decree of 1 January 1871, the decree of 24 October 1870 was understood to be in effect abrogated. See Edgard Rouard de Card, *Étude sur la naturalisation en Algérie* (Paris: Berger-Levrault, 1881), 114–16.

158. Ageron, *Histoire de l'Algérie contemporaine*, vol. 1, 451 n. 3.

159. Albin Rozet (1852–1915) was a Radical deputy from Haute-Marne from 1889 to 1915. Secretary of Algeria's commission to the Chamber of Deputies, he fought as early as 1902 for the rights of Muslims in Algeria.

160. Jean Mélia, *Le triste sort des musulmans indigènes d'Algérie* (Paris: Mercure de France, 1935), 33–34.

161. Henri Doizy (1869–1952) was a Socialist deputy from Ardennes from 1910 to 1919.

162. Maurice Viollette (1870–1960), a lawyer, was deputy mayor of Dreux from 1902

to 1919 and from 1924 to 1930, and finally senator from Eure-et-Loir from 1930 to 1939. One of the Chamber's specialists in colonial affairs, he was governor of Algeria from 1925 to 1927. In 1936 he submitted a bill intended to attribute citizenship to twenty thousand Muslims from the elite.

163. Maurice Viollette, *L'Algérie vivra-t-elle? Notes d'un ancien gouverneur général* (Paris: Félix Alcan, 1931), 425–38.

164. Bonnichon, *La conversion au christianisme de l'indigène musulman algérien*, 14.

165. See the statistical table in the Moutet report, 1919, reprinted in Victor Piquet, *Les réformes en Algérie et le statut des indigènes* (Paris: Émile Larose, 1919), 59–64.

166. *JO*, 21 February 1900, report to the minister of justice on the results of the application of the laws and decrees relative to nationality during 1899, 1198. It should be noted that the rejection of numerous naturalization requests made in Algeria also applied to the Italians, especially the Italian fishermen living in Algeria: they were accused of seeking naturalization only to practice their trade, which was reserved to the French. See *JO*, Déb. Parl. Ch. des Dép., session of 30 January 1899, intervention of Émile Morinaud, 86–89.

167. Decision of 27 October 1910 by the court of appeals of Indochina (Werner, *Essai sur la réglementation de la nationalité*, 45).

168. Zouhir Boushaba, *Être Algérien hier, aujourd'hui et demain* (Algiers: Mimouni, 1992), 45. On the confusion in the use of legal terms in connection with the situation of Algerian Muslims see also Laure Blévis, "Les avatars de la citoyenneté en Algérie coloniale ou les paradoxes d'une catégorisation," *Droit et Société* 48 (2001), 557–80.

169. Cited in Charles-Robert Ageron, "Le mouvement 'Jeune-Algérien' de 1900 à 1923," *Études maghrébines, Mélanges Charles-André Julien* (Paris: Presses Universitaires de France, 1964), 219 n. 4.

170. By the same token, the colonials opposed this extension of military service to Muslims.

171. The professors consulted were Eugène Audinet, Charles de Boeck, Arthur Giraud, Edgard Rouard de Card, and André Weiss. *Revue indigène* (July–August 1911), nos. 63–64. The authors invoke in particular the Muslims' declining practice of customs that differentiated them from the French: in 1911 there were only 55,000 polygamous marriages as compared with 149,000 in 1891. In 1912 fewer than 10 percent of Muslim marriages involved two, three, or four wives (source: Moutet report).

172. Ageron, *Histoire de l'Algérie contemporaine*, 230–32.

173. Marius Moutet (1876–1968), lawyer and founder of the League of the Rights of Man in 1898, was a Socialist deputy from Rhône from 1914 to 1929, then from

Drôme from 1929 to 1940. From 1918 he played a role in all the colonial questions; on 4 June 1936 he was appointed minister of the colonies in the Popular Front government.

174. Moutet report.

175. It was also necessary that he had not been subjected to certain condemnations and that he had lived for more than two years in France or in a French colony or protectorate.

176. Citations from the interventions of Morinaud and Barris du Penher, *Procès-Verbaux des délégations financiers*, May–June 1918. Cited in René Gantois, *L'accession des indigènes algériens à la qualité de citoyen français* (Alger: La Typo-Litho, 1928), 75.

177. Morinaud motion, cited in the report prepared by Marius Moutet in the name of the Commission on Foreign Affairs, Protectorates, and Colonies concerning the bill on the access of native Algerian Muslims to French nationality (hereafter cited as Moutet report 2), annex 4664, *JO*, Doc. Parl. Ch., session of 2 August 1918, 1309.

178. Bill on the access of Muslim Algerian natives to political rights, annex 4663, session of 14 May 1918, *JO*, Doc. Parl. Ch., 613–15.

179. See Charles-Robert Ageron, *RHMC*, April–June 1959, 121–51.

180. Ageron, *Histoire de l'Algérie contemporaine, 1871–1954*, vol. 2, 275. Dominique Colas gives other examples of the restricted application of the law of 1919, especially by the Supreme Court, in "La citoyenneté du risque de la nationalité," *La démocratie en France*, vol. 2, *Les limites*, ed. Marc Sadoun (Paris: Gallimard, 2000), 182–83.

181. Bonnichon, *La conversion au christianisme de l'indigène musulman algérien*, 3.

182. These calculations were based on information from the statistical annual of France.

183. In certain communes, this meant that less than 5 percent of the European population would continue to be represented by two thirds of the municipal council, while more than 95 percent would be represented by only one third.

184. Passerieu motion, in Moutet report 2, 1309.

185. Unpublished letter cited in Ageron, *Histoire de l'Algérie contemporaine*, vol. 2, 1208. Hubert Lyautey (1854–1934) was then the resident general in Rabat.

186. See Guy Pervillé, "La politique algérienne de la France (1830–1964)," in Lydia Flem, *Juger en Algérie 1944–1962* (Paris: Le Seuil, 1997), 27–37.

187. Ahmed Henni, "La naissance d'une classe moyenne paysanne musulmane après la Première Guerre Mondiale," *RFHOM* 83, no. 311 (1996), 47–63.

188. Ageron, *Histoire de l'Algérie contemporaine*, vol. 1, 276.

189. Algerian immigration appeared in metropolitan France at the end of the nineteenth century. On the eve of the First World War an administrative investigation
revealed the presence of four to five thousand Algerians (counted in the census
mostly in Marseille, Pas-de-Calais, and Paris). On these points see Pierre Laroque
and François Ollive, *Le problème de l'émigration des travailleurs nord-africains en
France*, report of the High Committee on the Mediterranean and North Africa,
mimeographed document, March 1938.

190. Stora, *Histoire de l'Algérie coloniale*, 4.

191. See the bill pertaining to the exercise of political rights by certain categories of
French subjects in Algeria, Ch. des Dép. Doc. parl., annex 1596, session of 30
December 1936.

192. See Jean-Louis Planche, "Le projet Blum-Viollette au temps du Front populaire,
et du Congrès musulman," *De Dreux à Alger: Maurice Viollette, 1870–1960*, ed.
Françoise Gaspard, preface by François Mitterrand (Paris: L'Harmattan, 1991),
135–50.

193. The decision made by the prefectoral council in 1929 is reproduced in Viollette,
L'Algérie vivra-t-elle?, 430–36.

194. The law of 5 February 1958 thus instituted a single college.

195. A decree of July 1958 granted the right to vote to Muslim women (Collot, *Les
institutions d'Algérie*, 16–17).

196. Concerning the senatus-consulte of 1865: between 1865 and 1915, 2,396 naturalizations were recorded (see the Moutet report); between 1919 and 1942, 1,176, for
a total of 3,572, to which should be added the naturalization decisions made between 1915 and 1919 and between 1943 and 1962. For the procedure of 1919 there
were a total of 2,395 according to the statistics published each year in *Exposé de
la situation générale de l'Algérie* (Algiers, Publication annuelle du gouvernement
générale de l'Algérie). There were thus a little more than six thousand Algerian
Muslims who had acquired full French nationality by one or the other of the two
procedures and had transmitted it to their children. By an order of 30 December
1907 the Supreme Court had recognized in fact, against the opinion of the court
of Algiers, that the naturalization of the father of a native family carried with it
the naturalization of his minor children. On 23 June 1949 the Supreme Court ruled
that children with just one parent subject to common law status were fully French.
In 1972 the number of Algerian Muslims benefiting from French nationality was
estimated at twenty thousand. *Le Monde*, 26 August and 11 October 1972.

197. According to the terms of the order of 21 July 1962. Finally, the persons subject to
a "particular status" who were not granted Algerian nationality (this was the case
for Jews who had not been included in the Crémieux decree or could not prove
that they had been) remained French. See Lagarde, "La rénovation du Code de la

nationalité," 217–20; see also Simone Massicot, "Effets sur la nationalité française de l'accession à l'indépendance de territoires ayant été sous la souveraineté française," *Population* 3 (1986), 533–46.

198. Source: Depoid, *Les naturalisations en France*, 45.

199. See Isidore Alauzet, *De la qualité de Français, de la naturalisation et du statut personnel des étrangers* (Paris: Marchal, Billard, 1880), 2nd edn., 137.

200. The opinion of the Council of State, designated at the time by the Assembly, was nevertheless required.

201. Article 2 of the law of 29 June 1867.

202. Article 3 of the law of 1889 made the minimum waiting period one year.

203. Naturalized persons who carried out their military service through active duty in the army benefited from a general exception.

204. It seems, however, that one professional ineligibility already existed, dating back to a law of 18 Germinal, Year X: according to article 16 of that law, only someone who was French from birth could be named a bishop. See Despagnet, *Précis de droit international privé*, 299.

205. See Ralph Schor, *L'opinion publique et les étrangers en France, 1919–1939* (Paris: La Sorbonne, 1985), 600–602. In addition, a law of April 1933 limited the practice of medicine to French people alone, or to people who had come from countries that had been placed under a French protectorate, provided that their medical doctorate had been earned in France. When a request for naturalization came from a doctor (or a dental surgeon or a student in medicine or dentistry) it had to be the object of a consultation between the Ministry of Health and the local doctors' or dentists' union, which generally resulted in a negative ruling. See Rémy Estournet, *La pratique de la naturalisation depuis la loi du 10 août 1927* (Montpellier: Imprimerie de la presse, 1937), 5.

206. *JO*, Doc. parl., Ch. des Dép., annex 3,737, report of M. Louis Rolland, 30 June 1934, 1117.

207. Foreigners naturalized by virtue of article 64 of the Nationality Code were relieved of this restriction, however.

208. Stanley Hoffmann, a well-known professor of political science at Harvard University, was in this situation. An Austrian Jew who had come to France with his mother in the mid-1930s, he went through the French school system, survived the war, and became French in 1947. Since he was not eligible to take the entrance examination for the École Nationale d'Administration until 1952, he earned a doctorate in law, took courses at Harvard University, and became a professor there in the late 1950s. See Stanley Hoffmann, "To Be or Not to Be French," *Ideas and Ideals: Essays on Politics in Honor of Stanley Hoffmann*, ed. Linda B. Miller and Michael Joseph Smith (Boulder: Westview, 1993), 19–46.

TABLE 10

Acquisitions of Nationality by Persons Aged 13 to 18 Born in France to Foreign Parents, 1999–2005

	1999	2000	2001	2002	2003	2004	2005	2006
Ages 13–15	19,399	17,593	16,807	18,413	19,160	10,855	19,855	20,301
Ages 16–18	23,034	18,290	14,264	11,869	10,259	9,017	7,403	6,580
TOTAL	42,433	35,883	31,071	30,282	29,419	29,872	27,258	26,881

Source: Ministry of Justice.

Chapter 9: How Does One Become or Remain French?

1. See Olivier Beaud, "Le souverain," *Pouvoirs* 67 (1993), 33–45.
2. They can also become French before that date: children whose parents are naturalized will be included in the parents' naturalization decree.
3. Article 3 of the law of 16 March 1998, article 21.8 of the Civil Code.
4. See table 10.
5. Since acquisitions of nationality at the age of eighteen are automatic, they cannot be counted directly. They can be estimated, however, by counting the number of certificates of nationality delivered to young people when they reach age eighteen (Civil Code, article 21.7).
6. See Ministry of Social Affairs, *La politique de la nationalité en 1993* (Paris: Ministère des Affaires sociales, de la Santé et de la Ville, 1994), 55.
7. See table 18, pp. 405–6.
8. More favorable conditions are provided in Catholic than in Protestant countries: one year of marriage with four years of residency, or two years of marriage with three years of residency in Austria as opposed to ten years for the normal procedure, one year instead of ten in Spain, three instead of ten in Portugal.
9. It should be noted that the declaration takes effect as of the date the application was submitted (in other words retroactively, as it were). In 2005 the average gap between the date of marriage and the application date for a declaration of nationality was seven years and four months, higher for Europeans (nine years and one month) than for Asians (five years and ten months). Source: Sous-direction des naturalisations, *La politique de la nationalité en 2005: données chiffrées et commen-*

taires (Paris: Ministère de l'Emploi et de la Cohésion Sociale, 2005), 61. See table 11.

10. Twenty cases brought before the Council of State, with eighteen favorable rulings and two unfavorable.

11. Ibid. See table 12.

12. This means that someone who comes to the United States with student status and stays four years, for example, and then prolongs his stay with an HB1 visa to work in computer science for six years before getting a green card, can be naturalized only after a minimum of fifteen years' residency.

13. French must also be their native language or else they must have attended schools for at least five years where French was the language of instruction—the latter provision was introduced in the law of 1993.

14. The services were instructed to apply the provisions of article 64 5° only to people from the Seychelles: "for people from other countries or fractions of countries *it would be inappropriate and detrimental to apply these provisions*" (note from the Sous-direction des naturalisations, 23 May 1995).

15. *JO*, Déb. Parl., Senate, 2nd session, 20 June 1961, 595.

16. To be precise, part of St. Kitts and Nevis, Grenada, St. Vincent, Dominica, Tobago, St. Lucia, St. Dominique.

17. Alabama, Arkansas, Illinois, Indiana, Iowa, Kansas, Kentucky, Michigan, Minnesota, Mississippi, Missouri, Montana, Nebraska, North Dakota, South Dakota, Ohio, Oklahoma, Tennessee, Wisconsin, and Wyoming.

18. The areas of Italy involved were Piedmont (1802), Liguria (1802), Parma and Tuscany (1808), and the state of Rome (1810).

19. Catalonia was annexed by a decree of 26 January 1812. The list of territories covered by this provision was the object of an exchange of letters between the Ministry of Social Affairs and the Ministry of Justice on 19 November 1984 and 27 March 1985.

20. Patrick Weil, "Bill Clinton: The French Years," *New York Times*, 10 January 2001.

21. This average length of stay in France is declining, from seventeen years and eight months in 2001, to seventeen years in 2003, to sixteen years and one month in 2004.

22. In the past, for special cases (refugees from Southeast Asia, Jews from Morocco or Tunisia) the administration adopted a more active approach. Between 1978 and 1982 those in this category seem to have been required to request naturalization at the time they requested residency and a work permit, by virtue of a secret agreement known as the Stoléru accords (Archives publiques privées).

23. Such is the "perverse" effect of a provision of memorandum DPM 2000–254 of 12 May 2000, which specifies that "particular attention must be paid to the infor-

TABLE II

Acquisitions of Nationality by Declaration since 1998
on the Basis of Marriage with a French National

	Men	Women	Total
1998	11,842	10,271	22,113
1999	12,559	11,529	24,088
2000	12,925	13,131	26,056
2001	11,243	11,773	23,016
2002	12,513	12,711	25,224
2003	14,768	14,840	29,608
2004	16,441	16,690	33,131
2005	9,964	10,750	20,714
2006	13,765	14,409	28,174

Source: DPM.

TABLE 12

Refusals to Register Declarations of Nationality on the Basis of Article 21.2 of the Civil
Code, 2000–2004

	2000	2001	2002	2003	2004	2005	2006
Declarations recorded	26,056	23,016	25,225	29,608	33,131	20,690	28,175
Refusals to record declarations	1,094	1,462	1,878	3,023	3,408	2,472	3,287
Percentage of examined declarations refused	4.8	6.0	6.9	9.3	9.3	10.7	10.4

Source: Direction de la population et des migrations, Sous-direction des naturalisations.

mation given when foreigners come to the prefecture. The agents responsible for receiving them must not simply hand over the request form along with an information sheet, but must be prepared to offer help in putting together the file." The goal, which was to keep the applicant from having to "come several times to the prefecture or having his file returned to him because it was incomplete," has thus been subverted.

24. Interview with François Galard, underdirector of naturalizations, 13 September 2001. The waiting period varies a great deal between the treatment of "youth" dossiers — which can be handled in a few days — and that of the others — which can take fourteen or fifteen months.

25. Source: population census of 2004. See Catherine Borrel, "Près de 5 millions d'immigrés à la mi-2004," *Insee Première*, no. 1098 (August 2006), 1–4. It was 31.4 percent in 1990 and 36 percent in 1999.

26. Irene Bloemraad, "The North American Naturalization Gap: An Institutional Approach to Citizenship Acquisition in the United States and Canada," *International Migration Review* 36, no. 1 (2002), 195–228.

27. Article 21-25-1 of the Civil Code provides for a maximum wait of eighteen months, which can be extended for three months while the file is being handled.

28. The Council of State was given the exclusive authority to take action against naturalizations by a Supreme Court decision on 1 August 1836; see Isidore Alauzet, *De la qualité de Français, de la naturalisation et du statut personnel des étrangers* (Paris: Imprimerie et Librairie Générale de Jurisprudence, 1880), 152.

29. Georges Olekhnovitch with the collaboration of Christian Quaglia, *La jurisprudence actuelle du Conseil d'État en matière d'acquisition, de retrait et de perte de la nationalité française*, Ministère des Affaires Sociales, de la Santé et de la Ville, Direction de la population et des migrations, Sous-direction des naturalisations, February 1994.

30. Directive of 28 February 2000, 1. This directive dealing with naturalization, reintegration, and loss of French nationality by a decision of the public authorities was issued by Martine Aubry, minister of employment and solidarity.

31. In a memorandum dated 17 October 2000 (DPM/SDN, no. 2000/530), the ministry set forth its decision to simplify and accelerate the naturalization of young people between the ages of eighteen and twenty-five who had arrived in France before the age of six and had had all their schooling there. The young people in this category were exempt from the interview intended to verify their assimilation, and from the police background check. Their files were given priority as soon as they were transmitted to the Naturalization Bureau. The success of the procedure can probably be explained by its simplicity but perhaps also by the end of obligatory national service, which in the past deterred many young men from requesting

naturalization before the age of thirty (at the time, avoiding national service was very often a reason for deferring the request). But this priority treatment also led to a slowdown in the treatment of other files, and the Ministry of the Interior had reservations about eliminating police background checks. This decision was abrogated by memorandum no. 2003-418 of 1 September 2003. Source: Sous-direction des naturalisations.

32. Ben Mansour decision, 5 May 1999.

33. Directive of 28 February, 9.

34. See for example Conseil d'État, 30 March 1984, Ministre des Affaires Sociales et de la Solidarité Nationale c/M. Abecassis, no. 40735.

35. Source: Sous-direction des naturalisations, "Acquisitions et pertes de la nationalité française," annual report, 2005. The decrease in percentage reflects an increase of applicants after only a few months of residence owing to a better knowledge of the special provision mentioned above, p. 231.

36. Bruno Maresca and Isabelle Van de Walle, *Les caractéristiques socio-économiques des naturalisés* (Paris: Centre de recherche pour l'étude et l'observation des conditions de vie [CREDOC], 1998).

37. Ibid., 43.

38. Source: statistical reports, Haut Conseil à l'intégration.

39. The agreement of 6 May 1963 "relating to the reduction of cases of plurinationality" has been replaced by a Council of Europe agreement dated 6 November 1997, which is much more open in this area.

40. See Karen Knop, "Relational Nationality: On Gender and Nationality in International Law," *Citizenship Today: Global Perspectives and Practices*, ed. T. Alexander Aleinikoff and Douglas Klusmeyer (Washington: Carnegie Endowment for International Peace, 2001), 89–124.

41. In the absence of government authorization, they would also lose it if they accepted civil service positions abroad, entered into relationships with any foreign corporation that presupposed distinctions by birth, or settled in another country "without the idea of returning" (Civil Code, article 17).

42. Fearing the effects of this measure, moreover, many people born on the left bank of the Rhine, who were thus formally French, gave up their positions in the service of the Prussian or Austrian state. On this point see Andreas Fahrmeir, "National Colours and National Identity in Early Nineteenth Century German," *Napoleon's Legacy: Problems of Government in Restoration Europe*, ed. David Laven and Lucy Riall (Oxford: Berg, 2000).

43. Claude Goasguen, "Les Français au service de l'étranger sous le Premier Empire: législation et pratique" (LL.D. diss., University of Paris II, 1976), 133–39.

44. The law of 1927 specified that authorization was required if the man was at least

twenty-one and if he had begun his active military service no more than ten years earlier.

45. National Assembly, 1952 session, report no. 4485 by Deputy Henri Lacaze, in the name of the commission on justice, and the legislation regarding the bill modifying ordinance no. 45-2441 of 19 October 1945, annexed to the minutes of the meeting of 24 October 1952, 2.

46. Paul Lagarde, *La nationalité française*, 3rd edn. (Paris: Dalloz, 1997), 150–51.

47. Ninety-six persons repudiated their French nationality in 2000, in application of article 23 of the Civil Code.

48. In certain countries, where French law speaks of withdrawal (*retrait*), the term revocation (*déchéance*) is used instead. Different terminologies also exist to designate déchéance in other countries.

49. In the United States a federal court had ruled in 1890 that even in the absence of explicit legislation, the federal government could take a naturalized person to court in view of obtaining an annulment of the naturalization in cases of fraud: U.S. v. Norsch 42 F. 417. Even today, American law allows denaturalization on the basis of article 15 of the law of 1906; no time limit is set for this procedure, but it is subject to strict control by the Supreme Court. See T. Alexander Aleinikoff, David A. Martin, and Hiroshi Motomura, *Immigration Process and Policy*, 3rd edn. (St. Paul: West, 1993), 1015–45.

50. Today, by virtue of article 27-2 of the Civil Code, naturalization can be withdrawn by decree within a one-year period if the naturalized person proves not to satisfy the legal conditions. In case of fraud the decision to withdraw naturalization can be made within a period of two years after the fraud is discovered, thus without a time limit with respect to the naturalization decree. See Lagarde, *La nationalité française*, 141–44.

51. This rule, applicable in civil law to prevent conditional donations, for example, is thus invoked by the Socialist deputy Auguste Reynaud in the discussion of the law of 1927 (*JO*, Déb Ch., 31 March 1927, 1212).

52. John L. Cable, *Loss of Citizenship, Denaturalization, the Alien in Wartime* (Washington: National Law Book, 1943).

53. For a comparison of the provision on revocation (*déchéance*) in other legislation see Catherine Kessedjan, "Un fondement international au droit des déchéances," *Les bons sentiments, Le Genre humain*, no. 29 (1995), 149–62.

54. See Jules Valéry, *La nationalité française: commentaire de la loi du 10 août 1927* (Paris: LGDJ, 1927), 74–75.

55. See Robert Kiefe, *La nationalité des personnes dans l'Empire britannique* (Paris: Arthur Rousseau, 1926), 69–80.

56. *JO*, Déb. parl., Ch. des Dép., session of 28 January 1915, 9. Jules Delahaye (1851–

1925), Boulangist deputy from Indre-et-Loire from 1889 to 1903, then deputy from Maine-et-Loire from 1907 to 1919, had become famous for getting a commission created to investigate the Panama scandal. In 1906 he had been the driving force behind the "Catholic Resistance League," which sought without much success to bring Catholics together on the political level. He abstained from ratifying the Versailles treaty, which had the disadvantage, according to him, of leaving Germany unified.

57. At the Senate's request, the law of 7 April 1915 also provided for a review of the 758 naturalizations granted after 1 January 1913; 94 were withdrawn. See Maurice Bernard, annex 2291, Doc. parl. Ch., session of 7 July 1916, 1057 n. 1.

58. Taking into account the German legislation according to which any return, even for tourism, suspended the period of ten years' residency abroad that brought about, according to a German law of 1870, automatic loss of German nationality for German expatriates, the administration judged that all Germans who returned to Germany regularly could be viewed as having kept their German nationality; the Council of State did not agree.

59. See Maurice Bernard, annex 2291, 1057.

60. Ninety-four persons had their nationality withdrawn by virtue of article 2 of the law of 7 April 1915, twenty-nine by virtue of article 1, and 427 by virtue of the law of 1917; the files of the last group had been investigated under the regime of the law of 1915. See Pierre Depoid, *Les naturalisations en France (1870–1940)* (Paris: Imprimerie Nationale, 1942), 42–43, and Maurice Bernard, annex 2291.

61. See Georges Gruffy, "La naturalisation et le préjugé de la race," *RPP* (1919), 8 n. 3. For partial information on these cases see also AD, CAC n. 324.

62. Chamber of Deputies, eleventh legislature, annex 511 to the minutes of the meeting of 14 January 1915, bill designed to modify the conditions of naturalization, Jean Lerolle, deputy.

63. Source: AMJ.

64. Report of Frédéric Eccard on the bill concerning the withdrawal of the quality of being French. Doc. parl. Senate, 7 December 1922, no. 734. See the correspondence between Eccard and the Ministry of Justice in CAC 19950165/10.

65. The decisions of the Supreme Court, which recognized the applicability of foreign law in cases of divorce or child custody — see Géraud de Geouffre de la Pradelle, "Nationalité française, extranéité, nationalités étrangères," *Mélanges dédiés à Dominique Holleaux* (Paris: Litec, 1990), 134–55 — or the functional approach of the positive clash of nationalities defended recently by Paul Lagarde (in relation to the Dujacque decision of the 1st Civil Chamber, 22 July 1987, RE DP 1988.29), can thus be perfectly inscribed within this French conception of dual nationality, contrary to what Yves Lequette indicates in "La nationalité française dévaluée,"

L'avenir du droit: mélanges en hommage à François Terré (Paris: Presses Universitaires de France/Dalloz, 1999), 350–92.

66. British law still allows for revocation in three instances: if during the five-year period following naturalization, the person has been sentenced to prison for a period of more than one year, unless that person would then become stateless; in cases of fraud; finally, in cases of lack of loyalty to the sovereign or connivance with the enemy during a war (British Nationality Act, section 40). See Nicholas Blake, "British Nationality Law," Le droit de la nationalité dans l'Union européenne, ed. Bruno Nascimbene (Milan: Butterworths and Giuffré, 1996), 708, 742–43.

67. Beyond the ten-year waiting period after the issuance of the naturalization decree, as provided in the law of 1927, or the ten-year period after the offending incident, as provided by the decree of 1938, it indicated that all acquisitions of nationality granted since 1927 could be contested.

68. The idea of revocation for unworthiness is found in the decree of 27 April 1848, which attached that sanction to slave trading, and which remained in force for nearly a century, until the ordinance of 18 October 1945. See Henri Batiffol, Traité élémentaire de droit international privé (Paris: LGDF, 1949), 149. That automatic revocation prevented the descendants of a certain Repaire de Truffin, for example, from claiming the quality of being French in 1928 (AD, Contentieux, Affaires diverses, 377).

69. Ministry of Justice, Direction of Civil Affairs and the Seal, Commentaire de la loi du 10 août 1927 sur la nationalité, Paris, 14 August 1927, 3.

70. Source: Depoid, Les naturalisations en France, 45. The statistics on revocation of nationality are found in Liste alphabétique des personnes ayant acquis ou perdu la nationalité française par décret, années 1921–1930, 1931–1940, 1941–1950, 1951–1960 (Paris: Imprimerie Nationale, 1931, 1941, 1951, 1961).

71. Gérard Noiriel, in Les origines républicaines de Vichy (Paris: Hachette Littératures, 1999), defends the continuity of Vichy's policy with that of the Third Republic from a different standpoint. It should also be noted that under Vichy the procedure for revocation between 1927 and 1938 was maintained by the services for the cases that fit the framework of these texts; these procedures concerned more than one hundred persons, whose revocations of nationality, unlike naturalizations, were not annulled after Liberation.

72. This passage draws heavily upon Janine Ponty, Polonais méconnus: histoire des travailleurs immigrés en France dans l'entre-deux guerres (Paris: La Sorbonne, 1988), 196–97, 297–99.

73. Ponty reports that in Pas-de-Calais seventy foreigners, including fifty-three Poles, were expelled in 1931 for political reasons, and ninety, including sixty-eight Poles, were expelled in 1932.

74. Cass., Chambre Civile, 7 March 1933 (1st ruling) Dal. D.H. 1933 217.

75. After spending eleven years in Moscow and on the eastern front, he returned to Poland in 1945 and played a leading role in party politics; he died in 1959.

76. CAC 19950165/10, letter from the Office of Civil Affairs and the Seal to the Ministry of the Interior, 14 December 1948. The response from the minister of justice incited the Ministry of the Interior to prudence, recalling that article 98-4 I° "[presupposed] that three conditions [had] been fulfilled: 1° acts to the profit of a foreign state; 2° acts incompatible with the quality of being French; 3° acts prejudicial to France's interests," and that the Council of State, whose concurrence was required, was the body that would assess whether those conditions had all been met.

77. Between 1947 and 1953, 143 open files were classified as tabled by the Ministry of Justice (for example, those of Communist militants); 560 were submitted for the approval of the Council of State, which rejected 81 of them (Archives de la Sous-direction des naturalisations).

78. AN, F1a3255.

79. See table 13.

80. Since 1938 the possibility of revocation for disloyalty has been extended in addition to any French person who has a foreign nationality. The current legislation thus specifies that any French person "who *behaves in fact like a national of a foreign country* can, *if he or she has the nationality of that country*, be declared, with the concurrence of the Council of State, to have lost the quality of being French" (Civil Code, article 23-7; emphasis added).

TABLE 13

Procedure for Deprivation of French Citizenship

Article of the Nationality Code	Discontinuance of proceedings	Opinion of the Council of State	Included in a decree
96	40	158	149
981	34	181	151
983	7	77	73
984	72	86	60
985	8	58	46
TOTAL	161	560	479

Source: ASDN.

81. Dautet report, BB30/1741.

82. See bill no. 3053 presented by André Honnorat, Chamber of Deputies, 23 February 1917.

83. This was not the case up to then, which means that in the course of a trial in which it became important to determine nationality for the application of a given rule of law, an Assize Court or another penal jurisdiction could settle the question by declaring Mr. X. to be French, while before another tribunal he could be declared to be a foreigner.

84. See Joseph Champcommunal, "Une réforme législative nécessaire: la preuve de la nationalité à organiser," *Revue du droit international privé*, 1919, 234; Georges Gruffy, "Nationalisation et francisation," *Journal de Clunet* 43 (1916), 1106, 1526; Édouard Lévy, "L'état civil et la nationalité," *RPP* 103 (April 1920), 108.

85. AN, 50AP27, letter from Georges Gruffy to André Honnorat, 6 August 1926.

86. Memorandum of 12 October 1941, AMJ.

87. See Jacques Maury, "Les lois récentes sur la nationalité. II. Les droits réservés à certains Français," *La Semaine juridique: Études doctrinales*, no. 169, 11.40 (November 1940).

88. The judge must consult the chancellery only in three cases: if nationality has been acquired through the tacit option (a child born in France to foreign parents who has not made a declaration before reaching majority); if a person has enlisted voluntarily in the army; if a foreign woman married to a French man declares that she has become French through her marriage.

89. This means that if a question of nationality is raised in a trial (except in an Assize Court), the tribunal must abstain from ruling and refer the case to a justice of the peace.

90. If a person invokes his or her quality of being French to prevent an order of expulsion from being applied to him or her, the responsibility for proving nationality falls upon that person.

91. Maury, Faculté de droit de Toulouse. Droit international privé, 3e année, cours professé par M. Maury, 1945–46, 57.

92. These departments constituted the territories annexed to the German Empire and were returned to France by the treaty of Versailles.

93. Out of a population of 1,831,000 in 1910, residents originating in Alsace-Moselle numbered 1,082,000. There were 513,000 German immigrants, chiefly from eastern Prussia, whose move had been encouraged by the Empire; 183,000 foreigners; and 183,000 persons born of mixed marriages.

94. The treaty provided for the possibility of claiming French nationality by declaration (available to descendants and spouses of French nationals, any person born

before 1871 to foreign parents and that person's descendants, and Germans enrolled in Allied armies); the request, which had to be made at the *tribunal de bailliage* before 15 January 1921, could be denied on an individual basis. Finally, the other inhabitants of the region — mostly of German origin — could often take advantage of a less rigorous naturalization procedure if they had arrived in Alsace-Moselle before 1914 and been legal residents there during the three years following the armistice of 11 November 1918. Other foreigners were subject to the normal naturalization procedure then in force — ten years of residency in France counting from the date of the armistice.

95. See Report no. 1676, annexed to the session of 28 April 1971, by Raymond Zimmermann, intended to complete the provisions of article 7 of the law of 22 December 1961 pertaining to the recognition of French nationality in persons born in the departments of Haut-Rhin, Bas-Rhin, and Moselle before 11 November 1918, 8.

96. See memo no. 94/16, 27 June 1994, BO Justice no. 54, 1 April–30 June 1994.

97. See Cass. 1st civ., 22 March 1960, *JCP* 61 II 1 1917).

98. Law no. 95-125 of 8 February 1995 transferred the authority to deliver certificates of nationality from civil court judges to head clerks; the authority in question is administrative and not jurisdictional.

99. See Lagarde, *La nationalité française*, 246.

100. Memorandum no. 98/14, 20 August 1995, pertaining to the modalities through which the law of 16 March 1998 would go into effect (*JO*, 21 August 1998).

101. The writer Jacques Laurent has recounted the ordeals that the judge of the sixth arrondissement in Paris put him through when he was simply trying to renew his identity card ("Jacques Laurent est-il français?," *Le Monde*, 11 July 1985).

102. See Philippe Bernard, "Afin de lutter contre la multiplication des contrefaçons et falsifications, la carte d'identité informatisée sera généralisée en 1995," *Le Monde*, 4 February 1994, 10.

103. In 1991, after a memorandum specified that it was possible to request a certificate of nationality in cases of "serious doubt" at the time one requested a renewal of one's national identity card, there were a number of incidents. See Philippe Bernard, "Français suspects," *Le Monde*, 27 May 1992, 10.

104. Philippe Bernard, "Le renouvellement de la carte d'identité est devenu une course d'obstacles," *Le Monde*, 6 February 1996, 9.

105. Since 1995 the chief clerk rather than the civil court judge has been the one who delivers certificates of nationality, and the conditions of delivery have been improved owing to a recent memorandum (no. 98/17, 24 December 1998). The fact remains that French nationals who are not French through filiation find it more difficult to prove their nationality than others do.

Conclusion

1. On Sumner see David H. Donald, *Charles Sumner and the Rights of Man* (New York: Alfred A. Knopf, 1970); see also Auguste Laugel, "Le sénateur Charles Sumner, un homme d'État américain," *Revue des Deux Mondes*, 15 June 1874, 721–49.

2. Francis Lieber (1798–1872), a jurist and a professor of law and political economics at the University of South Carolina (1835–56), Columbia College (1857–65), and Columbia Law School (1865–72), wrote most notably *The Political Ethics, Nationalism and Internationalism* (New York: Charles Scribner, 1868). For the United States government he wrote what was to become the first legal code of war. See Franck Freidel, *Francis Lieber: Nineteenth Century Liberal* (Baton Rouge: Louisiana State University Press, 1947).

3. See Bernard Crick, *American Science of Politics: Its Origins and Conditions* (London: Routledge and Kegan Paul, 1959), 15–18.

4. Charles Sumner papers, microfilms, box 84, letter dated 8 March 1872, Library of Congress.

5. See Donald, *Charles Sumner*, 149.

6. Congressional Globe, 38th Congress, 1st session, pp. 1488–89, cited in Donald, *Charles Sumner*, 151.

7. Cited in Donald, *Charles Sumner*, 149.

8. He added: "When a monarch extends his dominion by conquest, he soon learns to consider his old and new subjects on the same footing; because, in reality, all his subjects are to him the same. . . . The provinces of absolute monarchies are always better treated than those of free states." David Hume, "That Politics May Be Reduced to a Science," 1777, in *Moral and Political Philosophy*, ed. H. D. Aiken (New York: Hafner, 1948), 298–99, cited in Peter Sahlins, *Boundaries: The Making of France and Spain in the Pyrenees* (Berkeley: University of California Press, 1989), 113.

9. David Blackbourn, *Fontana History of Germany, 1780–1918: The Long Nineteenth Century* (London: Fontana, 1997), 261–62.

10. Philippe Bernard, "Le renouvellement de la carte d'identité est devenu une course d'obstacles," *Le Monde*, 6 February 1996, 9.

11. Cf. Patrick Weil, "The History and Memory of Discrimination in the Domain of French Nationality: The Case of Jews and Algerian Muslims," *Hagar* 6, no. 1 (spring 2005), 49–75.

12. On the Crémieux decree and its effects on the relation between Algerian Jews and France, see Jacques Derrida, *Monolinguism of the Other; or, the Prosthesis of Ori-*

gin, 2nd edn., trans. Patrick Mensah (Stanford: Stanford University Press, 1998), 14–18.

13. Benjamin Stora, *Le transfert d'une mémoire: de l'"Algérie française" au racisme anti-arabe* (Paris: La Découverte, 1999).

Glossary

1. According to law no. 95-125 of 8 February 1995.

2. On this subject see François Terré, "Réflexions sur la notion de nationalité," *RCDIP* 64, no. 2 (April–June 1975), 194–214.

3. See Peter Sahlins, *Unnaturally French: Foreign Citizens in the Old Regime and After* (Ithaca: Cornell University Press, 2004).

4. Paris: Auguste Durand, 1845, 149–50.

5. Antonin Dubost, "Rapport sur la nationalité," Chambre des Députés, no. 2083, 7 November 1887, 25.

6. See Tronchet in the debates over the Civil Code (chapter 1).

7. See Yann Thomas, "Le droit d'origine à Rome: contribution à l'étude de la citoyenneté," *RCDIP* 84, no. 2 (April–June 1995), 253–90.

8. *État, nation, et immigration: vers une histoire du pouvoir* (Paris: Belin, 2001), 150.

9. London: Peltier, 1807, book 14, 395.

10. Oscar Bloch and Walther von Wartburg, *Dictionnaire étymologique*, 4th edn. (Paris: Presses Universitaires de France, 1964). See Anne Lefebvre-Teillard, "Jus sanguinis: l'émergence d'un principe (Éléments d'histoire de la nationalité française)," *RCDIP* 82, no. 2 (April–June 1993), 223–50.

11. Copy of the report addressed by the mayor of the city of Bastia to the review council on 11 August 1821 (AN, F9/170).

12. Benoît Guiguet, "Citoyenneté et nationalité: limites de la rupture d'un lien" (Ph.D. diss., European University Institute, Fiesole, 1997), 52.

13. Vol. 1, 3rd edn., enlarged (Dijon: Victor Lagier, 1842).

14. Paris: Maresque aîné, 1847.

15. I thank Serge Slama for pointing this out to me.

16. Eugène Pierre, *Traité de droit politique, électoral et parlementaire*, 842.

17. S. de Dainville-Barbiche, "Les archives du sceau, naturalisations, mariages, changements de nom, titres," *Gazette des Archives*, nos. 160–61 (1993), 127–51.

18. Georges Tessier, "L'audience du sceau," *Bibliothèque de l'École des Chartes* (1951).

19. Note from Joseph Barthélemy to Marshal Pétain (AN, BB 30 1707).

MAPS AND DOCUMENTS

MAP I

The Extension of French Territory during the Revolutionary and Imperial Periods.

Source: Jacques Godechot, *Les institutions de la France sous la Révolution et l'Empire* (Paris: Presses Universitaires de France, 1951; 5th edn., 1998).

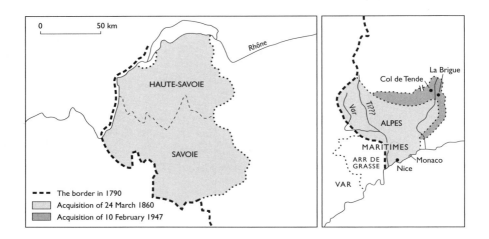

MAP 2

The Southeastern Border, 1790–1947

The Alpes-Maritimes department was established by combining the county
of Nice (annexed in 1860) with the arrondissement of Grasse (detached from
the Var department).

Source: *Atlas historique de la France contemporaine (1800–1965)* (Paris: Armand Colin, 1966).

The Loss of Alsace-Moselle: 1870–1918
——— The border in 1869
- - - The border in 1871
· · · · Borders of the annexed departments
▨ Former department of Moselle
▢ Former department of Meurthe
▨ Region where German was taught in schools in 1870

MAP 3

The Loss of Alsace-Moselle, 1870–1918

The arrondissement of Belfort, detached from the Haut-Rhin
department when the department was annexed, was established
as the territory of Belfort and created as a department.

The cantons of Schirmeck and Saales, which had belonged to
the former Vosges department and were annexed to Germany in 1871,
were reattached to the Bas-Rhin department in 1918.

Map prepared by G. Dupeux, based on *Histoire de la Lorraine* (Nancy:
Berger-Levrault, 1939).

Source: *Atlas historique de la France contemporaine (1800–1965)*
(Paris: Armand Colin, 1966).

Institut für Staatsforschung
an der Universität Berlin
Direktor: Prof. Dr. Höhn.

Auf Schreiben vom 7.10.1943
III A.3 - 803 - 151/43 -

Berlin-Wannsee, den 16.10.1943
Königstr. 71
Fernruf, 807083

Betr.: Stellungnahme zum Entwurf eines franz. Staats-
angehörigkeitsgesetzes.

Brigadeführer L.

Ich habe auf Anforderung des Amtes III zum Entwurf eines franz.
Staatsangehörigkeitsgesetzes wie folgt Stellung genommen:

I. Der Entwurf und das geltende franz. Staatsangehörigkeitsrecht.

Der Entwurf verwirklicht weder bestimmte, von völkischen Gesichtspunkten an ein modernes Staatsangehörigkeitsrecht zu stellende
Anforderungen, noch bringt er irgendwelche Neuerungen, die vom
Standpunkt des geltenden, formal staatlich ausgerichteten franz.
Staatsangehörigkeitsrechtes bemerkenswert sind. Er führt viel-
mehr das franz. Staatsangehörigkeitsrecht grundsätzlich auf den
vor dem Erlass des Staatsangehörigkeitsgesetzes vom 10.8.1927
geltenden Rechtszustand zurück.

Ziel des Entwurfs ist im wesentlichen die Beseitigung der
Erleichterungen, die durch das Staatsangehörigkeitsgesetz vom
10.8.1927 im Einbürgerungsverfahren zur Erhöhung der Zahl der
franz. Staatsangehörigen geschaffen worden waren. Gleichzeitig
verarbeitet der Entwurf die seit 1927 erfolgten vom Standpunkt der
Besatzungsmacht uninteressanten Novellierungen zum franz. Staatsangehörigkeitsrecht mit einer bemerkenswerten Ausnahme: Das
Gesetz vom 28.2.1941, das die Grundlage für die Aberkennung der
Staatsangehörigkeit der Dissidenten bildet, ist nicht eingearbeitet

SS Brigadeführer   Der Entwurf stellt also keine Neuschöpfung des franz. Staats-
Ohlendorf   angehörigkeitsrechtes dar. Mit der Rückführung des franz.
Berlin S. 68   Staatsangehörigkeitsrechtes auf den im Jahre 1927 geltenden
Wilhelmstr. 102   Rechtszustand reiht er sich in die von Marschall Petain befolgte
                     Generallinie ein, unter Beseitigung der Rechtsschöpfung, die

FIGURES 1.1–1.5

Note from the Institut für Staatsforschung of the University of Berlin
proposing the rejection of the Vichy government's nationality bill
(7 October 1943), with translation.

Source: CARAN — AJ40/547.

für die franz. Volksfrontregierung typisch waren, das formale
kleinbürgerliche Verfassungsrecht der Republik mit einer
konservativen Grundhaltung, dem typischen Zeichen des be-
sitzenden Bürgertums fortzubilden.

II. Der Entwurf und die Interessen des Deutschen Reiches.

Die mit übersandte Stellungnahme zum Entwurf eines franz.
Staatsangehörigkeitsgesetzes stellt die Bestimmungen des
Entwurfes, die deutsche Interessen berühren, m.E. richtig und
mit einer Ausnahme erschöpfend zusammen: Das Interesse des
Reiches erfordert m.E. auch eine vom gegenwärtigen franz.
Staatsangehörigkeitsrecht abweichende Regelung der Staatsangehörigkeitsverhältnisse der Kinder, die von deutschen Soldaten während des gegenwärtigen Krieges in Frankreich mit Frauen
franz. Staatsangehörigkeit erzeugt werden.

Nach den zu ergreifenden Massnahmen müssen die deutsche
Interessen berührenden Bestimmungen des Entwurfs eines franz.
Staatsangehörigkeitsgesetzes in zwei Gruppen aufgegliedert
werden:

1. Bestimmungen, die die Interessen des Reiches als kriegsführen-
de Macht berühren und bis zu ihrer Änderung die Aufrechterhal-
tung des gegen den Entwurf vorsorglich eingelegten deutschen
Einspruchs erfordern:

a) Der Entwurf und die Einbürgerung von Juden. Der Entwurf
schliesst an keiner Stelle die Angehörigkeit der jüdischen
Rasse vom Erwerb der franz. Staatsangehörigkeit aus. Auch
in Zukunft kann also nach dem Entwurf jeder Jude bei Er-
füllung der sonstigen Voraussetzungen die franz. Staatsangehörigkeit erwerben.

Eine solche Neukodofikation in einem unter deutscher Be-
satzungshoheit stehenden Lande widerspricht m.E. sowohl
dem unmittelbaren militärischen als auch den aussenpoli-
tischen Interessen des Reiches.

b) Der Entwurf und die Staatsangehörigkeitsverhältnisse der
Dissidenten. Der Entwurf lässt eine Bestimmung vermissen,
die eine klare gesetzliche Grundlage für die Aberkennung
der Staatsangehörigkeit der Dissidenten schafft. Nach Ar-
tikel 12 § 1 Ziff. 1 des Entwurfs kann die franz. Staatsangehörigkeit zwar Franzosen aberkannt werden, die einer
ausländischen Macht unterstehen oder sich ihr unterstellen.
Da die Dissidenten aber von unsern Feinden völkerrechtlich
als freie franz. Macht anerkannt sind - Sowjetrussland hat
den Befreiungsausschuss in Algier sogar als die einzige Ver-
treterin der franz. Republik anerkannt - kann die gegenwärtige
Fassung des § 12 Abs. 1 Ziff. 1 des Entwurfs den Attentisten
in der Vichy-Regierung nur allzu leicht zur Behauptung Anlass
geben, die von der deutschen Besatzungsmacht unwidersprochene
Fassung des § 12 Abs. 1 Ziff. 1 gebe in Zukunft keine Mög-
lichkeit, die Staatsangehörigkeit der Dissidenten abzuerkennen.
In der gleichen Linie liegt, dass die Bestimmungen der Art.
13 § 1, 14 § 3 Abs. 2 und 14 § 3 Abs. 3 des Entwurfs, die
Erleichterungen für die Wiedereinbürgerung ehemaliger franz.
Staatsangehörigen vorsehen, auch weiterhin auf Dissidenten und
ihre Angehörigen, die die franz. Staatsangehörigkeit aufgrund
des Gesetzes vom 28.8.1940 verloren haben, anwendbar sind.
Auch hier erfordert m.E. das Interesse des Reiches als krieg-
führende Macht eine klare gesetzliche Grundlage, die die Aberkennung der Staatsangehörigkeit der Franzosen, die auf Seiten
der militärischen Gegner des Reiches kämpfen oder sie sonstwie
unterstützen, ermöglicht und die Anwendung der Bestimmungen
über die erleichterte Wiedereinbürgerung ehemaliger Franzosen
auf Dissidenten und ihre Angehörigen - wenigstens bis zu
einem bestimmten Zeitpunkt nach Friedensschluss - ausschliesst.
                    die
Bestimmungen, die zwar biologischen Interessen des deutschen Volkes
berühren, zweckmässigerweise aber nicht bei der Neukodifizierung des
franz. Staatsangehörigkeitsrechtes durch das Reich als Besatzungsmacht beanstandet, sondern im Zusammenhang mit der grundsätzlichen

Regelung der Stellung Auslandsdeutscher in Frankreich anlässlich
der Friedensverhandlungen endgültig geregelt werden sollen.

Wie das bisherig franz. Staatsangehörigkeitsrecht folgt
auch der Entwurf weitgehend dem jus soli - Prinzip.

Eine Reihe hierauf zurückgehender Bestimmungen des Entwurfs
wird naturgemäss den Anforderungen, die das Reich an die Erhal-
tung der in den angrenzenden europäischen Staaten wohnenden Volks-
deutschen zu stellen hat, nicht gerecht. Sie erfüllen auch nicht
die Forderungen, die das Reich hinsichtlich der Regelung der
Staatsangehörigkeitsverhältnisse der Kinder stellen muss, die
von deutschen Soldaten während des gegenwärtigen Krieges mit
Frauen franz. Staatsangehörigkeit - zumindest in den blutmässigen
germanischen Provinzen Frankreichs - erzeugt werden.

Für die zweckmässige Regelung der staatsrechtlichen Stellung
der deutschen Volksgruppen in den angrenzenden europäischen
Staaten sowie der von deutschen Soldaten während des Krieges mit
Frauen nichtdeutscher Staatsangehörigkeit erzeugten Kinder werden
die mit den bisherigen Einzelregelungen gewonnenen Erfahrungen
von grosser Bedeutung sein. Da dieser ganze Fragenkreis bei
Friedensschluss oder in nachfolgenden Staatsverträgen wenn auch
nicht übereinstimmen, so doch nach einheitlichen Gesichtspunkten geregelt werden muss, halte ich es für u zweckmässig, bei Behandlung
des vorliegenden Entwurfs eines franz. Staatsangehörigkeitsgesetzes auf diese Fragen abzuheben und die Zustimmung des Reiches
als Besatzungsmacht zum Entwurf von der Aufnahme entsprechender
Bestimmungen abhängig zu machen. Mit unserm Siege werden diese
Fragen von selbst die Regelung finden, die wir wünschen.

III. Vorschlag:

Das RSHA schlägt dem Herrn Militärverwaltungschef in Paris vor,
die Zurückziehung des gegen den Entwurf eines franz. Staatsangehörigkeitsgesetzes vorsorglich eingelegten deutschen Einspruchs von
der Aufnahme ergänzender Bestimmungen abhängig zu machen, die

1. die Einbürgerung von Juden in Zukunft unmöglich machen,
2. eine klare gesetzliche Grundlage für die Aberkennung der franz.
   Staatsangehörigkeit der Dissidenten sowie die Ausschliessung
   der Anwendung der Bestimmungen über die erleichterte Einbürgerung ehemaliger Franzosen auf Dissidenten und ihre Angehörigen
   schaffen.

Der dem Amt III z.H. von SS Obersturmbannführer Dr. Gengenbach
übersandten Stellungnahme ist eine vom Institut angefertigte deutsche
Übersetzung des Entwurfs eines franz. Staatsangehörigkeitsgesetzes
beigeschlossen.

> Heil Hitler!
>
> Ihr sehr ergebener
>
> gez. Hofmann.

Copy of copy.

Institute for State Research	Berlin-Wannsee, 16 Oct. 1943
at the University of Berlin	Königstr. 71
Director: Prof. Dr. Höhn	Telephone 807083

Re. your letter of Oct. 7, 1943	*Subj.*: Position statement on the
III A 3 – 803 – 151/43 –	Draft of a French Nationality Act

Brigade Leader,

At the request of Office III, I have taken a position on the Draft of a French Nationality Act as follows:

I. THE DRAFT AND CURRENT FRENCH NATIONALITY LAW.

The draft does not fulfill certain prerequisites for a modern nationality law from ethnic points of view, nor does it offer any significant innovations as compared with the current, procedurally state-oriented French nationality law. Rather, it takes the law back, in effect, to its status prior to the passage of the Nationality Act of 10 August 1927.

The *goal of the draft*, essentially, is to do away with the measures for simplifying the naturalization process that were introduced in the Nationality Act of 10 August 1927 to increase the number of French citizens. At the same time, the draft assimilates the amendments to the French Nationality Act passed since 1927, which are uninteresting from the viewpoint of the occupying power with one notable *exception*: The act passed on 28 February 1941, which forms the legal basis on which dissidents can be deprived of their citizenship, has not been incorporated.

ss Brigade Leader
Ohlendorf
Berlin S7 68
Wilhelmstr. 102

Thus, the draft does not represent a reform of French nationality law. In taking French nationality law back to its 1927 status, it follows Marshal Pétain's general policy of continuing to develop the Republic's procedural constitutional law along conservative lines as it affects the lower middle classes, the typical hallmark of a property-owning bourgeoisie, doing away with the legal innovations that had typified the French Popular Front government.

II. THE DRAFT AND THE INTERESTS OF THE GERMAN REICH.

The position statement on the Draft of a French Nationality Act that you sent along lists correctly and exhaustively, in my opinion, the provisions of the draft that affect German interests, with one exception: In my opinion, the interests of the Reich also call for changing the provision under existing French nationality law pertaining to the nationality of children begotten during the present war by German soldiers in France with women of French nationality.

As for the measures to be taken, the provisions of the Draft of a French Nationality Act affecting German interests must be differentiated into two groups:

1. *Provisions that affect the interests of the Reich as a warring power and require the preemptive lodging of German objections to the draft until they are changed:*

a) *The draft and the naturalization of Jews.* Nowhere does the draft rule out the acquisition of French citizenship by members of the Jewish race. Thus, even in the future, according to the draft, any Jew who meets the other requirements can acquire French citizenship.

In my opinion, such a revision of the code in a country under German occupation and sovereignty conflicts with the immediate military interests as well as the foreign-policy interests of the Reich.

b) *The draft and the citizenship status of dissidents.* The draft lacks a provision creating a clear legal basis on which dissidents can be deprived of their citizenship. According to Article 12 § 1 No. 1 of the draft, French citizens who are subject to, or who submit to, a foreign power can be deprived of their citizenship. But since dissidents are recognized by our enemies as a free French power under international law — Soviet Russia has actually recognized the Liberation Committee in Algiers as the only representative of the French Republic — the current wording of

§ 12 Par. 1 No. 1 of the draft, unopposed by the German occupying power, makes it all too easy for those in the Vichy government following a wait-and-see policy to claim that dissidents cannot be deprived of their citizenship in the future. Along the same line, the provisions of Articles 13 § 1, 14 § 3 Par. 2, and 14 § 3 Par. 3 of the draft, which simplify the restoration of citizenship to former French nationals who lost their citizenship on the basis of the act of 28 February 1941, now apply to dissidents and their families as well. Here too, in my opinion, the interests of the Reich as a warring power call for the establishment of a clear legal basis on which French nationals who fight on the side of military enemies of the Reich or otherwise support them can be deprived of their citizenship, and for the ruling out of any possibility that the provisions simplifying the restoration of citizenship to former French nationals can be applied to dissidents and their families—at least until a specified point in time after the signing of a peace agreement.

2. *Provisions that, although they affect the biological interests of the German people, the Reich as an occupying power does not object to in the revision of French nationality law, for the sake of expediency, but that should ultimately be resolved in the peace negotiations in connection with a general ruling on the status of German nationals in France.*

Like current French nationality law, the draft largely follows the principle of *jus soli*.

A number of draft provisions that rest on this principle inherently fail to meet the demands that the Reich must make to preserve the citizenship of ethnic Germans living in bordering European states. Nor do they meet the Reich's demands in regard to the nationality of children begotten during the present war—at least in the ethnically German provinces of France—by German soldiers with women of French nationality.

For appropriate legislation governing the position under constitutional law of German ethnic groups living in bordering European states, and of children begotten during the war by German soldiers with women who are not German citizens, it is very important that we consider experience gained with current individual provisions. Because this entire group of questions will have to be resolved in a peace agreement, or in subsequent international treaties, through standardized, if not identical, provisions, I consider it pointless to address these issues in a discussion of the present Draft of a French Nationality Act or to make approval of the draft by the Reich as occupying power contingent on the inclusion of such provisions. Once we are victorious, these questions will automatically be resolved as we wish.

III. PROPOSAL:

The RSHA [Reich Security Main Office] suggests that the head of the military government in Paris make withdrawal of the Germans' preemptively lodged objection to the Draft of a French Nationality Act contingent upon the inclusion of additional provisions that

1. make the naturalization of Jews henceforth impossible, and that

2. establish a clear legal basis on which dissidents can be deprived of their French citizenship and rule out any possibility that provisions simplifying the restoration of citizenship to former French nationals can be applied to dissidents and their families.

Enclosed along with the position statement sent to Office III for the attention of ss Senior Storm Unit Leader Dr. Gengenbach is a German translation of the Draft of a French Nationality Act prepared by the Institute.

Heil Hitler!
Your very devoted
(signed) Hofmann.

Forces françaises libres

Registre de Nationalité
(deuxième exemplaire)

1ère Partie. — Acquisition conservation
ou consolidation de la
nationalité française.

IIème Partie.. — Perte de la nationalité
française ou obtenue en
faveur d'une autre nationalité

Ce Registre de
Nationalité
a été ouvert
au
Quartier-général des
Forces françaises
libres

à Londres - Carlt... Gardens 4

Le 23 septembre 1940

Il est tenu en double exemplaire
pour le bureau de la nationalité
R. Cassin

FIGURES 2.1–2.3

Excerpt from the register of nationality inaugurated on 23 September 1940 by
René Cassin at the Free French forces headquarters in London.

Source: ASDN.

Ière Partie
— x —

Acquisition, maintien ou consolidation
de la nationalité française

Nº 1 — Acquisition de la nationalité française par le
23 septembre mariage d'une femme étrangère avec un
1940 Français.

Mademoiselle Watson, Jacqueline, Emma,
Marie-Laure, Réine
née à Henry-Vannes (Belgique) le 26 juin 1919
domiciliée à Polaggio (Suisse) Jardin
de nationalité britannique
a demandé le 11 septembre 1940 à acquérir la
nationalité française,
par l'effet de son mariage avec le lieutenant
Millet-Dard, Philippe, Jérôme ... des Forces françaises
libres, autorisé par le Général de Gaulle, dont
célébration doit avoir lieu le 23 septembre 1940
en l'église de Our Lady, St. John's Wood.

Réquisite lui a été adressé le 23 septembre
1940. Domicile actuel, 100 Aristole Rd. Liverpool
Dossier annexé

Nº 2 Acquisition de la nationalité française.
par le mariage d'une femme étrangère avec
un Français

Mademoiselle Tombet, Lunette, alias Laura,
Emma, Prunella
née à Carouge (Suisse) le 23 juin 1917
domiciliée à Pinksbenny Mille, London Road,
Camberley (Surrey) ...
de nationalité suisse
a demandé le 10 novembre 194... à acquérir la nationalité française par l'effet de son mariage
avec le sergent Trochon ... Julien, Eugène,
Abité Camp Care, ... Aldershot
dont la célébration a eu lieu le 12 août 1940
au Registar Office, City of Westminster, Londres

Réquisite adressé le 15 novembre 1940

Dossier annexé

N° 5

Conservation de la nationalité
française acquise par naturalisation -
Déclaration de fidélité à la France
faite par un réfugié français en Angleterre

Monsieur Jarecki Sigismond
né le 11 juin 1881 à Lemberg (Anc.) Pologne
entré sur le sol français en 1907
marié le 6 janvier 1914 à Paris, Mairie du IV
d'origine polonaise
devenu français par décret de naturalisation
N° 61029 X 28, en date du 11 novembre 1930
engagé volontaire pour la durée de la guerre au
Bureau de Recrutement de la Seine en 1939
actuellement domicilié à Londres, 21 ...
Gardens, W.2.
a adressé un acte de fidélité à la France libre
le 18 octobre 1940
et demande à demeurer Français qui qu'il arrive

Récépissé lui a été adressé le 1er novembre 1940

Dossier annexé

N° 4

Conservation de la nationalité
française acquise par naturalisation
Déclaration de fidélité à la France
faite par une réfugiée française en Angleterre

Madame Jarecka Hélène, Jeanne, Jarecki
née le 10 août 1880 à Lemberg (Anc.) Pologne
mariée le 6 janvier 1914 à Paris, Mairie du IV
d'origine polonaise
devenue française par décret de naturalisation
N° 61029 X 28, un date du 11 novembre 1930
actuellement domiciliée à Londres, 29 ...
Gardens, W.2.
a adressé un acte de fidélité à la France libre
le 18 octobre 1940
et demande à demeurer Française qui qu'il arrive

Récépissé lui a été adressé le 1er novembre 1940

Dossier annexé

FIGURES 2.1–2.3 *translation*

This Register of Nationality
Was opened
at the
Headquarters of the
Free French Forces
In London – Carlton Gardens 4
23 September 1940
It is maintained with a copy
by the bureau of nationality
[signed] R. Cassin

Free French Forces Register of Nationality
(Second copy)

Part I. Acquisition, retention
or consolidation of
French nationality

Part II. Loss of French
nationality or options
in favor of another
nationality

Acquisition, maintenance or consolidation of French nationality

No 1.

1360 DX 267/12

September 23 1940

Acquisition of French nationality, by the marriage of a foreign woman to a French-man. Mademoiselle Watson, Jacqueline, Fernande, Marie-Laure, Hélène, born in Heusy-Verviers (Belgium), 26 June 1919 residing in Polegate (Sussex) of British nationality asked on 21 September 1940 to acquire French nationality by virtue of her marriage to Lieutenant Miller-André Philippe, of the Free French Air Forces, authorized by General de Gaulle, the wedding being scheduled to take place on 23 September 1940 in the Church of Our Lady, St. John's Wood

Receipt sent her on 23 September 1940
Current residence, 60 Croxteth Road-Liverpool
Dossier appended

No 2.

230/9h DX 40

Acquisition of French nationality by the marriage of a foreign woman to a Frenchman Mademoiselle Tombet, Laurette, Alias Laure,–Emma, Pervenche born in Carenge (Switzerland) 28 February 1917 residing in Portesberry Hill, London Road, Camberley (Surrey) of Swiss nationality requested on 10 November 1940 to acquire French nation-ality by virtue of her marriage to Sergeant Trochon, Lucien, Eugène, Delville Camp Cove, near Aldershot, the wedding having taken place on 17 August 1940 at the Register Office, City of Westminster, London

Receipt sent 15 November 1940
Dossier appended

No 3.

61028 X 28

Retention of French nationality acquired through naturalization. Declaration of fidelity to France made by a French refugee in England

M. Jarecki Sigismond

Born 11 June 1881 in Lemberg (Lvov) (Poland) entered French territory in 1907 married 6 January 1916 in Paris, City Hall, 6th arrondissement of Polish origin became French by naturalization decree no 61029 X 28, dated 11 November 1930 enlisted voluntarily for the duration of the war at the Seine Recruitment Bureau in 1938 currently residing in London, 29 Gloucester Gardens, W 2 addressed an act of fidelity to Free France on 10 October 1940 and asks to remain French under any and all circumstances

Receipt sent him on 1 November 1940
Dossier appended

61029 X 28

No 4.
Retention of French nationality acquired through naturalization. Declaration of fidelity to France made by a French refugee in England

Mme Kuezabinska Hélène, spouse Jarecki
Born 10 April 1886 in Lemberg (Lvov) Poland married 6 January 1916 in Paris, City Hall, 6th arrondissement of Polish origin became French by naturalization decree no 61029 X 28, dated 11 November 1930 currently residing in London, 29 Gloucester Gardens, W 2 addressed an act of fidelity to Free France on 10 October 1940 and asks to remain French under any and all circumstances

Receipt sent her on 1 November 1940
Dossier appended

TABLES 14–19

TABLE 14

Acquisitions of French Nationality Registered According to the Procedures in Effect from 1945 to 2002

	Total acquisitions registered	Manifestations of intent	Acquisitions by decree				Acquisitions by declaration			
			Total	Naturalization	Reintegration	Collective effect (children naturalized with parents)	Total	Through marriage	During minority	Other
1945	17,884		4,983	3,377	903	703	12,258	976	11,282	
1946	38,869		18,114	14,154	744	3,216	20,275	5,187	15,088	
1947	111,736		85,243	67,737	1,899	15,607	26,087	11,992	14,095	
1948	70,925		60,009	48,955	1,186	9,868	10,694	3,269	7,422	3
1949	61,270		52,407	41,701	1,411	9,295	8,642	479	8,137	26
1950	43,790		35,964	27,912	977	7,075	7,654	270	7,255	129
1951	25,257		19,462	14,897	502	4,063	5,645	194	5,386	65
1952	28,139		20,998	15,707	493	4,798	6,765	211	6,534	20
1953	34,824		26,477	19,078	650	6,749	8,103	188	7,880	35
1954	39,308		27,886	20,410	593	6,883	11,172	164	10,992	16
1955	44,972		29,577	21,506	452	7,619	14,933	248	14,658	27
1956	38,040		24,704	17,263	350	7,091	13,088	233	12,726	129

1957	36,890	25,590	17,620	514	7,456	11,118	377	10,549	192
1958	34,452	24,452	17,205	458	6,789	9,823	702	8,904	217
1959	34,098	24,780	17,278	497	7,005	9,113	924	8,113	76
1960	29,683	19,208	13,192	253	5,763	10,342	2,035	8,184	123
1961	25,954	15,952	10,774	167	5,011	9,845	1,770	7,993	82
1962	28,149	16,894	11,120	157	5,617	11,155	1,234	9,686	235
1963	30,648	20,307	13,443	115	6,749	10,240	917	9,167	156
1964	27,289	17,810	11,890	147	5,773	9,403	764	8,479	160
1965	41,487	30,859	20,029	205	10,625	10,525	735	9,575	215
1966	30,488	22,874	15,652	204	7,018	7,522	635	6,707	180
1967	57,231	45,663	30,415	222	15,026	11,463	668	10,469	326
1968	38,387	29,935	19,876	520	9,539	8,273	520	7,299	454
1969	38,397	30,116	19,457	702	9,957	8,211	536	7,556	119
1970	35,000	27,986	18,002	784	9,200	6,962	372	6,498	92
1971	39,989	32,554	20,531	952	11,071	7,381	363	6,916	102
1972	35,254	27,851	17,235	823	9,793	7,321	282	6,945	94
1973	33,662	26,651	17,434	761	8,456	6,965	464	6,175	326
1974	36,050	24,028	16,241	711	7,076	11,955	5,984	5,226	745
1975	41,388	26,674	18,006	1,021	7,647	14,664	8,394	5,348	922
1976	45,131	30,667	20,140	1,538	8,989	14,421	9,181	4,107	1,133
1977	48,135	32,906	21,610	1,676	9,620	15,176	9,885	4,198	1,093
1978	50,977	34,105	22,439	1,670	9,996	16,833	10,849	4,623	1,361
1979	46,810	30,982	20,164	1,562	9,256	15,808	10,044	4,245	1,519

TABLE 14
Continued

	Total acquisitions registered	Manifestations of intent	Acquisitions by decree				Acquisitions by declaration			
			Total	Naturalization	Reintegration	Collective effect (children naturalized with parents)	Total	Through marriage	During minority	Other
1980	52,129		31,504	20,203	1,977	9,324	20,599	13,767	4,836	1,996
1981	54,030		34,400	21,541	2,811	10,048	19,611	13,209	4,600	1,802
1982	48,835		28,459	18,073	2,349	8,037	20,368	14,227	4,473	1,668
1983	39,714		19,990	13,213	1,557	5,220	19,705	13,213	4,793	1,699
1984	35,575		20,056	13,635	1,599	4,822	15,517	10,279	4,201	1,037
1985	60,688		41,588	26,902	2,708	11,978	19,089	12,634	5,088	1,367
1986	55,975		33,402	21,072	1,986	10,344	22,566	15,190	6,312	1,064
1987	41,758		25,702	16,205	1,649	7,848	16,052	9,788	5,486	778
1988	54,313		26,961	16,762	2,251	7,948	27,338	16,592	9,937	809
1989	59,528		33,040	19,901	2,961	10,178	26,468	15,489	9,711	1,268
1990	64,991		34,889	20,827	3,462	10,610	30,077	15,627	12,041	2,406
1991	72,242		39,445	23,177	3,710	12,558	32,768	16,333	13,551	2,884

Year									
1992	71,601		39,346	22,792	4,205	12,349	32,249	15,601	14,383	2,265
1993	73,170		40,739	23,283	4,299	13,157	32,425	15,246	15,476	1,703
1994	126,341	33,255	49,499	28,936	4,946	15,567	43,633	19,493	21,750	2,390
1995	92,412	30,526	40,867	24,718	4,108	12,041	21,017	16,659	1,492	2,866
1996	109,940	29,845	58,098	34,650	6,525	16,923	21,880	19,127	156	2,597
1997	116,286	32,518	60,485	35,703	6,311	18,471	23,191	20,845	81	2,265
1998	112,461	25,549	58,123	34,697	5,753	17,673	29,089	22,113	5,300*	1,676
1999	136,435		67,569	39,832	6,512	21,225	68,866	24,088	42,433	2,345
2000	141,455		77,478	45,485	7,340	24,653	63,977	26,056	35,883	2,038
2001	121,631		64,595	39,394	5,765	19,436	57,036	23,994[a]	31,957	1,085
2002	122,834		64,081	38,440	5,712	19,929	58,753	26,351	30,282	2,170
2003	139,930		77,102	43,572	7,830	25,701	62,828	30,922	29,419	2,487
2004	165,121		99,368	56,727	9,648	32,993	65,753	34,440	29,872	1,441
2005[b]	151,861		101,785	58,629	10,155	33,001	50,076	21,527	27,258	1,291
2006	145,315		87,878	51,431	8,138	28,309	57,437	29,276	26,881	1,280

[a] As of 2001, totals in this column include the children of foreigners who have become French after their parent has acquired nationality by declaration following a marriage with a French person: 978 persons in 2001, 1,126 in 2002, 1,313 in 2003, 1,308 in 2004, 812 in 2005, and 1101 in 2006.

[b] In addition, 2,553 certificates of nationality were delivered in 2005 to young people who had been born in France to foreign parents and had reached the age of 18. It is thus fair to say that 147,868 foreigners acquired French nationality in 2005.

* Estimated.

Source: Direction de la population et des migrations, Sous-direction des naturalisations et Ministère de la Justice.

TABLE 15

Attribution of Nationality at Birth in Selected Countries in Europe and North America

	Original nationality	
	Jus soli (date of inclusion)	Jus sanguinis (date of inclusion)
Austria	No	Yes (1811)
Belgium	Yes (for the third generation, 1992)	Yes (1831)
Denmark	No	Yes (1898)
Finland	No	Yes (1941)
France	Yes (for the third generation, 1889)	Yes (1803)
Germany	Yes (1999, with conditions: dual nationality)	Yes (Prussia: 1842)
Greece	No	Yes (1856)
Ireland	Yes (1935, on condition of a parent's legal residence since 2005)	Yes (1935)
Italy	No	Yes (1865)
Luxembourg	No	Yes (1804)
Netherlands	Yes (1953, for the third generation)	Yes (1888)
Portugal	Yes (for the third generation [2006] and on condition of parents' residence, 5 years)	Yes (1822)
Spain	Yes (for the third generation, 1982)	Yes (1837)
Sweden	No	Yes (1984)

TABLE 15

Continued

	Original nationality	
	Jus soli (date of inclusion)	Jus sanguinis (date of inclusion)
United Kingdom	Yes (on condition of parents' residence)	Yes (no transmission to the third generation unless residence is established in the United Kingdom before the child's birth)
United States	Yes (according to the Constitution, 1868)	Yes (no transmission to the third generation unless residence is established in the United States before the child's birth)

Source: Weil, "Access to Citizenship," and collection of French citizenship laws.

TABLE 16

Access to Nationality by Children of Immigrants in Selected Countries in Europe and North America

	Right to nationality	Existence of a specific provision	Residence	Age	Other information
Austria	Yes	Yes	6 years instead of 10	—	Naturalization
Belgium	Yes	Yes	Parents residents for 10 years	Before 12	Declaration
			One year before option and between ages of 14 and 18, or 9 years in all	Between 18 and 30	
Canada	Yes	Yes	Automatic	At birth	
Denmark	No, except for Nordic Countries citizens	Yes	10 years	18–23	Declaration, absence of prison sentence
Finland	Yes	Yes	10 years	21–23	Declaration
France	Yes	Yes	5 years (not necessarily continuous)	After 13	With parental consent at 13; on request at 16; automatic at 18

Germany					
born in Germany	Yes	Yes	Parents permanent residents	At birth	At 23; renunciation of dual nationality
not born in Germany	Yes	Yes	8 years, of which 6 in primary education and 4 in secondary	16–23	Renunciation of dual nationality, declaration, and absence of prison sentence
Greece	No	No			
Italy	Yes	Yes	Continuous since birth	18	
Luxembourg	Yes	Yes	5 years	18	Declaration
Netherlands	Yes	Yes	At least since age 4	18–25	Declaration
Portugal	Yes	Yes	No	Any age	Declaration
Spain	Yes	Yes	1 year	18–20	Parents residents for 10 years, or 6 years if from a Portuguese-speaking country
Sweden	Yes	Yes	1 year	18–20	Declaration
United Kingdom	Yes	Yes	Parents legal residents	At birth	
United States	Yes	Automatic	No	At birth	

Source: Weil, "Access to Citizenship," and collection of French citizenship laws.

TABLE 17

Access to Nationality through Naturalization in Selected Countries in Europe and North America

	Residence	Knowledge of history	Knowledge of language	Loyalty oath	Adequate income	Investigation of morality	Absence of conviction of crime	Renunciation of previous nationality
Austria	10 years	No	Yes	Yes	Yes		Yes	Yes
Belgium	3 years	No						No
Canada	Permanent, 3 years out of 4 before the request	Yes	Yes	Yes			Yes	No
Denmark	9 years	Yes	Yes	Yes	Yes	Yes	Yes	Yes
Finland	6 years	No	Yes		Yes	Yes	Yes	No
France	5 years		Yes		Yes	Yes	Yes	No
Germany	Permanent, 8 years		Yes	Yes	Yes	No		Yes, with exceptions
Greece	5 years after the request, or 10 out of 12 before plus 1 year after			Yes		Yes		No

Country	Residency requirement						
Ireland	5 of last 9 years; illegal residency or residency as student or asylum seeker not counted	No		Yes			No
Italy	10 years	No		No	Yes		No
Luxembourg	5 years, continuous	Yes		No		Yes	Yes
Mexico	5 years	Yes	Yes				Yes
Netherlands	Permanent or habitual for 5 consecutive years before the request	Yes		Yes	Yes		Yes with exceptions
Portugal	6 years	Yes		Yes	Yes		No
Spain	10 years	Yes		Yes			Yes
Sweden	5 years	No		Yes			No
United Kingdom	5 years	Yes		Yes			No
United States	5 years of permanent residence	Yes		Yes			Yes

Source: Weil, "Access to Citizenship," and collection of French citizenship laws.

TABLE 18
Access to Nationality through Marriage in Selected Countries in Europe and
North America

	Existence of a specific provision	Residence	Waiting period	Other requirements
Austria	Yes	5 years of marriage plus 6 years of residence	1 year	Loss of previous nationality
Belgium	Yes	3 years		
Canada	No			
Denmark	Yes	6 to 8 years		Naturalization
Finland	Yes	3 years	4 years	
France	Yes	No	4 years (5 if nonresident in France)	Declaration
Germany	Yes	2 years of marriage and 3 years of residence		Naturalization
Greece	Yes	3 years of marriage and residence		Naturalization
Ireland	Yes		3 years	
Italy	Yes	After marriage, 6 months in Italy or three years abroad		No access if convicted of certain infractions
Luxembourg	Yes	3 years of marriage and residence		Loss of previous nationality

TABLE 18
Continued

	Existence of a specific provision	Residence	Waiting period	Other requirements
Netherlands	Yes	3 years		
Portugal	Yes	3 years		
Spain	Yes		1 year	
Sweden	Yes	2 years of marriage and 3 years of residence, or 10 years of marriage without residence	2 years	
United Kingdom	Yes	3 years		
United States	Yes	3 years		Same provisions as for other foreigners

Source: Weil, "Access to Citizenship," and collection of French citizenship laws.

TABLE 19

Categories of Persons Authorized to Acquire French Nationality by Declaration

1795: Year III Constitution	Resident in France, born abroad: automatic French nationality seven years after declaration		
1799: Year VIII Constitution	Resident in France, born abroad: automatic French nationality ten years after declaration (in effect until 1809)		
1803 (Civil Code)		Children born in France to a foreign father: if they resided in France, they could become French in the year following majority	
1889		Registration possible for young people born in France up to age of 22	
1927		Registration by minors born in France	Foreign women married to French men

TABLE 19
Continued

1945	Registration by minors born in France	
1973	Registration by minors born in France	Foreigners (women or men) married to French nationals
1993	Registration by minors between the ages of 16 and 21 born in France	Foreigners (women or men) married to French nationals
1998	Registration by minors between the ages of 13 and 18 born in France	Foreigners (women or men) married to French nationals

Source: Compiled by Patrick Weil.

Bibliography

In the public archives of France, the Ministry of Justice maintains no records that could serve as sources for reconstituting the history of French nationality policy. The impossibility of gaining access to the nineteenth-century naturalization files to carry out quantitative studies was a secondary handicap for this research.

Access to the archives kept by the Bureau of Nationality within the Ministry of Justice (AMJ) and by the Naturalization Bureau in Rezé (Loire-Atlantique) was extremely valuable. (Most of the AMJ archives have since been transferred to the Center of Contemporary Archives in Fontainebleau under the call numbers 1995 0165/10 to 1995 0165/13.) Systematic research in the archives of the national or departmental administrations with which the Ministry of Justice was in communication, in archives of politicians and jurists who contributed to nationality policy over the last two centuries, and also in foreign archives allowed me to bring this project to fruition. The archival documents mentioned here are the ones cited in the book; they represent only a small fraction of those I consulted.

For the study of the contemporary period, given the role I was able to play in the development of the law adopted in 1998, I decided to rely primarily on secondary sources that I knew to be very well informed.

INTERVIEWS

Albin Chalandon, 25 January 2001

Jean Foyer, 4 December 2000

Reinhard Höhn, 12 April 1996 (telephone interview conducted by Franz Mayer)

Marceau Long, 20 November 2001

Pierre Mazeaud, 30 October 2001

Mme Ménard, daughter of M. Boulbès, former head of the Bureau of Seals in the Ministry of Justice, 18 January 1997

Odile Pichat, former division head of the Commission on Laws in the National Assembly, 14 December 2000

Mme Thin, daughter of M. Aymond, former head of the Bureau of Seals in the Ministry
of Justice, 30 April 1997

Georges Vedel, 7 June 1998

GERMAN ARCHIVES

Geheimes Staatsarchiv, Stiftung Preußischer Kulturbesitz, Berlin-Dahlem

Rep. 80 I Nr. 62 Bd. I

Rep. 80 I Nr. ad 62a

Archives of Humboldt-Universität, Berlin

Institut für Staatsforschung file UK 827

Institut für Staatsforschung Assistenten file Nov 35-Feb 46 UK 828/

University personnel files, Höhn dossier

AMERICAN ARCHIVES

Library of Congress, Washington

Charles Sumner papers, microfilms

Georgetown University, Washington

Alexis Carrel papers

FRENCH ARCHIVES, PUBLIC

Archives Nationales, Centre historique des Archives nationales (CARAN)

Ministère de la Justice

BBII 2: requests for letters of naturalization (1789–92)

BBII 3 and 4: naturalizations (1808–11)

BBII 76–90: files pertaining to establishment of residency in France (Year XI: 1809)

BBII 91: establishment of residency: royal ordinances (1820–21)

BBII 94–95: naturalizations (1812–13)

BBII 96: admissions to residency (1808–10)

BB18 3366: Notes and correspondence from the criminal division of the Ministry of
Justice and memoranda about measures to be taken with respect to foreigners and
naturalized persons

BB30 649: correspondence with various ministries about matters pertaining to the
Bureau of Seals (1815–28)

BB30 1163–2: memoranda from the Ministry of Justice

BB30 1604: French nationality (1816–48)

BB30 1605: documents from 1934

BB30 1707: papers of the Secretariat General of the Ministry of Justice (1940–44)

BB30 1711: French nationality (1940–44)

BB30 1713: texts submitted by the Ministry of Justice to the Occupation authorities (1940–44)

BB30 1714: status of civil servants

BB30 1731: work by the general study commission on questions of justice

BB30 1741: general inspection of services: Dautet report

Ministry of the Interior

F1a 3346: administrative measures pertaining to foreigners (1945–47)

F1a 3255: naturalizations and miscellaneous

F7 12574: relations with Italy

F7 12731: surveillance of foreigners during the war (1914–18)

F7 14885: papers found in the office of Yves Fourcade, director of police administration (1940–44)

F7 15322: review of acquisitions of nationality, information about the applicants

Military Affairs

F9 170: recruitment, general correspondence, Corsica (1792–1810)

F9 171: recruitment, general correspondence, Corsica (1810–33)

F9 227: recruitment, general correspondence, Nord (Year V–1821)

F9 228: recruitment, general correspondence, Nord (1822–31)

Présidence du Conseil

F60 490: Israelites under the Vichy government (1940–41)

F60 491: Israelites under the Vichy government (1942–44)

F60 493: internment camps under the Vichy government

F60 494: reports on the meetings of the High Committee on Population

F60 499: High Committee on Population, legislation on naturalizations (1937–47)

F60 1038: Public Health, organization of the Ministry (1944)

F60 1440: status of Jews, development and discussion of bills and their effects (1940–44)

F60 1480/2: DGTO (Delegate General of the French government in the occupied territories), ambassador de Brinon's cabinet, correspondence with the keeper of the seals (1940–44)

F60 1485: DGTO, ambassador de Brinon's cabinet, political and social life in the occupied zone, files on Jews and foreigners

F60 1507: DGTO, military cabinet: administrative, political, and social situation in the occupied zone: files on refugees and foreigners

"French State" Archives of the Civilian Cabinet

2AG/450: proposed constitutions (1941–44)

German archives from Second World War

AJ40/547: bill and law on nationality (1941–44)

High Court Files

2w66: testimony of M. Mauco at the Riom trial

3w46: Raphaël Alibert

3w144: Georges Dayras

3w334: Frédéric Roujou

Archives of the Council of State

AL 2357: transcript of the discussion in plenary session of the proposed decree pertaining to French nationality in the colonies, 23 April 1896

Cases

223 768: bill designed to modify the nationality law of 10 August 1927

223 773: proposed decree modifying the nationality decree of 10 August 1927

229 733: proposed decree on the application of the law of 2 June 1941 designed to control the access of Jews to commercial, industrial, or artisanal professions

229 744: proposed decree designed to control the access of Jews to agricultural professions

Files Pertaining to Requests for Derogation from the Status of Jews

224 015: request for derogation of M. Lévy-Brühl

224 016: request for derogation of M. William Oualid

224 027: request for derogation of M. Albert Michel Lévy

224 029: request for derogation of M. Jacques Valensi

224 030: request for derogation of M. Marc Klein

224 035: request for derogation of M. Léon Hermann

224 036: request for derogation of M. Jean Wahl

224 044: request for derogation of M. Claude Lévi-Strauss

224 238: request for derogation of M. Robert Weill

224 239: request for derogation of M. Ancel

224 630: derogation file of M. Claude Roger-Marx

229 948: derogation file of M. André Meyer

229 949: derogation file of de M. Georges Mossé

Centre des Archives contemporaines de Fontainebleau

1982 0774/ art. 1-10: general delegation for national "equipment"

1995 0165/ art. 10-13: litigation concerning nationality

1986 0269/ art. 1-7: archives of the High Advisory Committee on Population and the Family

2000 0145/21: Ministry of Justice

2000 0145/23: Ministry of Justice

Some fifty boxes containing naturalization files were consulted. They are included under the call numbers 1977 0623/68 and 1977 0904/133.

Diplomatic Archives

International administrative conventions and litigation, litigation subset (1807–1950)

No. 387: foreigners and children of foreigners in France, law of 1874 (1867–1931)

No. 324: law of 7 April 1915 (1915–18)

No. 354: files pertaining to the German law of 1913 (1913–19)

No. 367: law of 10 August 1927

International Unions, 1st Installment

No. 277: labor and immigration (1940–42)

International Unions, 3rd Installment (1944–50)

No. 452: revocation of French nationality

Administrative series C

Vol. 138: nationality, questions of principle (dual nationality, denaturalization), 1945–47

Vol. 366: law of 10 August 1927

Personal Series

Vols. 310–11: Liberation, purge commission

1939–45 War, Vichy Europe

Series C, vol. 199: naturalizations (23 July 1940–31 July 1944)

1940 Papers

Bureau d'études Chauvel (a think tank), vol. 5: bibliography

Berlin Collection

Series C, art. 84

Archives of the Legal Committee of Free France (Council of State)

9912/1: record of business (26 August 1943–1 August 1945)

9938/2: chronology of the opinions of the Legal Committee

Centre des Archives d'Outre-Mer (Aix-en-Provence)

Ministerial collection. Cabinet, carton 37: Free French Forces; headquarters, office of French nationals abroad (1940–41)

Ministerial collection. Political affairs 877: Jewish affairs, abrogation of the Crémieux decree

Ministerial collection. Political affairs 889 bis: withdrawal of French nationality

F80 2043: naturalizations (1838–88)

General Government of Algeria collection. Administrative organization 8 H 10, miscellaneous files 12 H 6, denizenship, electoral representation of the natives

Military Archives (Historical Service of the Land Army)

3R485–3R488: naturalization files (1950s)

3R595: National unworthiness: military personnel sentenced to this punishment, list of names, individual files

3R598: File 1, discharge of officers as a disciplinary measure, especially under the Vichy government, for desertion or presumption of dissidence

File 2, French nationality: military obligations of binationals, naturalizations, withdrawals of French nationality (1941–45)

7T 408: naturalizations of foreigners and status of foreigners granted French nationality (1939–67)

Senate Library

Transcript of the meetings of the Sénat Conservateur (Constitutional Court), 21 and 22 Ventôse, Year X of the Republic

Archives of the Paris Police Headquarters

DA 430: general council (miscellaneous files)

DA 745: foreigners, regulations and memoranda (1917–50)

DA 781: French nationality, principles

DB 336: war of 1914, foreigners, nationality

Isère Departmental Archives

61 M 16: investigation ordered by the Ministry of War (1915) into the application of the law of 1893

127 M1: naturalizations, instructions and memoranda

127 M2: nationality, typical cases (1927–38)

128 M3–34: information and correspondence regarding foreigners requesting naturalization

Nord Departmental Archives

M 495-7 to 495-9: naturalizations (1870–1910)

1 R 47: nationality laws, instructions and dossiers (1888–1907)

Dunkerque Sub-prefecture

5 Z 332: naturalizations, miscellaneous information (1931–34)

5 Z 333: naturalizations, miscellaneous information (1931–34)

Valenciennes Sub-prefecture

7 Z 18: naturalizations (1848–51)

Bas-Rhin Departmental Archives

8M25–28: admissions to residency, naturalizations: memoranda and instructions (Year VIII: 1870)

Archives of the Fondation Nationale des Sciences Politiques (National Political Science Foundation)

Fonds MRP

MRPS 50: transcripts of meetings of the MRP parliamentary group

FRENCH ARCHIVES, PRIVATE

Louis Canet (Diplomatic Archives, agents' papers)
 Vol. 27: commission charged with examining the status of Jews (minutes of opinions)

René Cassin (National Archives, CARAN)
 382AP74, work of the provisional government: official correspondence and legal work (1944–45)

Jean Donnedieu de Vabres (National Archives, CARAN)
 539AP1: work of the provisional government (1944–46)
 539AP2: legal affairs, general matters, naturalizations (1945)

Antonin Dubost (Isère departmental archives)
 1J940

André Honnorat (National Archives, CARAN)
 50AP27: naturalizations
 50AP63: Foyer français

Emile Laffon (Diplomatic Archives, agents' papers)
 Vol. 1: notes to the minister, September 1944–45

Georges Mauco (National Archives, CARAN)
 577AP2: 1939–40 war
 577AP3: High Advisory Committee on Population
 577AP4: immigration questions
 AP577/5: articles on immigration before 1945
 AP577/6: controversies provoked by Mauco's article in *L'Ethnie française* (1940–47)

Emmanuel Sieyès (National Archives, CARAN)
 284AP/5: Notes regarding the constitution of Year VIII

François-Denis Tronchet *(Supreme Court library)*
 Consultations no. 1441 and no. 1783

Other Primary Sources

Archives parlementaires (AP), M. Mavidal and E. Laurent. Archives parlementaires de 1787 à 1860. Recueil complet des débats législatifs et politiques des chambres françaises. 1st series, 1787–94.

René Barenton. *Dictionnaire biographique des Préfets. Septembre 1870–mai 1982*, Archives nationales, 1994.

Dictionnaire des Parlementaires français: Notices biographiques sur les ministres, députés, et sénateurs français de 1889 à 1940. 8 vols. Paris: Presses Universitaires de France, 1960–77.

Robert Adolphe, Edgar Bourloton, and Gaston Cougny, eds. *Dictionnaire des Parlementaires français.* Paris: Bourloton, 1891.

Benoît Yvert. *Dictionnaire des ministres de 1789 à 1989*. Paris: Perrin, 1990.

Liste alphabétique des personnes ayant acquis ou perdu la nationalité française par décret, années 1921–1930, 1931–1940, 1941–1950, 1951–1960. Paris: Imprimerie Nationale, 1949, 1950, 1953, 1963.

Ministère de la Justice. *Compte général de l'administration de la justice civile et commerciale en France*. Annual publication.

SECONDARY SOURCES

L'acquisition de la nationalité française par la procédure de manifestation de volonté pour les jeunes étrangers âgés de 16 à 21 ans: Cahiers de l'Observatoire régional de l'intégration et de la ville, no. 22, Région Alsace. Strasbourg, 1997.

Ageron, Charles-Robert. *Les Algériens musulmans et la France (1871–1919)*. Paris: Presses Universitaires de France, 1968.

———. *France coloniale ou parti colonial*. Paris: Presses Universitaires de France, 1978.

———. *Histoire de l'Algérie contemporaine, 1871–1854*. Vol. 2. *De l'insurrection de 1871 au déclenchement de la guerre de libération*. Paris: Presses Universitaires de France, 1979.

Akzin, Benjamin, and Suzanne Basdevant, eds. *La nationalité dans la science sociale et dans le droit contemporaine*. Paris: Sirey, 1933.

Alauzet, Isidore. *De la qualité de Français, de la naturalisation et du statut personnel des étrangers*. Paris: Imprimerie et Librairie Générale de Jurisprudence, 1880.

Aleinikoff, T. Alexander, David A. Martin, and Hiroshi Motomura. *Immigration Process and Policy*. 3rd edn. St. Paul: West, 1995.

Alteroche, Bernard d.' *De l'étranger à la seigneurie à l'étranger au Royaume*. Preface by Anne Lefebvre-Teillard. Paris: LGDJ, 2001.

Ansky, Michel. *Les Juifs d'Algérie du décret Crémieux à la Libération*. Paris: Centre de Documentation Juive Contemporaine, 1950.

Azimi, Vida. "Le suffrage 'universaliste,' les étrangers et le droit électoral de 1793." *La Constitution du 24 juin 1793, l'utopie dans le droit public français?* Proceedings of a colloquium held in Dijon, 16–17 September 1993, ed. Jean Bart, Jean-Jacques Clère, and Michel Verpeaux, 204–39. Dijon, 1997.

Barthélemy, Joseph. *Ministre de la Justice, Vichy, 1941–1943*. Paris: Pygmalion / Gérard Watelet, 1989.

Bar-Yaacov, Nissim. *Dual Nationality*. London: Stevens and Sons, 1961.

Batiffol, Henri. *Traité Élémentaire de Droit International Privé*. Paris: LGDJ, 1949.

Bauböck, Rainer, Eva Ersboll, Kees Groenendijk, and Harald Waldrauch, eds. *Acquisition and Loss of Nationality*. Amsterdam: Amsterdam University Press, 2006.

Blanc-Chaléard, Marie-Claude. *Les Italiens dans l'est parisien: une histoire d'intégration, 1880–1960*. Rome: École Française de Rome, 2000.

Blatt, David S. "Immigration Politics and Immigrant Collective Action in France, 1968–1993." Ph.D diss., Cornell University, 1996.

Bleich, Erik. *Race Politics in Britain and France: Ideas and Policymaking since the 1960s.* Cambridge: Cambridge University Press, 2003.

Blévis, Laure. "Les avatars de la citoyenneté en Algérie coloniale ou les paradoxes d'une catégorisation." *Droit et société* 48 (2001), 557–80.

Bloch, Marc. "A Contribution towards a Comparative History of European Societies." *Land and Work in Medieval Europe: Selected Papers by Marc Bloch*, 44–81. Berkeley: University of California Press, 1967.

Bloemraad, Irene. "The North American Naturalization Gap: An Institutional Approach to Citizenship Acquisition in the United States and Canada." *International Migration Review* 36, no. 1 (2002), 193–228.

Bonnet, Jean-Charles. *Les pouvoirs publics français et l'immigration dans l'entre-deux-guerres.* Lyon: Université de Lyon II, 1976.

Bonnichon, André. *La conversion au Christianisme de l'indigène musulman algérien et ses effets juridiques (un cas de conflit colonial).* Paris: Sirey, 1931.

Borgetto, Michel. "Être français sous la Révolution." *Crises* 2 (1994), 80–88.

Boulbès, Raymond. *Commentaire du Code de la nationalité française (ordonnance du 19 octobre 1945).* Paris: Sirey, 1946.

———. *Droit français de la nationalité.* Paris: Sirey, 1957.

Boushaba, Zouhir. *Être Algérien hier, aujourd'hui et demain.* Algiers: Mimouni, 1992.

Bredbenner, Candice Lewis. *A Nationality of Her Own: Women, Marriage and the Law of Citizenship.* Berkeley: University of California Press, 1998.

Brubaker, Rogers. *Citizenship and Nationhood in France and Germany.* Cambridge: Harvard University Press, 1992.

Bruschi, Christian. "Droit de la nationalité et égalité des droits de 1789 à la fin du XIXe siècle." *Questions de nationalité: histoire et enjeux d'un code*, ed. Smaïn Laacher, 57–89. Paris: CIEMI–L'Harmattan, 1987.

Cable, John L. *Loss of Citizenship, Denaturalization, the Alien in Wartime.* Washington: National Law Book, 1943.

Camiscioli, Elisa. "Intermarriage, Independent Nationality, and the Individual Rights of French Women: The Law of 10 August 1927." *French Politics, Culture and Society* 17, nos. 3–4 (1999), 52–74.

Carbonnier, Jean. *Essai sur les lois.* 2nd edn. Paris: Répertoire du Notariat Defrénois, 1995.

Cassin, René. "L'inégalité entre l'homme et la femme dans la législation civile." *Annales de la faculté de Droit d'Aix*, new series, no. 3 (1919).

Chattou, Zoubir, and Mustapha Belbah. *La double nationalité en question: enjeux et motivations de la double appartenance.* Paris: Karthala, 2002.

Club de l'Horloge. *L'identité de la France*. Paris: Albatros, 1985.

Cluzel, Gaston. *De la nationalité des enfants mineurs d'étrangers dans la législation française*. Paris: Arthur Rousseau, 1901.

Cogordan, George. *Droit des gens: la nationalité du point de vue des rapports internationaux*. Paris: Larose, 1879.

Colas, Dominique. *Citoyenneté et nationalité*. Paris: Gallimard, Folio, 2004.

Colas, Dominique, Claude Emeri, and Jacques Zylberberg, eds. *Citoyenneté et nationalité: perspectives en France et au Québec*. Paris: Presses Universitaires de France, 1991.

Collot, Claude. *Les institutions de l'Algérie durant la période coloniale*. Paris: CNRS, Office des Publications Universitaires, 1987.

Crémieux-Brilhac, Jean-Louis. *La France Libre: de l'appel du 18 juin à la Libération*. Paris: Gallimard, 1998.

Crépin, Annie. *La conscription en débat ou le triple apprentissage de la Nation, de la Citoyenneté, de la République (1798–1889)*. Arras: Artois Presses Université, 1998.

Darras, Loïc. "La double nationalité." University of Paris II, 1986.

Debré, Robert, and Alfred Sauvy. *Des Français pour la France*. Paris: Gallimard, 1946.

Depoid, Pierre. *Les naturalisations en France (1870–1940)*, Études démographiques, no. 3, ed. Service national des statistiques Ministère des Finances, Direction de la statistique générale. Paris: Imprimerie Nationale, 1942.

Derainne, Pierre-Jacques. "Le travail, les migrations et les conflits en France: représentations et attitudes sociales sous la Monarchie de Juillet et la Seconde République" (Ph.D. diss., University of Bourgogne, 1998–99).

Despagnet, Frantz. "Du rôle du Conseil d'État dans la naturalisation d'après la loi du 22 juillet 1893." *Revue de droit public et de la science politique*, 1894, 101–14.

———. *Précis de droit international privé*. 4th edn. Paris: Librairie de la Société du Recueil Général des Lois et des Arrêts, 1904.

Dietrich-Chénel, Karin, and Marie-Hélène Varnier. "Intégration d'étrangers en France par naturalisation ou admission à domicile de 1790/1814 au 10 mai 1871." Ph.D. diss., University of Aix-Marseille I, 1994.

Divine, Robert A. *American Immigration Policy, 1924–1952*. New Haven: Yale University Press, 1957.

Dubost, Jean-François, and Peter Sahlins. *"Et si l'on faisait payer les étrangers"*: *Louis XIV, les immigrés et quelques autres*. Paris: Flammarion, 1999.

Estournet, Rémy. *La pratique de la naturalisation depuis la loi du 10 août 1927*. Montpellier: Imprimerie de la Presse, 1937.

Fahrmeir, Andreas. *Citizens and Aliens: Foreigners and the Law in Britain and the German States, 1789–1870*. London: Berghahn, 2000.

Feldblum, Miriam. *Reconstructing Citizenship: The Politics of Nationality Reform and Immigration in Contemporary France.* Albany: SUNY Press, 1999.

Fenet, Pierre-Antoine. *Recueil complet des travaux préparatoires du Code civil.* 15 vols. Paris: Videcoq, 1827–36.

Foelix, Jean-Jacques-Gaspard. *Traité de droit international privé.* 4th edn. Paris: Marescq aîné, 1866.

Fulchiron, Hugues, ed. *Être Français aujourd'hui: premier bilan de la mise en oeuvre du nouveau droit de la nationalité.* Lyon: Presses Universitaires de Lyon, 1996.

————. "'Rétablissement du droit du sol' et réforme du droit de la nationalité: Commentaire de la loi no. 98–170 du 16 mars 1998." *Journal de droit international* 2 (1998), 343–88.

Gantois, René. *L'accession des indigènes algériens à la qualité de citoyen français.* Algiers: Typo-Litho, 1926.

Gastaut, Yvan. *L'immigration et l'opinion en France sous la Ve République.* Paris: Le Seuil, 2000.

Gérardin, Lucien. *De l'acquisition de la qualité de Français par voie de déclaration: étude sur le bienfait de la loi.* Paris: Larose, 1896.

Glasberg, Alexandre. *À la recherche d'une patrie: la France devant l'immigration.* Paris: Réalités, 1946.

Goasguen, Claude. "Les Français au service de l'étranger sous le Premier Empire: législation et pratique." LL.D. diss., University of Paris II, 1976.

Godechot, Jacques. *Les institutions de la France sous la Révolution et l'Empire.* Paris: Presses Universitaires de France, 1951; 2nd edn., revised and enlarged, 1968.

Gosewinkel, Dieter. *Einbürgern und Ausschließen: Die Nationalisierung der Staatsangehörigkeit vom Deutschen Bund bis zur Bundesrepublik Deutschland.* Göttingen: Vandenhoeck and Ruprecht, 2001.

Grawert, Rolf. *Staat und Staatsangehörigkeit: Verfassungsgeschichtliche Untersuchung zur Entstehung der Staatsangehörigkeit.* Berlin: Duncker and Humblot, 1973.

Gruffy, Georges. "La naturalisation et le préjugé de la race." *Revue politique et parlementaire* 100 (July–September 1919), 36–51.

Guichard, Éric, and Gérard Noiriel, eds. *Construction des nationalités et immigration dans la France contemporaine.* Paris: École Normale Supérieure, 1997.

Guiguet, Benoît. "Citoyenneté et nationalité: limites de la rupture d'un lien." Institut Universitaire Européen, 1997.

Halpérin, Jean-Louis. *L'impossible Code civil.* Preface by Pierre Chaunu. Paris: Presses Universitaires de France, 1992.

Hansen, Randall, and Patrick Weil, eds. *Towards a European Nationality: Citizenship, Immigration and Nationality Law in the EU.* Houndmills: Macmillan, 2001.

—————. *Dual Nationality, Social Rights and Federal Citizenship in the U.S. and Europe: The Reinvention of Citizenship*. London: Berghahn, 2002.

Heuer, Jennifer. *The Family and the Nation: Gender and Citizenship in Revolutionary France*. Chicago: University of Chicago Press, 2005.

Hoffmann, Stanley. "To Be or Not to Be French." *Ideas & Ideals: Essays on Politics in Honor of Stanley Hoffmann*, ed. Linda B. Miller and Michael Joseph Smith, 19–46. Boulder: Westview, 1993.

Institut National d'Études Démographiques. *Documents sur l'immigration*. Paris: Presses Universitaires de France, 1947.

Jennings, Eric T. *Vichy in the Tropics: Petain's National Revolution in Madagascar, Guadeloupe, and Indochina, 1940–44*. Stanford: Stanford University Press, 2001.

Joppke, Christian. *Immigration and the Nation-State: The United States, Germany, and Great Britain*. Oxford: Oxford University Press, 1999.

Julien, Charles-André. *Histoire de l'Afrique du Nord: Tunisie, Algérie, Maroc*. Preface by Stéphane Gsell. Paris: Payot, 1931.

—————. *Histoire de l'Algérie contemporaine*. Vol. 1. *La conquête et les débuts de la colonisation (1827–1871)*. Paris: Presses Universitaires de France, 1979.

Kessedjan, Catherine. "Un fondement international au droit des déchéances." *Les bons sentiments, le genre humain*, no. 29 (1995), 149–62.

Kiefe, Robert. *La nationalité des personnes dans l'Empire britannique*. Paris: Arthur Rousseau, 1926.

Klarsfeld, Serge. *Le calendrier de la persécution des juifs en France*. Paris: Les Fils et filles des déportés juifs de France / Beate Klarsfeld Foundation, 1993.

Knop, Karen. "Relational Nationality: On Gender and Nationality in International Law." *Citizenship Today: Global Perspectives and Practices*, ed. T. Alexander Aleinikoff and Douglas Klusmeyer, 89–124. Washington: Carnegie Endowment for International Peace, 2001.

La Pradelle, Géraud de Geouffre de. "Nationalité française, extranéité, nationalités étrangères." *Mélanges dédiés à Dominique Holleaux*, 134–55. Paris: Litec, 1990.

—————. "La réforme du droit de la nationalité ou la mise en forme juridique d'un virage politique." *Politix*, no. 32 (1995), 154–71.

—————. "Sang et nationalité." *Revue juridique de l'Île-de-France*, no. 30 (1993), 37–54.

Laacher, Smaïn. *Questions de nationalité*. Paris: CIEMI–L'Harmattan, 1987.

Lagarde, Paul. "À propos de l'arrêt Dujacque de la Iʳᵉ Chambre civile du 22 juillet 1987." *Revue critique de droit international privé* (1988), 29.

—————. *La nationalité française*. 3rd edn. Paris: Dalloz, 1997.

—————. "La rénovation du Code de la nationalité par la loi du 9 janvier 1973." *Revue critique de droit international privé* (1973), 431–69.

Laguerre, Bernard. "Les dénaturalisés de Vichy 1940–1944." *Vingtième Siècle* 20 (1988), 3–15.

Lambert, Charles. *La France et les étrangers (dépopulation-immigration-naturalisation)*. Paris: Delagrave, 1928.

Lavisse, Ernest. *Études sur l'histoire de Prusse*. 3rd edn. Paris: Hachette, 1890.

Le Bras, Hervé. *Le sol et le sang*. La Tour d'Aigues: L'Aube, 1994.

L'Ébraly, Charles. *De l'admission à domicile et des droits qu'elle confère à l'étranger qui l'obtient*. Paris: Larose, 1898.

Lefebvre-Teillard, Anne. "Jus sanguinis: l'émergence d'un principe (Éléments d'histoire de la nationalité française)." *Revue critique de droit international privé* 82, no. 2 (1993), 223–50.

Lequette, Yves. "La nationalité française dévaluée." *L'avenir du droit: mélanges en hommage à François Terré*, 350–92. Paris: Presses Universitaires de France / Dalloz. 1999.

Leroy-Beaulieu, Paul. *L'Algérie et la Tunisie*. Paris: Guillaumin, 1887.

Lévy-Ullmann, Henry. "Rapport sur le projet de loi portant refonte des textes relatifs à l'acquisition et à la perte de la nationalité française." *Extrait du Bulletin de la Société d'études législatives*. Paris: Rousseau, 1918.

Lippe, Hans Heinrich. "Die preußische Heimatgesetzgebung vom 31. Dezember 1842." 2 vols. LL.D. diss., Göttingen and Hanover, 1947.

Lochak, Danièle. *Étrangers de quel droit?* Paris: Presses Universitaires de France, 1985.

Long, Marceau, et al., eds. *Être Français aujourd'hui et demain*. 2 vols. Paris: Union Générale d'Éditions, 1988.

Marrus, Michael R., and Robert O. Paxton. *Vichy France and the Jews*. New York: Basic Books, 1981.

Martial, René. "Politique de l'immigration." *Mercure de France*, 15 April 1935.

Mauco, Georges. *L'assimilation des étrangers en France: leur rôle dans l'activité économique*. Paris: Société des Nations, 1937.

———. *Les étrangers en France: étude géographique sur leur rôle dans l'activité économique*. Paris: Armand Colin, 1932.

Maupas, Jacques. *La nouvelle législation française sur la nationalité*. Issoudun: Éditions Internationales, 1941.

Maury, Jacques. "Droit international privé." Toulouse: Faculté de droit, 1946–1947.

———. *La Semaine juridique, études doctrinales*, no. 165, 10.40 (1940).

———. *La Semaine juridique, études doctrinales*, no. 169, 11.40 (1940).

Milza, Pierre. *Voyage en Ritalie*. Paris: Plon, 1993.

Mondonico, Cécile. "La loi du 26 juin 1889 sur la nationalité." Master's thesis, University of Paris I (Panthéon-Sorbonne), 1990.

Morère, Hélène. "La loi du 10 août 1927 sur la nationalité." Master's thesis, University of Paris 1, 1985–86.

Muñoz-Perez, Francisco, and Michèle Tribalat. "Mariages d'étrangers et mariages mixtes en France: Évolution depuis la Première Guerre." *Population* 3 (1984), 427–62.

Nascimbene, Bruno, ed. *Le droit de la nationalité dans l'Union européenne*. Milan: Butterworths / Giuffrè, 1996.

Nathans, Eli. *The Politics of Citizenship in Germany*. Oxford: Berg, 2004.

Niboyet, Jean-Paulin. *Traité de droit international privé français*. Vol. 1. *Sources, nationalité, domicile*. Paris: Sirey, 1938.

Noiriel, Gérard. *État, nation, et immigration: vers une histoire du pouvoir*. Paris: Belin, 2001.

———. *The French Melting Pot: Immigration, Citizenship, and National Identity*, trans. Geoffroy de Laforcade. Minneapolis: University of Minnesota Press, 1996.

———. *Les origines républicaines de Vichy*. Paris: Hachette Littératures, 1999.

———. *La tyrannie du national: le droit d'asile en Europe, 1793–1993*. Paris: Calmann-Lévy, 1991.

Orentlicher, Diane F. "Citizenship and National Identity." *International Law and Ethnic Conflict*, ed. David Wippman. Ithaca: Cornell University Press, 1998.

Oualid, William. *Législation industrielle*. Paris: Les Cours du Droit, 1936–37.

Pairault, André. *L'immigration organisée et l'emploi de main-d'oeuvre étrangère en France*. Paris: Presses Universitaires de France, 1926.

Ponty, Janine. *Polonais méconnus: histoire des travailleurs immigrés en France dans l'entre-deux-guerres*. Paris: La Sorbonne, 1988.

Redlich, Fritz. "Towards Comparative Historiography: Background and Problems." *Kyklos* 11, fasc. 3 (1958), 362–89.

Renan, Ernest. *Qu'est-ce qu'une nation? (et autres textes choisis et présentés par Joël Roman)*. Paris: Presses Pocket, 1992.

Rosanvallon, Pierre. *L'État en France de 1789 à nos jours*. Paris: Le Seuil, 1989.

———. *Le sacre du citoyen: Histoire du suffrage universel en France*. Paris: Gallimard, 1992.

Rouard de Card, Edgard. *La nationalité française*. Paris: Gallimard, 1922.

Ruby, Maurice. *L'évolution de la nationalité allemande d'après les textes (1842 à 1953)*. Baden-Baden: Wervereis, 1954.

Saada, Emmanuelle. *Les enfants de la colonie: les métis de l'Empire français entre sujétion et citoyenneté*. Paris: La Découverte, 2007.

Sahlins, Peter. *Boundaries: The Making of France and Spain in the Pyrenees*. Berkeley: University of California Press, 1989.

————. "La nationalité avant la lettre: les pratiques de naturalisation en France sous l'Ancien Régime." *Annales HHS*, no. 5 (2000), 1081–1108.

————. *Unnaturally French: Foreign Citizens in the Old Regime and After*. Ithaca: Cornell University Press, 2004.

Saint-Joseph, Anthoine de. *Concordance entre les codes civils étrangers et le code Napoléon*. Paris: Charles Hingray / Leipzig: Brockhaus und Avenarius, 1840.

Savigny, Friedrich Karl von. *Traité de droit romain*. 8 vols. Paris: Firmin-Didot, 1840–51.

Sayad, Abdelmalek. *La double absence: des illusions de l'émigré aux souffrances de l'immigré*. Preface by Pierre Bourdieu. Paris: Le Seuil, 1999.

————. *L'immigration et les paradoxes de l'altérité*. Brussels: De Boeck, 1991.

Schnapper, Bernard. *Le remplacement militaire en France: quelques aspects politiques, économiques et sociaux du recrutement au XIXᵉ siècle*. Paris: SEVPEN, 1968.

Schnapper, Dominique. *Community of Citizens: On the Modern Idea of Nationality*, trans. Séverine Rosée. New Brunswick: Transaction, 1988.

————. *La France de l'intégration*. Paris: Gallimard, 1994.

Schneider, William H. *Quality and Quantity: The Quest for Biological Regeneration in Twentieth-Century France*. Cambridge: Cambridge University Press, 1990.

Schor, Ralph. *L'opinion publique et les étrangers en France, 1919–1939*. Paris: La Sorbonne, 1985.

Schwartzfuchs, Simon. *Les Juifs d'Algérie et la France, 1830–1855*. Jerusalem: Institut Ben Zvi, 1981.

Spire, Alexis. *Étrangers à la carte: l'administration des étrangers (1945–1975)*, 33–58. Paris: Grasset, 2005.

Spire, Alexis, and Dominique Merllié. "La question des origines dans les statistiques en France." *Le Mouvement social*, no. 188 (1999), 119–30.

Spire, Alexis, and Suzanne Thave. "Les acquisitions de nationalité depuis 1945." *Synthèses: regards sur l'immigration depuis 1945*. Paris: INSEE.

Stora, Benjamin. *Histoire de la guerre d'Algérie (1954–1962)*. Paris: La Découverte, 1993.

————. *Histoire de l'Algérie coloniale (1830–1954)*. Paris: La Découverte, 1991.

————. *Le transfert d'une mémoire: de l'"Algérie française" au racisme anti-arabe*. Paris: La Découverte, 1999.

Taguieff, Pierre-André. "Catégoriser les inassimilables: immigrés, métis, juifs, la sélection ethnoraciale selon le docteur Martial." *Recherches sociologiques*, no. 2 (1997), 57–83.

————. *L'antisémitisme de plume, 1940–1944: études et documents*. Paris: Berg International, 1999.

————. "L'identité française." *Regards sur l'actualité*, nos. 209–10 (1995), 13–28.

Terré, François. "Réflexions sur la notion de nationalité." *Revue critique de droit international privé* 64, no. 2 (1975), 197–214.

Thomas, Elaine Renée. "Nation after Empire: The Political Logic and Intellectual Limits of Citizenship and Immigration Controversies in France and Britain, 1981–1989." Ph.D. diss., University of California, 1998.

Thomas, Yan. "Le droit d'origine à Rome: contributions à l'étude de la citoyenneté." *RCDIP* 84, no. 2 (1995), 253–90.

———. *"Origine" et "Commune Patrie": étude de droit public romain (89 av. J.-C.–212 ap. J.-C.)*. Collection de l'École Française de Rome, vol. 221. Rome: École Française de Rome, 1996.

Tribalat, Michèle. *Faire France: une enquête sur les immigrés et leurs enfants*. Paris: La Découverte, 1995.

Tribalat, Michèle, ed. *Cent ans d'immigration: étrangers d'hier, Français d'aujourd'hui*. Paris: La Découverte, 1993.

Trinh, Dinh Thao. *De l'influence du mariage sur la nationalité de la femme*. Aix-en-Provence: Paul Roubaud, 1929.

Troper, Michel. "La notion de citoyen sous la Révolution française." *Études en l'honneur de Georges Dupuis, Droit public*, 301–22. Paris, 1997.

Vanel, Marguerite. "Le Français d'origine dans l'ancien droit français (XVe–XVIIIe siècle)." *Revue critique de droit international privé* 35 (1940–46), 220–31.

———. *Histoire de la nationalité française d'origine: évolution historique de la notion de Français d'origine du XVIe siècle au Code civil*. Preface by Jean-Pierre Niboyet. Paris: Ancienne Imprimerie de la Cour d'Appel, 1946.

Viet, Vincent. *La France immigrée: construction d'une politique, 1914–1997*. Paris: Fayard, 1998.

Viollette, Maurice. *L'Algérie vivra-t-elle? notes d'un ancien gouverneur général*. Paris: Félix Alcan, 1931.

Watson, Alan. *Legal Origins and Legal Changes*. London: Hambledon, 1991.

———. *Legal Transplants*. Edinburgh: Scottish Academic Press, 1974.

Weil, Alfred. "Des ambiguïtés de la dénationalisation allemande." *Journal de droit international* (1916), 69–72.

Weil, Patrick. "Access to Citizenship: A Comparison of Twenty-Five Nationality Laws." *Citizenship Today: Global Perspectives and Practices*, ed. T. Alexander Aleinikoff, and Douglas Klusmeyer, 17–35. Washington: Carnegie Endowment for International Peace, 2001.

———. *La France et ses étrangers: l'aventure d'une politique de l'immigration, 1938–1991*. Paris: Calmann-Lévy, 1991.

———. "Races at the Gate: A Century of Racial Distinction in American

Immigration Policy (1865–1965)." *Georgetown Immigration Law Journal* 15, no. 4 (2001), 625–48.

———. *Rapports au Premier ministre sur les législations de la nationalité et de l'immigration*. Paris: La Documentation Française, 1997.

———. "The Return of the Jews in the Nationality or in the Territory of France (1943–1973)." *The Jews Are Coming Back: The Return of the Jews to Their Countries of Origin after World War II*, ed. David Bankier, 58–71. New York: Berghahn, 2005.

———. "The History and Memory of Discrimination in the Domain of French Nationality: The Case of Jews and Algerian Muslims." *Hagar* 6, no. 1 (2005), 49–75.

Weiss, André. *Traité théorique et pratique de droit international privé*, 2nd edn. 6 vols. Paris: Larose et Tenin, 1907–13.

Werner, Auguste-Raynald. *Essai sur la réglementation de la nationalité dans le droit colonial français*. Toulouse: Boisseau, 1936.

Wihtol de Wenden, Catherine, ed. *La Citoyenneté*. Paris: Edilig, 1988.

INDEX

Abbas, Ferhat, 223

Abd el-Kader, 214, 223

Abetz, Otto, 99

Action Française: newspaper, 61, 69, 72, 77, 114; movement, 90, 106

Age of majority: as criterion for active citizenship, 13; as criterion for automatic conferral of French nationality, 42, 49, 52, 58, 94–95, 102, 159–68, 193–94, 207, 213–14; as criterion for requesting or repudiating French nationality, 31–32, 38, 43, 48, 57–60, 162, 165, 198, 213–14, 325 n. 87, 329 n. 129

Ageron, Charles-Robert, 221

Algeria, 48–49, 53, 87, 127–28, 150–58, 165, 194, 207–25, 231, 252–54

Alibert, Raphaël, 4, 91, 98, 301 n. 2, 311 n. 106

Allegiance, 256; bonds of, 113, 155, 176, 241; as criterion for nationality, 5, 168; "feudal," 12, 30, 52–53, 178; to Free France, 126–27; oath of, 90, 159, 303 n. 16, 337 n. 32; perpetual, 31, 182, 187, 238

Alsace, 34, 166, 251

Alsace-Moselle, 54, 72, 166, 183, 241, 247–48, 343 n. 103

Ancillon, Johann Peter, 175–77

Anti-Semitism: in Algeria, 216; in French nationality legislation, 88–89, 94, 128–29, 315 n. 155; in Vichy government policy, 118, 122, 132, 169

Ardennes (department), 36, 41, 282 n. 39

Armenians, 66, 79, 95, 104–6, 132, 135, 147, 322 n. 56

Assimilation: absence of or deficiencies in, 90–91, 97, 105, 109, 130–31, 140, 146–47, 156–57, 230, 236, 306 n. 44; of Algerian Jews and Muslims, 209–12, 219; assessment of, 71–73, 76–77, 81–83, 93, 141, 149, 232–35, 322 n. 53, 365 n. 31; as criterion for naturalization, 55, 68, 136–37, 141, 227; efforts to facilitate, 69, 185; of Jews, 88–90; legal, 93, 243; power of, 136, 344 n. 109; traditional instruments for, 163; of women, 197

Asylum, 78, 82, 208,

Austria, 176–77, 182

Austrians (Austro-Hungarians), 36, 78–80, 226

Azimi, Vida, 20

Bainville, Jacques, 61

Balladur, Édouard, 162

Bardoux, Jacques, 147, 332 n. 40

Patrick Weil is a senior research fellow at the Centre National de Recherche Scientifique (Centre d'Histoire sociale du XXᵉ siècle, Université de Paris I-Panthéon-Sorbonne) and a professor at the Paris School of Economics. He is the author of *La France et ses étrangers: l'aventure d'une politique de l'immigration de 1938 à nos jours* (Paris: Gallimard, coll. Folio Histoire, new edn. 2005), *La république et sa diversité, Immigration, Intégration, Discriminations* (Paris: Le Seuil, coll. La république des idées, 2005), and *Politique de la Laïcité au 20ème siècle* (Paris: Presses Universitaires de France, 2007). He recently published *Migration Control in the North Atlantic World* (New York: Berghahn, 2003) with Andreas Fahrmeir and Olivier Faron, and *L'esclavage, la colonisation et après . . . ? (Une comparaison, États-Unis, France, Grande-Bretagne)* (Paris: Presses Universitaires de France, 2004) with Stéphane Dufoix. He was a member of the Haut Conseil à l'Intégration from 1996 to 2002 and a member of the commission charged with deliberating on the application of the principle of *laïcité* (secularism) in the French Republic in 2003. In 1997, at the request of Prime Minister Lionel Jospin, he submitted two reports on nationality and immigration law that became the basis of two laws in 1998: *Mission d'étude des législations de la nationalité et de l'immigration* and *Rapports au Premier ministre*, both published by La Documentation française in 1997. Under its original title, *Qu'est-ce qu'un Français?*, *How to Be French* won the François Furet Prize (France, 2003) and the H-Soz-u-Kult prize for the best book on modern history (Germany, 2004).

Library of Congress Cataloging-in-Publication Data

Weil, Patrick, 1956–
[Qu'est-ce qu'un français? English.]
How to be French : nationality in the making since 1789 /
Patrick Weil ; translated by Catherine Porter.
p. cm.   Includes bibliographical references and index.
ISBN 978-0-8223-4348-6 (cloth : alk. paper)
ISBN 978-0-8223-4331-8 (pbk. : alk. paper)
1. Citizenship — France — History.
I. Porter, Catherine, 1941– II. Title.
KJV4184.W45 2008   342.4408′3 — dc22
2008028480